TICS AND CULTURE IN MODERN AMERICA

Series Editors:

rgot Canaday, Glenda Gilmore, Michael Kazin,
Stephen Pitti, Thomas J. Sugrue

series narrate and analyze political and social change in the
ons from 1865 to the present, including ideas about the ways
and wielded power in the public sphere and the language and
ics at all levels—local, national, and transnational. The series is
ire to reverse the fragmentation of modern U.S. history and to
ic perspectives on social movements and the state, on gender,
abor, and on intellectual history and popular culture.

The F   PO

                                          N

Volumes in th
broadest dimen
people have soug
institutions of po
motivated by a d
encourage synth
race, an

The Port Huron Statement

Sources and Legacies
of the New Left's Founding Manifesto

Edited by
Richard Flacks
and
Nelson Lichtenstein

PENN

UNIVERSITY OF PENNSYLVANIA PRESS

PHILADELPHIA

Published by
University of Pennsylvania Press
Philadelphia, Pennsylvania 19104-4112
www.upenn.edu/pennpress

Printed in the United States of America
on acid-free paper

1 3 5 7 9 10 8 6 4 2

Library of Congress Cataloging-in-Publication Data

A catalogue record for this book is available from
the Library of Congress.

ISBN 978-0-8122-4692-6

Contents

Introduction

Richard Flacks and Nelson Lichtenstein

The United States was a very different country when a group of politically active young people drafted the Port Huron Statement more than half a century ago. The fact that this manifesto, from Students for a Democratic Society (SDS), continues to live in our political and social imagination is truly remarkable. Its afterlife has been far longer than that of any other document emanating from the American left over the past century, and it has some of the iconic quality of other works that have helped define the American agenda, like W. E. B. Du Bois's *Souls of Black Folk,* Rachel Carson's *Silent Spring,* Betty Friedan's *Feminine Mystique,* or earlier manifestos such as the 1848 Seneca Falls "Declaration of Rights" and the 1892 Omaha Platform of the Populist Party. First drafted by Tom Hayden, a twenty-two-year-old graduate of the University of Michigan, this 25,000-word statement was debated and revised by fifty-plus people who met in the rustic buildings of a Michigan lakeside encampment for almost a week in June 1962. The many conferences and essays that have appeared to mark Port Huron's fiftieth anniversary testify to the long shadow cast by this document. It still lives, retaining considerable moral power, cultural resonance, and political relevance.

The essays collected in this volume seek to explain why this is so. They probe the origins, content, and contemporary influence of the Port Huron Statement. Most were first written for a February 2012 conference commemorating the fiftieth anniversary of the Statement held at the University of California, Santa Barbara. Presenters at that conference included Port Huron participants Dick and Mickey Flacks, Tom Hayden, Charles McDew, Steve Max, Charles Payne, Robert Ross, and Michael Vester, along with historians, sociologists, and contemporary activists whose scholarship and praxis shed light on the context, meaning, and legacy of the Statement.

Two themes emerged most forcefully from the conference and the essays assembled in this book. The first demonstrates the symbiotic relationship between radicalism and liberalism that for at least a brief moment in the early 1960s proved both creative and energizing, not only to a generation of college youth but to their elders as well. Although the Port Huron Statement constituted a forceful protest against many of the complacent ideas and stolid institutions that seemed so well rooted in Cold War America, the Statement also made its influence felt as the most advanced and adventuresome assertion of a racial liberalism and humane internationalism that was making its presence known in the years after 1956. As Tom Hayden puts it in the lead essay in this volume, "Most of the participants were shaped and informed in part by Marxist traditions. But the convention was never intended as a revival ceremony for Marxism." The document, writes Hayden, would bring together "liberals and socialists, the former for their relevance and the latter for their sense of thoroughgoing reforms in the system." The Port Huron writers thus envisioned young people as shock troops, helping to build "a new governing majority," composed of liberal Democrats, peace groups, organized labor, and the civil rights movement. "The buoyancy of this strategy," remembers Hayden, its hopeful innocence, "was a momentous break from the culture of the left in those times." Indeed, immediately after the Port Huron conferees adopted the Statement, Hayden and a few others drove to Washington, D.C., in hopes of seeing the President. They handed a fresh copy to Arthur Schlesinger, Jr., who apparently did send it on to John F. Kennedy.

That symbiotic relationship between liberalism and radicalism, highlighted in this volume, has too often been obscured by a well-remembered conflict that took place during and immediately after the Port Huron meeting. The Statement's first audience was the group of old social democrats in charge of SDS's parent organization, the League for Industrial Democracy (LID). They were often linked to the needle trades unions, and some had feuded with the Communists since the 1920s. The LID was represented at the Port Huron gathering by Michael Harrington, a thirty-four-year-old "elder" who had nevertheless been something of a guru for Tom Hayden and other SDS founders. Harrington read Hayden's draft as a betrayal—since it contained sharp criticism of anti-communism as a divisive and destructive feature of left-wing discourse. Hayden had been dismayed in the preceding months by the ways in which veteran civil rights stalwarts in the South were being labeled and marginalized by Harrington and other social democrats because of their alleged pro-communist tendencies. He and other SDS founders, seeing the communist-oriented left as a dying force, wanted, as well, to reach out to the children of members of the U.S. Communist Party (CPUSA), the "red-diaper babies" of the old left who were themselves looking for a new left political home. And, like many in the emerging peace movement, they wanted to move beyond the Cold War political culture. But for Harrington and his political comrades, language in the draft document that moved in these directions was heresy.

Harrington's concerns were extensively discussed, after he left, as the convention unfolded. Dick Flacks, who as a "red-diaper baby" was deeply interested in the new directions Hayden and company were seeking, helped craft new language for the final Statement that would hopefully assuage Harrington, while sustaining the political creativity expressed in the original document about communism and the Cold War. But in the weeks after the gathering, and before the new draft had been written, Harrington convinced the LID board to virtually destroy the nascent SDS. Fortunately, the new SDS national council, with the aid of some LID board members, including the venerated Norman Thomas, managed to get that decision reversed. Harrington, by the end of summer 1962, made some apology, and a few years later freely admitted that the Port Huron Statement's formulations were in fact valid.[1] Indeed, in long retrospect, the stance taken in the Statement on these matters anticipated by several years what eventually became conventional wisdom among liberals and social democrats in Europe and the United States. SDS, of course, became the leading force among white students nationally, pioneering student involvement in community organizing efforts and mobilizing campus uprisings against the Vietnam War and the draft.

The second theme present in this volume concerns the meaning, both historical and contemporary, of the concept of participatory democracy, a phase indelibly linked to the essence of the Statement itself. The phrase—participatory democracy—appears but once in the entire document, toward the end of the "Values" section, but its definition and ethos are pervasive. The Statement defines and evokes the idea in many ways: "Human relationships should involve fraternity and honesty"; "As a social system we seek the establishment of a democracy of individual participation"; "Politics has the function of bringing people out of isolation and into community."[2]

And there is much more, a conjoining of individualism and solidarity that can fuse libertarian, anarchist, and pacifist strands in American radicalism with the socialist tradition.

The concept of participatory democracy has had at least two distinct meanings. They are not mutually exclusive, but one historicizes the concept as a mode of movement building and political engagement that was largely a product of the late 1950s and the first several years of the 1960s; the other sees participatory democracy as a set of ideas and practices that have roots deep in American political culture and which remain available and valuable to activists on the left, even in the twenty-first century.

In the first instance and as a way to vitalize the democratic process at the end of the stolid 1950s, the participatory democracy advanced by the authors of the Port Huron Statement stood counterposed to a more ortho-dox concept, the pluralist theory of democracy, which in the 1940s and 1950s had enjoyed its greatest academic and organizational influence. Mod-ern democratic practice, argued John Kenneth Galbraith in his influential 1952 study *American Capitalism: The Concept of Countervailing Power*, functioned best when large, powerful interest groups jockeyed for power and resources. A set of competing elites, sometimes elected but often self-appointed, were thought to speak on behalf of and represent the interests of a normally more passive and atomized populace. Some writers, notably sociologist C. Wright Mills and philosopher Arnold Kaufman, had force-fully challenged such a schema, and Hayden, among others, imported the radical and skeptical views of these academics into the Statement. In this sense, the idea that a more genuine and effective form of democratic deci-sion making might prove attractive to a new generation of citizens helped fuel the assault on pluralism that left-wing intellectuals, both young and old, successfully waged from the late 1950s onward.

Participatory democracy was also a formulation that could allow the young left a way to transcend Cold War cant. It provided a visionary per-spective and a point of ideological resistance that enabled adherents to reject the fiction that a set of "people's democracies" stood on one side of the Iron Curtain, the "free world" on the other. Moreover, it provided a way of organizing that was fundamentally opposed to the Leninist van-guardism that had characterized the internal life of the old left well into the postwar era. Likewise, the participatory culture fostered by this mode of direct action politics would soon help nurture a feminist critique of patriar-chal structures and styles of the male left, both old and new.

In constructing such a participatory and radical organizing model, mid-twentieth-century pacifists, war resisters, and Quakers offered important guidance. But the most influential and inspiring example was that of African American students, soon organized into the Student Nonviolent Coordinating Committee (SNCC), whose lunch counter sit-ins in the winter and spring of 1960 captured the imagination of thousands in the North. "Here were four students from Greensboro who were suddenly all over *Life* magazine," recalled Rennie Davis, an Oberlin student who would become a key SDS activist in the mid-1960s. "There was a feeling that they were us and we were them, and a recognition that they were expressing something we were feeling as well."[3]

As a participant at our conference and in his award-winning history of the Mississippi freedom struggle, *I've Got the Light of Freedom*, Charles Payne emphasized the extent to which, out of sheer necessity, SNCC invented a radically democratic form of decision making, essential to the clandestine and dangerous organizing initiatives that only infrequently burst into the headlines and broadcasts. SNCC activists and sage elders like Ella Baker, Septima Clark, and Myles Horton "were committed to participatory political forms because people develop by participating, not by being lectured to or told what to do." They were localists, but hardly parochial. "What Bob Moses said about Ella Baker could have been said about all of them: they were taking the style and substance of the rural South and elevating it to another level."[4]

Like so many others of his political generation, Tom Hayden caught a life-changing sense of this powerful dynamic when he and Paul Potter, an SDS vice president, joined SNCC organizers in Klan-invested McComb County, Mississippi, early in the fall of 1961. There they were beaten by local whites and jailed by the police but also inspired by the audacity and steadfastness of hundreds of high school students protesting atrocious conditions, and by the quiet courage of local African American leaders, heretofore voiceless, oppressed, and fearful. Hayden titled his report from the deepest South "Revolution in Mississippi," referring to a revolution that was not yet victorious against a racist social or political structure, but which had made great strides in the minds and bodies of those SNCC organizers and community activists who sought to transform it. He saw a melding of direct action and democratic ethos, a combination that would soon animate large sections of the Port Huron Statement: "They have decided it is time right now—not in a minute, not after this one more committee meets, not after we have the legal defense and the court costs promised—to give blood and body if necessary for social justice, for freedom, for the common life, and for the creation of dignity for the enslaved, and thereby for us all."[5]

For virtually every early member of SDS, the rural, southern African American movement as exemplified in SNCC was both political model and moral exemplar. "In northern movement circles, the names of SNCC leaders became legendary," wrote Todd Gitlin, a Harvard SDS leader, "along with the sites of SNCC's passion, the Delta, Parchman Penitentiary, and the rest. The southern martyrs became our saints; cherishing them, we crossed the Mason-Dixon line of imagination, transubstantiated."[6] Port Huron veteran Paul Booth shared that vision. As he put it in a subsequent interview, "If everything could be restructured starting from the SNCC project in McComb, Mississippi, then we would have participatory democracy."[7]

Of course, that moment did not last. SNCC metamorphosed into a very different sort of organization, and as the growth of African American militancy and escalation of the Vietnam War radicalized millions in the late 1960s, a more "revolutionary" conception of leadership and organization emerged within the New Left. In that context, many activists saw the Port Huron Statement as merely "reformist," and some, in SDS and other organizations, once again found persuasive the Bolshevik posturing that the Port Huron generation had tried to sweep into history's dustbin.

Did participatory democracy survive that period of eclipse? Most of the contributors in this volume argue in the affirmative, in part because this mode of political and social engagement has had such deep roots in American culture. The values and ideas inherent in participatory democracy are found in the writings of Henry David Thoreau and Alexis de Tocqueville in the nineteenth century and in the essays and books of philosopher John Dewey and those working in his tradition a century later. Participatory democracy proved useful—and controversial—not only to the early SDS, but to the environmentalists, feminists, and gays who would create their own movements in the decades ahead as well as those social justice activists who assembled in Puerto Allegro and Zuccotti Park in the next century.

This volume is divided into four parts plus an appendix that presents the entire Port Huron Statement as SDS first published it in pamphlet form. Part I discusses the diverse intellectual and cultural roots of the Statement, some present only in the 1950s, while others ran back for more than a century. Part II describes the complex but creative circumstances that made it possible for liberals and radicals to cooperate in the birth of an American New Left and then bitterly divide just as it became a mass movement a few years later. In Part III, four writers explore how the concept of participatory democracy was defined and deployed during those movement-building years of the 1960s. And in Part IV, the concluding section of the book, four social scientists discuss the extent to which participatory democracy remains a resonant and operational democratic construct in our own time.

The historical essays assembled here largely endorse and enrich Tom Hayden's understanding of what made the Port Huron moment unique in the history of American radicalism. Michael Kazin argues that we should characterize Hayden, Flacks, and the other drafters of the Statement as a "young" left rather than a "new" one. This is because their quest for an authentic, even an existential sense of selfhood, combined with a set of programmatically specific reforms, mirrored and advanced a deeply rooted tradition of American radicalism that stretched back from the abolitionists and suffragists of the nineteenth century to the Jewish Bundists and social reformers of the Progressive era, in which individuals as resonate and "American" as William Lloyd Garrison, Frederick Douglass, Charlotte Perkins Gilman, and Emma Goldman have been celebrated and embraced. To Kazin, therefore, Port Huron was not so much a break with the radical tradition as it was an artful meld of what remained fresh and stirring in the often tortured history of the American left.

Lisa McGirr also links the Port Huron Statement to a young left, albeit a new one, but she emphasizes the way in which the events of 1956—Nikita Khrushchev's denunciation of Stalin, the Hungarian Revolution, Ghanaian independence—generated an international moment that gave rise to a whole series of left-oriented youth rebellions that spread throughout the world during the early 1960s. These mobilizations shared ideas, networks, repertoires of protest, and a sense of an imagined community. These New Left movements and moments rejected Stalinism, but they also decentered a Marxism that seemed overly structural if not mechanical. What stands out, writes McGirr in her survey of the New Left impulse in Germany, Japan, France, and the United Kingdom, is a new and central preoccupation with an existential and subjective search for an understanding of modern "selfhood." Thus, Port Huron's call to "find a meaning in life that is personally authentic," its search for community, was echoed in Japanese students' calls for "self-negation," as well as in a bohemianism that was hostile to both materialism and a purely individualistic solution to life's problems.

With Hayden, she recognizes that this moment would pass as the radicals of the 1960s confronted structures of power that were hardly amenable to substantial reform, but that moment was nevertheless a potent one that shaped a generation.

Read closely and sympathetically, the Port Huron Statement was also an important document that linked a new generation of young intellectuals to the emotions and affectations that would give the 1960s their distinctive cultural coloration. This is the insight put forward by Grace Hale, who argues that only if we historicize such otherwise intangible emotions as "love" and "authenticity" can twenty-first-century men and women understand why and how the Statement had such a dramatic and compelling impact on an earlier generation of young people. Why, in truth, should a cohort of college-educated intellectuals, moderately affluent and largely white, have identified so profoundly with the aspirations of the rural, poor, southern population of African Americans who were making a civil rights movement? Because participants, journalists, and historians have so often taken this for granted, we have not bothered to either stand aside and marvel at the phenomenon or analyze its meaning.

Hale argues that "love, the emotions, affect—these are the neglected threads in the histories of the 1960s social movements." By the mid-twentieth century a new definition of authenticity and realism had gained traction far beyond the world of avant-garde art or music. A novel, a song, a photograph, or even a political manifesto could be authentic if it was true in an emotional sense. It was beginning in the early 1960s, not the late, that young activists embodied left political goals in new modes of self-performance and style. They infused a sense of social justice into these new subjective, interior understandings of what constituted the authentic and the true. "And they did all this," writes Hale, "in part, by falling in love with the mostly black student activists of the southern civil rights movement."

In Part II, historians Nelson Lichtenstein and Dan Geary emphasize the extent to which the drafters of the Port Huron Statement shared a set of ideas and expectations with the older generation of liberals whose own impatience with American political culture had grown more urgent from the mid-1950s onward. The fact that the Statement was drafted at a labor education camp was hardly a fluke. In the early 1960s Walter Reuther and the coterie of ex-socialists and frustrated radicals that advised him were desperate to break out of the political and organizational straightjacket into which big labor had been drawn during the previous twenty years. As

Lichtenstein makes clear, there were a remarkable number of parallels between the programmatic initiatives proposed in the Statement and the kind of resolutions that the United Auto Workers (UAW) leadership wrote and passed at their union conventions. The Reutherites therefore welcomed this new generation of campus-based radicals and funded several SDS educational and organizing projects.

Likewise, as Geary shows us, a group of Harvard intellectuals, of whom sociologist David Riesman was most prominent, were thinking along very similar lines to those who composed the Port Huron Statement. At a time when the Kennedy administration relied on the "best and the brightest" to develop and justify its policies, both SDS and the Riesman academics, who published a blog-like newsletter, *The Correspondent*, imagined that they were organizing a group of counter-intellectuals "to challenge technocratic experts and turn policy issues into matters for democratic deliberation." Within two or three years both the Reutherites and the Riesman circle would find themselves estranged from SDS radicalism, but Geary makes the important point that the Port Huron Statement might well be understood not as the birth of an authentically radical New Left but rather as a promising start for a broad left-liberal alliance that failed to fully materialize. He writes that "we must recognize that liberalism and radicalism have been most successful in American history when they have established a synergistic relationship characterized by mutual respect for working within the system and for seeking to challenge its most fundamental structures."

Among American conservatives, and especially that heavily academic and journalistic variant once labeled neoconservative, it has become a truism that the New Left stood in an antagonistic relationship to the university and its humane purposes, not just in the violence-touched era after 1968, but during the otherwise more moderate early years of that decade. Certainly, writes Robert Cohen, one can find in the Post Huron Statement much denunciation of the mid-century university, both as an institution linked to military and business interests and as a breeder of apathetic, apolitical students. Two years later Free Speech Movement (FSM) leader Mario Savio would famously describe it as a factory-like institution, a machine whose operation "becomes so odious, makes you so sick at heart, that you can't take part; you can't even passively take part, and you've got to put your bodies upon the gears and upon the wheels, upon the levers, upon all the apparatus, and you've got to make it stop."[8]

But Cohen argues that a close reading of the Port Huron manifesto and other SDS and FSM documents of that era reveals a more complex picture, and a cluster of attitudes toward the university that included not merely negativism, but also hopefulness. It was a "love-hate relationship with a campus world that is at once profoundly undemocratic and yet houses the most hyper-democratic critics of our increasingly plutocratic social order." While the early sections of the Port Huron Statement focused on the university only to criticize it, the manifesto ends with an elaborate and upbeat argument about the university's potential to serve as a fount of humane culture and a vehicle for democratic change. Indeed, the Port Huron Statement articulated a radically reformist ethos regarding the university, which reflected early SDS optimism that a transformed university could help transform American society. This is a view to which even University of California president Clark Kerr and other academic liberals might well have subscribed.

If the relationship between radicals and liberals, between an authentic sense of personhood and politics, represented one important dimension by which we can calibrate the Port Huron Statement, then the concept of participatory democracy represents another. Indeed, many observers, then and now, conflate the manifesto with participatory democracy as a useful and imaginative form of movement building and decision making, especially since most of the programmatic sections of the Statement have long been rendered partially obsolete by a new set of social and political imperatives.

Part III of this volume explores how the Port Huron Statement, and in particular the concept of participatory democracy, was deployed and understood during the first few years after it was written. Robert Ross, an SDS veteran, explains that participatory democracy should not be confused with decision making by consensus or endless meetings. Instead it constituted an approach to politics and social issues that sought to link the frustrations and dilemmas of daily life to a resolution of, and to collective action about, the most profound societal problems. It was an aspiration, argues Ross, even a "kind of redemption," but as a method of decision making, participatory democracy had much in common with older forms of democratic practice. Therefore, as an activist fully engaged in University of Michigan student government and later as a participant in crucial SDS meetings, Ross became something of an expert on parliamentary procedure. He found Robert's Rules of Order not an obstacle but a vehicle for the

realization of what his comrades and he saw as a robust and effective participatory politics. "Usually we made decisions in small groups, and votes
were not required, but when the meetings were large and the decisions
weighty we voted, counted hands, and declared a winner."

Participatory democracy was a plastic concept with a sometimes transformative impact on those who practiced it. In her essay, Barbara Haber,
who was present at the Michigan lake-side meeting, finds seeds of 1960s
feminism in the values and sensibility embedded in the Port Huron Statement. On the face of it, the document can easily be dismissed as "hopelessly
sexist," writes Haber. The pronouns are all in the male gender, and there is
not a word acknowledging any of the issues upon which feminists would
soon shine a spotlight: reproductive freedom, sexual violence, unequal pay
and opportunities at work, or the assumption of male supremacy in family
affairs, in politics, and in the movement itself.

And yet Haber finds in the Statement themes, values, and outlooks that
"seem to prefigure early feminist thinking." She notes the decision to open
the document not with a structural analysis of power and politics, but with
"an evocative description of our own lives and the moral lessons we had
derived from them," hallmarks of a feminist approach to social issues, later
encapsulated in the catchphrase "the personal is the political." Indeed, for
Haber the Statement's emphasis on a participatory and democratic mode
of discussion and decision-making would prove entirely consonant with
how the women's movement in the late 1960s would raise consciousness,
build solidarity, and fight for radical change in gender relations. The male
leadership of SDS would soon come in for plenty of criticism from women
inside and outside the ranks, but in the long run, holds Haber, "the Port
Huron Statement may have played a catalytic role in developing feminist
consciousness."

Participatory politics also played a role in structuring and transforming
the SDS approach to the empowerment of African Americans in the urban
North. In her study of SDS community organizing in Chicago, Cleveland,
Newark, and Boston, Jennifer Frost finds that a dynamic series of encounters, negotiations, and conflicts between New Left organizers and local residents shaped both the organizational meaning and the political content of
participatory democracy in these antipoverty projects. For example, when
in 1963 Carl Wittman and Tom Hayden authored *An Interracial Movement
of the Poor?*, they imagined that jobless men demanding employment would
constitute a highly motivated and politically radical constituency, but

young SDS organizers on the ground soon found that women concerned with welfare, schools, housing, and safe streets ended up forming the largest and most active membership and providing the most consistent leadership in the projects. In the process, SDS activists came to redefine what constituted the political, broadening the definition to encompass not just efforts to push and prod the state to take action, but service activities within the community that enhanced the dignity, development, and participation of heretofore isolated and atomized individuals. In this regard the years of SDS community organizing in the North served as an ideological and organizational bridge between the "beloved community" envisioned by southern civil rights pioneers and the Great Society's brief determination that antipoverty programs would require the "maximum feasible participation" of those most affected by such governmental action. That Office of Economic Opportunity gambit is now long past, but such participatory imperatives have not entirely vanished, even in the twenty-first century, from the rhetoric that accompanies the way virtually every domestic governmental program is conceived and implemented.

The Port Huron Statement made its influence felt in continental Europe as well. Michael Vester, in 1962 already a national leader of the German Socialist Student Federation, offers an insightful analysis of how the American SDS and civil rights movement praxis had a considerable impact on the young left in West Germany. Vester was a participant in the Port Huron discussions and played a large role in shaping the Statement's foreign policy brief on Berlin, the division of Europe, and the Cold War, but from his perspective the idea of a creative and nondogmatic participatory democracy proved the most exciting and useful part of the SDS worldview that he could explain and deploy in his native country. Germany was fertile soil for such ideas because the social democratic tradition there already maintained institutions amenable to an opening from the left. There was first of all the Social Democratic Party itself, a mass organization that sustained a large and sometimes radical student presence. Most unions, especially IGMetal, also maintained large educational departments, in which many radicalized students found at least temporary posts. And finally there was the postwar development in many key industries of *Mitbestimmung*, or codetermination. Whatever its bureaucratic features, this law was predicated upon the idea that workers should participate in virtually all those workplace decisions that in the United States were the exclusive prerogative of top management.

However, Vester notes that the most important transplant that the German student left took from the United States—and also from the British academic left—came in the realm of political culture. Orthodox German leftists often found themselves in a strange but de facto alliance with some Frankfurt School Marxists, who saw mass culture and the contemporary media/entertainment complex as stultifying, oppressive, and demobilizing. Only a solid socialist set of organizations could counter such a regime. But Vester argues that participatory democracy implied that such a degree of cultural and social stratification could be broken by a disparate set of autonomous social movements, not unlike those typical of the United States in the mid-1960s, that emerged from the everyday frustrations and hypocrisies of daily life. And under such conditions German liberals and centrists might well be enlisted in the cause. This dispute generated a 1965 conflict within Germany's SDS (Sozialistische Deutsche Studentenbund)— the orthodox labeled Vester an "anarchist" for holding such views—but his side ultimately prevailed, which helped give rise not only to the mass radicalism that characterized German youth politics in the late 1960s but also to the profound liberalization of German culture, social policies, and even foreign policy that accompanied Willy Brandt's election as chancellor in 1969.

In Part IV we consider the extent to which the Port Huron Statement, and in particular the idea of participatory democracy, still resonates in contemporary consciousness. When we held our conference commemorating the Port Huron Statement in early 2012, Occupy Wall Street was on the minds of many who saw its radical spirit and communal governance structure as an evocation in the twenty-first century of the participatory democracy idea. In their essays, Jane Mansbridge and James Miller consider that sense of equivalence and the degree to which participatory democracy can function as a template for experimental collectives as well as insurgent social movements. Mansbridge, a political scientist, notes that by the early 1970s thousands of participatory experiments—free schools, food co-ops, women's centers, drug crisis hotlines—had formed across the country. But were they truly democratic and egalitarian, or did the iron law of oligarchy apply to them as well? Mansbridge found, in these collectives as well as in Occupy Wall Street, that participation and power were never equally distributed, but the real question was the extent to which those inequalities eroded mutual respect and a commitment to a common purpose. Unlike a state structure, these collectives were almost always voluntary associations that attracted people in common cause and hence a sense of mutual respect. Mansbridge argued, along lines similar to those of Robert Ross, that "when a group has relatively common interests on many issues that come before them for decision, it is often not useful to insist on political equality in those moments." Indeed, she thinks consensus decision making can become dysfunctional if some members of these groups remain stuck in the self-protective uses of equality and consensus that are unnecessary given the shared values and goals of such voluntary organizations.

James Miller, whose book *"Democracy Is in the Streets": From Port Huron to the Siege of Chicago* (1987) was important in reviving interest in the Statement twenty-five years after, takes a close look at Occupy Wall Street to test Mansbridge's argument and see if a twenty-first-century participatory democracy might work for a movement that exploded in size and for a brief few months seemed to put questions of finance capitalism and social inequality at the top of the national agenda. Miller acknowledges that the young people who drafted the Port Huron Statement never meant to propose rule by consensus as a working definition of participatory democracy. But that understanding, which evolved later in the decade, nevertheless became a working definition of one important meaning of participatory democracy.

Miller argues that Occupy Wall Street is but the latest example of a social movement that came to grief because they failed to confront seriously the toughest challenge to democratic ideas in a complex and modern society. "That challenge," writes Miller, "is one of coping with participants who hold radical, often incommensurable differences of opinion, including different views on whether or not social justice requires less income inequality, never mind the abolition of capitalism." Unlike the governance of a collective or a commune, Occupy's concerns, including systemic debt, structural unemployment, global warming, and the unfettered power of finance capital, involve dilemmas that can be addressed best by new forms of transnational regulation and governance, not by local assemblies. Participatory democrats have always found problems of scale and political economy difficult.

Sociologist Erik Olin Wright confronts these issues in his essay, "Radical Democracy as a Real Utopia." Here he seeks a way of thinking about social transformation that simultaneously holds on to our deepest utopian aspirations for a just and humane world and embraces the practical tasks and dilemmas of real-world institution building. Such a project shares with ordinary policy reform the goal of finding concrete ways to change existing institutions and create new organizational modes that transform everyday life, connecting immediate reforms with a broader vision of systemic transformation, immediate steps with a final destination. Wright points to participatory budgeting, the Mondragon worker cooperatives of Spain, community-controlled land trusts, Wikipedia, and open-source software as contemporary experiments leading to a set of "practical utopias" that seem to have avoided some of the dysfunctionalities that both Mansbridge and Miller found when a participatory democracy frame was applied to modern techno-organizational problems.

In the final essay, Dick Flacks transcends the debate about the mechanics of decision making for those engaged in participatory institutions and moves the discussion to the nature of consciousness as it is mediated through a radical democratic process. Here he explicates the work of John Dewey, Arnold Kaufman, and C. Wright Mills, the key intellectuals most influential in shaping the thought of those who wrote the Port Huron Statement. With Flacks, they sought to vitalize democracy by making malleable and therefore subject to political discussion and decision realms of human existence too often walled off by the market, the class structure, and the institutions of the national security state. To banish apathy and atomization, argued Mills and Dewey, required an engaged public in command of its own fate. But the Port Huron Statement was not just a recapitulation of the thought of these two figures. In contrast to Dewey, who always had an ambiguous relationship to radical reform, the authors of the Statement were certain that major transformations were necessary in American society. And unlike Mills, who had grown pessimistic about the capacity of a mass movement to provide the agency necessary to alter society, the Port Huron activists were profoundly inspired by the creativity and courage of the southern student movement (some of whose leaders came to Port Huron), seeing it as an inescapable moral challenge to more privileged youth—and also as a possible opening wedge for a new progressive alliance. The hopes then expressed have not been fulfilled, and yet the statement seems to remain relevant because to some considerable degree it charted some key elements of the social change that followed: the civil rights movement did transform American politics and much else; the terms and discourses of the Cold War were superseded; a new left based in the university did emerge—and the university we now inhabit is far more connected to social movements of the day. Moreover, as Flacks's essay tries to suggest, participatory democracy offers possibilities for theory, action, and organization that await new trial and error.

Chapter 1

Crafting the Port Huron Statement: Measuring Its Impact in the 1960s and After

Tom Hayden

We are now in the sixth decade since publication of the Port Huron Statement, the founding declaration of Students for a Democratic Society, issued as a "living document" in 1962. The SDS call for a participatory democracy echoes today in student-led democracy movements around the world, even appearing as the first principle in the September 17, 2011, declaration of the Occupy Wall Street (OWS) protesters.

As a signpost of the early 1960s, the Port Huron Statement is worth treasuring for its idealism and for the spark it ignited in many an imagination. The Port Huron call for a life and politics built on moral values as opposed to expedient politics; its condemnation of the Cold War, echoed in today's questioning of the "war on terror"; its grounding in social movements against racism and poverty; its first-ever identification of students as agents of social change; and its call to extend participatory democracy to the economic, community, and foreign policy spheres—these themes constitute much of today's progressive sensibility.

The same spirit of popular participation that inspired OWS drove the electoral successes of Latin American nations emerging from dictatorships in the 1990s. It appeared among the demands of young people in Tunisia, Egypt, and other Middle Eastern countries in the Arab Spring of 2011. Spontaneous democratic demonstrations have also erupted in Russia, Israel, Brazil, and Iran, organized on Facebook by young people seeking honest elections and a more equitable distribution of wealth. The

Statement was even prophetic in condemning the 1 percent, who in 1962 owned more than 80 percent of all personal shares of stock. It may be sobering for today's Wall Street critics to read in the Statement original draft that despite the radical reforms of the 1930s, the share of wealth held by the 1 percent in 1960 had remained constant since the 1920s.

On the other hand, there are sources of hope now that we could not imagine in 1962. The technological revolution of the Internet and social media is propelling a global revival of participatory democracy. Facebook and Twitter are credited with a key role in movements from Cairo to the volunteer campaign for Barack Obama. For the next generations, perhaps the most important issue for participatory democracy will be ownership and control of the means of producing and distributing information. These issues were prefigured in the Statement in the briefest of complaints about computerized problem solving and in the outcry two years later from Berkeley students in the Free Speech Movement, who claimed they were being processed like IBM punch cards. The Statement criticized the profit motive behind automation while noting that the new technology, if democratically controlled, could eliminate much drudgery at work, open more leisure time, and make education "a continuing process for all people."

According to Kirkpatrick Sale's *SDS*, published in 1973 and still the most comprehensive history of the organization, the Statement "may have been the most widely distributed document of the American left in the sixties," with 60,000 copies printed and sold for twenty-five cents each between 1962 and 1966. Sale made two observations about the Statement. First, the Statement contained "a power and excitement rare to any document, rarer still in the documents of this time, with a dignity in its language, persuasiveness in its arguments, catholicity in its scope, and quiet skill in its presentation . . . a summary of beliefs for much of the student generation as a whole, then and for several years to come." Second, "it was set firmly in mainstream politics, seeking the reform of mainstream institutions rather than their abolition, and it had no comprehension of the dynamics of capitalism, of imperialism, of class conflict, certainly no conception of revolution. But none of that mattered."[1] More recently, historian Michael Kazin wrote that the Statement "is the most ambitious, the most specific, and the most eloquent manifesto in the history of the American Left."[2]

Who We Were, What We Said

I wrote the first notes for the Port Huron Statement in December 1961, when I was briefly in an Albany, Georgia, jail cell after a Freedom Ride to fight segregation in the South. The high school and college students engaged in direct action there changed my life. I had never met young people willing to take a risk—perhaps the ultimate risk—for a cause they believed in. Quite simply, I wanted to live like them. Those feelings, and the inspiration they gave me, might explain the utopian urgency of the Statement's final sentence: "If we appear to seek the unattainable, as it has been said, then let it be known that we do so to avoid the unimaginable." (I have no recollection of where this exhortation originated.)

Even today I find it hard to explain the "power and excitement," the "dignity" and the "persuasiveness" of this document, which sprawls over 124 pages in book form.[3] Though I was already a student editor and a budding pamphleteer, I remember myself, just twenty-two, as a kind of vessel for channeling a larger spirit that was just in the air—blowin' in the wind—and coursing through the lives of my friends.

The Port Huron attendees insisted that it begin with an emphasis on "we," to be followed immediately by a section on values. And so we described ourselves as a new generation "raised in modest comfort, looking uncomfortably at the world we inherit." This was an uncertain trumpet compared with, say, the triumphal tones of *The Communist Manifesto*. Why did it resonate with so many activists?

In fact, a few sons and daughters of former Communist Party members were present, but their previous family dogmas and loyalties lay shattered by the crushing of the democratic Hungarian revolution in 1956 and the revelations about the Stalinist gulag by Soviet leader Nikita Khrushchev. There were also children of New Deal democratic socialists now experiencing liberal middle-class lives, and there were plenty of mainstream idealistic student leaders, graduate sociology students, a few pacifists, and a number of the spiritually inspired.

Though they were not at Port Huron, there were other philosophical searchers at the time who practiced participatory democracy. Bob Moses, perhaps the single greatest influence on the early SDS and SNCC (the Student Nonviolent Coordinating Committee), could be described as a philosophical existentialist given to the democratic method. The Free Speech Movement's Mario Savio described himself as a non-Marxist radical shaped by secular liberation theology who was "an avid supporter of participatory democracy." We were all influenced by Ella Baker, an elder adviser to SNCC with a long experience of organizing in the South for the National Association for the Advancement of Colored People (NAACP). Ms. Baker, as everyone referred to her, was critical of the top-down methods of black preachers and organizations, including her friend Dr. Martin Luther King Jr. She argued that SNCC should remain autonomous and not become a youth branch of the older organizations. She spoke of and personified participatory democracy.

SNCC played a direct role in shaping my values, as it did with many SDS founders. SNCC's early organizing method was based on listening to local people and taking action on behalf of their demands. Listening and speaking in clear vernacular English was crucial. Books were treasured, but where you stood, with whom, and against what risks was even more important, because if the people you were organizing could not understand your theories, you had to adjust. This led to a language and a form of thinking cleansed of ideological infection, with an emphasis on trying to say what people were already thinking but had not put into words.

The right to vote was no intellectual matter, as it was for many on the left who felt it was based on illusions about where real power lay. Again and again, SNCC organizers heard rural black people emphasize how much they wanted that right. Typically they would say, "I fought in World War II; I fought in Korea; and all I want before I die is the right to vote." (Many decades earlier, twenty-two-year-old Emma Goldman learned from a similar experience, after an early lecture in which she had scornfully dismissed the eight-hour day as a stupid token demand. When a worker in her audience replied that he could not wait for the overthrow of capitalism but that he also needed two hours less work "to feel human, to read a book or take a walk in daylight," the experience gave Goldman the consciousness of a great organizer.)[4]

The "Values" section of the Statement reflected our eclectic, existential, sometimes apocalyptic, take on life. "We have no sure formulas, no closed theories." We would accept no hand-me-down ideologies. "A first task of any social movement is to convince people that the search for orienting theories and the creation of human values is complex but worthwhile." We agreed with French existentialist novelist Albert Camus, who argued that a previous generation of revolutionaries had sometimes rationalized horrific slaughters in the name of future utopias like "land reform." Still, we wanted to argue, carefully, for a restoration of the utopian spirit amid the deadening compromises all around us. We wrote that "we are imbued with urgency, yet the message of our society is that there is no viable alternative to the present" (the same phrase later employed by Margaret Thatcher). Our diagnosis of the prevailing apathy was that deep anxieties had fostered "a developed indifference" about public life but also a yearning to believe in something better. "It is to this latter yearning, at once the spark and engine of change, that we direct our present appeal."

We even thrashed out basic views of human nature day after day, not the usual subject of political platforms. We asserted a belief that "men [are] infinitely precious and possessed of unfulfilled capacities for reason, freedom and love." (Use of the term "men" was unquestioned; Betty Friedan's *Feminine Mystique* was one year away.) This formulation followed long discussions in which we repudiated doctrines of pessimism about the fallen human condition, as well as the liberal humanist belief in human "perfectibility." It may have been influenced also by the Vatican II reforms then sweeping the Catholic Church. The formulation about "unrealized potential" was the premise for believing that human beings were capable of participating in the decisions affecting their lives, a sharp difference from the dominant view that an irrational mass society could be managed only by experts, or the too hopeful Enlightenment view of Tom Paine that our world could be created anew.

What Participatory Democracy Meant

Much was omitted because in 1962 awakenings just around the corner were not anticipated. Many of us read Doris Lessing and Simone de Beauvoir, but the first women's consciousness-raising groups were two years in the future and would be provoked in part by our own chauvinism. American combat in Vietnam was unseen over the horizon, though the Statement opposed U.S. support for the "free world's" dictators, including South Vietnam's Ngo Dinh Diem and Cuba's Fulgencio Batista. Rachel Carson's *Silent Spring* was published just two months after Port Huron, but all the Statement observed about the environment was that "uncontrolled exploitation governs the sapping of the earth's physical resources." There was no counterculture, no drug culture, no hippies—all that was to come. The folk music revival was at its peak; the Beatles were just ahead. The Statement would need major updating, but its passionate democratic core was of permanent value.

What did we mean by participatory democracy? Obviously the concept arose from our common desire to participate in making our own destiny, and in response to the severe limitations of an undemocratic system that we saw as representing an oligarchy. At its most basic, it meant the right to vote, as Henry David Thoreau once wrote, "not with a mere strip of paper but with one's whole life." It meant simplicity in registration and voting, unfettered from the dominance of wealth, property requirements, literacy tests, and poll taxes. It meant exercising the right to popular initiatives, referendums, and recalls, as achieved by Progressives in the early twentieth century. And it meant widening participation to include the economic sphere (workplace democracy and consumer watchdogs), neighborhood assemblies, and family life itself, where women and children were subordinates. It meant a greater role for citizens in the ultimate questions of war and peace, then considered the secret realm of experts.

Participatory democracy was a psychologically liberating antidote to the paralysis of the apathetic "lonely crowd" depicted by David Riesman, Nathan Glazer, and Reuel Denney in the 1950 sociological study by that title. The kind of democracy we were proposing was more than a blueprint for structural rearrangements. It was a way of empowering the individual as autonomous but interdependent with other individuals, and the community as a civic society. Without this empowerment on both levels, the Statement warned, we were living in "a democracy without publics," in the phrase of C. Wright Mills, the rebel sociologist who was one of our intellectual heroes.

The Statement's economic program was an extension of the New Deal and a call for deeper participatory democratic reform. Proposals for a government-led poverty program and "medical care . . . as a lifetime human right" anticipated the Medicare legislation that came in 1965, and the Statement's concept of a government-led antipoverty program foreshadowed the Office of Economic Opportunity, a project envisioned by John F. Kennedy and adopted by Lyndon Johnson.

But the Statement also called for *economic* democracy, as distinct from the New Deal's more bureaucratic approach: the major resources and means of production should be "open to democratic participation and subject to democratic social regulation." There was a danger of "bureaucratic coagulation" and too much emphasis in Kennedy's New Frontier belief that "problems are easiest for computers to solve." There should be experiments in decentralization, we said, devolving the power of "monster cities" to local communities seeded with more developmental incentives. Returning to the Statement's moral focus, since a human being's economic experience has "crucial influence on habits, perceptions and individual ethics," we insisted that there be incentives beyond money or survival, ones that are "educative, not stultifying; creative, not mechanical; self-directed, not manipulated; encouraging independence, a respect for others, a sense of dignity, and a willingness to accept social responsibility."

Not that Marxism was irrelevant to the Port Huron gathering. Most of the participants were shaped and informed in part by Marxist traditions. But the convention was never intended as a revival ceremony for Marxism. The document at one point mentioned a need to bring together "liberals and socialists, the former for their relevance and the latter for their sense of thoroughgoing reforms in the system." Even those at Port Huron who were children of the Old Left had concluded that moral values and democracy were more important than any ideological renovation of Marxism, Leninism, Trotskyism, Maoism, or anarchism. It seemed we agreed that we were something new: a movement, perhaps an embryonic blessed community. When those from an earlier tradition pointed out, sometimes vehemently, that we were not only not new but descendants of the left, the New Left became our hybrid brand. No one had complained when that label was suggested in 1960 by C. Wright Mills, in his open "Letter to the New Left."

Breaking the Political Stalemate

In his *American Dreamers: How the Left Changed a Nation*, Michael Kazin argued that the role of the American left has been to make lasting cultural and normative contributions while never actually coming to power. We were dreamers too, but dreamers who had a plan for achieving political influence and power.

The Kennedy administration was in a crossfire between two opposing forces: the civil rights movement versus the dinosaurs of the Dixiecrat South, on which the party depended for its national majority. By risking their lives daily in sit-ins and voter drives, SNCC and rural black people would soon crumble the foundation of Dixiecrat power.

The Port Huron Statement articulated a strategy of "political realign-ment," in which the goal was to end the "organized stalemate" in Washing-ton and open the possibility of a more progressive party. Realignment was embraced by King, Bayard Rustin, and Michael Harrington, and it was the implicit agenda of the vast March on Washington for Jobs and Freedom in August 1963. Soon northern students were streaming south in 1964 for the Mississippi Summer Project, whose aim was to unseat the state's white Democratic delegation and replace it with a democratically chosen slate, the Mississippi Freedom Democratic Party, at the convention that year in Atlantic City. By 1965 the Voting Rights Act was passed, establishing federal oversight of Deep South voting patterns.

The energy of some SNCC and SDS organizers also overflowed into the nascent farmworkers' organizing efforts in the Southwest at around the same time. The Statement condemned the disenfranchisement of migrant workers while also citing them as a potential base for rebirth of a "broader and more forceful unionism." In 1964 the government's hated *bracero* pro-gram was forced to its end. Political realignment was advanced that same year when the Supreme Court decreed that voter representation must be based on population rather than the land holdings of growers. By 1966 the United Farm Workers (UFW) were bringing new energy to the labor movement; that same year, Congress moved to include minimum-wage protections for farmworkers, who had been excluded for the previous twenty-eight years under the Fair Labor Standards Act. We saw the UFW's four-year global consumer boycott of grapes as a channel of participatory democracy that attracted thousands of new activists.[5]

One link between these events was the leadership of United Automobile Workers (UAW) president Walter Reuther; his brother Victor; and a top UAW officer, Mildred Jeffrey, the mother of a key SDS founder at Port Huron, Sharon Jeffrey. The Reuthers helped fund and support the early SDS as well as the UFW, SCLC and the southern voter registration cam-paigns and marches.

The overall strategy of realignment envisioned participatory democracy directly connected to a new social movement, one capable of forging a new governing majority on a national scale, with young people as shock troops building a "bridge to political power" composed of liberal Democrats, peace groups, organized labor, and the civil rights movement. For the first time, students were thinking of themselves as "agents of social change." The buoyancy of this strategy, perhaps carried on the innocence of the young, was a momentous break from the culture of the left in those times, which was dispirited by McCarthyism, bogged down in poisonous factional disputes, and weighted with the ideological language and baggage of a Marxism that remained foreign to most Americans.

Assassination and Vietnam Destroy the Great Society

The Port Huron vision of winning seemed entirely possible to those who debated the strategy and set forth earnestly to carry it out. But even the "best and brightest" among the young radicals were thwarted by our inability to predict the future.

First, there was the assassination of John Kennedy, which devastated any rational basis for strategy. The assassination of a president simply was not factored into any models we took seriously about reform or revolution. Whether or not the Kennedy killing was part of a larger conspiracy, as many still believe, a mood of paranoia took root in the New Left, in which it seemed that any notions of peaceful democratic transfers of power were illusory. It may be wishful thinking, but I believe the evidence is that Kennedy would not have sent 100,000 ground troops to Vietnam, as his successor did (after promising not to).[6] For most of us, Kennedy, as well as other national leaders assassinated that decade, including JFK's brother Robert, Martin Luther King Jr., Medgar Evers, and even Malcolm X, had been central figures in the transformation we hoped to see. The power of the independent movement came first, but it was also necessary to pressure the president to follow, to recognize, legitimize and legalize the victory and pursue a transition to a more participatory and egalitarian democracy.

The Port Huron Statement correctly predicted that if nuclear war with the Soviet Union could be prevented, there still would be an ongoing "international civil war" between proxies of the United States and the Soviet Union. Cuba was one such focal point, and Vietnam became another. The Vietnam War diverted public attention and drained resources from the budding War on Poverty. I was one of many hundreds who moved into inner-city neighborhoods to engage in community organizing against poverty, establishing groups that took over local boards in Newark, New Jersey. But Vietnam wrecked all that, plunging our young movement into five years of draft and war resistance, and provoking an escalated militancy against the war makers. The Vietnam escalation was accompanied by hundreds of uprisings in black communities, with the cost in lives still uncounted and billions of dollars wasted. Any possibility, however remote or delusional, of our being the left wing of Johnson's Great Society was rendered impossible and was rejected in disgust.

The consequences for realignment were far different from our predictions. As a result of the civil rights movement, there came a generation of white liberal politicians like Jimmy Carter, Bill Clinton, and Al Gore, along with a huge complement of black elected officials from the South, from local sheriffs to Congressmen like John Lewis (a SNCC member) and James Clyburn (vice chair under Charles McDew of the South Carolina State student movement in 1960). The climate of officially sponsored terrorism ebbed in the South, and leaders like the Reverend Jesse Jackson would eventually run impressive presidential campaigns where none had been possible in the previous century. Barack Obama, born in 1961, the year the Freedom Rides began, very much owes his election to the voting rights reforms that brought about this realignment. As Attorney General Eric Holder said at SNCC's fiftieth reunion in 2010, "there is a direct line from that lunch counter to the Oval Office and to the . . . Department of Justice where the attorney general sits."

On the other hand, as Richard Flacks, a principal author of the Statement, has noted, we underestimated another realignment: the flight of white southern voters from the Democratic Party, predicted by Johnson and encouraged by Richard Nixon's 1968 "Southern strategy." This resulted in two backlash victories by Republicans (Nixon, Ronald Reagan) and the transformation of the white South from solid Democratic to solid Republican. The civil war between so-called red and blue continues to this day, with the red lines eerily drawn around the Old Confederacy and much of the West where the Indian wars were fought.

I believe the Port Huron vision of a progressive alliance would have succeeded in bringing a new governing majority to power in 1964, with a likelihood of avoiding the Vietnam War, were it not for the murder of Kennedy and Johnson's subsequent policy of military escalation. This argument may be criticized as purely hypothetical, but it tries to capture the immensity of our dream and how close it seemed to our grasp. It is also a measure of the depths of despair we fell to in the years to come, a despair that lingers today among those who experienced both the beautiful struggle and the bitter fruit.

There was a third obstacle to the Statement dream, besides the assassinations and the Vietnam War. For want of another term, it was the system itself, or the powerful paradigm we defied but could not defeat. By "system" I mean the intersecting (though not coordinated) hierarchies of banks, corporations, the military, media, and religion, dominant then as now (though there are far more women and people of color at the upper levels today). This was the "power elite" described by C. Wright Mills. His concept of power was broader than that of an economic ruling class. It was an establishment far more flexible, even liberal, that had presided over the growth of the white middle class in the 1950s.

By "paradigm" I mean an understanding of power as cultural hegemony or dominance, a thought system in which there seems to be no alternative. The oppressive paradigm the Statement tried to discredit was the Cold War between two blocs engaged in nuclear brinkmanship. We were the first generation in history to grow up with the Bomb, to learn to hide under desks or in bomb shelters, to be exposed to the mad logic of "mutual assured destruction" and the cynical realpolitik of "free world" and Soviet blocs controlling alliances of servile authoritarians. We went through a near-death experience during the Cuban missile crisis. And we knew the grim math: the trillions spent on weapons were dollars that could have been invested in economic development, health care, and education. President Eisenhower had a name for this system—the military-industrial complex—and we noted that he dared name it only as he was leaving office. This paradigm at first froze us in fear. The legacy of McCarthyism, if continued in the 1960s, would mean that all our work, from the sit-ins to the Freedom Rides to the Port Huron Statement, would be marginalized as taking the wrong side in the Cold War.

The Statement therefore included a twenty-page attack on this Cold War mentality, half devoted to a proposal for phased nuclear disarmament, half to a welcoming attitude toward anticolonial revolutions. Our proposal was to de-escalate the bipolar nuclear confrontation. We differed with most of the left-liberalism of the time by suggesting that our own government was partly to blame for the Cold War, and by denying that the Soviet Union sought to take over the world by force. There was a growing peace movement, which many in our ranks eagerly joined. Despite, or perhaps because of, the nuclear near-miss over Cuba in 1962, President Kennedy became an important critic of the Cold War before his assassination. It appeared that the SDS demand for new priorities was being recognized when Kennedy initiated and signed a partial nuclear test ban treaty with the Soviet Union in October 1963.

SDS, the CIA, and the Power Elite

As the killing of JFK and the Vietnam escalation were burying the original hopes of SDS, a new radical resistance was taking root, and with it new ideological searching. The second generation of SDS, and the movement generally, was learning hard lessons from experiences not available to us in 1960–62. Black people who played by the rules would see those rules changed when power was threatened. Leaders were assassinated if they moved in a progressive direction. Politicians lied about taking us to war. Vietnam seemed to prove that militarism and imperialism were central to American society, whether liberals or conservatives were in power.

And finally, the power elite ruled beyond, or behind, elected officials. To take one example among many, official disclosures in 1984 revealed that John McCone, Kennedy's director of the Central Intelligence Agency (CIA), head of the Atomic Energy Commission, and Bechtel executive, conspired with the Federal Bureau of Investigation (FBI) in a "psychological warfare campaign" against the Free Speech Movement, in part designed to elect Ronald Reagan governor of California.[7] Rampant conspiracy theories seemed to negate the prospects of popular movements and peaceful transitions through elections. But even if the paranoia went too far, as it usually did, there were still grounds for believing that manipulators were behind the curtain.

In 1961 at a National Student Association convention I found a yellow pad with a chart identifying SDS in a box on the left, Young Americans for Freedom on the right, and an entity called Control Group in the center top. Six years later *Ramparts* magazine revealed that the secretive Control Group included CIA agents whose work was to promote a pro–Cold War global student movement. The CIA also ran covert operations through the AFL-CIO's international affairs department. Tom Kahn, special assistant to AFL-CIO president George Meany and later director of the federation's foreign operations, was the very person at the League for Industrial Democracy who in 1962 tried to fire Al Haber and myself, locking us out of SDS headquarters in New York because he believed the Statement was soft on the Soviets.

The CIA's role in the AFL-CIO and foreign policy came to light as the by-product of hearings into tax-exempt foundations by Representative Wright Patman in September 1964, confirming our worst suspicions. AFL-CIO staff were also involved in the U.S. invasion of the Dominican Republic in 1965 and in controlling Saigon's labor federation, protecting the flow of U.S. military supplies into South Vietnam's ports during the war.

The importance of this sojourn into left-wing history is that SDS and SNCC (and King, among others) were unaware of the company we were keeping. The unmovable obstacle to the coalition we hoped to build with organized labor was the secret pro–Cold War element within liberalism, directly and indirectly tied to the CIA, which was fiercely opposed to our break from Cold War thinking. On the one hand, the UAW's Reuther brothers helped fund and provide conference quarters at Port Huron, supported the March on Washington and the early UFW organizing effort, and were frustrated by Meany's archconservative views. On the other hand, the right-wing AFL-CIO foreign affairs department carried on the anticommunist crusade with its covert operations. The Reuther wing was tied to Johnson's leadership and unwilling to break from Meany. There was no way, in other words, that the New Left could have joined organized labor in 1964–65 around the Port Huron foreign policy vision, because the AFL-CIO was shackled to the CIA without our knowledge. The Reuthers were the great hope, but they were loath to break from Johnson over the Mississippi delegation battle in Atlantic City and over Vietnam. When the UAW finally broke from Meany and demanded a cease-fire in Vietnam, SDS and SNCC were too radicalized and factionalized for it to matter anymore. Death, our old nemesis, also intervened. On May 9, 1970, one week after the National Guard killed four students during a protest at Kent State, and after Walter Reuther demanded an immediate withdrawal from Vietnam, he and five others were killed in a charter-jet crash.[8]

Marxism Replaces Participatory Democracy

While the Port Huron Statement was criticized by an older generation as too far left, an opposite attack came from the mid-1960s generation. In 1966 new SDS leaders rejected the Statement as "too reformist." It was certainly true; the Statement did envision reforms—substantive rather than token, rapid though not overnight—and revolution was seen more as an undefined aspiration or long-term hope. Radical reform depended on independent social movements in combination with awakened progressives within political institutions rather than any revolutionary conquest of state and corporate power. The new generation claimed that this strategy was based on delusional liberal hopes.

Why was it so necessary for SDS leaders to reject Port Huron as "reformist"? The main reasons were external—the escalation of the Vietnam War and the draft by the liberal Democrats—but there was an internal dynamic as well. The new SDS leaders, in search of an ideology, turned steadily to Marxism, then to Marxism-Leninism and Maoism.

This was a stunning turn for a "new" left, because it implied a broad rejection of many of the new social movements as basically "reformist" too, since none of them were led by Marxists and none (except the Black Panthers) favored vanguard parties. The implication was that no genuine explanatory framework existed for a radical U.S. social movement outside Marxism, a thesis that ignored or downplayed deep historical currents of populism, pacifism, religious reform, and slave rebellions in American history. Most of the thinkers who inspired the early SDS—Mills, John Dewey, Camus, Lessing, James Baldwin—were shelved in search of an ideology that only Marxism seemed to offer.

Soon the open, participatory structure of the early SDS was being penetrated and disrupted by the Progressive Labor Party, a tightly disciplined, highly secretive organization dedicated to recruiting SDS members in support of a communist revolution on the inspiration of China and Albania. It proved impossible to dislodge from the organization, and it pushed all internal discussions in a poisonous sectarian direction.

Beginning in 1968, the Weatherman faction (later the Weather Underground) surfaced as new "communist revolutionaries," inspired by the revolutions in Vietnam and Cuba and the Black Panthers at home. Instead of the Port Huron concept of a majority progressive coalition, they favored forming clandestine cells behind enemy lines, a formulation that regarded the white American majority as hopelessly racist and privileged. Their ideological heroes included Lin Piao, a leader of the Chinese Revolution, along with Che Guevara and the young French intellectual Regis Debray, with his *foco* theory that small bands of armed guerrillas could set off popular revolutions and their vision of a "tri-continental" alternative to the "revisionist" Soviet Union. For an American hero, the Weathermen turned to John Brown, who led a suicidal though heroic uprising against slavery. That uprising was vindicated to the Weathermen (and many African Americans) by the vast swelling of support for John Brown during and after his martyrdom. Perhaps it would take a vanguard of martyrs to incite an American revolution, or so the thinking went.

These were compelling notions to many SDS radicals desperate to stop the Vietnam War and disillusioned with liberalism's default. But by 1969, less than eight years after its founding, SDS fell victim to the factional wrangling.

The Movements Rise Again, with SDS Underground

I am not describing these post–Port Huron Marxist tendencies as mad delusions, as many have. That brief generation tried to make sense of the terrible and traumatizing events of the time. Nor was their deep paranoia unjustified. In late 1967 Johnson screamed at his top advisers, "I'm not going to let the Communists take this government, and they're doing it right now!" Fifteen hundred Army intelligence officers, dressed as civilians, conducted surveillance on 100,000 Americans. Two thousand full-time FBI agents were deployed, with massive use of informants and counterintelligence programs. J. Edgar Hoover's orders to "neutralize" protest leaders are well documented. Scores of young people were killed or wounded, well beyond the widely remembered shootings at Kent State and Black Panther offices. One victim of an assassination attempt in 1969 was Richard Flacks, a key participant at Port Huron. He was targeted politically by Hoover and the Chicago police "red squad" before being attacked in his office with a claw hammer by someone who was never apprehended. SDS was banned on many campuses. Police or troops occupied at least 127 campuses, and 1,000 students were expelled in the spring of 1968 (which, as Kirkpatrick Sale notes, made them instantly draftable). Softer counterinsurgency techniques included the screening-out of the "protest prone" by admissions officers and the use of psychological counseling to "treat" alienated students. Making the paranoia all the more justified was the palpable sense among many of us that we had been abandoned by our parents; a 1969 Gallup survey indicated that 82 percent of Americans wanted student demonstrators expelled. If that was true, what was the point of depending on mainstream public opinion?

But the heightened militancy became disconnected from a comprehensible narrative that the wider public might have understood. In abandoning the Port Huron vision and strategy as times worsened, SDS was offering a fringe analysis at best, and was no longer able to invest leadership and organizing resources in the vast swelling of campus and public protest.

Indeed, the greatest outpouring of youth, student, GI, liberal, feminist, and environmentalist sentiment—of perhaps any previous era in American history—occurred *after* SDS had closed its doors. It included the November 1969 Moratorium against the war, up to that point the largest peace march in American history; Earth Day 1970, for which 20 million turned out; and the May 1970 student demonstrations against the invasion of Cambodia, in which 4.3 million took part at half the colleges in the country.

Less than two years later, the Democratic Party was taken over by progressive forces, and the old insiders like Chicago Mayor Richard Daley and George Meany were suddenly outsiders. This was much too rapid and radical for most voters, as the 1972 presidential election results showed, but the Statement prophecy of realignment had proven to be more feasible than anyone had imagined.

The 1960s movements stumbled to an end largely because we had won the major reforms that were demanded, thus causing our popular base to ebb: the 1964 and 1965 civil and voting rights laws, the end of the draft and the Vietnam War, passage of the War Powers Resolution and the Freedom of Information Act, Nixon's environmental laws, amnesty for war resisters, two presidents forced from office, the eighteen-year-old vote, union recognition of public employees and farmworkers, disability rights, the decline of censorship, the emergence of gays and lesbians from a shadow existence . . . perhaps never in U.S. history had so many changes occurred in so short a time, all driven by the vibrancy of participatory democracy.

Those who warned us of the system's unbendable durability, like Howard Zinn, a mentor I dearly loved, seemed at times to undervalue these achievements while celebrating the very movements that made them possible. For Zinn, the reforms at best were reluctant concessions "aimed at quieting the popular uprisings, not making fundamental changes."[9] But were all those reforms meaningless? Or were they democratic improvements, as I would argue? As if to prove Zinn's thesis, the global Cold War quickly morphed into the rise of neoliberal globalization, the militarized war on narcoterrorism, and, by 2001, the "global war on terror." The old threat of international communist conspiracies was replaced by alleged new threats from the narcoterrorists and global jihadists. The secrecy of the state expanded even in times of peace. And in response, new movements arose across the planet against war, sweatshops, hunger, and environmental destruction. The elite of the World Economic Forum, flying into Davos on corporate jets, were challenged by the World Social Forum, in which thousands of campesinos, indigenous people, workers, students, and artists made their way to Porto Alegre, Brazil. Porto Alegre showcased a model of "participatory budgeting," in which local citizens are directly involved in decisions to allocate public funds for neighborhood needs.

Starting in the 1980s, pro-democracy movements flourished across Latin and Central America in the wake of guerrilla campaigns. After these democratic transitions came the uprisings across the Arab world. Where the uprisings were repelled or derailed, the only unifying forward path still seemed to be through and toward participatory democracy. In 2009 came a movement echoing the 1961 Freedom Rides: undocumented students taking the risk of deportation while demanding passage of the DREAM Act. The 2011 revolt against Wisconsin Governor Scott Walker, which saw thousands occupy the state house for nearly a month, was another show of participatory democracy in action.

Participatory Democracy and Occupy Wall Street

The Occupy Wall Street phenomenon rose and fell so rapidly that it is hard to determine what lessons it might hold for participatory democrats. I do not know whether history begins anew or just repeats its sputtering cycles again and again. What is clear enough is that the Occupy movement began without pundit predictions, without funding, without organization, with only determined people in tents, countless Davids taking on the smug Goliath in spontaneous planetary resistance. While Occupy could not and would not agree on making detailed demands, it did agree, as noted earlier, on "direct and transparent participatory democracy" as its first principle.

Occupy's very existence made clear that across the Western world, the smoldering division is becoming one between unelected wealthy and foreign private investors and the participatory democracies of civic societies with their faltering elected governments. Of course, there are differences between the Port Huron Statement and the Occupy Wall Street manifesto, but they should not be overstated. One of the major differences has to do with anarchism, or "direct democracy," which plays a major role in the thinking, structure, and practice of many Occupy activists. The early SDS certainly identified with the Wobblies, the anarchists who organized the 1912 Bread and Roses strike in Lawrence, Massachusetts; the Haymarket Square martyrs; and the historic wildcat strikes across the Western mining country. We sang of Joe Hill; knew all about "Big Bill" Haywood, Emma Goldman, and Mother Jones; and lamented the executions of Sacco and Vanzetti. But we believed that social movements should insist on the democratic reform of state and corporation, not expect their overthrow or implosion. We carefully avoided adopting any of the previous ideologies of the left, including anarchism, in our search for something new. Ours was a democratic populist heritage, in which, we naively believed, many factions could bloom but none could choke our growth.

On the other hand, strict anarchist theory suggests that reforms merely legitimize and strengthen structures that should be toppled or dissolved. But the early SDS saw no alternative to winning reforms from the state and corporate sectors, or revitalizing a stagnant labor movement. We were fully aware of the dangers of being co-opted into the system, the managed cooling of street heat, the predictable countermovements that would rise up against us, like the Birch Society then and Tea Party today. Even a philosophical anarchist (or "libertarian socialist") like Noam Chomsky has argued that "There is a state sector that does awful things, but it also happens to do some good things." Anarchist effort to minimize "the state means strengthening the private sectors. It narrows the domain within which public influence can be expressed."[10]

I do not mean to say that all Occupiers opposed reform. But there is a broad suspicion of seeking reforms that require alliances with top-down organizations, especially with progressive elected officials. The same dilemmas arose in the 1960s in the relationships between SNCC and the national civil rights leadership, and between SDS and the liberal Democrats we blamed for starting the Vietnam War. Today, some Occupy theorists are equally suspicious of such progressive coalition building. For example, Micah White, a brilliant editor at *Adbusters*, writes that "an insurrectionary challenge to the capitalist state" will be mounted by "culture-jammers" who create "fluid, immersive, evocative meta-gaming experiences that are playfully thrilling and [that] as a natural result of their gameplay" a social revolution will arise as "pure manifestation of an anonymous will of a dispersed, networked collective."[11] It is as if the pure insurrectionary act, memorialized as performance art, is more important than the construction of any alliances, or any consequences that flow from it.

It is certainly true that an engine of decentralized democratic power is today available to *Adbusters*, Occupy, Facebook, and WikiLeaks that was not present at Port Huron. When I first saw a computer in 1964 it was the size of a room, and the professor who predicted microprocessors seemed nuts. We have come a long way from the Free Speech Movement's outrage at IBM cards to the exploding vista of instant information and interaction that has played a critical role, from the Zapatista uprising and the Battle of Seattle to the recent eruptions of interactive, live-streaming, participatory democracy all over the world.

But it is utopian to believe that downloading and freeing information, especially secret information, will bring about a decentralized revolution—anonymously, as one might say. The download replaces the overthrow in the imagination of some in this new movement. The invention of open-source technology may be the single greatest pathway to participatory democracy in our lifetimes, not only in coordinating social movements but in making democratic decision making possible without passing through representatives or gatekeepers. But like it or not, organizing the reform of existing institutions is also needed, if only to protect the open source or the whistleblowers. Such a participatory future cannot be protected without engaging in some sort of politics in the present.

A useful model was implicit in the Port Huron Statement, one transmitted from our parents' generation, the last until now to weather Wall Street scandal, foreclosures, bankruptcies, and unemployment (without any safety net). Our parents wanted a New Deal and Franklin Roosevelt to meet their basic needs, just as black people in Mississippi wanted the vote and Kennedy, and workers wanted the eight-hour day in Emma Goldman's time. After waiting several years for Wall Street to self-correct, the people of the 1930s began demanding what became the Wagner Act, Social Security, the Works Progress Administration, the Civilian Conservation Corps, and the Federal Writers Project, which made life better for generations to come.

These reforms came about, as Zinn would rightly warn, as pragmatic institutional responses or concessions meant largely to restore order. But the New Deal itself was driven by a chaotic, eclectic, sectarian, combative, fanatic, and passionate energy, and included anarchists, communists, musicians, muralists, liberals, progressives, prairie populists, industrial union organizers, and, yes, reformers, from Al Smith to Upton Sinclair to Eleanor Roosevelt. What became the New Deal was pushed from below by insurrectionary strikes in Seattle, factory occupations in Flint, and writings and art from government-subsidized poets and intellectuals who interviewed the poor, the migrants, and the unemployed, and who created great works like "This Land Is Your Land" and *The Grapes of Wrath*. It was a splendid bedlam of participatory democracy, which led neither to socialism nor fascism but to Keynesian economics and a vision of the state as an instrument that can sometimes be bent to the popular will and public interest. After twenty years of celebration, we decided in 1962 that those New Deal reforms were stagnating and insufficient, and that it was time to begin again.

We are not as badly off as Americans were in the 1930s, of course, if only because of the safety net reforms that were achieved in that earlier dangerous time. Globally, however, the unfettered appetites of capitalism have created an intolerable human condition. It is time for a participatory New Deal, to bring the banks and corporations under the regulations and reforms they have escaped through runaway globalization. The challenge is far greater when one considers the climate crisis, which is forcing us to build a democratic political economy without dependence on fossil fuels or nuclear power. The gluttony of Wall Street and the failures of capitalism will not be fixed by an election, but that is beside the point. Elections produce popular mandates, mandates spur popular activism, and new thinking emerges in the creativity of activism. Since the Occupy moment, we have seen the elections of Sen. Elizabeth Warren and Mayor Bill De Blasio, both successes the eventual political outcomes of the earlier uprising. Sadly, the 2000 election stolen from Al Gore would have moved us forward to the first environmental presidency. In a time when it is possible again to organize a progressive majority and win, the vision and strategy of Port Huron is worth considering as a guide.

PART I

Intellectual and Cultural Foundations

Chapter 2

Two Cheers for Utopia

Michael Kazin

The Port Huron Statement of Students for a Democratic Society is the most ambitious, the most specific, and the most eloquent manifesto in the history of the American left. It is also, at just over 25,000 words, undoubtedly the longest one. But it had to be lengthy to accomplish its aim—to propose an entire "agenda for a generation." Consider the variety of topics about which Tom Hayden and his fellow delegates to that SDS meeting in June 1962 had intelligent and provocative things to say: moral values, American politics, the U.S. economy, the nation's intellectual and academic life, the labor movement, the Cold War, the nuclear arms race, the anticolonial revolution, and a vivid description of why the black freedom movement was so pivotal to the birth of a new left. All this was informed by a sensibility attuned to what one might call the national psychology. And that is just a summary of the first half of the Statement.

The second part—"What Is Needed"—glowed with passion and elegance. What was needed, according to the fifty-five or so young drafters, included both such strategic aims as consolidating the Democrats into a principled liberal party by expelling the Dixiecrats and details fine-grained enough to delight the heart of any policy analyst. To wit: "there were fewer mental hospital *beds* in relation to the numbers of mentally ill in 1959 than there were in 1948."[1] In addition, the Statement combined varieties of prose not commonly featured in one document: existential longings inspired by Albert Camus, a quote from an encyclical by Pope John XXIII, urgent descriptions of the most serious issues facing humankind (then known as "mankind"), and far-reaching proposals for how to go about the prodigious task of democratizing the nation and the world.

Remarkably, most of the activist-intellectuals who accomplished all this were still in their early twenties. Hayden, at twenty-two, was the age at which most students are preparing to graduate from college. The previous year, *The Activist*, an obscure magazine edited at Oberlin College, had published Hayden's "A Letter to the New (Young) Left." After Port Huron, that article read like a textbook example of false modesty: "It is not as though we even know what to do," Hayden wrote in *The Activist*, "we have no real visionaries for our leaders, we are not much more than literate ourselves."[2] Somehow, he and his comrades figured it out. I cannot imagine a group of Americans, of any age, writing such a manifesto today. In our era of high anxiety and blasted visions, we could certainly use one.

But, for all its brilliance, Port Huron was not so much a break with the radical tradition as it was an artful meld of what remained fresh and stirring in the often tortured history of the American left. Thus, "young," the adjective Hayden had placed in parentheses, was more accurate than "new," which remains the word nearly everyone since has affixed to the movement in which SDS played a vital part.

The Statement managed to fuse two types of ideological advocacy that are often viewed as antagonists: first, the romantic desire for achieving an authentic self through crusading for individual rights and, second, the yearning for a democratic socialist order that would favor the collective good over freedom of the self. This fusion was wrapped in language whose utopian tone resembled that articulated by other messianic movements in American history—from the abolitionists and Owenite socialists to the Wobblies and Debsian Socialists to such radical feminists as Charlotte Perkins Gilman and Emma Goldman.

The similarity to the language of the abolitionists was particularly strong. Consider this bold assertion from the "Values" section of the Statement: "The goal of man and society should be human independence: a concern not with . . . popularity but with finding a meaning in life that is personally authentic. . . . This kind of independence does not mean egotistic individualism—the object is not to have one's way so much as it is to have a way that is one's own." Compare it to the late-life reflection by antislavery crusader Theodore Weld: "The starting point and power of every great reform must be the reformer's self," declared Weld, "He must first set himself apart its sacred devotee, baptised into its spirit, consecrated to its service, feeling its profound necessity, its constraining motives, impelling causes, and all [the] reasons why."[3] Devout Christians were a distinct minority at the FDR camp; evangelical Protestants were, I believe, entirely absent. But members of SDS were expressing the same ultra-romantic idea that a free society can be built only by individuals who define that freedom for themselves that had inspired fervently Protestant abolitionists more than a century earlier.

In this sense, Port Huron demonstrated how the new, young left—in its rebellion against a managed society and its hunger for an authentic one—was beginning to turn back, if unintentionally, to similar impulses that had inspired Weld and such fellow crusaders as his wife, Angelina Grimke, as well as William Lloyd Garrison, Frederick Douglass, and David Walker. Both groups insisted that one had to live one's politics as well as preach them. Both took delight in smashing taboos about interracial sex, about the proper roles of men and women, and even about dress and diet. Both experimented with styles of communal living they believed would allow individuals to realize their "true" nature and to find happiness in doing so.

Whether pious or secular, radicals before the Civil War and their counterparts during the Cold War struggled fiercely both to free their minds and bodies from an evil society and to fill the world with individuals who aspired to perfection. The passion for self-improvement in the cause of social transformation could be found nearly everywhere in the young left in the 1960s and 1970s. "I had to find out who I am and what kind of man I should be, and what I could do to become the best of which I was capable," confessed Black Panther leader Eldridge Cleaver. In 1970, Marshall Berman, in his *Politics of Authenticity*, observed, "The New Left's complaint against democratic capitalism was not that it was too individualistic, but rather that it wasn't individualistic enough."[4] In 1977, the black lesbians in the Combahee River Collective asserted, "Our politics . . . sprang from the shared belief that Black women are inherently valuable, that our liberation is a necessity not as an adjunct to somebody else's but because of our need as human persons for autonomy."[5] So the final American left of the industrial age gestured back, in spirit, to the first.

At the same time, long stretches of the Port Huron Statement echo not just the spirit but the letter of the social democratic tradition, which these young radicals were determined to transcend. One sees this in the Statement's harsh attack on corporate power and its vision of an egalitarian society that would expand civic participation rather than restrict it, as in both capitalist and communist nations. Michael Harrington bridled at the "anti-anti-Communism" of the section on the Cold War, but he could have found little to argue with in the lengthy list of proposals for economic planning, party realignment, mobilizing black voters, and more.

Even when the Statement criticized organized labor, it did so in a tone of disappointment and with hope for its renewal. "Labor continues to be the most liberal—and most frustrated—institution in mainstream America," SDS members commented. Then they noted that, although union members showed little enthusiasm for politics, "there are some indications . . . that labor might regain its missing idealism": the threat of automation, splits among union leaders over nuclear testing, and the demand by black activists for labor to take a clear stand for equal rights and to organize interracial unions in the South and elsewhere. The Statement continued, "Either labor continues to decline as a social force, or it must constitute itself as a mass political force demanding not only that society recognize its rights to organize but also a program going beyond desired labor legislation and welfare improvements." Members of SDS were, of course, not in thrall to what C. Wright Mills called "the labor metaphysic," the idea that only the proletariat could bring to birth a new world from the ruin of the old. But of organized labor's significance, the Statement left no doubt: "a new politics must include a revitalized labor movement."[6]

At the time, not coincidentally, that not-so-vital movement was keeping SDS in business. The United Auto Workers and other unions were the main contributors to SDS's modest budget, and the FDR camp, where the Port Huron meeting took place, was owned by Michigan AFL-CIO. Moreover, as Nelson Lichtenstein pointed out in his biography of Walter Reuther, most of the program outlined at Port Huron was already the "common coin of the UAW leadership strata."[7]

Thus, like socialists from Eugene Debs and Crystal Eastman to Norman Thomas and A. Philip Randolph, Hayden and his comrades understood the need to straddle the line between imagining a radically new society and improving the lives of the people who had to live in the deeply flawed old one. So it should not be startling to read in Hayden's memoir that, "immediately after the Port Huron convention, Al Haber and I drove to Washington to take our Statement to the White House. We met there for an hour with [historian and Kennedy adviser] Arthur Schlesinger . . . and he agreed to bring our views to the attention of the president. For the occasion, I wore a tie."[8]

Of course, early members of SDS did break with some hallowed traditions on the American left: they usually eschewed the socialist label and, most important, they followed the moral lead, the north star, of the black freedom movement. This was a clear break from the labor-centered vision and strategy of a social democracy created and led by white people. But, at the time the Statement was written, progressive union stalwarts like Reuther and Jerry Wurf of the American Federation of State, County, and Municipal Employees (AFSCME) were, at worst, the uneasy allies of most civil rights organizers. And at best, labor liberals and civil rights activists could rock the nation together, as they showed at the March on Washington for Jobs and Freedom just fourteen months after the campers had returned to their colleges and urban enclaves.

And is it even necessary to point out that close to a majority of the participants at Port Huron were secular Jews? That demographic fact also represented a continuity with both the socialist and communist lefts over the previous four decades. The association of radicalism with opposition to World War I and the ensuing rupture in the Socialist Party had led, fairly rapidly, to the desertion of most of the white working-class Christians who had been the majority in the People's Party, the pre-war SP, and the Industrial Workers of the World. Few of their grandchildren rushed to join SDS.

But Jews continued to be prominent in the white New Left out of all proportion to their numbers in the American population—just as they were in Marxist parties from the 1920s through the 1950s. Tom Hayden, Paul Potter, Jane Adams, Greg Calvert, and Diana Oughton, all of whom were raised as Christians, were outnumbered by the likes of Dick Flacks, Todd Gitlin, Paul Booth, Heather Booth, Paul Berman, Mark Rudd, Bernardine Dohrn, Robin Morgan, Abbie Hoffman, Karen Nussbaum, and Mike Klonsky—not to speak of middle aged Jewish mentors like Arnold Kaufmann, Howard Zinn, and Noam Chomsky. This ethnic continuity may help explain why, after SDS imploded and disappeared, its more historically minded survivors found much to praise in the Old Left tradition they had once been so keen to bury.

One aspect of the old Marxism that Port Huron mercifully interred was its twin faith in the inevitability that world capitalism would collapse and that a free and equal order would surely arise from the rubble. Carl Oglesby, in a brilliant essay published in 1969, called this faith "almost a carrion-bird politics. Distant and above it all for the moment, the revolutionary cadre circles, awaiting the hour of his predestined dinner."[9] The introduction to the Port Huron Statement replaced such grim delusions with the grim realism of the nuclear age: the next global conflict would destroy the human race, not liberate it.

The Statement then moved briskly to propose a fresh, utopian alternative to the old vision of state socialism that had been smashed into dust six years earlier by Khrushchev's not-so-"secret" speech and then by the bloody suppression of Hungary's revolt that he directed a few months later. SDS's alternative was "participatory democracy." As Jim Miller wrote insightfully, "p.d." was, at its creation, a profoundly ambiguous idea that did not become any more coherent over time. "It pointed toward daring personal experiments and modest social reforms," wrote Miller, "It implied a political revolution" but with a patriotic ring, evoking New England town meetings where neighbors debated and made the key decisions that affected their communities.[10]

What appealed to most of the young people who began to use the term was not so homespun a tradition. It was the promise of "participatory democracy" to utterly transform the society of overmanaged, bureaucratic, formally representative institutions they believed were stifling their independence of thought and action. That is why Mario Savio's famous speech in 1964 on the steps of University of California at Berkeley's Sproul Hall with his feverish plea to "put your bodies upon the gears and upon the wheels" of the "odious" machine became so emblematic and why consensus decision making turned into the process of choice for many SDS chapters and then for the growing radical feminist movement as well.

The merits of participatory democracy, as an ideal and a practice, should be obvious. Only when "the people" stand up for themselves in their neighborhoods, their workplaces, and the streets of their cities will they learn how power works ànd how they can use it to advance their own interests. The Port Huron Statement went further, arguing, in one of its most famous lines, that "politics has the function of bringing people out of isolation and into community, thus being a necessary, though not sufficient, means of finding meaning in personal life."[11] Aided by this implicit promise of psychic benefits, the white New Left, at its zenith in the late 1960s and early 1970s, convinced several million Americans to engage in modes of civic life—ranging from teach-ins to civil disobedience to consciousness-raising groups to running wild in the streets—that were educational, exhilarating, and at times, almost orgasmic.

However, "participatory democracy" was plagued by major blindspots too. Claimed as *the* path to the good society, it had no answer to the question of what happens to the vast majority of citizens who have little or no taste for politics. Only an activist aflame with the impatient desire for a revolution could believe that the apolitical masses are a bunch of alienated, sad human beings who would welcome liberation by young zealots they have never met. Most people, after all, prefer to have their orgasms in private.

It was also a serious mistake to equate democracy with participation in a social movement and to view all elected officials as either ineffectual cogs or corrupt parasites in an unjust system. The history of the American left from the abolitionists to the civil rights movement proves that only when representative and participatory forms of democracy work together do egalitarian reforms succeed and political leaders emerge who can be held accountable to the will of their constituents. Tom Hayden recognized this himself in the mid-1970s when he took to wearing a tie on a daily basis in his new career as a progressive and often successful Democratic politician.

In 2011, we witnessed protests—from Tunisia to Madrid to Madison to Tel Aviv to Cairo to Moscow to Zuccotti Park—that were reminiscent of the kind of change the Port Huronites were advocating. Notwithstanding their vast differences, all these demonstrations sought to bring people out of isolation and into politics without requiring that they abandon their individual desires for the uncertain security of a hierarchical organization. Many of the protests were either organized by or helped to gestate mass movements. In the United States, the Occupiers took up the slogan "This is what democracy looks like."

Unfortunately, that is just a partial truth and one that contains the seeds of disillusionment, if not a movement's decline. *The New Republic*'s Leon Wieseltier is skeptical about nearly every mass protest, yet he did recently ask a good question: "Why do demonstrators always confuse the quality of their own experience, their mystical moments of unity, with the condition of their country, with its progress?"[12] Later in the 1960s, I was among the SDS members who imagined that our takeovers of campus buildings and our huge demonstrations in Washington, D.C., and other cities were the tip of a popular rebellion that would not stop with ending the war in Vietnam. In the 1970s, we discovered the need to identify and campaign for peace-minded politicians too. But by the time George McGovern was nominated for president in 1972, he was unable to mobilize the dwindling energies of the antiwar movement without being held captive to its popular image as a band of scruffy, violent anti-Americans.

Since most Americans were not about to become full-time political activists, it was natural for the writers of The Port Huron Statement to pin their hopes for a truly radical, fully democratic society on the only group whose members had the time, the vigor, and the inclination to dedicate their lives to bringing it about: college students of all races with a strong intellectual bent. Academia was "an overlooked seat of influence," they argued, because of its "social relevance, the accessibility of knowledge, and internal openness. These together make the university a potential base and agency in a movement of social change." The Statement added that, to grow, the New Left would require a partnership between liberals and socialists; the university was "a more sensible place than a political party for these two traditions to begin to discuss their differences and look for political synthesis."[13]

Just a few years later, that last goal sounded naive and outmoded when opposing the war in Vietnam consumed most SDS activists. Since liberal presidents and their appointees had planned and carried out the assault on Indochina, "humanist liberals," as Oglesby, then the president of SDS, called them in 1965, had to denounce that legacy or else become what he called "grudging apologists for the corporate state." Soon, on campuses from Palo Alto and Kent, Ohio, to Cambridge and Manhattan, SDS members were battling liberal administrators and forcing liberal professors to choose sides. The grand synthesis of liberalism and radicalism was stillborn.[14]

However, by the end of the 1960s, the reigning culture at universities was beginning to undergo a rapid and, for young radicals, a most salutary change. The delegates at Port Huron had not anticipated this. Ironically, they lodged a critique of academic life that was as damning as anything Allan Bloom, the idol of neoconservativism, would say a quarter-century later. "The actual intellectual effect of the college experience," they complained, "is hardly distinguishable from that of any other communications channel—say a television set—passing on the stock truths of the day. Students leave college more 'tolerant' than when they arrived, but basically unchallenged in their values and political orientations."[15]

While young radicals did not overthrow the System, they certainly helped alter what passed for "stock truths" in every humanities discipline and in most of the social sciences as well. Alas, the "long march through the institutions" that German SDS leader Rudi Dutschke had called for, was, in the United States at least, more successful in colleges and universities than anywhere else. Ironically, the former student activists who went on to careers in academia did more to create a refuge from the nation's rightward drift than a mass base for progressive social change. Kalle Lasn, the editor of *Adbusters* magazine who helped create Occupy Wall Street, declared, "Revolutions always start at universities." Perhaps—but they can end there too.

The emphasis at Port Huron and after on the radical potential of the young also obscured an analytical flaw beneath the undeniable excitement of a generation on the move. The fact that the New Left heralded itself as a *young* left was critical to its growth—and to its ultimate demise. Radical movements everywhere depend on the zealous energies of people who need little sleep and do not have to worry about the feeding, clothing, and sleep schedules of children. The average age of the Bolshevik leaders who took power in Petrograd in 1917 was all of twenty-six. But never before had an American left made youth itself a badge of rebellion—or prided itself on breaking away from its older predecessors. Jack Weinberg, the Berkeley radical who coined the famous line "We don't trust anyone over thirty" meant it as a rebuttal to the charge that subversive adults were pulling the strings. But few people, inside or outside of the movement, got the joke.[16]

The notion of a "revolution" made almost exclusively by the young was both brilliant and absurd. On the one hand, it expressed the self-confidence of activists from a generation that was both larger and better educated than any in U.S. history. College enrollment tripled during the 1960s to nearly ten million, and few students had experienced the privations of the Great Depression. For many Americans who believed that one can always remake one's life, the plain-spoken brashness of young radicals was often appealing, even when they disagreed with the point of their protests.[17]

Yet age has no intrinsic political merit, and the impatience of nearly all young radicals and the arrogance of some also led them astray. Contemptuous of liberals, they came to spurn the very idea of inter-class, interracial reform coalitions that was still a live option for the authors of the Port Huron Statement. Disenchanted with old formulas for remaking American society, they gave little thought to devising new ones. For the antiwar militants who flooded into SDS after 1965, "participatory democracy" seemed too hazy and abstract in both meaning and application to guide a revolution. Frustration at the lack of an alternative led an aggressive minority in the movement to take up one variety of Leninist dogma or another, while other activists sought to refashion a liberalism cleansed of Cold War hypocrisies. Neither project was successful.

So Port Huron's "agenda for a generation" devolved, perhaps inevitably, into a set of stirring principles for an activist, mostly white minority of that generation. And by the end of the 1960s, the visibility of the text itself had faded. Even as a much abridged pamphlet, the Statement was not high on the reading list at most SDS chapters. The radical movement had grown much larger, as well as much angrier and prone to an ideological rigidity that had been refreshingly absent at the convention camp. *The New Left Reader*, a popular anthology edited by Carl Oglesby in 1969, included documents by everyone from Louis Althusser and Fidel Castro to Huey Newton and Mark Rudd—but not a word of the Port Huron Statement.

And for all its capaciousness, Port Huron had nothing to say about three groups that would become major factors in American politics and culture by the end of the decade: environmentalists, feminists, and the New Right. It would be unfair to criticize the Port Huronites for failing to anticipate the coming of Earth Day or the emergence of the women's liberation movement; Rachel Carson's *Silent Spring* wasn not published until the fall of 1962, and Betty Friedan's *Feminine Mystique* did not reach bookstores until half a year later. But the conservative Young Americans for Freedom had roughly 30,000 members in 1962. That March, YAF sponsored a rally that filled Madison Square Garden. A few SDS members picketed the event. But in a text that devoted thousands of words to the shortcomings of liberalism, some attention might have been paid to what, even then, was its main opposition.

Still, what was produced at Port Huron has aged better than the apocalyptic, hypermilitant pronouncements that drew so much attention forty years ago yet elicit mostly puzzlement or derision today. "I liked both the longing for a total explanation and the uncertainty as to what it might be," Todd Gitlin recalled about his first reading of the Statement. Indeed, for radicals, a little self-doubt is a valuable thing. In the class I teach about the 1960s, I show undergraduates a film clip of Mario Savio shouting on the steps of Sproul Hall on the Berkeley campus about throwing his body on the machine. Then I ask, "What was this man so angry about?" They haven't got a clue, although his passion is rather compelling.[18] Huey Newton's talk of "revolutionary suicide" has, thankfully, no appeal at all. To young Americans who worked hard to elect Barack Obama in 2008 and sympathized with the Occupy uprising, the idea of building a movement to restructure the system instead of blowing the whole thing up just sounds like common sense.

But they need—we need—the utopian spirit of Port Huron as much we do its attention to posing practical solutions to the outrages committed by power elites at every level of society, in the United States and around the world. Fifty years ago, that band of twenty-somethings dared to imagine the making of a more decent, more humane, as well as a more democratic society. "We would replace power rooted in possession, privilege, or circumstance by power and uniqueness rooted in love, reflectiveness, reason, and creativity," they declared.[19] That one sentence captured the larger ideal that animated many civil rights organizers as well as the feminist and gay insurgencies soon to come. These movements greatly expanded the scope of individual freedom in America: to work wherever one is qualified, to live anyplace one can afford, and to love and marry anyone who loves and wants to marry you—to an extent unimaginable at the time the Statement was written.

Today, the international regime of freebooting capitalism has delivered neither material abundance, nor social harmony, nor security to most of the world's people. Failed states, religious wars, environmental disaster, austerity in the face of poverty, clashes between immigrants and the native born are common features of current history, as they were in previous eras. But the perception that there is no alternative to chronic crisis but, somehow, to muddle through only exacerbates the problems.

At the end of his book about the Port Huron Statement, Jim Miller rhapsodized, "For anyone who joined in the search for a democracy of individual participation—and certainly for anyone who remembers the happiness and holds to the hopes that the quest itself aroused—the sense of what politics can mean will never be quite the same again."[20]

For those who believe in and work for beneficial and enduring change, such longings should never be dismissed as merely "utopian." They are, instead, the very soul of realism—the only way to motivate large numbers of people to join and commit themselves to the lofty purposes of left-wing social movements. As the memorable coda of the Port Huron Statement put it, "If we appear to seek the unattainable . . . then let it be known that we do so to avoid the unimaginable."[21] Future writers of manifestos could do worse than to begin right there.

Chapter 3

Port Huron and the Origins of the International New Left

Lisa McGirr

The Port Huron Statement and the student movement in the United States that it helped inspire was part of a widespread international moment of left-oriented youth rebellion that spread around the world during the 1960s. These mobilizations shared ideas, networks, repertoires of protest, and a sense of imagined community. Transnational linkages fueled these movements' growth, as did social and economic developments affecting all of the core countries of the post–World War II capitalist West.[1] While distinctive political and social contexts within individual countries mattered most to understanding the grievances, character, strength, and trajectories of these diverse movements, an eye toward the global can help us better understand how these mobilizations took place in so many places simultaneously, what they shared, as well as how they differed. Taking off the national casements that often bind our historical narratives, in other words, allows us to see these global processes that contributed to this moment of "revolutionary" tumult. Building on recent scholarship, this essay places the Port Huron Statement within this global context to offer a more complete understanding of its meaning and its making.

Popular memory and participant accounts that once dominated understandings of the left-oriented social movements of the 1960s are now increasingly being replaced by a robust set of scholarly accounts that chart the strikes, university occupations, protests, and demonstrations that rocked cities and towns from Venice to Mexico City, Tokyo to Prague, and

London to Dakar. An outpouring of sociological studies in France has shaped (even if, according to Kirstin Ross, depoliticized) the collective memory of the great student and worker strike in Paris in May of 1968 that almost brought down the De Gaulle regime.[2] Mexican historians have charted how the intersection of a vibrant youth counterculture and the New Left in high schools and universities challenged state authority and government repression, culminating in the infamous Tlatelolco massacre that killed scores of students.[3] For Italy, Robert Lumley, among others, has analyzed the university as well as factory strikes stretching from Milan to Venice that blossomed within the waters of a broader Mediterranean world of student rebellion.[4] Scholars of Czech history and politics, building on the work of Gordon Skilling, have debated the factors that contributed to the Prague Spring, disagreeing on whether it was spurred more by reforms at the top or pushed from below by peasants, artists, writers, and university students. But they agree that in the fall of 1967, students did their part to protest old-style authoritarian rule, taking to the streets and calling for a "new socialism" with a "human face."[5] For Germany, Tim Brown has interrogated the intersection between the local and the global within the vibrant world of youth counterculture and its varied incarnations on both sides of the Wall in Cold War Berlin.[6] And breaking the long silence of Japanese scholars on the topic, Eiki Oguma in 2009 published a massive study of the vibrant, if extremely faction-ridden mobilization of Japanese students that led to occupation and strikes at more than one-third of universities in 1968.[7] For Senegal, Omar Gueye has made an important contribution tracing the protest, strikes, and riots of workers and students in his work on the tumultuous year of 1968 in Dakar and its ramifications more widely in West Africa.[8]

All of these accounts excavate in rich detail the vibrant and varied national incarnations of the student New Left. They now allow us to map the linkages between them of ideas, organizational ties, and sense of imagined community. Doing so deepens our understanding of the intersection of the local and the global in propelling youth protest in the 1960s and sets these movements in conversation with one another. Those historians that have begun to tease out these transnational connections highlight the rewards that can be reaped by expanding our frame of vision beyond local and national developments.[9] Essay collections such as *New World Coming: The Sixties and the Shaping of Global Consciousness* (2009), edited by Karen Dubinsky and others, as well as a forum on "International 1968" in the flagship journal of the discipline, the *American Historical Review,* published in 2009, point in this direction.[10] While the project of understanding the student New Left of the 1960s in international terms is in its early stages, with most studies focused on just a few places (predominantly West Germany and the United States), it has become clear that such an approach enriches our understanding of Port Huron, not by undermining its significance, but by decentering it.[11]

The scholarship produced thus far on the global 1960s, however, while opening a new internationalist angle of vision has weighted heavily toward charting the upheaval of 1968.[12] Those books that take a longer chronological approach, Martin Klimke's study of student protest in West Germany and the United States (2009), for example, and Gerd-Rainer Horn's comprehensive examination of protest in both Western Europe and the United States notable among them, highlight the rewards that can be reaped with a longer view. Still, the tendency of scholarship to focus on the revolutionary New Left social movement upheaval, shorthanded as "1968," has caused us to lose sight of the far longer trajectory of the global New Left that laid the groundwork for that tumultuous year. The origins of "international 1968" are best understood within a longer angle of vision, one that reaches back to the prior decade. Events during the latter half of the 1950s sparked the formation and consolidation of the global New Left between 1956 and 1962. The snowballing of the New Left thereafter fueled the year of revolutionary upheaval around the globe.[13] Making sense of "international 1968" requires a chronologically long transnational frame of vision.

The several dozen men and women gathered at Port Huron who drafted the "manifesto for a generation," and the international New Left they formed part of, drew their inspiration for a new movement out of a set of events that stretched back to the mid-1950s. The Khrushchev/Stalin revelations and the crushing of the Hungarian uprising in 1956 disillusioned a young generation of radicals, leading them to reject the dogmas of their fathers. The year 1956 was a watershed for left-leaning intellectuals and students from Asia, Western and Eastern Europe, Latin America, and the United States, both communist and non-communist. The disillusionment with the authoritarianism and factionalism of the left inspired calls for renewal and a search for new visions and models for left politics. Out of these reckonings, New Left movements took root and flourished around the world.

In Japan, students at the University of Tokyo disillusioned by the Communist Party's abandonment of militant policies soon abandoned the

Japanese Communist Party and forged the independent Kyosan Shugisya Domei, also known as the "Bund," in 1956.[14] The Bund soon took over the leadership of Zengakuren, the national student federation.[15] Eight hundred of those students occupied Haneda Airport in January 1960 to prevent Prime Minister Nobusuke Kishi from leaving for the United States to sign the U.S.–Japan Security Treaty, signaling the entry of the Japanese student New Left onto the national stage.

In Western Europe, left-oriented intellectuals sought to forge a new radicalism in the wake of the 1956 revelations. In Britain, academics and left intellectuals proposed a new middle way and a "humane socialism," leading to the founding of E. P. Thompson's *New Reasoner* in 1957 and Stuart Hall's *Universities and New Left Review* in 1958, later merged into the *New Left Review* in 1960. These calls modeled themselves in part on the "Nouvelle Gauche" in France, marked by flourishing journals of dissent from *Arguments* (1956–1962) to the *L'Internationale Situationniste* (1958–1969).[16] West German students affiliated with the Social Democratic Party soon critiqued what they saw as authoritarian tendencies within the party. Conflicts led to a split in 1961 and the crystallization of an independent student New Left.[17] The German SDS (Sozialistischer Deutscher Studentenbund) articulated their own debt to youth intellectuals in other parts of the world. They declared, as Martin Klimke highlighted, that "we feel that we belong to the movement which originates in England under the name New Left and in France is called 'Nouvelle Gauche.'"[18]

In Eastern Europe, in places such as Prague as well as Warsaw, Khrushchev's "secret speech" in the Soviet Union led intellectuals and academics to challenge party dogmatism and prompted calls for democratization of the political system and a "renaissance socialism."[19] Young people, both inside and outside of Czech and Polish universities, contributed to the dissent, calling for liberalization. And in the United States, the New Left arose out of the ashes of the old left, which had been dealt lethal blows by the combined impact of McCarthyism and the Khrushchev/Stalin revelations.[20] Young idealists heeded the call of iconoclasts such as C. Wright Mills, whose "Letter to the New Left" called for building an anti-authoritarian, nondogmatic alternative to the old left. Mills himself, however, as historian Dan Geary has revealed, was not solely a lone-wolf, iconoclast intellectual.[21] Mills's "Letter to the New Left," after all, was first published in a British journal, *New Left Review,* and Mills spent time in British New Left circles in 1957, traveling throughout Europe, even visiting with dissident intellectuals in Eastern

Europe.[22] Even this seemingly most "homegrown organic" New Left intellectual was part of global networks and global debates.

A longer temporal and wider geographical vision also brings to center stage the importance of the newly independent block of nations that emerged from the ashes of colonialism to the tumultuous upheavals of those years. It was in 1955, after all, that twenty-nine Asian and African nations came together at the Bandung Conference in Indonesia to chart a "third way"—and embrace an identity as the "third world." At this moment, as historian Vijay Prashad has written, "the colonized world emerged to claim its place in world affairs."[23] These nations sought to pursue newly independent paths of development determined by their alignment with neither the Soviet Union nor the United States. Those emergent "third-world nations" that linked their struggles for national liberation with a vision of social revolution breathed new life into a new left that saw the Soviet Union as a moribund model of "real existing socialism."

The theme of solidarity championed by third-world leaders, no matter the actual problems of autocracy, corruption, and instability experienced by emerging postcolonial nations, inspired a young, radical generation in core capitalist countries. They identified with third-world nations' aspirations and the idea of the third world as a new possibility for building alternative revolutionary socialism. The idea of the third world as the future linked the European and American New Left with the politics of Africa, Asia, and Latin America.[24] The Port Huron Statement crystallized the sense of optimism inspired by decolonization and the revolutionary movements in the global South it sparked: "While weapons have accelerated men's opportunity for self-destruction, the counter-impulse to life and creation are superbly manifest in the revolutionary feelings of many Asian, African and Latin American peoples. Against the individual initiative and aspiration, and social sense of organicism characteristic of these upsurges, the American apathy and stalemate stand in embarrassing contrast."[25]

This new set of actors played an important role in the emergent activism of young students in core capitalist countries and gave credence to their hopes to make the world anew. Historian Quinn Slobodian has documented the importance of African and Iranian visiting students to the issues that galvanized West Germany's student movement. Van Gosse has examined the importance of Cuba to the movement in the United States. And Sean Mills has examined the influence of postcolonial struggles and ideas to 1960s political activism in Montreal.[26] From this angle of vision, middle-class students, whether in France, West Germany, Canada, the United States, or Japan, were on the "periphery" of the core theater of struggles—that of third-world revolutions and the United States', the Soviet Union's, and also China's efforts to contain and shape them. Indeed, Rudi Dutschke observed that the "anti-authoritarian revolt" of the young in West Germany took flight with a protest against the visit of Prime Minister Moise Tshombe of the Congo in 1964, successor to the hero-martyr Patrice Lumumba, whose challenge to United States and Belgian geopolitical and economic interests resulted in his assassination.[27] It was centrally, of course, in protest against U.S. military designs to control and direct one such anticolonial struggle for self-determination and social revolution in Vietnam that energized the New Left movement around the world. The very essence of the New Left was thus a newfound internationalism that seemed to contrast to the Soviet Union's and China's efforts to mold socialism into a nationalist project.

Rooting the student New Left within this longer and wider angle of vision also reminds us of the fundamental importance not simply of the struggles of new independent nations but also of the wider nonstudent progressive mass struggles, from worker movements in Italy and Senegal and the civil rights movement in the United States, to providing the broader supportive waters, inspiration, protest tactics, strategies, and models for collective social change. The black freedom struggle in the United States, in particular, from civil rights to the black power movement, resonated internationally. The importance of ordinary men and women taking to the streets and putting their own bodies on the line to challenge entrenched systems of oppression and power cannot be overstated as a motor force inspiring students toward social movement–building, whether in Frankfurt, Germany, or Ann Arbor, Michigan. In turn, civil rights actors and black nationalists in the United States shaped their ideas and strategies for struggle within the context of wider pan-Africanist and pan-Asian struggles, as Brenda Gayle Plummer has charted in her book *African-Americans in the Era of Decolonization, 1956–1974.*[28]

The nonstudent actors and organizations around the globe that contributed to the broader supportive waters in which the student New Left in the 1960s emerged had built significant transnational linkages as well. The broad-based international effort to end the spiraling arms race, for example, from the Campaign for Nuclear Disarmament in Britain, the Committee for a Sane Nuclear Policy (SANE) in the United States, and the massive peace movement in Japan of the late 1950s and early 1960s shared organizational ties, strategies, and tactics across national borders. These organizations flourished alongside and intersected with student New Left activism, with student peace organizations providing some of the first forays into activism for many students and contributing the broader activist protest milieu of the period.[29] All of these distinctive mobilizations happening simultaneously contributed to the dynamism of protest and the sense that change was possible. The post–World War II communications revolutions, moreover, instantaneously broadcast news of events and protest to televisions and newspapers worldwide. The increasing ease of air travel, moreover, facilitated transnational linkages between distinctive national movements.

The importance of nonstudent actors and organizations working for social change in the West and the East, North, and South begs the question of why it was that students came to identify themselves as a central motor force of change. The 1960s, after all, did not mark the first time students engaged in left politics. They did, however, represent the first time that students identified themselves as a social group with a special mission. The Port Huron Statement crystallized this sentiment in just few words: "We are people of this generation, bred in at least modest comfort, housed now in universities, looking uncomfortably to the world we inherit."[30]

Students' sense of their own positioning and *agency* was shaped by the structures of global capitalism that rose out of World War II. As renowned historian Eric Hobsbawm has written, this was the "golden Age of American capitalism."[31] The dramatic economic growth in the core capitalist countries from 1950 to 1970, underwritten in no small part by welfare-oriented social democratic states of the period, brought profound social transformations, massive urbanization, and tremendous population booms. Unprecedented economic growth contributed to widespread affluence and strong middle classes. To meet the growing needs for skilled workers as well as meet the rising expectations of their countries' growing middle classes, core capitalist states and newly industrializing nations expanded their systems of higher education, and student populations skyrocketed. The student population in the United States more than doubled, reaching 670,000 in 1967. Other nations saw even greater growth. France and Turkey's student populations exploded by 400 percent during those same years. West Germany's and Japan's student populations each tripled. And while not quite as dramatic, the numbers in Italy and the United Kingdom also more than doubled.[32]

This dramatic growth at the very least granted students a new social position. The growing numbers of students also meant challenges for university administrators that many were ill equipped to face. Students, whether in Alsace, France; Trento, Italy; Berlin, Germany; Berkeley, California; or Mexico City chafed against bureaucratic, top-down structures of university governance, rigid examination structures, and outmoded curricula. In some places, such as northern Italy, exploding numbers of students meant overcrowded dormitories and classrooms. In the United States, while students had been actively mobilizing on campuses for a number of years, concerns over the bureaucratic rules and limits on student speech of the new "multiversity" sparked the Free Speech Movement, demonstrating to administrators and public officials that students represented a powerful new collective voice to be reckoned with. In Trento, Italy, protests over curriculum led to calls for the "democratization of the university."[33] And it was concerns at the University of Tokyo over the internship requirements for medical students, and the administration's authoritarian response to their demands, that granted the student movement a new lease on life there.[34] Inadequate infrastructure also sparked student actions in Czechoslovakia: continued power outages at the Strahov dormitory in Prague in 1967 led students to pour into the streets chanting "we want light" and calling for a new socialism "with a human face."[35] Already politicized dissident students on campuses in the East and West responded to campus grievances (and to what they saw as university complicity in larger interlocking power structures), utilizing tactics pioneered by broader worker and civil rights movements that preceded and intersected with them, working to build radical campus activism.

As campuses themselves became sites for left-oriented students to protest the power dynamics, structures of capitalism, and universities' role in a larger military-industrial complex, so too did they provide spaces that facilitated transnational alliances. Universities, after all, provided travel opportunities for student exchange. Now, middle-class left-leaning students traveled to other campuses and built organizational ties, exchanged news, and established networks and friendships. One example, among many, was West German SDS activist Michael Vester. In 1961, he traveled as an exchange student to the United States, where he built ties to the U.S.-based SDS, attended Port Huron, and contributed to the creation of the foreign policy section of the Port Huron Statement.[36] As documented in another essay in this volume, Vester's international links, as for many other activists, remained critical to his vision of activism throughout the decade. Sometimes, student radicals traveled across borders to exchange tactics and strategies, such as when a group of Leuven students, already seasoned in university occupations, traveled to Paris to offer their advice to striking students.[37] Left-oriented student organizations and their media outlets, whether in Germany, Italy, or Japan, encouraged contacts, news, and ties with their brethren left students in other countries.

These exchanges contributed to the "world-wide phenomena" of "youthful dissidence," as a concerned 1967 Central Intelligence Agency memo described this turbulent moment of protest.[38] And, this movement, in contrast to the old left, was generation-specific to its core. Indeed, this generational identity, expressed through shared imagery, slogans, styles of dress, and its sense of imagined community, was one of the central dividing lines between the old and the New Left. American slogans such as "never trust anyone over thirty" were echoed, for example, by Japanese students' cries of "give me back my youth."[39]

Their sense of themselves as a group apart was fostered by the structures of global commercial culture that emerged after the war. With economic growth and rising prosperity, corporations hungry for new markets were quick to exploit the large numbers of youth as a promising niche. Cultural products like Hollywood movies, rock music, and magazines aimed at youth (like Italy's *Mondo Beat* and the satirical *MAD* magazine in the United States) tapped into youth sensibilities of disaffection and heightened young people's sense of participating in a broader youth culture.[40] Uta Poiger and Eric Zolov, among others, have charted how movies, fashion, and music, often but not always Anglo-American in origin, translated to new milieus, contributing to counter-hegemonic cultural modes and youth disaffection.[41] According to Eric Zolov, in Mexico, rock-and-roll music became a part of a "shared repertoire" that "linked youth psychically, if not materially to one another's struggles."[42]

Still, it is important not to overestimate the influence of this broader youth culture to the forging of the student New Left. While cultural products that appealed to youth may have contributed to youth's rebellious attitudes, their consumption lacked substantive political meaning, and their messages could be read in a number of ways and serve distinctive purposes depending on their audiences. Mexican parents, for example, might decry rock music's weakening of their children's "buenos costumbres," but they might also embrace it as a sign of their own family's modernity and their children's middle-class status.[43] Indeed, while segments of dissident Mexican youth created indigenous forms of rock music as a cultural critique, a broad segment of the student left rejected rock music as a foreign import and a tool of capitalist imperialists, favoring indigenous music instead.

While the global youth culture of the 1950s and 1960s, then, should not be understood in itself as a motor force in forging the international student New Left, it did shape its distinctive style and, more important, contributed to the New Left's emphasis on culture as a significant realm of action in its efforts to make the world anew. This emphasis on culture and on preformative politics marked a sharp contrast to the politics of the old left. "Men," emphasized the Port Huron Statement, "have unrealized potential for self-cultivation, self-direction, self-understanding, and creativity." Creative action and performativity became a means of young radicals to counter what the Port Huron Statement described as the "depersonalization that reduces human beings to the status of things."[44] This emphasis, of course, differed depending on the corner of the globe one points one's flashlight to. The powerful and radical student movement in Turkey, for example, tightly linked to the nation's radical worker parties, adhered closer to traditional Marxist analysis that fore-fronted class struggle. Movement tactics and strategies in distinct countries to foment social change also shifted over time, with all countries experiencing a marked radicalization at the turn of the decade. But, as a whole, the international student New Left, with some variation, distinguished itself from the old left by its thoroughgoing cultural critiques of modern capitalism.

In many countries witnessing tremendous economic growth, students positioning within the middle class did not displace but sidelined questions of economic inequality, class exploitation, and redistribution in favor of concerns over democracy, the hegemonic structures of modern consumer capitalism (or in the East, centralized state bureaucratic power), and the problem of forging meaningful dissent within these systems. As the authors of the Port Huron Statement lamented, "Beneath the stagnation of those who have closed their minds to the future, is the pervading feeling that there simply are no alternatives, that our times have witnessed the exhaustion not only of Utopias, but of any new departures as well. . . . The dominant institutions are complex enough to blunt the minds of their potential critics, and entrenched enough to swiftly dissipate or entirely repel the energies of protest and reform, thus limiting human expectancies."[45] In opposition, the generation of the New Left called for the forging of meaningful participatory democracy.

The short space of this essay cannot do justice to the wide and varied intellectual influences on the student New Left. Yet, arguably, no one contemporary intellectual contributor mattered more to the organizers of SDS in the founding moment of the New Left between 1958 and 1962 than C. Wright Mills. And, as the movement unfolded over the course of the decade and around the globe in the wake of Port Huron, Herbert Marcuse took pride of place along with Mills in forging a powerful critique of the structures of modern capitalism. His championing of students as possible agents of revolutionary change against the overwhelming powers of conformity, complacency, and difficulty of dissent not surprisingly resonated among the generations' global middle-class dissident youth.

Indeed, in places from Trento, to Paris, to Amsterdam, to Tokyo, and to Madison, C. Wright Mills and Herbert Marcuse crystallized and provided the theoretical framework to the actions and broader *Weltanschauung* of the movement. C. Wright Mills and Marcuse, picking up on Frankfurt School critiques, abandoned organized labor and workers as agents for revolutionary change: they had become conservative, sated by affluence and the trappings of consumer capitalism. Mills emphasized the agency of a "new class," students among them, who might be able to challenge the "power elite," the centralizing forces of state-military and corporate power within managerial capitalism that made real democratic decision-making impossible and crushed individualism. Marcuse's analysis in *One-Dimensional Man* (1964), while pessimistic about the possibility of breaking through the totalizing and hegemonic power of modern capitalism, called for a "Great Refusal." He argued that only the "lumpenproletariat," marginalized racial groups, outsiders, and the dispossessed could serve as agents of resistance (later, in a somewhat unlikely move, he included students within this group of outcasts as well).[46] His concerns over alienation and calls for an "optimism of the will" resonated with students' own search for meaning.

Mills and Marcuse were read widely on campuses by left activists in many places.[47] Although Mills died in 1962, his critiques of managerial society, of bureaucracy, and of the "power elite" rippled through the Port Huron Statement and in the demands and goals of students elsewhere, such as in Trento and in Tokyo. Marcuse too was widely read, and his ideas permeated the writings of influential New Left thinkers, such as French situationalist Guy Debord.[48] Marcuse's influence was made real not only through his writings but also through crowded campus lectures from

Rome, Amsterdam, Paris, and London. One former left Turkish radical remarked that Marcuse was "meaningless" for the movement there, which adhered tightly to Marxism. His very referencing of the New Left iconoclast, however, suggests Marcuse's broader influence.[49] Tellingly, sociology faculties were, not infrequently, the cradles of broader campus protest. This was the case, for example, in Trento, Italy, where students read a wide canon of American sociological texts, including, undoubtedly, Mills and Marcuse.[50] More work remains to be done to tease out the transmission, dissemination, and translation of left ideas in different places.

If one looks at the New Left internationally, what stands out is its new and central preoccupation, in contrast to the old left, with questions of "subjectivity." Its orientation was at least as much existential as it was political. The extent to which these diverse movements emphasized finding a new "selfhood" is deeply striking. The Port Huron Statement, for example, called for finding "a meaning in life that is personally authentic." It rejected "selfish" individualism in favor of community and human "interdependence."[51] These calls were echoed in a different cultural context when Japanese students called for "self-negation." New Leftists there called for students to remake themselves by denying their own privileged position as members of an elite and to identify with the oppressed. At the University of Tokyo, one prominent slogan was "Tokyo University within ourselves," a call not simply to outward critique but of one's own lived privilege and subjectivity. The leading Japanese scholar of the movement concluded that the movement was as much existential in orientation as seeking purely political goals.[52]

Such an orientation is revealed in a segment of the student New Left's embrace of the politics of the spectacle. The Dutch "Provos," the French "Situationist International," the antics and hype of Jerry Rubin's "Youth International Party," along with, arguably, the Japanese student New Left's "performance of violence" all exemplified variations on the theme of the spectacle of subversion.[53] This segment of the New Left sought to foment social change not through mass demonstrations and forging popular front movements, but by staging sometimes shocking performances of the street. Avant-garde artists and cultural theorists, such as French theorist Guy Debord, called for a comprehensive critique of modern society transcending Marxist theory and encompassing all aspects of human life. This tendency intersected with the "prefigurative" politics of the left: the effort to live out the society one hoped to create in the "beloved community." Such efforts, evident in SDS's Economic Research and Action Project (ERAP), were mirrored in experiments in communal living in multiple countries. West Berlin's Kommune I and especially Kommune 2, for example, linked their left political goals to cultural modes and styles of living that rejected materialism and abandoned the bourgeois norms of upward mobility and rigidity.[54]

The importance within this *Weltanschauung,* of an existential and deeply personal stance, as Tom Hayden averred, of "putting one's body on the line," may have contributed to another shared characteristic of the student New Left in multiple countries—namely, the romance with violence that marked so many of these movements by the decade's end. The non-dogmatic and open-ended vision of "participatory democracy" expressed in the Port Huron Statement in 1962 was, of course, displaced at its 1969 conference when disciplined cadres of radical Maoist Progressive Labor and the radical Weathermen split the organization, leaving SDS a shell of its former self. Such factionalism and radicalization was not simply a feature of the American student New Left. Indeed, looking to developments in multiple countries, rather than one country alone, suggests that the embrace by a small but significant segment of the New Left of terrorist methods was a pattern that marked the movements broadly.

The post-1968 legacy of fractures, state repression, and the frustration of failed goals, as well as an ideology that emphasized the importance of individual existentialist stance over pragmatic mass-based change, contributed to the establishment of revolutionary factions from the Weather Underground in the United States to the Brigate Rosse in Italy; from the Rote Armee Fraktion in Germany to Japan's United Red Army; and from Turkey's People's Liberation Front to Peru's Sendero Luminoso, nursed in the philosophy department at the San Cristóbal of Huamanga University and the student councils of the National University of San Marcos.[55] Faced with the violence of the state, the international student New Left turned to methods of violence, building terrorist movements with varying degrees of success. The Weathermen's call to "Bring the War Home" was short-lived and meager compared with the influence of violent left-wing factions in places like Germany, Japan, Turkey, and Peru, among other places. Indeed, no movement was more violent or faction ridden than the Japanese student New Left, with a subset of students trained to occupy positions as bureaucrats, instead traveling abroad to train for careers as terrorists. Japanese students' calls for a "total rejection of the existing system" and to "break

up the university," echoing Marcuse's "Great Refusal," may have failed to take down Japan's university system, but its sense of urgency contributed to the extreme violence that marked the movement. Japan's United Red Army insular internal dynamics led to a particularly shocking series of incidents. In a three-month period in 1972, the desperate remnant of the United Red Army executed twelve of its own members in a moment of "revolutionary self-cleansing," a traumatic set of events that has shaped the problematic legacy of the student movement in Japan.[56] While some scholars, such as Jeremy Varon, have compared the distinctive trajectories of New Left terrorist groups operating in more than one country (in this case West Germany and the United States), we have no comprehensive study of this particular turn.[57]

If the trajectory from the "years of hope" to the "days of rage" was shared by 1960s protest movements internationally, another shared element of the global New Left was the protest movement's gendered dynamics. Whether Rudi Dutschke in Germany, Daniel Cohn-Bendit in France, Mahir Cayan in Turkey (killed in a confrontation with the military in 1972), or Mark Rudd, Mario Savio, or Tom Hayden in the United States, the public face of the student New Left was indubitably male. The movement's leadership is just the most evident example of the masculine orientation of the student New Left. Indeed, while young men rebelled against the authority of their fathers and, in so doing, may have challenged constructions of manhood, they did not challenge gender hierarchies, sparking women within the movement to organize for their own liberation. But few studies have made gender central to their analysis of the international New Left of the 1960s.[58]

As this essay suggests, setting these varied mobilizations in conversation with one another reveals the dimensions they shared as well as their distinctive national motor forces, developments, and trajectories. Such a transnational analysis cannot do full justice to the "particularities of place, culture and political context," nor should it seek to.[59] This brief essay, moreover, cannot take account of the variety of movements that sprouted from Lima to Dakar. A more complete study of the origins and trajectory of the international student left should include accounts of the vibrant movements that took root in parts of Latin America, Africa, and Asia. It should also grapple with radical youths' role within the ordeal of China's cultural revolution as well as more fully explore the importance of Maoism to the direction student movements took in the late 1960s from Latin America to the

United States. It is impossible to make full sense of the meaning, making, and fate of "Port Huron" without this perspective. Teasing out these inter-linkages between the local and the global are just under way, but the studies that have been done suggest their promise. Shaking off a national lens for broader angles of vision promises to enrich our understanding of this inter-national turbulent moment of progressive social change, its successes and failures, and what we still have to learn from it.

Chapter 4

The Romance of Rebellion

Grace Elizabeth Hale

Somehow, amid the memoirs and anniversary conferences, the celebrations and the attacks, we have forgotten one of the most interesting facts about the early New Left: its radical act of the imagination. Young college student activists accomplished something unprecedented in U.S. history. They created a left political movement in a time of great prosperity. And they did it by imagining new conceptions of "we," new alliances that joined people across chasms of class, race, and region. What inspired those mostly middle-class, mostly white, and mostly not southern college students who created Students for a Democratic Society and Friends of SNCC (Student Nonviolent Coordinating Committee) to care about the experiences of mostly working-class black people in the South? The evidence that they did care is overwhelming, but it is difficult today to remember how radical this caring was in the context of the late 1950s and early 1960s United States. How do we measure and examine this emotion—in its simplest terms "love"—not in sexual terms, though there was plenty of that, but love in its broader meanings, love as deep feelings of attachment, pleasure, and interest?

Love, the emotions, affect—these are the neglected threads in the histories of the 1960s social movements. Participants often remember their sense of alienation from middle-class, white suburban America as a reason they became involved in "the Movement." Scholars and participants like James Forman, Sara Evans, Clayborne Carson, Todd Gitlin, and Doug Rossinow have examined how the search for authenticity and belonging inspired some young people to become activists. Clearly, many participants in the New Left were looking for and found meaningful emotions in their

political work. In particular, in solidarity with southern African Americans, some participants experienced belonging, security, and a sense of well-being: they experienced love. The history of Students for a Democratic Society (SDS) and the writing of its manifesto, the Port Huron Statement, is an important part of U.S. political and social history, but it is also an important moment in U.S. cultural history, and more specifically, the history of affect or emotions and the history of subjectivity or how people understand the nature of the self. This essay explores the role of feelings in the early history of SDS and in the Port Huron Statement. I begin by offering a brief account of the cultural context of the United States at mid-century and a quick primer on theories about affect and emotion. This theory and context then set up an examination of how activists learn to "be" real by learning to "feel" real and an analysis of the role of affect in SDS's manifesto with feelings, the Port Huron Statement. I conclude by exploring one powerful strain of backlash against this "love."[1]

Authenticity and Affect

For cultural historians and American Studies scholars, the profoundly changing meaning of authenticity and the nature of the real are key characteristics of the post-1945 world. On a broad continuum and with a great deal of overlap, people experienced and helped create a shift away from mimetic, external, strongly visual, and seemingly objective definitions of the real and toward experiential and emotional, internal, strongly aural, and seemingly subjective definitions of the real. This transition was never absolute, and both definitions of the real continued to circulate across the post-1945 period. But a profound transformation began in the late nineteenth century in the arts, as the invention and spread of photography (and later film) eroded an older meaning in which the real was the best possible copy. Paintings of landscapes, for example, that looked exactly like the scene were no longer as interesting once people could use photographs for this purpose. Increasingly, in the early twentieth century, artists and writers began to understand forms of cultural expression or artifacts as real when they were unique, when they somehow gave evidence of their maker's individual perspective. A painting in which an artist like Van Gogh interpreted a landscape was more "real" in these terms than a painting in which an

artist attempted mimesis. Abstract art—like Jackson Pollock's famous drip paintings—got rid of the object of representation altogether. Instead of painting something in the external world, some artists began to think about their images as their own inventions. Some critics and artists began to talk about artwork as the expression of the artist's own perspective or their internal world. Subjectivity, in this sense, became as or even more important than objectivity. By the mid-twentieth century, this definition of authenticity and realism had gained traction far beyond the world of avant-garde art. A novel, a song, a photograph, or even a political manifesto could be authentic if it was true in an emotional sense.[2]

Most members of the generation that created the New Left were not artists, art critics, or even fans of avant-garde art, however. They experienced and participated most directly in the redefinition of the real in other cultural arenas, especially in the late 1950s and 1960s folk music revival. As some young, middle-class folk fans also began to play folk music, a debate broke out within the folk music world and especially in the pages of folk music magazines like *Sing Out!* and *The Little Sandy Review* about what made a particular song or musician authentic. Initially, many participants thought about authenticity as a characteristic defined in material and geographic terms as outsiders' music. "Real" folk music was music made outside the music industry, and thus noncommercial, by people—the folk—who lived outside the modern world. As the ranks of the new musicians who often called themselves "citybillies" (a play on "hillbillies") grew, this definition of what made a folk musician or a folk song authentic no longer worked very well. Some musicians created a past to fit the old terms. Bob Dylan, for example, claimed to be an orphan and a hobo rather than a university dropout and the son of middle-class parents still very much alive in the small town of Hibbing, Minnesota.

Other young musicians, critics, and fans began to subtly shift the meaning of authenticity to make room for their own engagement with the music. An admirer of Joan Baez told a reporter, "Joan does not pretend to be a Negro or a British Maiden broken by a feudal lord. What she gives us are her own feelings about these people. She's like a passionate biographer; and more than that, she makes these songs contemporary by identifying with their emotional content as herself." As Baez told *Time* in 1962, "I don't care very much where a song came from or why—or even what it says. All I care about is how it sounds and the feeling in it. The songs are so clear emotionally that they can speak for themselves." This new emphasis on feelings helped transform authenticity into an internal rather than an external quality. Being alike on the inside, as people who shared emotions and the need for self-expression, could replace being alike on the outside, as people who shared a history of oppression and isolation. The folk music revival taught many young, middle-class Americans to think about authenticity in this new way.[3]

In the early 1960s, members of SDS and other early New Left groups like SNCC, CORE (the Congress of Racial Equality), and the Northern Student Movement helped import more subjective definitions of the real into left political thought. Young activists translated the ideas and practices of the old left into ideas, images, and stories that figured truth and authenticity in more emotional terms and that embodied left political goals in new modes of self-performance and style. They played an essential role in infusing a sense of social justice into this new subjective, interior sense of the authentic and the true. And they did all this, in part, by falling in love with the mostly black student activists of the southern civil rights movement.

SNCC played a complex, multilayered role in this romance of the rebellion. Individual white and black members of the organization became the objects of other young activists' feelings of identification and attachment. SNCC's practices—the hugely successful southern sit-in movement and later actions like the Freedom Rides and the Albany movement—inspired the theorizing that led to the Port Huron Statement. SNCC's actions also worked as a training ground for activists from outside the South who learned how to organize by conducting sympathy boycotts and pickets and creating Friends of SNCC groups or participating in later activities like Freedom Summer. As an organization, SNCC embodied the intersection of the civil rights movement, the folk music revival, and the New Left.

Theoretical models of emotions are useful tools for thinking through the role of love in the New Left. An inside-out model of how emotions work dominates American popular and scholarly discussions today. This understanding—which grows out of Freud, later psychoanalytic thinkers, and writers who popularized his theories—emphasizes the interiority of emotions. Feelings are centered in the individual and are subjective and a sign of self-presence. They must be expressed or communicated to be a social object. An alternative, the outside-in model of how emotions work, also circulated in the mid-twentieth century, although it had more traction in academic circles than in the broader culture. In this kind of thinking, feelings are social and cultural practices. Emotions come from without and move inward, and they have a social presence. Émile Durkheim is the key theorist here, especially as interpreted by mid-twentieth-century sociologists and anthropologists. Feelings do not originate in individual bodies but are instead what holds and binds the social body—the community—together.

While some members of SDS were surely exposed to the outside-in model in their college classes, the inside-out model had become increasingly hegemonic by the time SDS formed. Both of these models, however, assumed outside and inside as recognizable categories, as knowable geographies, as set spaces whether metaphorical or actual. Neither model fit a historical moment when the meaning of these geographic terms and associated ideas about the location of truth and authenticity were rapidly changing.

A more useful model has emerged in recent interdisciplinary thinking about affect. Brian Massumi has created a framework for understanding feeling as an activity that takes place in a body. Physiological changes often occur when a person is feeling or thinking: the heart rate shifts, blood vessels constrict and dilate, eyes blink and move, muscles twitch. Acts that register our consciousness of ourselves are literally embodied activities—they take place inside a body. When we think or feel, we move and these things happen simultaneously. Theorist Sara Ahmed provides a way to build a different understanding of emotions that takes into account this embodiment. Emotions, she argues, create the very effect of surfaces and boundaries, the very categories outside and inside, the psyche and the social. A surface, she insists, is the effect of an impression left by others: experiencing their emotions, sensing their movements, and reacting to their embodiment. Attachment takes place through physiological as well as psychological movement, through being literally moved. This model of how emotions work provides a way to think about the role of love in the New Left.[4]

On the Road to Port Huron: Learning to Feel, Learning to be Real

For the young activists who helped to create and build SDS, the road to Port Huron began, in emotional terms, with the feeling that something was missing. In the early twentieth century, philosopher Walter Benjamin argued that the experience of loss was an essential part of the political economy, society, and culture of modernity. Loss, he argued, mediated between and helped make individual and collective subjectivities. Modernity, then, urges its inhabitants to ask: Where do these losses that I am attached to come from? With whom do I share these losses? How does our shared loss connect us? To put this idea another way, modernity makes people think they are missing something. What was radical about the young SDS folks was not that they experienced a sense of loss. What was radical was what they did to ease those feelings.[5]

Their radical act of the imagination had its origins in their 1950s childhoods. The generation that made the New Left grew up with early rock-and-roll—with Chuck Berry and Little Richard and Elvis Presley and a love for what they thought of as black music, whatever the color of the musician performing it. They grew up with teenage rebel movies like *Rebel Without a Cause* and *Blackboard Jungle*. Many graduated to the Beats and *On the Road* and Jack Kerouac's lyrical longing to be a black man or a Denver Mexican or "even a poor, overworked Jap": "feeling that the best the white world offered was not enough ecstasy for me, not enough life, joy, kicks, darkness, music; not enough night." Others grew up with Pete Seeger sing-alongs at summer camp—he was their stealthy red Raffi. Seeger introduced many kids to vernacular music styles and to a vague hammer of justice, what remained of left politics after the red scare. Future white New Leftists grew up falling in love with rebels, especially African Americans, and rebellion.[6]

As they finished high school and entered college in the late 1950s and early 1960s, members of this generation became those folk music fans and "citybillies" who worked to change the meaning of authenticity. Among other musical forms, they increasingly listened to and played vernacular styles like the blues and hillbilly music originally created by early twentieth-century working-class whites and blacks. Like 1950s rock-and-roll, this music taught them to see African American and white working-class people as rebels. It also exposed them to people like Seeger, a living link to that old left coalition of socialists, communists, and others united under the popular front in the 1930s and again under the fight against fascism in the 1940s. In the early 1950s, House Un-American Activities Committee (HUAC) hearings and other forms of persecution destroyed most of this public old left network of people and organizations. Survivors who did not move to the center politically often abandoned organizing work and kept their beliefs quiet. Yet since leftists had actively used folk music as an organizing tool in what scholars often call the folksong revival, during the McCarthy era folk music acquired an aura of political danger. As John Cohen, photographer, filmmaker, and member of the revivalist string band the New Lost City Ramblers, told a reporter about the small group of Yale art and math students interested in folk music in the mid-1950s: "We heard of actual fist fights, held in dormitory rooms, where students tried forcibly to prevent their roommates from going to the hoots—on the grounds that it would seriously impair their future chances, particularly for Government jobs, if it were known that they associated with people like us."[7]

The early history of SDS and its organizers' early interest in the southern civil rights movement is well known today. We forget, however, how radical and deeply significant the white New Left's affective attachment to southern civil rights activists, another group of mostly black and seemingly authentic rebels, was in the 1960s. SDS survived and grew as an organization because founder Al Haber and early member Sharon Jeffrey and later member Tom Hayden brilliantly connected their fledgling organization to what was then often called the southern student movement, the phase of the southern civil rights movement that erupted with the Greensboro sit-ins and the founding of SNCC in 1960.[8]

In 1959, Haber was president of the University of Michigan student chapter of the Student League for Industrial Democracy (SLID), a once national old left student group dying out everywhere but Ann Arbor. That fall, Jeffrey and Haber decided to plan a spring conference aimed at campus activists on the topic of human rights in the North. Their timing was perfect. In February, Haber heard about the Greensboro sit-ins from the regular updates on student activism mailed to affiliated campus political organizations by the National Student Association (NSA), a group then at the height of its power on college campuses and not yet exposed as funded by the CIA. As the sit-ins spread quickly across the South, Haber and Jeffrey decided that the way to draw attention to their new organization was to invite participants in the Greensboro sit-ins to come to Michigan to speak at their conference. Jeffrey and other students also organized sympathy pickets at the Ann Arbor Woolworth and other local branches of chain stores that practiced segregation in the South. Tom Hayden, who had joined a few SDS protests that fall and was not yet committed to the organization, published a fiery editorial in the Michigan student paper linking the demonstrations there to the outpouring of student protest in the South and elsewhere. In the spring of 1960, just two weeks after the meeting that created SNCC, around 150 student activists including participants in the Greensboro sit-ins gathered in Ann Arbor for SDS's first conference. These delegates produced pages of ambitious resolutions in which SDS proposed nothing less than to make itself the national coordinating committee for all student civil rights activities across the country, a national version of the original regional vision of SNCC.[9]

Throughout the rest of 1960 and 1961, SDS continued to grow by connecting its own activities with the activism of those "real" student rebels, the southern civil rights activists. For Tom Hayden, a key SDS member and the primary author of the Port Huron Statement, meeting southern student activists changed his life. Unlike Haber and Jeffrey, he had not grown up with liberal political organizing, and his childhood was more characteristic of future SDS members than their own. In high school in a suburb of Detroit, he read Catcher in the Rye and saw Rebel Without a Cause. The year he started college, he read On the Road. Over the next three years, he recalled, he spent his vacations hitchhiking "to every corner of America, sleeping in fields here, doorways there, cheap hotels everywhere, embracing a spirit of the open road without knowing where I wanted to go." In a 1972 interview, he confessed being "very influenced by the Beat Generation." He admitted that, "politics was unimaginable to me. I'd never heard or seen a demonstration. . . . There was not a sense that there was something like a political form of protest, so whatever that was, it was mainly trying to mimic the life of James Dean or something like that. It wasn't political."[10]

For Hayden, direct experience was everything, and in the summer of 1960, he hitchhiked to the Bay Area, where in May large protests against the annual HUAC hearings had made the national news. Earlier that year, CORE activists had helped University of California at Berkeley students organize sympathy pickets of local Woolworth stores in support of the southern sit-ins. The Berkeley activists, in turn, took what they had learned about nonviolent mass protest and used this information to organize the anti-HUAC protests. Hayden wanted to meet them. In late August, he caught a ride to the National Student Association annual meeting, held that year at the University of Minnesota. Haber was also there, as well as about twenty-five SNCC members, including SNCC chairman Chuck McDew.

As conference participants hotly debated a resolution proposed by Haber endorsing the southern sit-in movement's civil disobedience, a graduate student and sit-in veteran from the University of Texas stood up to speak. Confronted with injustice, she argued, a person faces choices. She can do nothing, she can work within the law, she can act violently, or she can act nonviolently: "I cannot say to a person who suffers injustice, 'Wait.' Perhaps you can. I can't. And having decided that I cannot urge caution, I must stand with him. If I had known that not a single lunch counter would open as a result of my action, I could not have done differently than I did. If I had known that violence would result, I could not have done differently than I did." The sit-ins, she said, gave her the chance to turn her thoughts and feelings into actions. "While I would hope that the NSA congress will pass a strong sit-in resolution, I am more concerned that all of us, Negro and White, realize the possibility of becoming less inhuman humans through commitment and action." Sandra "Casey" Cason, in Sara Ahmed's terms, moved the room. She made an impression. People in the room heard her and reacted intellectually to what she was saying, but they also reacted to her emotionally. They sensed her physical movements, and they experienced the physical effects of her emotions as well as the emotions of other people in the room. Cason was not just a message—she was also a sound and an image, an embodied presence. And the members of that NSA audience heard and saw and felt her speak. Shared affect helped create a new sense of the connections and boundaries between outside and inside, body and psyche, self and other. NSA voted to issue the statement of support. Hayden committed himself to political activism, and he later married Cason.[11]

Looking back, Hayden described meeting SNCC members as a transformative moment. They "lived on a *fuller level of feeling* than any people I've seen, partly because they were making history in a very personal way, and partly because by risking death they came to know the value of living each moment to the fullest [emphasis mine]." He was moved, in other words, by their actions but also by their psychological intensity. For Hayden, the SNCC activists at the NSA convention and later in the South made it clear that feeling and acting were paired activities, that political work involved fear, elation, frustration, and even love as well as analysis and strategic thinking.[12]

Haber too left the NSA convention convinced that the way to move and then politicize students in the North was to connect them with southern activists. In a letter to Tim Jenkins, a member of SNCC and a NSA officer, sent about a month after the national conference, Haber wrote, "students in the North" want "greater personal knowledge of the movement. We must be able to know what is going on, to be able to identify personalities and *feel* some direct involvement in the struggle [emphasis mine]." News reports were not enough. Northern students did not want simply to know about the movement. They did not want simply to support the movement. They wanted a connection, emotional as well as political. They wanted to be a part of it. And their feelings worked to reconfigure their sense of the geography of identity and the boundary between outsider and insider.[13]

A little less than a year later, Hayden and Haber were both linking feelings and actions. In an article on campus activism Hayden wrote for the August 1961 issue of *Mademoiselle,* he quoted Haber, "Students have a mystique about action. They are thrilled by action per se. The passion usually associated with ideology is transferred to the actual doing of the deed." Feeling and acting together, for this generation, signaled commitment. That fall, Hayden started working full-time for SDS as a liaison to SNCC. He also began writing a series of reports from the South that gave readers both the facts about southern student activism and a vivid sense of what it was like to participate in their protests. Haber, in turn, edited these SDS "Southern Reports" and sent them to his campus contacts and to growing numbers of SDS members across the nation. SDS, he assured them, was working hard to bring students the news "in the face of an almost total news blackout." These reports, passed hand-to-hand on college campuses, spread word about SDS as well as the southern movement and greatly increased the circulation of SDS publications.[14]

In January 1962, SDS published *Revolution in Mississippi*, Hayden's in-depth account of activism in and around McComb, Mississippi, and his own experiences there, including being pulled out of a car and beaten in the street. At the very start, he emphasized the interconnectedness of thinking and feeling in both understanding the southern movement and in allying with it. "How do we make the situation *real* to outsiders—those who know not the people involved, the state, the country, and most of all, the social, political, economic, cultural, religious, historic pattern we have labeled segregation? . . . This report is intended to make the facts *real*." Outsiders to Mississippi, Hayden hoped, would read these facts and then ally themselves with the outsiders within Mississippi, local blacks, and SNCC activists. Together they would create a new political coalition, win the revolution in Mississippi, and create a truly democratic America.[15]

We forget today how truly remarkable it was for the young people that created SDS to understand themselves as connected to these activists fighting segregation in the South. Together, young activists imagined and worked to build a new alliance of outsiders, people alienated from a historic moment in which nuclear America dominated the world and white, suburban nuclear families dominated the nation. Members of their generation, no matter their class or racial or ethnic background or the source of their oppression, they suggested, all shared the sense of loss that characterized modern life. This common feeling, then, could be the ground of a new alliance, the New Left. Perhaps shared emotions could be a tool for making social change.

Sometimes what early members of the New Left wrote about their experiences in the early 1960s revealed their own investment in the inside-out model of emotions in which feelings originated in the individual and achieved a social presence through expression. What they actually did, however, made clear that for them, feeling and thinking and knowing as inseparable and embodied phenomena enabled them to imagine a new political terrain.

A Manifesto with Feelings

In the winter of 1962, Hayden began working on a speech that later became an SDS pamphlet called *Student Social Action: From Liberation to Community*. He wanted to think about politics through the prism of what he had learned in the South and his reading of intellectuals like Albert Camus and C. Wright Mills in order to construct a general program for student activism. "Student Social Action" offered a compelling vision of white middle-class college students as outsiders. The powerlessness of students on college campuses, Hayden argued, paralleled the powerlessness of African Americans in the segregated South. Both groups were deprived of political voice. Both groups experienced "deep alienation" in the decision-making institutions of society. College students should see southern African Americans and other oppressed groups as their allies in a new political coalition of the alienated. Together, they should work for "genuine independence": "a concern not with image or popularity, but with finding a moral meaning in life that is direct and authentic for the self." Following Mills, Hayden broadened his definition of independence to include psychological freedom and cultural determination, the right to self-expression, as well as economic security and political representation, the right to vote.[16]

This work, in turn, became the starting point from which SDS members collectively revised and in some sections wrote new sections of the document that became the Port Huron Statement. "Where," he asked readers in an SDS report, "does one begin thinking about manifestos?" Again, the radical act of the imagination on display here is stunning. Hayden asked, and fifty-nine student activists traveled to the AFL-CIO retreat on Lake Huron to provide an answer. Somehow, the young people at the 1962 SDS National Conference had the confidence, naiveté, and optimism to believe they were qualified to write and issue a proclamation to try to change the world.

In the SDS correspondence files, some members refer to the Port Huron Statement as a "manifesto of hope," a fitting name for a document full of dreams, wishes, and fears that imagines a political activism that can fight loneliness, estrangement, and isolation as well as racist oppression, nuclear annihilation, and poverty. Port Huron works to make readers feel as well as know its vision of reality, its truth. It does not simply try to inform people. It tries to move them, to make them care psychologically as well as intellectually. And despite the inclusion of analytical sections, the document starts with a call to feel as well as to know and returns to this point throughout.[17]

"We are people of this generation," the manifesto begins, "bred in at least modest comfort, housed now in universities, looking *uncomfortably* to the world we inherit [emphasis mine]." From the beginning, feelings are called into play: the world is not oppressive or unjust but "uncomfortable," which suggests feeling ill at ease or tense or awkward or confined. Coupled with the phrase "modest comfort" and verb "housed, " "uncomfortable" implies the feeling people who are not accustomed to unpleasantness experience—people of a generation, yes, but also of a particular class. The opening continues, "As we grew, however, our comfort was penetrated by events too troubling to dismiss. First, the permeating and victimizing fact of human degradation, symbolized by the Southern struggle against racial bigotry, compelled most of us from silence to activism." Clearly, they are not talking about southerners here. White or black, southern activists had grown up with segregation and did not need the civil rights movement— "our" struggle, or, on the other side, "our" resistance—to see it. The manifesto continues, "Second, the enclosing fact of the Cold War, symbolized by the presence of the Bomb, brought awareness that we ourselves, and our friends, and millions of abstract 'others' we knew more directly because of our common peril, might die at any time." The invention of nuclear weapons placed these middle-class young peoples' futures in jeopardy, despite their "modest" or greater standard of living amid post-1945 plenty. The bomb made them think about and feel the fate of humanity, of people everywhere. "We might deliberately ignore, or avoid, or *fail to feel* all other human problems, but not these two, for these were too immediate and crushing in their impact, too challenging in the demand that we as individuals take the responsibility for encounter and resolution [emphasis mine]." These feelings, the rest of the Port Huron Statement boldly claims, can be the ground on which we make a broad, new political coalition and movement.[18]

Often, the authors of the Port Huron Statement make bold and sweeping claims: "the search for truly democratic alternatives to the present, and a commitment to social experimentation with them, is a worthy and fulfilling human enterprise, one which *moves* us and, we hope, others today. On such a basis do we offer this document of our convictions and analysis [emphasis mine]." As Ahmed describes the work of emotions, movement—both physiological and psychological—creates the very "we" SDS members write out of and suggests the even larger "we" they hope their manifesto will help create. Being moved—feeling and thinking within a body—creates understandings of outside and inside and a geography of identity in which class and race do not divide the speakers from participants in the "Southern struggle" or from "abstract 'others'" anywhere.

In perhaps the most famous and often-quoted line, the authors of the Port Huron Statement assert, echoing a statement in Hayden's earlier work, "Men have unrealized potential for self-cultivation, self-direction, self-understanding, and creativity. . . . The goal of man and society should be human independence: a concern not with image of popularity but with finding a meaning in life that is personally authentic." The fact that the authors decided to modify "authentic" with the word "personal" suggests the degree to which the psychological and experiential definition of the term is still new in 1962. "Authenticity" still retains its material, mimetic, and objective qualities, its connection to concrete things in particular places and times, even as a new emphasis on affect and subjectivity grows. People who accept the problems of the modern world, from the oppression of racial segregation to the plastic conformity of popular culture, are not true or real in either the older or the newer meanings of the term. Alienation, the problem, has many sources. Authenticity, the solution, must grow out of independence, again a word that, like authenticity, has material as well as psychological meanings. For all their boldness, the young people who worked on the Port Huron Statement could never quite decide whether self-expression was enough. A productive contradiction remained. Their faith in self-expression and an inside-out model of how emotions work as the route to authenticity bumped up against their desire for a connection with southern activists, their belief in political coalitions, and their faith in collective action.

Near the end, the manifesto returns again to an emphasis on affect: "A new left must transform modern complexity into issues that can be understood and *felt* close up by every human being. It must give form to the *feelings* of helplessness and indifference." To make a new world, they are saying, we must enable people to feel and not just know the problems we face. The knowing and the feeling have to go together. The young SDS members who wrote the Port Huron Statement called their vision of the future a "politics of hope and vision."[19]

Too Much Love

To say that many New Leftists were motivated by romanticism, by their love for southern activists and especially African Americans is not to diminish the radicalism of their acts but to historicize them. Emotions make people move. They make people change. They make people subjects and objects. They set up oppositions and make categories: they create insides and outsides. SDS emerged as ideas about authenticity as realistic representation (looking right) gave way before new ideas about authenticity as an emotional state (feeling right). Love helped Students for a Democratic Society reach people increasingly thinking about reality and truth in these interior and subjective ways. In turn, SDS helped bring this key cultural shift into politics and radically changed U.S. politics as a result. This is the "new" in New Left and other movements of the time; not many scholars and critics would have us believe that these groups engaged in cultural politics—politics have always been cultural.[20]

Love helped some members of the New Left craft a view of the world in which they were allied with southern blacks (some of whom also saw themselves as participants in the New Left) and later with other groups like low-income urban blacks and Cuban, Chinese, and Vietnamese revolutionaries in fighting for a more democratic and just nation and world. But there were other emotions than love and alternative definitions of insides and outsides, of the real and the unreal, moving through the activism of the 1960s than those circulated by the early members of SDS. How, for example, did the people New Left activists imagined as allies feel about these New Left politics? While some participants imagined white and black college student activists feeling and thinking together, other participants in the same events did not share the same emotions. The turn toward black power and black nationalism by some African American civil rights activists provides an example of the deployment of alternatives. In the mid-1960s, some African American activists in the South and elsewhere began to publicly define inside and outside in different ways. Julius Lester's 1966 *Sing Out!* article, "The Angry Children of Malcolm X," spells out as clearly as any surviving document the way some black activists responded to some white activists' love.[21]

Lester was a former Fisk University student, a folk singer and organizer who helped Highlander Folk School's music director Guy Carawan collect, transcribe, and publish "Freedom Songs," wrote articles for folk music magazines, served as a song leader in the southern movement, and composed and wrote his own music. He also worked as an SNCC staff member and was in Mississippi for the 1964 summer project. Though he later moved to the right politically, in 1966 Lester spoke for many SNCC members as the organization embraced African American self-determination. The children of Malcolm X, he argued, were tired of singing. The title he chose played off the title of an earlier *Sing Out!* article, widely read and discussed among folk music fans and musicians, on the influence and legacy of folk singer Pete Seeger—"Pete's Children."

In 1966, blacks and whites, Lester argued, no longer shared a common parent, a common emotion, or a common sense of the goals of the struggle. The problem, he wrote, was the way some whites' love for blacks as authentic outsiders limited blacks' efforts to gain equality. "SNCC had been their romantic darling, a kind of teddy bear that they could cuddle. The time had come, however, when blacks could no longer be the therapy for white society." White liberals "had a cause, something that would put meaning into their lives, something that their country and society had not given them. They had it in the Negro. So they came south and they loved us when we got out heads beat, our asses kicked, and our bodies thrown in jail."

From this perspective, the early New Left's "love" for African American activists felt like another way white people denied African American equality. It felt like being in another kind of minstrel show, like being asked once again to play a part imagined by whites. Love, Lester insisted, was not the opposite of hate—it was its less brutal cousin. Indifference was the opposite of hate.

Sing Out! often published folk song lyrics as epigrams for its articles. Lester wrote his own: "Too much love / too much love / nothing kills a nigger / like too much love." There were other ways of looking at the early New Left's radical act of the imagination. One was to say NO, we do not want to be loved.

PART II

Liberalism and Radicalism
Conjoined and Divided

Chapter 5

The New Left and Liberalism Reconsidered:
The Committee of Correspondence
and the Port Huron Statement

Daniel Geary

There is a well-known story about the Port Huron conference. Students for a Democratic Society invited the prominent socialist Michael Harrington to address the meeting. Harrington lambasted SDS for its insufficient anti-communism. After the day's meeting, Harrington and Tom Hayden drank beer and engaged in an increasingly heated debate centered on the SDS stance on communism. When Harrington left the conference, he reported back to SDS's parent organization, the League for Industrial Democracy, which subsequently reprimanded SDS leaders for the statement drafted at Port Huron. The moral to this story characterizes a common historical understanding of the relationship between the New Left and its progenitors. It emphasizes the generational conflict between young radicals and their elders and suggests that the split between them, however regrettable, was inevitable.[1]

The story also suggests that the Port Huron conference offered a clean break with liberalism as the SDS pioneered the development of an American New Left. In fact, the early SDS was strongly influenced by key strands within postwar liberalism. Nelson Lichtenstein shows that the social-democratic vision of the United Automobile Workers was one such influence.[2] Another was the peace activism of the Committee of Correspondence, a small but influential organization advocating nuclear disarmament. When Hayden debated Harrington over beers, he was defended by Roger Hagan, editor of the Committee's newsletter.

Many of the characteristic positions adopted in the Port Huron State-ment were shared by the Committee. These included not only opposition to obsessive anticommunism and commitment to arms control but also criticism of the costs of the Cold War, belief that society should be orga-nized to allow individuals to pursue personally meaningful lives, and con-fidence in the political potential of intellectuals and universities. Most important, the early SDS and the Committee imagined leftists and liberals of various political stripes collaborating along a broad front to achieve shared goals. Examining SDS alongside the Committee allows us to recap-ture the cooperative relationships that early New Leftists had with liberals. That the possibilities for such collaboration contracted after the early 1960s was a tragedy for both the New Left and liberalism.

As the Port Huron Statement noted, the early New Left developed from two major struggles. The first, and most important, was the civil rights movement. The second, sometimes neglected by historians, was antinuclear activism in the United States and internationally. Indeed, the Port Huron Statement's first policy suggestion was "universal controlled disarma-ment."[3] Also emerging out of the peace movement revival was the Commit-tee of Correspondence, founded in March 1960 at the Bear Mountain Inn in New York's Hudson Valley. Later that year, the group issued its Bear Mountain Statement, which declared, "We have joined together because we fear that unless men can find an alternative to their present search for security through nuclear deterrence, civilization will be destroyed by war." The Bear Mountain meeting's principal organizers were radical pacifists from the Quaker-affiliated American Friends Service Committee (AFSC), a long-standing peace organization that had sought to spark opposition to the Cold War with its 1955 manifesto, *Speak Truth to Power*. AFSC leaders invited to the meeting prominent academics such as David Riesman and Erich Fromm, whom they hoped to recruit to more active involvement in the peace movement. Prominent Quaker pacifists such as A. J. Muste and Stuart Meacham were present at the meeting. Robert Gilmore, head of the New York AFSC and a leader of the principal U.S. antinuclear organization, National Committee for a Sane Nuclear Policy (SANE), played a leading role in the Committee's formation and served as its first president.[4]

Bear Mountain participants hoped to found a national organization with many local branches. Committee of Correspondence chapters did form in Berkeley, Chicago, Louisville, New York City, and Urbana, Illinois. However, the only lasting chapter, founded in Cambridge, Massachusetts, built on an existing network of intellectuals already concerned about nuclear issues. It consisted mainly of professors and graduate students affiliated with Harvard University, such as Everett Mendelsohn, an assistant professor of the history of science. Though the AFSC remained involved by helping to administer the organization from its New York office, for all intents and purposes the Committee came to be based in Cambridge. From its founding in 1960 to its dissolution in 1966, the Committee was an extremely informal organization. It relied heavily on donations of money and time from a small group of individuals; there were no professional staff or membership dues. In 1963, Riesman described it as "a small, struggling, amateur, and barely organized group whose principal function is editing a Newsletter."[5]

Riesman was the guiding force behind the Committee's activities. A Harvard sociologist, Riesman was best known as the lead author of the best-selling 1950 book *The Lonely Crowd,* which famously identified a shift in the American character from "inner-directed" to "other-directed" personalities. *The Lonely Crowd*'s depiction of the unfulfilled lives of affluent middle-class Americans resonated among New Leftists, as did its call for "utopian" thinking about how society might better be arranged to enhance individual autonomy. If there was an older liberal that young radicals could look up to in the early 1960s, it was Riesman. Indeed, Riesman worked closely with early New Leftists such as Todd Gitlin and Staughton Lynd.[6]

In Cambridge, the Committee formed part of a broader network of antinuclear activism. Its close ties to the student peace group Tocsin, founded at Harvard in 1960, indicate the close relationship that existed between older liberals such as Riesman and the nascent New Left. Tocsin proved an important forerunner to Harvard's SDS chapter; one of its leaders was future SDS president Gitlin. Riesman served as one of Tocsin's faculty advisers. The other, historian H. Stuart Hughes, ran for the U.S. Senate in 1962 as a third-party peace candidate, supported by the Committee and Tocsin. Riesman later explained that the Committee published its newsletter in part to influence "Tocsin and other students who are starting to fight their way to a clear idea about disarmament and foreign policy."[7] In turn, Tocsin's prospectus cited the Committee as an inspiring group that had "begun to evolve ideas adequate to challenge the principle of security through arms."[8]

These Harvard antinuclear groups were typical of the peace movement in that they were based in the affluent, educated middle class that populated cities, universities, and university towns. At the same time, peace activism in Cambridge had a special character given the close connections between Harvard University and policy makers in the federal government during the Kennedy administration. As Riesman later quipped, so many Harvard students came from such well-connected families that even freshman undergraduates were, "at most, but one person and a telephone away from being able to speak to the White House."[9] Thus, even small groups such as Tocsin and the Committee hoped to receive a hearing in the corridors of power in Washington.

In addition to lobbying contacts in the federal government, the Committee of Correspondence organized local events to educate the public about the dangers of nuclear war and the costs of the arms race. Its main activity, however, was publishing a newsletter. The newsletter began as an extremely informal publication, consisting of Riesman's diary entries on disarmament-related topics and events and reprints of personal letters between Riesman and his close circle of friends in the Committee. Riesman was one of the great correspondents of his day, a prolific writer of long and engaging letters that established deeply personal intellectual relationships. The newsletter bore the stamp of his unique personality.

The newsletter's early issues were mimeographed on cheap paper, often reproduced with handwritten notes and with little or no proofreading. Published at irregular intervals, they were distributed for free, initially to only about fifty people. Like personal letters, the newsletters were sent by first-class mail, a fact that Riesman believed ensured that recipients read them immediately as personal correspondence rather than saving them to read for later as they would with magazines.[10] Though the Committee of Correspondence's name consciously harkened back to the exchanges of letters among American Revolutionaries, the informality of the newsletter anticipated the blog format of today.

Over time, the newsletter grew in both circulation and professionalism, eventually shortening its name from *Newsletter of the Committee of Correspondence* to *The Correspondent*.[11] By 1965, its final year of publication, *The Correspondent* had become a standard format journal with a print run of 5,000.[12] Despite the Committee's small size, its newsletter garnered national and international attention. In 1962, *The Correspondent* boasted that in addition to its core audience of university students and faculty, it was distributed to several congressmen, members of the Kennedy administration, and editors of major magazines.[13] Reflecting the international nature of the peace movement, the newsletter was also read abroad, particularly in Britain, Canada, and Japan. Riesman reported that in Japan, where he traveled in 1961, "Our newsletter is one of the few American voices . . . which speak with different accents from the line purveyed by the most vocal segments of Congress."[14] A leading Japanese physicist used a *Correspondent* issue on civil defense as the basis for a published letter to the editor of *Asahi,* a major Japanese newspaper with circulation of four million.[15]

The *Correspondent*'s outspoken stance led to its denouncement in some American periodicals. An editorial in *Life* described the Committee as a left-wing version of the conspiratorial anticommunist John Birch Society, alleging that Riesman would "malign any Westerner who is willing to use nuclear weapons in defense of his freedom."[16] The conservative *National Review* attacked the Committee for its presumed "willingness for all of us to live under Communist domination."[17] Such negative attention suggests both the Committee's national prominence and the colossal challenge it faced in changing American attitudes about the Cold War.

The collaboration between Riesman and Hagan, a self-identified "radical," embodied *The Correspondent*'s cooperative exchanges between liberal and left, old and young. Born in 1934, Hagan was Riesman's junior by twenty-five years, but still nearly a decade older than the students at Port Huron. Hagan was a key figure in the early New Left at Harvard, helping to form a "new left club" that met for regular discussions. Hagan came to Harvard as a doctoral student in history, but dropped his studies to become editor of *The Correspondent.* He took over in early 1961, following a short-lived and unsuccessful editorial stint by Nathan Glazer, whom many Committee members deemed insufficiently critical of the Cold War.[18]

The Correspondent was notable for the ideological and generational breadth of its contributors. Through its newsletter, the Committee sought to facilitate "a high-level exploration of alternatives to deterrence involving radical pacifists, radical socialists and radical liberals."[19] Many established left-of-center intellectuals wrote for *The Correspondent,* such as Daniel Bell, Lewis Coser, Ronnie Dugger, Erich Fromm, Nathan Glazer, A. J. Muste, Bertrand Russell, William Appleman Williams, and C. Vann Woodward. A younger generation of leftists also wrote for the newsletter, including Gabriel Kolko, Staughton Lynd, Michael Walzer, and Howard Zinn as well as SDS leaders Richard Flacks, Todd Gitlin, Al Haber, and Tom Hayden.

The major ideas contained in *The Correspondent* bore striking similarities to those expressed by the early SDS. *The Correspondent* demonstrates that the common assumption that all postwar liberals were "Cold War liberals" is fallacious. Writers for *The Correspondent* criticized pervasive anti-communism for suppressing debate about the Cold War and the nuclear arms race, challenging what the Port Huron Statement called "unreasoning anti-Communism." Both SDS and the Committee of Correspondence believed it should be possible to question American foreign policy without being labeled a communist or fellow traveler. In one issue of *The Correspondent,* Riesman attacked "the new fundamentalists of anti-Communism, who are so often terrified of anything hopeful happening . . . that they would rather see the planet explode."[20] Writers for *The Correspondent* questioned whether the Soviet Union was inherently expansionist, a central tenet of Cold War thought that justified aggressive strategies of containment. Like SDS, the Committee advocated engaging in a détente with the Soviet Union in order to avoid the horrific danger of nuclear war. The Committee relentlessly criticized the Kennedy administration's foreign policy. After the U.S.-sponsored invasion of Cuba at the Bay of Pigs, *The Correspondent* asked, "Is the New Frontier a fraud?"[21]

Like the early SDS, *The Correspondent* linked discussion of disarmament to questions of American values. To both, the growth of a military-industrial complex reflected the distorted priorities of postwar American society. *The Correspondent* analyzed the Cold War as a distraction from difficult questions of how Americans might live meaningful lives in an affluent era. By providing a ready-made enemy in communism, it argued, the Cold War gave Americans a false sense of meaning. Hagan, for example, explained the appeal of "anti-Communist hoopla" to the "millions of Americans whose style of life, whose sense of meaning, and whose manner of economic endeavor and personal encounter have come to depend upon being publicly patriotic and firm."[22] A reduction in Cold War tensions, therefore, would allow Americans to focus on improving the quality of their lives. As Riesman concluded, "the release of energies in areas other than the arms race could serve to give Americans a sense of vitality and flexibility of our society" and "create a more tolerable plateau from which to raise more profound questions about the kind of a country and a world we would like to inhabit."[23] The Port Huron Statement developed a similar analysis, arguing that instead of investing in the Cold War, "America should concentrate on its genuine social priorities: abolish squalor, terminate neglect, and establish an environment for people to live in with dignity and creativeness."[24]

Thus, though focused on disarmament, *The Correspondent* raised broad questions similar to those addressed in the Port Huron Statement's first and most famous section on "Values." This section spoke of "unfulfilled capacities for reason, freedom, and love" and the importance of "finding a meaning in life that is personally authentic."[25] Though the "Values" section is rightly celebrated, its originality is sometimes overstated. One of the section's sources was the engagement with "quality-of-life" issues by postwar liberals. Riesman was one of the most prominent advocates of qualitative liberalism, which argued that the tremendous economic growth of the postwar period allowed Americans to adopt social and individual goals other than simply maximizing the quantity of economic goods produced. In *The Lonely Crowd,* Riesman imagined the possibilities for expanded individual autonomy in an age of affluence if only Americans could adopt new values to replace the economic individualism of the industrial age. The Committee of Correspondence set as a goal "altering the quality of life in industrial society, not merely in this or that detail, but drastically."[26]

"The American Crisis," a 1960 article co-written by David Riesman and a younger Committee member, Michael Maccoby, anticipated the Port Huron Statement's call for greater personal fulfillment and democratic participation. American society, Riesman and Maccoby argued, "must readjust to face the problems that have suddenly become visible because of abundance: lack of participation in life and lack of opportunity and education for self-expression." The Cold War, they claimed, had exposed the "failure of a style of life."[27] The history of "The American Crisis" demonstrates the interpenetration of liberal and left discourses at the start of the 1960s. Riesman and Maccoby presented it at the Bear Mountain meeting, but it was first delivered at a conference organized by the Liberal Project, an initiative that brought together intellectuals such as Riesman with liberal Democratic congressmen to challenge the assumptions of Cold War politics. The Liberal Project, which the Port Huron Statement dubbed "a hopeful beginning," was central to the revival of liberalism in the late 1950s and early 1960s.[28] "The American Crisis" was also reprinted in the pioneering British Marxist journal *New Left Review.*[29]

The Committee of Correspondence also shared the early SDS's confidence that intellectuals could revive public debate. Reinvigoration of the public sphere after a period of apathy, SDS believed, was vital to building participatory democracy. The Port Huron Statement, for example, concluded that "the university could serve as a significant source of social criticism and an initiator of new modes and molders of attitudes."[30] Similarly, *The Correspondent* contended, "intellectuals ha[ve] a crucial role to play in generating alternatives to nuclear war, in developing analysis and policy which might become the basis of political action toward a more safe and just world."[31] At a time when the Kennedy administration relied on the "best and the brightest" intellectuals to develop and justify its policies, both SDS and the Committee imagined organizing a group of counter-intellectuals to challenge technocratic experts and turn policy issues into matters for democratic deliberation. The Committee particularly contested the way that government and scientific experts monopolized debate about nuclear policy. It asserted the moral responsibility of intellectuals to engage public issues and not simply pursue specialized research interests. An early newsletter declared: "The CoC calls on the university communities to make their concern for survival an integral part of their concern as professional thinkers. . . . It is the purpose of the CoC to end the separation so often made by intellectuals between their public concern and their professional life which has led them so often to turn their backs on the most exciting questions of our time."[32]

Finally, like the early SDS, the Committee of Correspondence was non-sectarian in nature and stressed the need for collaboration between liberals and radicals. The Port Huron Statement emphasized that the New Left "must include liberals and socialists, the former for their relevance, the latter for their sense of thoroughgoing reforms in the system." "The university," it claimed, "is a more sensible place than a political party for these two traditions to begin to discuss their differences and look for political synthesis."[33]

The Correspondent similarly advocated working within the established system to seek reforms, the characteristic tactic of liberals, while agitating for more expansive programs that could not be immediately implemented. *Correspondent* contributors respected the benefits and limitations of liberal and radical ideas and strategies. Thus, Riesman, himself a liberal, acknowledged, "In the past, liberalism suffered from complacency and a lack of radical critique."[34] Hagan, more radical than Riesman, appreciated the newsletter's need to strike a "balance between radical criticism and the politics of influence." He argued that it must avoid becoming solely an organ of the "intellectual left" because it would then alienate prominent liberals in government and media. Hagan and radical pacifist Robert

Gilmore toned down their radicalism in the hope that their newsletter could serve as a bridge from the left to liberals with power and influence.[35] The early SDS similarly hoped to influence establishment liberalism; for example, it submitted the Port Huron Statement for publication in *Commentary,* then a leading liberal magazine, and personally delivered a copy to Kennedy adviser Arthur Schlesinger, Jr.

The broad front between leftists and liberals contracted after the early 1960s. Tensions were already evident in later issues of *The Correspondent.* In late 1963, for example, Riesman criticized Howard Zinn's article that argued for more aggressive enforcement of civil rights in the South. Like the drafters of the Port Huron Statement, Zinn hoped for a political realignment in which the Democratic Party would purge its southern segregationists and become a fully liberal force in American politics. Riesman worried, however, that such a strategy might elect the conservative Republican Barry Goldwater in 1964, with catastrophic results for liberal policies. Recollecting a visit by Hayden to Cambridge in which Hayden advocated party realignment, Riesman wrote, "As an older but not necessarily wiser man, I could not help hearing . . . the voice of German radicals who attacked the Weimar Republic . . . at the risk of putting Hitler into power." But Riesman promised to keep an open mind, concluding that Zinn and Hayden "may well be right."[36] In a later issue, Hayden responded, asserting that Riesman's profession of open-mindedness exemplified a "liberal posture" that was "an ideology of inaction and irresponsibility, pronounced from heights of shelter and sophistication."[37] With liberals drawing analogies to Nazi Germany and New Leftists attacking liberal tolerance, rhetorical tensions were high indeed.

Many reasons account for the demise of the Committee of Correspondence and *The Correspondent.* The organization's finances were always precarious, ironically more so after *The Correspondent* gained a wider readership since it lost money on every copy. Hagan worked full-time as editor but was only paid for part-time work. In late 1964, he decided to take a position in Seattle with King Broadcasting, whose president, Stimson Bullitt, had been a major donor to *The Correspondent.* For an organization heavily dependent on a few individuals and their personal relationships, overcoming the loss of Hagan proved impossible.

Yet it was little coincidence that the Committee disbanded at a time when relations between young radicals and liberals became acrimonious. Riesman quickly became a vehement critic of the New Left. In the last issue of *The Correspondent*, published in August 1965, Riesman charged young radicals with taking their critiques of American society to such extremes that they renounced the possibility of reform: "Among members of the Students for a Democratic Society and other groups on the student left, hostility to the concept of 'power politics' reflects a general hostility toward 'politics,' 'bureaucracy,' 'organization'—all of these symbols being seen as aspects of the corruption of our society." He charged that SDS wanted "to stand outside politics."[38] Riesman worried that the radicalization of the New Left and its rejection of the politics of influence would more likely provoke a right-wing reaction than energize liberalism. He predicted that New Leftists would help elect Ronald Reagan president.[39] In 1970, Riesman wrote to Hagan to rue the loss of the Committee of Correspondence and express antagonism to the radical student movement: "You can imagine how often I have wished there were still something like *The Correspondent* going but I would now write on 'intra-student divisions' weakening the anti-war movement."[40]

For their part, New Leftists became increasingly hostile to liberalism. The Port Huron Statement imagined a coalition of liberals and socialists. In 1962, "liberal" was still a positive word among New Leftists; for example, when the Port Huron Statement referred to labor as the most "liberal" force in mainstream American society, it was meant as a compliment. Early SDS strategy focused on allying with those liberals whom it could persuade to its side, reflecting an understanding that liberals did not constitute a monolithic bloc on issues such as the Cold War. The New Left's role, as imagined at Port Huron, was to bolster and energize genuine liberalism by holding liberals to their principles. As Richard Flacks put it, its strategy was to "inspire, catalyze, goad, and irritate the liberal and labor organizations."[41] By the mid-1960s, however, SDS grew increasingly impatient with liberalism. In a 1965 antiwar speech, then SDS president Carl Oglesby identified "liberals" as responsible for the Vietnam War and other problems in American society. Oglesby distinguished between "corporate liberalism," which advanced reforms merely to prop up the power of big business and the imperial state, and "humanitarian liberalism," which held true to its stated principles. Yet he saw little role for liberals working within the established system, implying that humanitarian liberals could serve no useful function unless they became New Left radicals. Increasingly over the course of the 1960s, much of the New Left came to see all liberals as corporate liberals who would co-opt any efforts at true social reform.[42]

Driving the New Left's alienation from liberalism was revulsion against the Democratic Party. The Kennedy and Johnson administration failed to protect civil rights activists in the South from violence and pandered to southern segregationists at the 1964 Democratic National Convention; they pursued imperialist Cold War policies in Cuba, the Dominican Republic, and Vietnam. Yet, New Leftists erred when they collapsed liberalism into a single category, identified it solely with the actions of Democrats in office, took for granted the genuine reforms accomplished under Kennedy and Johnson, and discounted liberals such as those in the Committee of Correspondence with whom they shared similar goals but who worked within the established system for gradual reform.

In 1972, the Democrats' Presidential nominee was George McGovern, a humanitarian liberal whose campaign platform included some of the proposals and much of the spirit of the Port Huron Statement. As McGovern's agenda indicated, the relationship between liberals and New Leftists was not always acrimonious after the early 1960s. By 1972, many New Leftists worked for political change through the liberal wing of the Democratic Party. The organizational implosion and radicalization that marked SDS by the late 1960s, when it splintered into factions such as the Weathermen and the Maoist Progressive Labor Party, never fully represented the later New Left. Even in the late 1960s, liberals and radicals in many areas collaborated in much the same manner as they had during the Port Huron moment. At Yale University, former Committee member Robert Lifton led a group of "Concerned Yale Faculty" who worked to ensure student radicals' right to protest peacefully. Partly due to his efforts, Yale avoided a destructive campus confrontation like those at Columbia that pitted radical students against mostly liberal faculty members.[43] One of the most sympathetic contemporary studies of the New Left, *Young Radicals* (1968), was written by a protégé of David Riesman's, Kenneth Keniston, who characterized himself as a liberal radicalized by his experiences with the New Left.[44] Nevertheless, the possibilities for collaboration between liberals and radicals were greater at the time of the Port Huron Statement than later in the 1960s. Thus, we might see Port Huron not as the birth of an authentically radical New Left but rather as a promising start for a broad left-liberal alliance that never fully materialized.

Collaboration between leftists and liberals remains of vital importance today. We should not urge radicals to accept the limits of the present political structure, nor should we force liberals to take to the barricades. But we must recognize that liberalism and radicalism have been most successful in American history when they have established a synergistic relationship characterized by mutual respect for working within the system and for seeking to challenge its most fundamental structures. Clearly, the fortunes of both liberalism and radicalism have sharply declined since fifty years ago. The best chance for their future revival depends upon the adoption of a broad front evident in the early 1960s in the overlapping goals of the Committee for Correspondence and the Port Huron Statement.

Chapter 6

A Moment of Convergence

Nelson Lichtenstein

In our effort to put the Port Huron Statement into historical context we properly pay close attention to two sections in the Statement, which collectively take up just a few pages. The first is the luminous prologue, from which the idea of "participatory democracy" and the commitment of a new generation "to make values explicit" have been remembered and celebrated through the decades. Of only somewhat lesser import has been the controversy that goes by the shorthand name "anti-anti-Communism," a formulation that does not appear in the Statement, but which encapsulates the break these young radicals sought to make with what was then denominated "Cold War liberalism." It generated a good deal of controversy then and to some degree continues to do so now.

But the Port Huron Statement contains a great deal more. It offers a sweeping survey of "the American scene" in all its economic, political, racial, and foreign policy complexity and it puts forth, on many issues, a concrete set of policy proposals. What is striking about so much of this is the extent to which the Statement tracks the debates then engulfing American liberalism. While it is remembered for its visionary appeal, much of the Statement itself is what we would today call "wonkish," a word that, thankfully, did not exist in 1962.

This observation is offered not to denigrate the Statement but to assert, contra Daniel Bell, that this species of radicalism was very much of this world as well as in it. Those who wrote the manifesto were hardly espousing the sort of socialism that Bell maligned as failing to "relate itself to the specific problems of social action in the here-and-now, give-and-take polit-ical world."[1] Indeed, this essay seeks to demonstrate the rootedness of the Statement in three ways. First, it explains the political and generational logic that put the week of discussion and debate over the Statement at a particular location, the trade union summer educational camp at Port Huron, Michigan. Then our discussion moves to a brief and selective com-parison between another document that appeared almost simultaneously with the Port Huron Statement: the resolutions passed by the United Auto-mobile Workers at their eighteenth constitutional convention, which began on May 4, 1962, little more than a month before those who would redraft Tom Hayden's manuscript assembled in Port Huron. The juxtaposition of these two highly ambitious documents illustrates the degree to which the radical liberalism that the Port Huron Statement represented tracked the programmatic politics of an institution that was so important to American liberalism in the early postwar decades.

But in demonstrating those political and ideological connections between the activist radicals and the older generation of labor-liberals, this essay also revisits a contradiction that stands at the heart of the Port Huron Statement, a conundrum that would bedevil the New Left itself during its most important and creative years. This is because the Statement itself embodies a high degree of tension between the expansive, visionary prom-ise of a new democracy offered by its principal authors and the prosaic and inadequate political strategy that the Statement puts forward as the path to that new world.

The New Left and Students for a Democratic Society had many support-ive parents: the communists and ex-communists who sent forth scores of highly effective and creative "red-diaper babies"; the needle trades socialists who were the primary funders of the Student League for Industrial Democ-racy; the neo-abolitionists, on issues of peace and racial politics, who often came out of the mainstream Protestant churches; and the United Automo-bile Workers, not so much the formal leadership, in the regions and locals, as the coterie of not-so-old socialists who were a highly imaginative "brain trust" surrounding fifty-five-year-old Walter Reuther. These included Reuther's youngest brother, Victor, who as director of international affairs, always stood slightly to the left of Walter; Irving Bluestone, a key collective bargaining aide who was also the father of Barry, soon to be active in the New Left; Brendan Sexton, the UAW educational director; Nat Weinberg, the union's research chief, and Mildred Jeffrey, the UAW director of community affairs, which put her in close contact with many Democratic Party activists. Jeffrey was the mother of Sharon, who as a Michigan undergrad had become part of the modestly large circle of students active in SDS on that campus.[2]

The latter proved fortuitous because as of late May 1962, SDS had not found a physical location where its members could assemble to discuss Tom Hayden's draft of an as yet unnamed manifesto. So SDS president Al Haber, a sometime Michigan grad student, made a desperate call to Sharon, who immediately called her mother to ask if Port Huron was available. Its official name was the FDR Labor Education Center, a set of 1940s-style rustic buildings near Lake Huron, sixty miles north of Detroit, and owned by the Michigan AFL-CIO. Walter Reuther would later call it a "recreational slum." But the UAW made use of its facilities for training and educational courses and camps far more extensively than any other union or labor-related group, and since Mildred worked almost daily with all the players at the state labor federation, she had no trouble securing it for a group still affiliated with the venerable League for Industrial Democracy.[3]

From the perspective of Mildred Jeffrey's generation, there was nothing unusual about a group of politically committed activists meeting at a summer education camp to pound out a detailed manifesto. The distinctive brand of UAW postwar liberalism had been birthed in a series of politically charged educational conferences and summer camps held periodically during the 1940s. There the legendary factional fights that consumed the first decade of the UAW's existence often reached a white-hot intensity. In the early postwar years, Victor Reuther, the UAW educational director, convened convention-sized conclaves of more than 2,000 attendees, where classes, workshops, and speeches offered a sophisticated brief for the Reuther caucus program. By 1947, when the Reutherites assumed full control of the union, the UAW enrolled more than 35,000 local leaders in educational institutes or summer schools established near auto plants across the Midwest. "First we must organize them, that's the easy part," remarked Walter Reuther of an era that now seems incredibly alien to twenty-first-century ears. "then we must unionize them, that's the hard part."[4]

It was hard because the UAW itself had over the early postwar years developed a highly ambiguous attitude toward places like Port Huron. This was true not so much of those in Reuther's brain trust as it was of the lower-and mid-level UAW officials and operatives. Local union leaders often held onto their offices in a tentative fashion since they bore the brunt of all the frustrations and complaints that boiled up from thousands of men and women who labored in factories that Reuther once described as the "largest glorified, gold-plated sweatshop in the world."[5] Since those who attended educational workshops tended toward the ambitious and committed, the attitude of many of these lesser officials might well be summed up as "Why spend money (to educate) people who may unseat us."[6] Workers' education at Port Huron therefore tended toward the prosaic: grievance handling, the mechanics of get-out-the-vote campaigns, time study techniques, and the like. In the mid-1950s, Roy Reuther is reported to have snapped at a young socialist who made reference to the "class struggle" at a Port Huron class, "Don't use that kind of sectarian Marxist crap in this school."[7]

Thus when Mildred Jeffrey and other once-radical UAW staffers read the Port Huron Statement, they were impressed and delighted: here was a new generation of activists to carry the torch, a group of free-spirited youth unconstrained by union procedures and tradition or demoralized by political defeat. Intimately aware of this attitude, Sharon Jeffrey prodded Hayden and other SDS members to apply for funding from the UAW. These proposals generated one favorable review after another. Irving Bluestone sent a memo to Reuther arguing that Bob Ross and SDS could be of "ultimate value to the liberal cause." Mildred Jeffrey described the organization as "the most important student organization in the country."[8] Both Bluestone and Jeffrey endorsed SDS's proposals to fight poverty via its Economic Research and Action Project, or ERAP.

And Walter Reuther agreed. As he told his executive board, whose average age was now past fifty, "We were once young and we were wild and we didn't believe you couldn't organize."[9] Early in 1963 he put Brendan Sexton in charge of a leadership study center at Solidarity House, the union's headquarters, and he funded a series of internships in Washington and Detroit for the new generation of campus radicals. In June 1963 the UAW executive board held a weeklong retreat in the Poconos, where speakers ranged from Tom Hayden to Norman Cousins of *Saturday Review*.[10] On one occasion Reuther turned down an SDS funding request, but only because he mistakenly thought too much money was earmarked for "education" and not enough for "organizing." In 1964 Reuther invited virtually the entire SDS leadership to the union's March 1964 annual convention. When he spoke with them during a break in the proceedings, the SDS contingent was impressed with the seeming militancy of the UAW leader. "We just sat there stunned because we thought we were the radicals, we were the tough kids," remembered a youthful Frank Joyce of that moment. "And this guy comes in and blows everybody away."[11] This love affair would be brief, but it was genuine while it lasted.

The Port Huron Statement was a lengthy and expansive manifesto. At the conference that gave rise to this volume, Richard Flacks remarked upon the chutzpah inherent in the ambition of a few dozen young people taking a stance on virtually all issues ailing the nation and then proposing a set of solutions, some grand, some petty, but all urgent. Leaders of the UAW were hardly to be undone on this score. The numerous resolutions adopted by delegates at the union's 1962 convention demonstrated just as much ambition as the set debated and adopted by their younger brothers and sisters in the emergent New Left.

The UAW passed fifty-eight such resolutions in all, many thousands of words in length, ranging from such obvious union issues as speed-up, plant location, and workman's compensation to a series of lengthy documents on civil rights, economic planning, international affairs, public education, housing and economic development, and the federal reserve board. Thus, for example, the preamble to the resolution on international affairs sounds as if it could have come right out of the Port Huron Statement. Entitled "The World in Crisis," it begins, "We, together with the rest of humanity, are in the middle of a world we must remake if we are to survive. At a time when the alternative to peace is annihilation, interest in world affairs is no longer a matter of voluntary choice for union members or anyone else." And it goes on: "Survival depends on solidarity—the solidarity of wage-earners in free unions voicing the moral strength of the people of the world against greed, against social injustice, and against all forms of tyranny that would enslave the human spirit."[12]

Two caveats are in order. First, many such resolutions contain a paragraph or two praising the Kennedy administration for taking steps in the right direction, inadequate as they might be. And second, it is highly doubtful that more than a handful of the 3,000 delegates bothered to either read or debate most of these resolutions, especially those concerned with international affairs, structural economic reform, or political issues not directly impacting the lives of these auto workers. The great exception here was the

resolution tackling civil rights, which had already begun to convulse the
UAW all the way from the composition of its executive board at the top to
the handling of thousands of racially fraught grievances in hundreds of
shop disputes all across the nation.[13]

The left has long been correct, in the unions and out, to condemn "res-
olutionary action." But the fact remains that the Reuther brain trust, and
in particular men and women like Nat Weinberg, Mildred Jeffrey, Irving
Bluestone, Jack Conway, Brendon Sexton, and Victor Reuther, took the
enormous time and energy to write these manifesto-like missives, then get
them passed by a fairly sophisticated resolutions committee and eventually
adopted at a huge convention. They are a testament to the long-lost ambitions of the American union movement and to the sense that its agenda
was properly that of the nation itself. So it is no wonder that the Reutherite
circle saw the Port Huron youth as a badly needed set of reinforcements in
a common battle for the soul of the nation.

Like the UAW resolutions, the Port Huron Statement backstops its
moral ambitions with a programmatic specificity. Thus in the section of the
Port Huron Statement dealing with poverty, the text asserts that any program must be just as sweeping as the nature of poverty itself. Hayden and
the other drafters of the statement then list a number of programs:
increased housing for low- and middle-income peoples, medical care for
all, and an extension of the welfare state. One line is devoted to the minimum wage, demanding that a standard of at least $1.50 should be extended
to all workers, including the 16 million, in agriculture and elsewhere, not
covered at all. Both the brevity of the proposal and its modesty are remarkable here.[14] At the time the Port Huron Statement was written, the minimum wage, which Kennedy had fought for as one of his first legislative
initiatives, was scheduled to rise to $1.25 an hour by 1963, bringing it to 83
percent of what SDS demanded. Moreover, the UAW actually stood to the
left of SDS on this issue, calling for the minimum wage to be "substantially
increased above the inadequate $1.25." And the union took it all very seri-
ously, devoting fourteen paragraphs to the issue in the resolution the UAW
passed at its 1962 convention.[15] Little more than a year later a minimum
wage of $2.00 an hour would be one of the demands put forward by the
coalition of unions and civil rights groups that organized the August 1963
March on Washington for Jobs and Freedom.

For the drafters of the Port Huron Statement, the text characterizing the
labor movement proved controversial. The basic stance of the document is

that labor has failed to fulfill its promise. Despite its size, capacity to raise real wages, and political influence, the very "successes of the last generation perhaps have braked, rather than accelerated, labor's zeal for change." Again and again the text bemoans this lost hope, at one point asserting that "Today labor remains the most liberal 'mainstream' institution—but often its liberalism represents vestigial commitments, self-interestedness, unradicalism. In some measure labor has succumbed to institutionalization, its social idealism waning under the tendencies of bureaucracy, materialism, business ethics." And perhaps most devastating is the judgment that the rank-and-file have themselves been "lulled to comfort by the accessibility of luxury and the opportunity of long-term contracts."[16] Here we get an echo both of C. Wright Mills's renunciation of the "labor metaphysic" as well as the complacency of liberals like Clark Kerr and John Kenneth Galbraith who saw the "labor question" as increasingly irrelevant because the unions themselves had become so functional to the system of bureaucratic industrialism that they thought characterized postwar America.

Indeed, the very concept of "participatory democracy" stood in rhetorical counterposition to the "industrial democracy" that in 1905, when student socialists had founded the League for Industrial Democracy, seemed such a radical and democratic vision. During the Great War and well into the 1930s the effort to give workers a role in the democratization of American industry had an unquestionably radical, if not a socialist flavor. But that radicalism seemed to quickly drain away once this aspiration devolved into the system of collective bargaining facilitated by the Wagner Act and practiced by the big unions and giant corporations in the postwar decades. To some liberals of that era, like Kerr, Galbraith, Seymour Martin Lipset, and Robert Dahl, this sort of interest group pluralism was as close to democratic practice as was possible in a modern society.

But the young radicals at Port Huron shared with other liberals a considerable disquiet. Arnold Kaufman's influential 1960 essay "Human Nature and Participatory Democracy" is in part an attack on the notion that all large organizations, including the unions, must of necessity conform to the iron laws of oligarchy.[17] Yet this viewpoint made the very existence of a set of stolid labor organizations all the more unacceptable. If the drafters of the Statement read the *New York Times* they were undoubtedly aware of the articles that had recently appeared under the byline of veteran labor journalist A. H. Raskin. Among them: "The Moral Issue That Confronts Labor," "New Issue: Labor as Big Business," and "Labor's Time of

Troubles: The Failure of Bread-and-Butter Unionism." Even more devastating was a *Commentary* article published that same year by Daniel Bell, "The Subversion of Collective Bargaining." Bell saw the great 1959 steel strike as a sham, largely useful to the corporations as a mechanism whereby the steel industry could "administer" a higher price schedule. "The desiccated language of collective bargaining is a trap," wrote Bell. It was no longer "an instrument for economic and social justice."[18] The Port Huron Statement mirrored such a critique two years later: "Labor has too often seen itself as elitist, rather than mass-oriented, and as a pressure group rather than as an 18-million-member body making political demands for all America."[19]

According to James Miller, quoting Bob Ross, the League for Industrial Democracy loyalists Rochelle Horowitz and Michael Harrington objected to such a text because it marginalized the role labor might play, the hegemonic role, in any new left. So to accommodate LID, two paragraphs in praise of labor were tacked on to Hayden's draft: "A new politics must include a revitalized labor movement: a movement which sees itself, and is regarded by others, as a major leader of the breakthrough to a politics of hope and vision. Labor's role is no less unique or important to the needs of the future than it was in the past."[20]

But if Horowitz and Harrington thought such paragraphs necessary to accommodate the sensibilities of those unionists in the New York needle trades, who were paying the bills, such rhetorical ransom was unnecessary when it came to the UAW, where even the most critical passages in the Hayden draft might have won a nod or two from the Reutherite intellectuals. Thus when Hayden asserted that it would be irresponsible not to criticize labor for losing much of the idealism that once made it a driving movement, he was practically channeling the speech Walter Reuther delivered the month before when he told the delegates at the union's 1962 convention, who were celebrating the twenty-fifth anniversary of the Depression-era sit down strikes, that "there is something quite sacred about that early period" that could still be put to practical use. "A labor movement can get soft and flabby spiritually. It can make progress materially, and the soul of the union can die in the process."[21] And if Reuther himself might not have signed on to Hayden's indictment, that "the labor bureaucracy tends to be cynical towards, or afraid of, rank-and-file involvement in the work of the unions," virtually the entire staff of the UAW would have agreed, if only because they were themselves engaged in an effort to build their own union-like staff organization during the early 1960s.[22]

A third perspective on this issue was also represented at the Port Huron conference. This was the somewhat muted voice of Kim Moody, a Johns Hopkins undergraduate who was then moving into the orbit of the Young People's Socialist League. Like Harrington and Horowitz he thought labor central to any revitalization of the left. He would soon write the SDS pamphlet "Toward the Working-Class," but unlike Horowitz and Harrington he was no apologist for the Meanyite union leadership. He identified with the "labor party" tendency inside the YPSL even thought he never actually joined that group, thinking it too sectarian. The "labor party" advocates privileged a new era of rank-and-file labor revolt, often in opposition to existing union leaders. They thought the effort to "realign" the Democratic Party, well endorsed in the Port Huron Statement, a futile and regressive effort.[23]

Indeed, the Port Huron Statement's emphasis on such a realignment strategy stands in a contradictory relationship to much of the analysis and almost all the spirit found elsewhere in the document. Like many liberals in Congress and the academy, Tom Hayden wanted to get the Dixiecrats out of the Democratic Party and into the Republican Party. And he hoped that northern Republicans of the Nelson Rockefeller, or at least the John Lindsay, stripe would soon join the more genuinely liberal party. This was no exercise in political speculation. Hayden had been jailed and beaten by southern Democratic sheriffs and other officials who were perfectly content to wield their stifling influence inside the same party that hosted John Conyers and Hubert Humphrey. He saw SNCC's heroic efforts to register African Americans in the deep South not just in terms of abstract justice and humanity, but as part of a concrete plan to revolutionize the region. "Linked with pressure from Northern liberals to expunge the Dixiecrats from the ranks of the Democratic party, massive Negro voting in the South could destroy the vise-like grip reactionary Southerners have on the Congressional legislative process"[24]—the Statement is saturated with passages of this sort denouncing the influence of the Dixiecrats.

Most are impassioned, as in this chastisement of liberal Democrats in the section "Towards American Democracy": "Every time the President criticizes a recalcitrant Congress, we must ask that he no longer tolerate the Southern conservatives in the Democratic Party. Every time a liberal representative complains that 'we can't expect everything at once' we must ask if we received much of anything from Congress in the last generation. Every time he refers to 'circumstances beyond control' we must ask why he fraternizes with racist scoundrels."[25]

But Hayden on occasion channels the most arid academic prose, as in this section, which might well have come right out of the 1950 report of the American Political Science Association, *Toward a More Responsible Party System*. So he writes:

> Two genuine parties, centered around issues and essential values, demanding allegiance to party principles shall supplant the current system of organized stalemate which is seriously inadequate to a world in flux. It has long been argued that the very overlapping of American parties guarantees that issues will be considered responsibly, that progress will be gradual instead of intemperate, and that therefore America will remain stable instead of torn by class strife. On the contrary: the enormous party overlap itself confuses issues and makes responsible presentation of choice to the electorate impossible. . . . The ideals of political democracy, then, the imperative need for flexible decision-making apparatus makes a real two-party system an immediate social necessity. What is desirable is sufficient party disagreement to dramatize major issues, yet sufficient party overlap to guarantee stable transitions from administration to administration.[26]

But here is the problem. Not all of America's difficulties could be solved by relying on the Democrats, even a more liberal and purified version thereof. In the section on the economy, largely written by Robb Burlage, a quasi-Marxist analysis details the deleterious influence of the growth in large corporations, the rise of the military-industrial complex, and the job-destroying impact of automation. None of these maladies seem resolvable by a realignment of the parties. The genuine realignment of the two parties that has taken place during the last third of a century has indeed polarized American politics, but not to the advantage of the liberals. "Be Careful What You Wish For," is the title of a 2007 article in the *Annual Review of Political Science* detailing the stalemate and conservative ascendency engendered by that realignment under Reagan, Clinton, and both Bushes.[27]

Even more important, realignment stood in contradiction to the visionary and insurgent spirit of the Port Huron Statement. It is true that in the American federalist system, with winner-take-all elections at every level, third parties or labor parties are doomed to defeat. But the costs of a realignment strategy are also exceedingly high, because it requires a kind of accommodative and coalition-building politics that was antithetical to the early New Left in its most creative and attractive moments.

All this became clear in the summer of 1964. At the very same UAW convention during which Walter Reuther hosted the SDS leadership, the Reuther brain trust was busy strategizing how they might assist in one of the boldest realignment gambits of the postwar era. The UAW strongly supported the challenge of the Mississippi Freedom Democratic Party (MFDP). Mildred Jeffrey and UAW counsel Joe Rauh were in close contact with Robert Moses, a leader of that effort, and veteran civil rights activist Ella Baker. Rauh thought it entirely possible that the convention might vote to seat both the MFDP and the segregationist Democrats from that state, in which case the racist delegation would undoubtedly walk straight out of the convention and into the arms of the Goldwater GOP. To this end Reutherite political operatives like Jeffrey, Jack Conway, and Bill Dodds rounded up an impressive number of delegate votes.[28]

As soon became very apparent, however, President Lyndon Johnson was determined to derail the MFDP challenge. He feared the loss of not just the intransigent white South, but the blue-collar voters George Wallace had begun to agitate in his sojourns north of the Mason-Dixon line. So LBJ put the hammerlock on Reuther, who in turn not only told his staff to cease their work on behalf of MFDP, but infamously provided the organizational muscle to subvert the challenge at Atlantic City. Reuther had been an advocate of realignment ever since he had abandoned his labor party dreams in the 1940s, but as Harvey Swados presciently remarked in a 1963 essay, "The UAW: Over the Top or Over the Hill," "One cannot complain, as one might with almost any other union, of an absence of intellect, or of a lack of application of that intellect to the problems of the age. What one can say, I think with justification, is that the UAW leadership no longer takes its own demands seriously."[29]

The same could not be said of SDS. The machinations of Johnson and Reuther at Atlantic City came as a sense of betrayal, a shock of recognition of where power and potential lay even at the height of America's liberal hour. "The rupture between the Democratic Party and the New Left would never heal," observed Tom Hayden, despite continued efforts, including his own, "to realign the party through the later Sixties."[30] Wrote Todd Gitlin, "To the New Left, Atlantic City discredited the politics of coalition— between militants and the liberal-labor establishment, between whites and blacks, between youth and elders." And to Staughton Lynd, Atlantic City represented a betrayal of direct democracy, of the rights of ordinary people. Its meaning, he declared, was that "coalitionism" was "elitism."[31]

SDS would soon make its greatest impact on the American polity, despite, or rather because, the politics of realignment were unworkable, certainly as long as LBJ was president and most Democrats marched in lockstep behind him. In subsequent decades, American politics would be transformed, but the tensions inherent between the expansive social vision of the American left and the constrained political terrain upon which it must struggle have never been resolved.

Chapter 7

The New Left's Love-Hate Relationship
with the University

Robert Cohen

From its opening sentence, the Port Huron Statement makes clear that its agenda for the 1960s generation was linked to and critical of the campus world: "We are people of this generation . . . , housed now *in universities,* looking uncomfortably to the world we inherit."[1] Part of this inherited world of Cold War America that made the Port Huron Statement's authors uncomfortable was the university itself, which they saw as an instrument of the national power elite, complicit in the creation of the warfare state and in the failure of America to address the social order's glaring inequities and injustices. The Port Huron Statement's lead section on "Values" begins with a scathing critique of university faculty and administrators for failing to bring "moral enlightenment" to students.[2] The next section, "The Students," is devoted entirely to the campuses, offering an indictment of the mindless, avaricious, apolitical character of America's dominant student culture and the way university authorities sustained that culture.[3] Nor did such SDS criticism of the university begin with Port Huron. Tom Hayden, the Port Huron Statement's main author, had already developed many of these criticisms and was speaking out about the nature of student life and politics well before the Port Huron conference. Tom Hayden's most influential speech at the University of Michigan during the semester before Port Huron (subsequently published as a widely circulated SDS pamphlet, *Student Social Action*) focused primarily on in loco parentis and the ways the university discouraged serious dissent and political engagement among students.[4]

In the pages of the Port Huron Statement, university administrators were portrayed as self-interested bureaucrats so eager to enrich their institutions that they more closely resembled businessmen than educational leaders. They were presiding over "a shift within the university toward the value standards of business and the administrative mentality. Huge foundations and other private financial interests shape the . . . colleges and universities . . . making them more commercial." To avoid antagonizing their patrons in the corporate world and the Pentagon, these administrators gladly "sacrifice controversy to public relations," leading universities that were becoming "less disposed to diagnose society critically, less open to dissent."[5]

Equally damaging, according to the Port Huron Statement, was the way in which the university's growing bureaucracy and increasingly corporate management style socialized students into political passivity. The "cumbersome academic bureaucracy . . . [was] contributing to the sense of outer complexity and inner powerlessness that transforms the honest searching of many students to a ratification of convention, and, worse, to a numbness to present and future catastrophes."[6] Since the university was led in top-down fashion, in the mode of a business corporation, students were effectively barred from the campus decision-making process, schooling them to be not active citizens in a democracy but compliant corporate employees deferring to the authority of managers. Thus the Port Huron Statement notes that "with administrators ordering the institution . . . the student learns by his isolation to accept elite rule within the university, which prepares him to accept later forms of minority control."[7]

The faculty, the Port Huron Statement implies, not merely had failed to resist these alarming trends but were actually complicit in them. Much of the faculty had abandoned the ideal of a critical university and dissident intelligentsia and so had allowed "academic resources . . . [to be] used to buttress immoral social practice."[8] Some had done so out of rank opportunism, as was the case with faculty in defense-related fields, who had allowed their "skills and silence" to be "purchased by investors in the arms race."[9] So instead of articulating alternatives to Cold War militarism, academics accepted huge "defense contracts [to] make the universities engineers of the arms race." The Port Huron Statement drew parallels with the way faculty expertise was enlisted to service big business, using "modern social science as a manipulative tool," via "human relations" consultants to "the modern corporations, who introduce trivial sops to give laborers feelings of 'participation' or 'belonging,' while actually deluding them in order to further exploit their labor."[10]

While accusing some faculty of having sold out, the Port Huron Statement criticized other professors for becoming overly specialized. They had morphed into narrow, insular technocrats incapable of serving as public intellectuals. Such faculty could not inspire their students to engage critically with serious social questions, much less become agents of democratic social change. In the classrooms of these narrow academics, the Port Huron Statement charged, "passion is called unscholastic" and learning disengaged from

> questions we might want raised, [concerning how] . . . to change society. . . . Social reality is "objectified" to sterility, dividing the student from life. . . . Specialization . . . has produced an exaggerated compartmentalization of study and understanding. This has contributed to an overly parochial view, by faculty, of the role of its research and scholarship, to a discontinuous and truncated understanding, by students, of the surrounding social order; and to a loss of personal attachment, by nearly all, to the worth of study as a humanistic enterprise.[11]

In the hands of such faculty, the curriculum changed "more slowly than the living events of the world," leaving students intellectually and politically impoverished. Instead of being centers of critical thought, universities had descended into knowledge factories and vocational training outlets that bred conformity, with students surrounded by "dull" teaching, "irrelevant" research, and "paternalistic" rules. Thus the Port Huron Statement concluded that the university's "real function . . . as opposed to its more rhetorical function of 'searching for truth' is to . . . help the student get by, modestly but comfortably, in the big society beyond."[12] College, life then, was in no sense transformative since "the actual intellectual effect of the college experience is hardly distinguishable from any other communications channel—say a television set—passing on the stock truths of the day. Students leave college . . . basically unchallenged in their values and political orientations."[13]

The Port Huron Statement's portrait of the university is at points so unflattering that at first glance it might seem to support the view of critics of the New Left who have depicted the student movement of the 1960s as implacably hostile toward the university and higher education, and even anti-intellectual. But a close reading of this SDS manifesto reveals a more complex picture, and a cluster of attitudes toward the university that included not merely negativism, but also hopefulness. While the early sections of the Port Huron Statement focused on the university only to criticize it, the manifesto ends with an elaborate and upbeat argument about the university's potential to serve as the ideal base for the New Left and democratic change. Indeed, without acknowledging the one-sidedness of its previous indictment of the university, the Port Huron Statement's closing section asserts that "social relevance, the accessibility of knowledge, and internal openness—these together make the university a potential base and agency in a movement of social change."[14]

The Port Huron Statement's authors reveal here that however jaded they may have sounded earlier in their biting critique of the campus status quo, they nonetheless held an almost romantic ideal of what a university could and should be. There was both hope for change and radical disappointment that so much of the university was failing to fulfill its potential to do good.[15] Such disappointment was evident when the Port Huron Statement rebuked the "many social and physical scientists "who did contract research for big business and the military—deeming them guilty of "neglecting the liberating heritage of higher learning."[16]

This phrase about "the liberating heritage of higher learning" was not empty rhetoric; it reflected a sense that the university could foment progressive change and point the way toward a better society if its faculty (and students) focused on generating searching social criticism and new ideas about how to democratize the American social order and its educational institutions. Such a vision of a politically engaged and radically democratic faculty was by no means utopian or merely hypothetical. There were, in fact, important left and liberal academics whom the Port Huron Statement's authors admired and emulated.

Although the generational rhetoric of the Port Huron Statement—and the fact that it was written by and for students—gave the document a student- and youth-centered tone, its ideas about the university, American capitalism, and democracy were influenced by progressive and radical academics. In virtually all the retrospectives that Hayden and other Port Huron veterans have written, they generously credit campus-based left and left-leaning intellectuals who inspired some of the key ideas that went into the Port Huron Statement. The most well-known inspiration was radical sociologist C. Wright Mills of Columbia University, who shaped the way that Hayden, Richard Flacks, and other Port Huron authors saw such key issues as power, class, and student apathy. Also important was philosopher Arnold Kaufman, of the University of Michigan, whose ideas about participatory democracy helped define the basic ethos of Port Huron. The educational reform ideas of Harold Taylor, former president of Sarah Lawrence College, influenced Hayden, and both Kaufman and Taylor were present at Port Huron.[17]

Having been so influenced by these dissenting figures in academia, the Port Huron Statement's authors knew that higher education could generate important dissident ideas. So they had good grounds for coupling their criticism of university cupidity, conformity, and military technocracy with a vision of a university transformed into the kind of institution in which progressive critics, like Mills, Kaufman, and Taylor, would be setting its tone rather than serving as dissidents. What this means, in effect, is that the Port Huron Statement's critique of the university was itself a legacy of American higher education, the academic left, which though weak in numbers was strong in radical ideas, ranging from Mills's critique of the power elite to Kaufman's articulation of a more robust form of democratic association, to Taylor's indictment of academia's commercialization.

Though far less well remembered today than Mills, Taylor is in some ways the most striking source of the Port Huron Statement's indictment of the technocratic and commercialized university. Taylor, after all, was coming from a part of the academic establishment—albeit a fading one—the presidency of a respected liberal arts college. He embodied the tension between the small liberal arts college, with its ideal of the community of scholars, and the giant multiversity devoted to servicing the military-industrial complex. His book *On Education and Freedom* (1954) had bemoaned the loss of community, the lack of focus on student learning in large institutions of higher learning—and how the presidents of those institutions had been reduced to bureaucrats and fundraisers. His vision of the president of a college or university was that of an engaged intellectual promoting educational community, "a faculty member with additional responsibilities."[18] Hayden had imbibed Taylor's critical ideas about higher education not simply from writings but also from personal contact. As an undergraduate, Hayden, while editor of Michigan's student newspaper, had met Taylor when he came to speak at Ann Arbor. Taylor befriended Hayden and became in Hayden's words "a kind of personal mentor/father figure."

Hayden had been "inspired by Cardinal Newman's vision of a small university," "passed along" to him "by Harold Taylor." He came to believe that Taylor's humane vision of the university as an intimate community of critical thinkers was "the perfect view for a university leader"—and one that was sadly lacking in America's massive academic knowledge factories.[19]

Along with the Tayloresque idealism about the university's potential as a beacon of useful ideas for democratic social change, the Port Huron Statement's closing arguments in favor of a university-based New Left reflected a sophisticated sociological sensibility, a realistic estimation—and an almost prophetic vision—of the strategic place and value of the university in what would soon be known as postindustrial society and the information age.[20] "The unchangeable reliance by men of power on" academics and the campus as "storehouses of knowledge . . . makes the university functionally tied to society in new ways, revealing new potentialities, new levers for change."[21] This connected up to the insight Hayden had gleaned from the writings of C. Wright Mills that in this emerging postindustrial society organized labor could no longer be seen as the primary agent for progressive social change. So Mills argued for a New Left that would kick the "labor metaphysic," look to a new youthful intelligentsia as a base for radicalism, a new generation that was centered on college campuses.[22] These sentiments were echoed in the Port Huron Statement's conclusion that the university "is an obvious beginning point" for such youth organizing. The fact that college students were relatively privileged economically did not lessen the Port Huron Statement's faith in their radical potential because students too, in the face of "modern complexity," experienced feelings of "helplessness and indifference," so the left could help them see that such feelings could be addressed by organizing "to change society. In a time of supposed prosperity, moral complacency, and political manipulation, a new left cannot rely on only aching stomachs to be the engine force of social reform."[23]

In light of all that the Port Huron Statement borrowed from such radical faculty as Mills, it may seem odd that the Statement did not mention the academic left and the tradition of campus dissent of which he was a part. This silence reflected the one-sided nature of political polemics and manifesto writing. If you are trying to organize a student movement to promote change in the university and society, your fundamental task is to make clear what needs to be changed. This implies a need to focus on what is wrong with the university (and society), not what is best about it. This is why much of the Port Huron Statement's discussion of the university is so negative; it is why one has to wait to almost the end of the document for acknowledgment of a more positive side of the university, its progressive potential. And it is also why the university's role in housing progressive faculty who helped to foster student dissent is never discussed in the Statement.

This rhetorical strategy makes sense politically, but it does lead to a truncated view of the university. It preempted candid, detailed autobiographical expressions in the Port Huron Statement by its authors—cutting us off from their potential insights. So, for example, the Port Huron Statement depicts students as too apathetic to "even give a damn about . . . apathy," without explaining how it was that Tom Hayden and the Port Huron Statement's other authors emerged from their college lives so politicized, revolting against campus apathy and laboring to build and lead a national student movement.[24] Where did their dissident ideas come from? Who inspired them to become activists? Answering such questions would have led them to quite a different take on the university than the one offered at Port Huron, since their ideas came in part from, as we have seen, a small but dynamic and eloquent academic left. One of the hallmarks of American higher education in the twentieth century (and since) has been that while many of its faculty and programs support the military-industrial complex, the university also houses faculty, graduate students, and undergraduates who oppose such service to the establishment. These dissidents interact and learn from each other, strengthening their oppositional stance and culture. So, for example, Hayden, as an undergraduate at Michigan, learned of C. Wright Mills from social psychology doctoral student and SDS co-founder Richard Flacks. Hayden would go on to earn a master's degree in political science at Michigan, and, fittingly, wrote his thesis on Mills.[25] The university, then, not only had the *potential*—as the Port Huron Statement acknowledged—to generate dissent in the future, it was *already* in 1962 responsible for helping to generate the dissident campus left that made the Port Huron Statement possible.

The modesty of the Port Huron Statement's claims about the state of campus dissent in 1962 is striking, and it is a reminder that although it is always, and appropriately, remembered as a document advocating and prophesying the student revolt of the 1960s, the Port Huron Statement was a document conditioned by the more politically placid 1950s. The Port Huron Statement represented SDS's call to action to move the politics and culture of America's students away from the apathy inherited from the "silent generation" of undergraduates of the Cold War 1950s, so as to banish from campus the ghost of Joe McCarthy—whose politically repressive crusade had generated much of the fear that helped to silence them. But having lived amid a student culture dominated by 1950s-style apathy left the Port Huron Statement's authors guarded even in their assessment of the campus impact of the most successful student insurgency of the early 1960s, the sit-ins against Jim Crow lunch counters in the South. The Port Huron Statement praised the sit-ins as events in which "thousands of American students demonstrated that they . . . felt the urgency of the times. They moved actively and directly against racial injustices."[26] But the Statement nonetheless made it clear that such dissidents were still on the outside of the white-bread campus world, that while thousands of students had become active, millions were not, so the protesters were at best "breaking the crust of apathy and overcoming the inner alienation that *remain the defining characteristics of American college life.*"[27] Rather than crowing, as one might from the perspective of the mid- or late 1960s, about the sit-ins launching the civil rights revolution and transforming student politics, the Port Huron Statement more soberly noted that they "succeeded in restoring a small measure of controversy to the campuses after the stillness of the McCarthy period. . . . Student movements for change are still rarities on the campus scene."[28] It was not until the Port Huron Statement's closing pages that the activists would go a bit further, briefly suggesting that civil rights activism might signal something transformative on campus—that "the power of students and faculty united is not only potential; it has shown its actuality in the South."[29]

Concerned, almost overwhelmed by the overarching pattern of student apathy, the Port Huron Statement's authors sounded most hopeful not when they discussed academia's past or present, but rather as they envisioned a more activist future for the university. Discussing that future, the Port Huron Statement articulated a radically reformist ethos regarding the university, which reflected early SDS optimism about the prospects for a transformed university helping to transform American society. This was clearly displayed in the Port Huron Statement's strategic discussions about campus organizing. That strategy avoided campus insularity and centered on coalition-building both within and far beyond the university. The Port Huron Statement urged:

national efforts at university reform by an alliance of students and faculty. They must wrest control of the educational process from the administrative bureaucracy . . . make fraternal . . . contact with allies in labor, civil rights, and other liberal forces outside the campus. They must import major public issues into the curriculum. . . . They must make debate and controversy, not dull pedantic cant, the common style for educational life . . . [and] consciously build a base for their assault upon the loci of power.[30]

Admitting that reaching out to the labor movement would be "made more difficult by the problems left over from the generation of silence"—meaning the anti-radicalism that was a legacy of the 1950s generation—the Port Huron Statement nonetheless urged students to "open the campus to labor through publications, action programs, curricula, while labor opens its house to students through internships, requests for aid (on the picket line, with handbills, in the public dialogue) and politics."[31] Recognizing that the university itself was an employer whose labor relations needed to be democratized, the Port Huron Statement urged student involvement in unionization drives for campus workers: "university employees can be organized," and student participation in that organizing can become "an important element in the education of the student radical."[32]

Looking back on the Port Huron Statement, Tom Hayden sees its understanding and critique of the university as among the strongest parts of the manifesto. Hayden claims that of "all the contributions of the Port Huron Statement, perhaps the most important was the insight that university communities had a role in social change." Early SDS had, in Hayden's view, built on Mills's insight of the need for the left to drop the "labor metaphysic," recognizing that in postindustrial America, students had great potential to become agents of social change, that "universities had become as indispensable in what we called the automation age as factories were in the age of industrial development. . . . We saw the possibilities, therefore, in challenging or disrupting the role of the universities in the knowledge economy." Hayden credits the Port Huron Statement's "most eloquent passages" with tapping into youthful angst, "the alienation that impersonal mass universities bred among idealistic youth searching for 'relevance,'" "and offering a way of overcoming it via activism on behalf of democratic vision of a reformed university that could in turn reform the larger society.[33]

Hayden claims that the Port Huron road map led not merely toward expanded student activism but also toward significant reform in higher education, at least regarding the curriculum. As Hayden put it:

> We wanted participatory education in our participatory democracy, truth from the bottom up, access to colleges and universities for those who had historically been excluded. Gradually, this led to a fundamental rejection of the narratives we had been taught, the myths of the American melting pot, the privileged superiority of (white) Western Civilization, and inevitably to the quest for inclusion of "the other"—the contribution of women, people of color, and all those who had been marginalized by the march of power.[34]

Hayden's claims may sound boastful, attributing a prophetic quality to the Port Huron Statement, in which the key challenges to the university status quo and changes in American higher education in the mid- and late 1960s and 1970s were all anticipated. But, in fact, it is striking how right Hayden is in much of this. The slow pace of curricular change was one of the first criticisms the Port Huron Statement made of the university, and this was the same grievance aired by those championing black studies, Latino studies, Native American studies, women's studies, gay studies, and other innovative programs designed to diversify the curriculum in and since the late 1960s—all of whom echoed the Port Huron Statement's call for "social relevance" in education.[35] Similarly, the issue of democratizing education access, which became so central to the Black Power movement on campus in the late 1960s, was raised in the Port Huron Statement's lament that "only one of 20 'nonwhite' students go to college as opposed to the 1:10 ratio for white students."[36] In its critique of campus administrators and calls for efforts to "wrest control of the educational process from the administrative bureaucracy," the Statement anticipated the challenge that Berkeley's Free Speech Movement would make in 1964 to the Kerr administration—which Mario Savio had denounced as "an autocracy which runs this university."[37]

Beyond the changes that were championed successfully later in the 1960s and 1970s, the Port Huron Statement also anticipated campus struggles that proved much more difficult to win, most notably the protests against war-related programs and Pentagon-contracted research at universities in the Vietnam era. The question of whether the university ought to be part of a war machine, which was raised politely at Port Huron in 1962, would be central to some of the most disruptive campus protests of the mid- and late 1960s.[38] It is an issue that has resurfaced in the past few years as leading university administrators have called for a return of the Reserve Officers' Training Corps (ROTC) to their campuses. And the question of whether the university should serve as a think tank, a research and development arm, for corporations that exploit labor—whether in the name of academic freedom, "academic resources" ought to be "used to buttress immoral social practice"—endures into the present, as the lines between corporatizing universities and their big business partners have become far murkier in the twenty-first century than they were in the twentieth.[39]

It is striking how much of the Port Huron vision for the university came, at least temporarily, to resemble campus reality in the late 1960s and early 1970s. Recall that that vision was one that considered the "ideal university" as "a community of controversy within itself and in its effects on communities beyond." Certainly by the time of Kent State there was no question that campuses had become centers of controversy and debate about the war. The same was true of Black Power on campus. In fact, by the time of the Kent State and Jackson State massacres in 1970, polls showed that the majority of Americans saw student unrest as the nation's number-one problem.[40] But such controversy elicited a harsh response from the state and tragic consequences that the authors of the Port Huron Statement never envisioned: the use of troops and deadly force to suppress student unrest.

The one problem with Hayden's retrospective discussion of the Port Huron Statement and educational change on campus is that his model of change is so student-centered. The curricular innovations that the Port Huron Statement anticipated were not merely the work of student activists. They were also made possible by the pioneering scholarship and organizing done by faculty in many of the new fields of education that emerged in the 1960s and 1970s. Here Hayden had inadvertently repeated the main shortcoming of the portrait of the university offered in the Port Huron Statement itself: the academic left, radical faculty, were never mentioned in the document.

But Hayden's larger point, that the Port Huron Statement, as one of the New Left's founding documents, helped orient the student movement of the 1960s toward involvement in reforming the university—and had a positive impact on American higher education—is an important one. It contradicts the view, widely held by the New Left's detractors in and since the 1960s, such as Allan Bloom in his Reagan-era best-seller *The Closing of the American Mind* (1987), that the student movement of the 1960s played a very destructive role with regard to higher education.[41] As such, it offers a useful entry point for moving beyond SDS and Port Huron and reconsidering the larger relationship between the student movement of the 1960s and the university.

Hayden's argument, and my own rereading of the Port Huron Statement's indictment of university administrators and faculty on the fiftieth anniversary of that document, brought to mind a conversation I had back in 1999 with one such critic of the New Left, Clark Kerr. As president of the University of California in 1964, Kerr did battle with the Free Speech Movement (FSM)—the New Left's first mass student rebellion on campus—an experience that led him to conclude that FSM's leader, Mario Savio, hated the university. In 1999 Kerr was drafting his memoir, and invited me (and historian Reginald Zelnik, who had been a pro-FSM faculty member at Berkeley in 1964) to discuss with him his (Kerr's) account of the Berkeley rebellion, in which his image of Savio the university-hater figured prominently. In our conversation, Kerr clung to that image even as I challenged its accuracy.[42]

Kerr based his negative judgment of Savio in part on a misreading of the Free Speech Movement leader's most famous speech, given from the steps of Berkeley's administration building, Sproul Hall, on December 2, 1964, just before the FSM's culminating sit-in. Kerr claimed that Savio had denounced the university as "odious," when in fact what he was denouncing was not the university but *its administration* for what Savio saw as its authoritarian management style, trampling of student free speech rights, and subservience to a plutocratic, unelected board of regents.[43] I pointed out to Kerr that Savio's indictment of the administration derived not from a hatred of the university but his radical idealism about what the university could become if it lived up to its high ideals about the pursuit of truth. Savio thought the university could and should emerge as a center of searching social criticism and a base for movements promoting egalitarian change. For this to occur, the university's own governing structure first needed to be democratized so that it was dominated not by professional administrators but by faculty and students, who made up the community of scholars that in actuality constituted the university. Savio hoped that a truly self-governing university would be able to free itself from the corrupting influence of big business and the Pentagon, which had made it a service station for the military-industrial complex, and align itself instead with the civil rights movement and other struggles for progressive social change. A brilliant student of philosophy and physics, Savio, contrary to Kerr's claim, was not hostile to the academy and in fact made lifelong friends on the Berkeley faculty. Savio would go on to spend his professional life as a teacher at the university level.[44] None of these arguments changed Kerr's mind, however, and so in Kerr's memoir Savio comes across as a demagogic New Left leader who loathed the university.[45]

Rereading the Port Huron Statement's passages about the university prodded me to rethink the way I had understood Kerr's stubbornness in insisting that Savio detested the university. At the time I had thought of Kerr as hopelessly partisan and unable to think in a nuanced way about Savio's critique about higher education simply because he wanted to place his former nemesis in the worst possible light. Kerr's memoir was, after all, colored by his lingering resentment of the way Savio and the Free Speech Movement had fomented a crisis that overwhelmed Kerr's UC administration in 1964 and set in motion the unraveling of Kerr's liberal presidency of the University of California—culminating in his firing by the newly elected right-wing governor of California, Ronald Reagan, in 1967.[46] Even so, I now think of it as simplistic to dismiss Kerr's censorious view of Savio as merely a reflection of his personal bitterness. After all, both Savio's public expressions about the university in 1964 and most New Left documents, including the Port Huron Statement and its successors, essentially constituted a literature of complaint. Being the target of such complaints and facing oppositional mass movements bent on challenging their authority, movements that used rhetoric that was often scornful and heated, it was not unreasonable for Kerr and his fellow university administrators to conclude that these movements and their leaders hated the university. Yes, there was a loathing for the status quo at the university that Savio and the Port Huron Statement both expressed—and in that limited sense Kerr was right. But what Kerr missed was the flip side of this opposition, that even if one insists on using the word hate, it was a *love*-hate relationship. How else can one explain why Savio endured suspension, arrest, and a prison term to change the university? Similarly, with all its biting criticism of the university, the Port Huron Statement nonetheless ends up devoting its entire closing section, "The Universities and Social Change," to champion-ing the notion that the university could be the center of a New Left move-ment to democratize America, a conclusion that reflects enormous hopefulness about the potential of higher education to lead the way toward positive social change.[47]

Though the Port Huron Statement was written two years prior to the emergence of both the Free Speech Movement and Savio as that move-ment's most famous orator, it displays an almost identical sensibility regarding the university to the one Savio articulated at Berkeley in 1964—sharp criticism of the university's undemocratic failings coupled with ideal-ism about the university's potential to become a center of democratic renewal.[48] Critics of the New Left, such as Kerr, were so offended by the hypercritical side of the movement—and its indictment of the academic order over which they presided—that they could not see the movement's idealistic side, its genuine and even passionate interest in university reform.

Kerr's tendency to equate criticism of the university's bureaucratic lead-ership with corrosive disdain for the university itself distorted his thinking about not only the New Left but also its faculty allies. In our interview and in the first draft of his memoir, Kerr had started out terming Berkeley faculty who supported the Free Speech Movement "anti-university," and those who supported his administration "pro-university." Reginald Zelnik, who was part of this dialogue with Kerr, objected to these labels because he and other faculty who sided with the FSM saw their support of the free speech fight as an effort to expand political liberty on campus and build a better university, and so it was not appropriate to label it as "anti-university."[49] In response to Zelnik's critique, Kerr modified his terminology, calling the pro-FSM faculty "pro-cause" instead of "anti-university." But Kerr was unwilling to give up the other half of his labeling, and so continued to term faculty supporters of his administration "pro-university." And of course in maintaining that label, the implication is still there that faculty who opposed him and the "pro-university" faculty by aiding the FSM were in effect anti-university.[50] This issue of labeling is important, because we are never going to understand the Port Huron Statement, the Free Speech Move-ment, the New Left and its faculty allies' educational vision unless we get beyond pejoratives and the tendency to confuse the New Left desire to reform or transform the university with an impulse to destroy it.

The Port Huron Statement's vision for the university and its place in a larger New Left tradition of criticism, questioning, and calls for change in academia have been all but forgotten. It is as if that whole tradition was erased from popular memory by the dramatic campus violence of the late 1960s and early 1970s—especially the torching of ROTC buildings, the bloodshed at Kent State and Jackson State, and the bombing of the Army-Math building at the University of Wisconsin. Such dramatic events leave many narrative histories of the 1960s sounding much like Clark Kerr did with regard to Savio, depicting a student movement at war with the university.[51]

There was, of course, a small ultra-militant faction in the late 1960s New Left that had no use for the university. This faction, as Mark Rudd recounts in his memoir, regarded the university as a decadent bourgeois institution not worth reforming.[52] But this hyper-revolutionary mindset—articulated by a very small group on the far left of the movement, some of whom ended up in the Weather Underground—was never a popular view among most 1960s student activists.[53] Indeed, at almost the same time that the Weather faction was rejecting the university, more senior New Left veterans were moving in the opposite direction, forming the New University Conference, in the hope that movement veterans who had become faculty could help make the university a base for radically democratic change.[54] And, of course, when the New Left was still new, in the first half of the 1960s, before the polarization and massive brutality of the Vietnam War seeded Weather's frenzied brand of ultra-militancy, just about nobody in the New Left was so dismissive of the university. The Port Huron Statement, like Savio, better reflects the New Left rank-and-file and the larger student movement's view of the university—a view that was complex and deeply critical but also reflected a genuine interest in democratizing the university so its considerable resources and intellectual firepower could become catalysts for egalitarian social change.[55]

Hayden, much like Savio, did not hate the university but was part of its left academic tradition. Hayden revered C. Wright Mills, the preeminent left sociology professor of his day, as a father figure and intellectual inspiration.[56] For Hayden, Mills represented a dissident academic tradition that he admired, even loved. Mills offered Hayden a model of a politically engaged intellectual, one who provided conceptual tools for understanding and organizing against the inequities, the bellicose nationalism and militarism of Cold War America.[57]

Whatever its flaws, the Port Huron Statement offered a brilliant critique of the university's Cold Warriorism, commercialism, undemocratic governance, and disengagement from progressive social struggle. It interrogated the purposes of higher education in ways that were serious and searching. It raised questions about the meaning of education and the state of society that one would hope students of every generation would engage: "what is really important? can we live in a different and better way? if we wanted to change society, how would we do it?"[58] Still, it would be a mistake to use the Statement's fiftieth anniversary to read it in isolation from the larger political culture of the New Left that paved the way for this document and whose educational thought the Port Huron Statement helped to stimulate.

While the Statement is an excellent starting point, if one is to understand the New Left's evolving relationship with the university, there are many SDS and other radical statements from the 1960s that illuminate this relationship and need to be compared with the Port Huron Statement. In fact, Hayden's own pre–Port Huron talk, "Student Social Action," probed the nature of student culture and student apathy regarding politics in more depth than did the Port Huron Statement. Six months after Port Huron, SDS founders Al Haber and Richard Flacks wrote *Peace, Power, and the University*, which more elaborately than the Port Huron Statement set the university into social context, urging the peace movement to end its marginalization by centering its organizing on campus, so as to have access to mainstream America. Also in 1963 SDS published a pamphlet by Paul Potter, *The University and the Cold War*, which was far more skeptical than the Port Huron Statement about the possibility of ever freeing the university from the military-industrial complex, a point Potter further developed in a subsequent SDS pamphlet, *The Intellectual as an Agent of Social Change*.[59]

That the New Left's interest in university reform did not end with the Port Huron Statement was made obvious by the Free Speech Movement's critique of political repression, authoritarian governance, impersonal lecture courses, and unresponsive bureaucracy at the University of California—which it publicized in its pamphlets, newsletters, and in Savio's headline-making speeches.[60] The SDS pamphlet by Paul Booth, *A Strategy for University Reform* (1964/1965), was literally a primer for the building of SDS chapters via mobilization of students interested in democratizing the university. And the stream of university change-oriented documents continued unabated throughout the late 1960s; they can be sampled via the two-volume *University Crisis Reader* that Immanuel Wallerstein and Roger Starr edited and published back in 1971—going way beyond SDS to include the black campus rebellions as well.[61] All of this points to the conclusion that the Port Huron Statement has to be seen as a founding document in a

New Left political culture whose engagement with the university and the cause of democratic, anti-imperialist education extended way beyond 1962. It is a culture whose educational thought has been neglected by historians. Not a single historian has published a book devoted to probing the New Left's national impact on educational reform and the university.[62]

There are some legitimate reasons for this neglect. New Left historians are directed off the campuses because a dynamic and important part of SDS saw the university as only one arena for change, and not even the most important one. As Todd Gitlin has pointed out, some New Left organizers saw the university as a middle-class enclave that was like a "cage" they needed to break out of if they were to connect with workers and the poor.[63] SDS's mid-1960s focus on inner-city organizing of the poor via its Education Research and Action Project reflected such thinking, and it was one indication that the New Left's priorities were not confined to the campuses.[64]

As alluded to earlier, the pyrotechnics of late 1960s campus militancy and violence seems to have played a role in obscuring the history of New Left reimagining of the university. This is not to deny that the Vietnam War poisoned the political atmosphere, especially in the darkest days of the Nixon administration. In those years New Left resistance to the war ended in arson, destruction of campus property, and disruption of academic life at scores of colleges and universities.[65] Certainly New Left anger and hostility on campus with regard to military research, recruitment for chemical warfare work, and the ROTC is part of the history of the student movement's relationship to the university. But if we are to move beyond the Kerr-like assumption that the New Left–university relationship can be dismissed as a simple tale of hatred, we need to explore the wealth of educational ideas and reforms championed by the New Left. Some of these reforms were additive, expanding the curriculum, extending student rights, securing a larger student and faculty role in campus governance. Others were restrictive, pushing to make the university a Pentagon-free zone in which war technology and research and military training had no place. Still others envisioned freer alternatives to the universities, from experimental colleges to free schools. The Port Huron Statement's fiftieth anniversary seems an appropriate moment to call for historians to rediscover this lost heritage of educational criticism and innovation in all its complexity since the Port Huron Statement was itself a prime example of just such New Left educational criticism, innovation, and complexity.

In the spirit of Port Huron as a living document (rather than as a closed and dated ideological tract), it seems fitting to end this discussion with questions rather than just pronouncements about the connections between past and present. With regard to the university, the key questions are those regarding legacies. Reflecting upon our own century, which university or university ideal has prevailed? The one that the Port Huron's authors loathed, in which the campuses, captained undemocratically by hierarchical administrators, serve as adjuncts to corporate America and the military? Or the university that the Port Huron Statement hoped to build, a center of dissent, social criticism, and progressive activism?

If you read the burgeoning academic literature on corporatization of the university, the partnerships with big business, the privatization of once publicly supported universities, the soaring salaries of campus administrators, and the endless tuition hikes, you could easily conclude that most of the criticisms of academia in the Port Huron Statement remain timely and the document's democratic vision unfulfilled.[66] Yet it is also true that the academic left, which in the early 1960s was still frail—and only beginning to recover from McCarthyism—is in our own century considerably larger and more influential, at least in the humanities and social sciences. Were C. Wright Mills alive today, he would not be, as he was in the 1950s and early 1960s, an isolated dissenter, but an icon on the academic left.[67] However exaggerated the right's attacks on political correctness at the university may be—and however melodramatic David Horowitz's anti-radical screed, *The 101 Most Dangerous Academics in America*—the fact is that campuses today remain one of the few places where the American left thrives.[68] Student involvement in the Occupy Wall Street movement has not been massive, but it does indicate that the "crust of apathy" has been broken in our own decade, much as it was broken by the sit-ins of the early 1960s. It seems evident, then, that *both* universities still exist, so that those committed to the democratic ideals of Port Huron still have good reason to continue to maintain a love-hate relationship with a campus world that is at once profoundly undemocratic and yet houses the most hyper-democratic critics of our increasingly plutocratic social order.

PART III

Putting Participatory Democracy into Practice

Chapter 8

The Democratic Process
at Port Huron and After

Robert J. S. Ross

Participatory democracy, the central idea of the Port Huron Statement, is today more relevant than ever before. The assaults on labor rights in Wisconsin and Michigan, the rise and fall of Occupy Wall Street as a movement against inequality, and the continuing institutionalization of global capitalism and financial capital's power within it—all these beg the question: what does the concept of participatory democracy mean in our era of crisis and hardship? Indeed, questions of organization and decision making are relevant at all times when ordinary people seek to organize themselves for political and social action, so here I shall focus on the meaning of participatory democracy as we understood it and practiced it during an earlier era when we also sought to build a movement that could change the world, both at home and abroad. In the process I want to correct some propositions about that decision-making process that have, in my view, more currency than accuracy.

Some Background

In the spring of 1960 I joined the picketers in Ann Arbor, Michigan, who were supporting the national call for a boycott of Woolworth and Kresge stores. This boycott and the picketing on its behalf were in support of the sit-ins that had begun in Greensboro, North Carolina, by students at the

North Carolina Agriculture and Technology College pressing for desegregation of regional lunch counters. After the picketing at the local Ann Arbor
Woolworth's and Kresge stores had begun, a Conference on Human Rights
in the North was convened in Ann Arbor in April 1960.

Robert Alan "Al" Haber had planned this meeting before—repeat,
before—the southern sit-ins (which began on February 1, 1960) had
changed the landscape of social action. This was but one of Haber's far-
sighted plans that has ever after earned him the adjective prophetic (other
instances follow below). Al had understood, even before the southern student sit-ins had launched the new era of civil rights activism, that the
"human rights" of African Americans—then referred to as Negroes—were
a national, not just a regional issue.

Haber was a long-term Ann Arborite; his father, William, was a prominent New Deal economist and eventually became dean of the liberal arts
college (1963–68) at the University of Michigan. Al became involved in
SDS's predecessor, the Student League for Industrial Democracy (SLID),
through its Michigan chapter, the Political Issues Club, and rose to some
responsibility in SLID's small national membership.[1] Having been introduced to activism by the picketing in support of the southern student sit-
in movement, I attended the April conference (after contacting Haber and
asking him to suspend the registration fee, which I could not afford; he
did).[2] Afterward, Haber asked a number of the picketers and those who had
been active at the conference to join him in the new incarnation of SLID,
which he would call SDS. We students that Haber recruited were very
young; I was finishing my first year in college, and so too was my future
roommate and successor as SDS chapter leader, Dickie Magidoff. Sharon
Jeffrey, with whom I would soon co-chair the chapter, was a second-year
student. She was the daughter of ex-socialist Mildred Jeffrey, one of UAW's
key political strategists. Haber had succeeded through patient, long, one-
on-one conversations in convincing us that democracy itself was a radical
idea—the ultimate radical idea—and the schisms and sectarianisms of the
past could be laid aside for a new vision.

At the June 1960 convention of the newly named SDS, we reconstituted
the SDS Executive Committee. At the tender age of seventeen I became a
member of the National Executive Committee, and soon thereafter that
body named me vice president. I note with some amusement and humility
that according to Robert's Rules of Order I was nominated and voted in to
fill a vice-presidential vacancy created by the resignation of a member of

the Yale chapter who distrusted the new activist turn of SDS. The total number of voters in this election was three.

Through the summer of 1960 I volunteered after hours in the SDS office (after my seven-day-a-week job as a lifeguard and tennis court attendant). For me, journeying to Nineteenth Street in Manhattan from work and home in the South Bronx to stuff envelopes or to help with production of newsletters was a bit like taking a summer course in political theory and praxis, with Al the Socratic seminar leader.

Over the next two years, we organized several chapters, the most vigorous and successful of which was at the University of Michigan, where VOICE, a mass political party, campaigned and won leadership within the student government. Tom Hayden and his associates Ken McEldowney and Andy Hawley, all senior editors at the *Michigan Daily*, had been the instigators and first organizers of VOICE, but Sharon Jeffrey and I made it a successful winner of elections and campaigns.[3] As leaders of the SDS chapter, Sharon and I brought the organization—initially called the Political Issues Club—into VOICE and then led VOICE to affiliate with SDS.

Hayden had returned from a summer at the University of California at Berkeley impressed by the pioneer New Left student organization SLATE, which had done the counterintuitive thing for student radicals and taken student government seriously. Largely the province of the Greek-letter organizations, student governments were somewhere between the sandboxes for political toddlers and training grounds for future Young Democrats and Republicans. Hayden saw the possibility of making the student government a representative voice for students in real governance—and Sharon and I thought it was just the right thing if democracy was the centerpiece of your thinking.

Democratic Practice in Founding Chapters

Even before Port Huron, then, a local practice was emerging in Ann Arbor and other soon-to-be-affiliated SDS chapters, which saw democratic practice as relevant to university governance and educational issues. We butted heads with conservatives and centrists in the student government who opposed our desire to have the student council make pronouncements on political issues of national and international consequence—for example, passing a resolution against the Bay of Pigs invasion. But we were also vitally concerned with campus issues, and thus we campaigned to prohibit racial discrimination in the Greek-letter societies that wished to use university facilities (which was all of them). Another issue was our campaign against the principle and practice of in loco parentis, whereby universities acted in place of parents and thus enforced curfews that applied to women and constrained our lives with other regulations we considered far too intrusive. We eventually won this fight, and the dorms were "liberated."

Given some of the contentions about process that emerged in the 1960s and afterward, it is important to note that as Sharon Jeffrey and I took up our positions as elected members of the Student Government Council (keeping in mind that there were 25,000 eligible voters; it was a really "formal" body), we were subjected to a crash course on parliamentary procedure. From that time, I became, willy-nilly, one of the movement's experts on running large meetings.[4] Our own SDS/VOICE chapter settled decisions—when there was division—by a formal vote at a membership meeting. Usually we made decisions in small groups, and votes were not required, but when the meetings were large and the decisions weighty we voted, counted hands, and declared a winner.

I do have one vivid memory of such an occasion. During the Cuban missile crisis of October 1962, to say that our leftist community in Ann Arbor was tense is an understatement. Tom Hayden, Dick and Mickey Flacks, and others were huddled around the shortwave radio of a friend of ours, social psychologist Bill Levant, listening to the English-language broadcasts of Radio Moscow; they somehow thought these broadcasts would provide new or different information than that which came from U.S. media sources. Mickey headed for Washington, D.C., to demonstrate with the group Women Strike for Peace, which wanted a solution mediated by the United Nations. Meanwhile, fully resigned to being momentarily powerless, I drafted the VOICE political party platform for the upcoming elections to student government. In my draft, I included a condemnation of the Kennedy administration threat to start a nuclear war. When the VOICE membership later met to consider the draft, we took formal majority votes on each part. (Unfortunately, I am unable to remember if this plank survived the vote or not.)

Our practice as campaigners running for student government office in no way restricted our practice as social movement activists. Our local organizing in support of SNCC and our demonstrations against the arms race continued apace. One virtue of the student government campaigns was that they caused us to bring our ideas about democracy in the university and democratic participation in the society and economy face-to-face to thousands of folks who otherwise would never have come to a leftist rally or encountered our ideas.

In the course of reorganizing the old SLID, Haber, Hayden, and the rest of us were making what had been a fairly inert "discussion club" into a more activist organization. We also had to deal with SLID/SDS's heritage as an extension of the social democratic movement, which had staked out an anti-Communist and, for better or worse, nonrevolutionary social democratic position. In December 1961, members of the National Council aligned with the Young People's Socialist League (YPSL, often pronounced "yipsel"), the Socialist Party youth group, vigorously challenged the inclusionary attitude—anti-anti-Communism—taken by the new SDS leadership. They questioned the critique we were developing of those liberals and laborites who had acquiesced in the arms race and the Cold War.

For Tom, Al, and Sharon, each of different heritages, none from Communist parentage, the social democratic fixation on anti-Communist purity on the left was an overly sectarian and narrow view of the need for social reform in the United States. The old antagonism, either within the European left or the New York–headquartered League for Industrial Democracy, was a sea anchor retarding our capacity to move with the winds of change.

For those of us whose parents had been influenced by the Communist movement, this social democratic heritage was an insulting and threatening slur and a scary attack on our parents and their friends. Known as "red-diaper babies," we thought of our elders—mostly rank-and-filers—as ultimately democratic and gave little credence to the Cold War anti-Communist charges that they were the carriers of totalitarianism. In fact, the culture that surrounded the young people in, around, and formerly of the Communist movement seemed so committed to democracy that when Haber preached democracy as the bedrock idea for radicalism, we felt comfortable despite SDS's anti-Communist social democratic parentage.[5]

Port Huron and Participatory Democracy

When the YPSL-oriented members of SDS raised their challenge in December 1961, it became apparent that some sort of defining statement, a manifesto, was needed to articulate a vision for a New Left. Tom Hayden, Al

Haber, and I were named to a drafting committee, but it immediately became clear that Tom was the writer and (not speaking for Al) my job was encouragement.

If democracy was the radical umbrella, though, what was wrong with what we—the United States—had then and have now? Our critique of contemporary democratic practice leading up to Port Huron can be summarized briefly: citizenship as broadly understood was part time and passive. You listened, you voted, and you were done. Democratic rights did not extend to the economy, so power over everyday life was exercised by corporate bureaucracies beyond the reach of workers and community members. Democratic rights excluded black people by law and practice, while economic inequality excluded the poor from the community of citizens. And finally, the political parties were morally compromised and politically inert; potential opposition was entombed in Cold War orthodoxy and unable to challenge—to speak truth to power.[6]

Participatory Democracy

Tom read numerous statements from independent left thinkers. We were all influenced by C. Wright Mills,[7] but Hayden was an omnivorous reader, and among those who particularly influenced him was one of our professors at Michigan, Arnold Kaufman, a social philosopher. At the core of Kaufman's thought was the proposition that we can be more than isolated, self-absorbed, and narrow beings, and that democratic participation can expand human capacities. Democratic activism, thought Kaufman, is a kind of redemption. These reflections on democracy and human capacity, which found their way into the very early "Values" section of the Port Huron manifesto, are followed by discussion of the economy, poverty, segregation, the danger of nuclear war, and the stifling of the developing world.[8] A section focuses on the segregationist Dixiecrat influence in the Democratic Party and calls for the ouster of racist tribunes from that party. This was in fact a part of the social democratic strategy favored by Mike Harrington, designed to "realign" the Democrats as a more consistently liberal-left party.

When we assembled at Port Huron, attendees were confronted with the task of amending, absorbing, and making Tom Hayden's forty-eight page draft their own. There and at virtually every SDS convention that was to follow, adherence to forms of parliamentary procedure and representation were normal.[9] Early on, the participants decided on a bones-and-flesh strategy of amendment and discussion. The document was broken down into sections, and these were assigned to committees. For example, I participated in the group working on the labor movement and its relation to the student movement. Each group was to break down its section into "bones"—that is, essential political or strategic points. These points were matters to be debated and revised. The proposed changes were brought to a final plenary in the form of instructions to a subsequent (post-convention) Drafting Committee. So, each committee, in charge of a section, brought its proposals to a final plenary, in a process that lasted almost all night. While the committees, which were small, worked more or less informally, the plenary was composed of thirty or forty people who voted in a highly formal manner to pass, reject, or amend these bones.

One of the moments most memorable for me occurred during the discussion of the section on the arms race and the Cold War. A member of the YPSL accused the section and many of the participants (pointedly myself) as "paranoiac anti-anti-communists." A majority vote defeated his attempt to change that "bone."[10]

The idea of participatory democracy was not originally or essentially about how to conduct meetings; it was about how to organize society and to conceive of citizenship. The Statement contrasted "domination of politics and the economy by fantastically rich elites" with the alternative of "shared abundance."[11] Acknowledging the labor movement's central role in improving workers' lives and as the most democratic institution of the mainstream, the Statement said that, nevertheless, "'Union democracy' is not simply inhibited by labor leader elitism, but by the unrelated problem of rank-and-file apathy to the tradition of unionism." Way ahead of its time, the Statement notes that "the contemporary social assault on the labor movement is of crisis proportions."[12] The formulation that I used in those days (and now) is that participatory democracy was an American term to encompass socialist democracy. In those days, many of us also had an interest in a range of specifically worker-oriented democratic innovations, ranging from the German co-determination law (putting union representatives on corporate boards) to Yugoslavian workers' councils.[13]

Between Port Huron in June 1962 and the March on Washington to End the War in Vietnam in November 1965, SDS became steadily more well known through the work of its campus chapters and the writing and speaking of its talented national leaders, including Hayden, Haber, Todd Gitlin, and Paul Potter. Throughout this period—and beyond—internal decisions were made by more or less standard parliamentary procedures and representative democracy. The Statement was widely circulated through the traditional mimeograph duplication process and also by the first typeset publication of the Statement in the Methodist collegiate magazine *Motive*.

The 1963 National Convention considered and adopted (by formal majority votes) a document entitled "American and the New Era," referred to as ANE.[14] Unfortunately neglected by scholars, ANE is a better guide than the Statement to subsequent SDS views and behavior. ANE identifies the Kennedy administration as "corporate liberalism"—note the parallel to the later leftist usage "corporate globalization"—and calls for a politics of "local insurgency."[15]

Beginning in 1964, most intensely with the Swarthmore College chapter, SDS began to think about community organizing as a radical practice.[16] Economic Research and Action Projects (ERAP) were launched in the summer of 1964 in ten cities. About six of these survived as ongoing, multiyear projects, and several were to have long-range impact on their cities and on the left: Newark, Cleveland, and Chicago. The ERAP initiative meant there were ex-student SDSers, who were now off campus in nonchapter groups, making up a large fraction of the de facto if not de jure leaders of the organization.

This transition was the setting for a dramatic and critical incident in which the future of SDS and the antiwar movement hinged upon an obscure parliamentary maneuver. I tell this tale both because it is fun to remember, and also because it so thoroughly refutes the idea that SDS advocated a democratic process without strong procedures or majority votes.

Robert's Rules Save the Day

On December 31, 1964, the SDS National Council convened in lower Manhattan. Late in the evening, a member from New York, Jim Brook, then working as a letter carrier, made an impassioned call for SDS to initiate a demonstration against the impending escalation of the war in Vietnam. In

August 1964 the notorious incident in the Gulf of Tonkin had given President Lyndon Johnson and Defense Secretary Robert McNamara the excuse they apparently wanted to escalate U.S. intervention. After alleged, and highly contested, attacks upon the destroyers *Turner Joy* and *Maddox,* the United States, for the first time, undertook a massive and openly acknowledged bombing of North Vietnamese targets. Plans for a major escalation in the use of U.S. ground forces were in the works.

Brook came before the Council at roughly 11:00 p.m. Some of the women had already begun setting up food and drink for a New Year's party at the back of the room. In opposition to Brook's anti-imperialist plea for action, a number of the more senior and well-respected leaders of SDS, who were now situated in ERAP community organizing projects, rose to express doubt about the proposal. They argued that antiwar work would make SDS too focused on a single issue, not the comprehensively radical organization it had always aspired to be, and they also thought that the effort to organize antiwar work would not connect to the poor white and black constituents of the ERAP projects and thus would detract from the work of the community organizers.[17]

Among other highly influential people expressing these doubts, Tom Hayden figured prominently. It is more than a bit ironic given his future role as a major leader of antiwar action during the Vietnam conflict and later, but Tom made a Buddha-like intervention that wondered what would happen if we called for a demonstration and nobody came. (I note openly that Tom has a different memory of this moment than I do.)

The motion to sponsor the March failed, with people like me, with one foot in community organizing and another on campus as a graduate student, torn. I voted against.

While the meeting recessed for party preparations, my former roommate Dickie Magidoff, then working in the Cleveland ERAP project, pulled me aside. This is a big deal, was the burden of his whispered plea. We cannot let this pass by. We have got to change it.

And I was the man to do it because I had learned the techniques of parliamentary procedure as a University of Michigan student government leader. One of Robert's Rules of Order's escape hatches is this: an individual may move to reconsider a question if and only if he or she has voted on the prevailing side. Dickie knew this, as did I.

As the clock approached midnight and we prepared for partying, the meeting reconvened to finish things off. I moved to reconsider. I cannot claim to have made any important intervention in the debate. SDS National Secretary Clark Kissinger, a University of Wisconsin radical who had attended Port Huron, made the last and most persuasive plea about the moral responsibility to oppose an outright imperialist war. On a reconsideration vote, the motion passed, and history was bent through the use of Robert's Rules of Order.

Thus on April 17, 1965, SDS led the first big Washington demonstration against the war in Vietnam. At that time it was the largest demonstration against an American war policy since the Spanish-American War. The Old Guard of anti-Communist social democrats was scandalized by the nonexclusionary policy—which welcomed anyone against the war in Vietnam. They were more concerned that Communists would join the March than they were that the March would succeed. That the March did galvanize public opinion and mobilize a new wave of public opposition to the war was perhaps the definitive sign that the Cold War on the left was over—or irrelevant—and that the New Left was now the culturally and politically hegemonic left.

For SDS the March—indeed the very act of calling for the March—was transformative. At the University of Chicago, where I was forming a new chapter in my first year of graduate school, our meetings of fifteen to twenty-five people became meetings of a hundred people. We sent five buses to Washington from Chicago. We had one chapter in Chicago before the March; by the time the buses returned we had at least three, including those at Roosevelt and Northwestern. SDS had, overnight, become a mass organization.

Reflecting on Participatory Democracy

These reflections on how individual SDS chapters governed themselves and on how the national body came to call for a March on Washington to End the War in Vietnam set in motion an alternative understanding of what has all too often become a canonical interpretation of what we—at Port Huron—meant by participatory democracy. In subsequent years many commentators have trivialized the idea of participatory democracy or defined it as impractical and utopian in the worst sense.

While rigorous participation and direct involvement in decisions was the ideal, the notion that no one could or should be represented—that voting for a representative was inherently undemocratic—would have been viewed as silly by Port Huron participants. We voted for our national officers; we voted for chapter leaders; we voted for resolutions and for constitutional alterations. Whatever I may say below about the problems of democracy in a global setting, Port Huron veterans and those who joined SDS in later years were not silly. We thought of ourselves as vigorously participating citizens and—some, at some times, would have said—revolutionaries.

How did participatory democracy come to be trivialized as a meeting rule for small groups? One guess is through mistakes by journalists and misinterpretations by newbies. A journalist who came to a small local chapter meeting might observe a kind of consensus-seeking process taking place. Given the prominence of the rhetoric about "participatory democracy," this might then become what the journalist thought it was all about. By reporting it, the idea became a self-fulfilling prophecy. Alternatively, and in addition, SDS grew incredibly rapidly, and there was little "socialization" of newer members by older members.[18] A kind of naive literalism was fueled by a cultural memory resonating, romantically perhaps, out of America's own anarcho-syndicalist past. New Leftists venerated the memory of the Industrial Workers of the World; many agreed with the famous IWW motto "We are all leaders."[19] There was also a sort of cultural affinity between a rejection of representation and the hyper-individualism of parts of American culture at that time: "I am unique; no one can represent me."

By the second decade of the twenty-first century, the notion of participatory democracy as a philosophy of group process had enough currency to be adopted uncritically by the Occupy Wall Street (OWS) anarchist tendency. They too found an American phrase for a European-origin ideology, but this time it was not socialism but rather a variant of anarchism. This was sustained by a certain cultural ambience that has been a factor of continuity between SDS and successor organizations—like OWS—who claim its heritage. Former SDS vice president and quipster Paul Booth once made the semifacetious remark that SDSers think "freedom is a constant meeting." Another time he said we might be "students for a small society." The point of continuity here—rather than formal rules—is the emphasis on process, community, and participation.

The most trivial interpretation of participatory democracy understands it as a way to conduct face-to-face meetings. Usually this interpretation conjures up consensus-seeking as the fundamental goal, and invents a variety of procedures for reaching it. What procedural, majoritarian voting rules that protect minority rights accomplish, however formal and forbidding their procedures may be—such as the venerable Robert's—is to protect majority rule while preserving minority rights through procedural safeguards. But a doctrine of consensus allows obstinate minorities to obstruct the will of the majority. Cases in point abound, including the highly consequential use of a sixty-vote requirement for cloture in the U.S. Senate. A more absurd example came during an Occupy meeting in Atlanta one morning in October 2011 when an eccentric individual blocked Representative John Lewis from speaking, an obstruction at variance from what appeared to be the will of an overwhelming majority of those present.[20]

Of course, meeting facilitators and prudent activists will seek consensus under many circumstances. These include situations when there are very small groups of decision makers, or when the stakes are extremely high and the members of the group risk legal or physical jeopardy, for example. Paradoxically, when the stakes are very small, the only thing that counts is getting a task accomplished.

What did participatory democracy evoke as a phrase for the Port Huron cohort that, following Tom Hayden's writing, made it their own? My claim is that it was broadly an American language for socialism and in particular for, of all things, industrial democracy. I can testify directly to the many conversations I had with comrades about worker control, German co-determination laws, the Yugoslav industrial example, and Wobbly syndicalist ideas. If C. Wright Mills's dim view of bureaucratic power was Satan, and Paul Goodman's simple anarchism was Eden, we were the democratic Adam as yet innocent.

Democracy at Scale

If participatory democracy and the Port Huron Statement envisioned both social and economic democracy, and envisioned empowered working people in alliance with educated youth, it nevertheless did not have, and the American left still does not have, an adequate response to the problem of scale. It is all very well to say that one wants to have a say in the decisions that affect one's life. Does that mean a group of upper-class property own-ers on Nantucket Sound should be able to frustrate a state's or nation's desire for wind-powered energy? Does democracy mean that a board of selectmen or town meeting should be able to deny a building/zoning permit to a halfway house for emotionally disturbed juveniles? Or a Planned Par-enthood facility? Leftists harken when working-class neighborhoods resist toxic waste sites, but we don't have a consistent decision rule for when a small group should decide or when larger groups should decide. The State-ment is not a guide to the problem of scale, and none of us—so far as I know—have thought this through to decision-rule conclusion. The future of democratic movements and theory is open in other and even more dra-matic ways than this.[21]

For all its vision, the Statement—as did every other mid-1960s under-standing of global affairs—missed the impending change in the structure of global capital. The Statement is fairly naive about industrialization and its potential growth in those new nations that were once European or American colonies. It does not contemplate the use of lower-income coun-tries to pound down standards of living of workers in nations bordering the North Atlantic.

So the problem of the Race to the Bottom is a whole new frontier for today's democratic movements, the reconciliation of workers' needs on a global basis. The matter has become increasingly painful. The distance between the key decision-making institutions like the central banks, the international financial institutions, the financial conglomerates, the regula-tory agencies that have been captured by the regulated financial institutions, and transnational political institutions, like the European Union or the World Trade Organization—in other words, the distance between bureau-cratic and oligarchic power elites and ordinary citizens—is truly titanic. Accountability, no less participation, seems more exotic a hope each week. Democrats everywhere await—or should work to hasten—the day that workers of the world understand and find ways to cooperate so they all lose their chains.

Chapter 9

A Manifesto of Hope

Barbara Haber

A half-century of mostly hard political times can put a halo of nostalgia on any experience. The words of old timers about the good old days are and ought to be suspect. I begin by pleading guilty: the Port Huron convention is high on my list of most cherished memories. I pride myself immensely on having had the good sense to get there, and I carry a special warmth and respect for those who were there with me that has withstood later political differences, personal animosities, and long years of separation.[1]

But the glow Port Huron carries for me is not newly coined. The people who gathered were impressive, smart, humorous, politically experienced, energetic, and committed. We held a shared assumption that through collective thinking we could understand the world, and that with passionate dedication we could change it.

We understood our project to be momentous—no less than the reshaping of political discourse, moving beyond both liberalism and socialism into something profoundly *new* and *radical*. We brought to Port Huron an astounding breadth and depth of knowledge about world events and moral philosophy, an unabashed confidence in our own abilities, and a determination to place intellection fully in the service of radical social change. We yearned for self-transformation and high-stakes venture, both of which many of us had tasted in civil rights organizing. The high spirits born of shared moral purpose, a sense of historic mission, and the sweet company of kindred souls were infectious.

The centerpiece of the convention was the Manifesto, later called the Port Huron Statement. Drafts had been circulating for discussion throughout the spring. Revising it was the task that drew us together, the framework that structured our thinking, the medium within which we began to shape our collective political vision. Since then I have seen political organizations founder over the hacking out of dreary one-page lists of "principles of unity." That was not what we were about. In our cultivated naiveté, we intended to create a piece of *literature*, well written, in clear American English, something that would actually be read, reflected upon, remembered. We had no interest in creating a litmus test of political correctness. Our aims were more generous: to freshly envision the radical possibilities of political culture, to provide ourselves with a rough map by which we could guide our political lives, and to fire the political imaginations of our contemporaries.

We were a group of perhaps fifty young people (and a few elders), mostly white (a few of our black civil rights comrades attended) mostly from elite schools, more men than women (although the numbers are distorted by sexism; no one kept records, and the women have tended to be forgotten). We were mostly handpicked by SDS insiders. We were experienced organizers, veterans of the civil rights movement, peace movement, and student organizations. Some of us were red-diaper babies, and a few of us had earlier discovered socialism on our own. I had been aware of SDS for about two and a half years. As an officer of the Brandeis Socialist Club, I had been recruited by an SDS organizer.

We drew our inspiration from others—most significantly from blacks struggling for equality in the South, but also from the cultural rebels of the Beat Generation and an eclectic array of intellectuals, C. Wright Mills, Albert Camus, and Karl Marx. We had come together to build a political community rooted in our own perceptions of the world and our own discontents without prescribed social destinies. We saw ourselves not as bit players in a social drama dominated by blue-collar workers, but as bona fide agents of change. We reasoned (correctly, I believe) that in a society increasingly dominated by information and high technology, students—who would serve as technicians, managers, and professionals—occupied a strategically vital position.

We were not, at Port Huron, asserting student hegemony over social change; we aspired to the role of catalyst, and we claimed without shame our rightful place as a legitimate segment of a social movement. As students, we saw our primary and immediate task to organize students. As civil rights veterans, we knew our own courage and zeal, and we insisted on our prerogative to utilize them in the service of movement-building.

For many of us the civil rights movement had already begun a transformative process within. The black struggle, and the vibrant communities that sprang up within it, were the harsh mirror in which we saw reflected the banalities and complacency of white middle-class life. We had tasted the heady brew of life (or at least moments) lived within communities of protest. We compared that with the lives of our parents' generation and the stereotypic social niches that were waiting for us, and we were repelled. We had already found something better. The task was to translate that something better into a society in which all people could live lives of meaning, vitality, and, yes, adventure. Privatism, alienation, and conformity were the chief demons in our white middle-class hell (though the Port Huron Statement reflects considerable grasp of economic and military factors). Community, founded on political engagement, was the antidote. In an age when traditional bases of community—the extended family, the stable neighborhood, the church—had waned, and their remnants looked uninviting, we saw shared political commitment as the only viable basis for community, and community as the only context within which the individual could find fulfillment and meaning.

Changing history, an honorable and deeply desired project in itself, was for many of us also the means by which our personal lives could be transformed. Long before we discovered that the personal was political, we had embraced the political as personal. The confluence of desire for personal transformation and political agency lies at the center of New Left politics, and it was the source of both strengths and weaknesses. Our intoxication with risk and our disdain for the ordinary led at times to overvaluation of extravaganza and to limitations in our ability to form alliances and endure slow processes of change. But the existential gusto with which we offered ourselves to the political process was the source of our incisive critique of our own culture and our experimental brashness in action. Without these, the many accomplishments of the New Left would not have happened.

From our civil rights experience we had also gained a sense of how change could come. Not yet a strategy (SDS never did achieve that), the Port Huron Statement suggested a raw, tactical game plan rooted in a distrust of the long, plodding processes of mainstream institutions that kept things as they were. The great leap forward, most of us believed, would come not in the halls of Congress (though there was a small but potent realignment faction in SDS, whose views are included in the Port Huron Statement) or through the mainstream labor movement (though here too the Port Huron Statement pays lip service). Change would come through a combination of tough, unyielding, grassroots organizations spread throughout society, coupled with dramatic acts of protest and courage that would *demonstrate* to the world, in irresistible images, the themes and demands on which we wanted to focus attention. Although in its purest form this view of tactics proved needlessly divisive and destroyed potentially valuable alliances, in the main it was a smart idea and an important contribution in its time, one that is still valid today.

My idyllic sense of in-tuneness at Port Huron was unmarred by any consciousness of sexism. I did not know about sexism when I went to Port Huron. I do not believe the word had yet been invented. Although, in retrospect, I can visualize scenes in which sexism was manifest at the convention, at the time the kind wool of ignorance shielded my eyes. Not only did the state of my own consciousness obscure sexism, however; there was a real atmosphere of inclusion and respectfulness extended to women. The process itself, at least in the "values" committee where I spent much of my time, exemplified the ideals, soon to be articulated, of the feminist movement. We met in a small group to collectively understand, modify, and accept a part of the Port Huron Statement. Much care was expended to encourage reticent members to express their views. Ideas and questions were responded to without condescension or acrimony. Good-naturedness, tolerance, and curiosity characterized our discussions. In plenaries, though there were hot and heavy debates (mostly participated in by men), trust, affection, and the desire to make it work seemed to predominate. It would not be long, however, before my eyes opened: a mere few weeks after the convention, I would find myself enraged at experiences in the SDS national office, where I had started working, for which I had no name. Slowly, over the next three years, first in informal "bitch sessions" with other SDS women, later through formal meetings and papers, I would learn, reluctantly, about sexism.

On the face of it, the Port Huron Statement itself can be dismissed as hopelessly sexist. The pronouns are all in the male gender; there is no acknowledgment of the oppression of women; issues of family life, child-rearing, reproduction, sexual violence, and unequal opportunity and pay, so crucial in today's feminist movement, all are missing. Yet as I reread the Port Huron Statement so many years later, I am struck by the many elements that seem to prefigure early feminist thinking. It occurs to me that the Port Huron Statement may have played a catalytic role in developing feminist consciousness. The Statement's critique and vision contain the seeds of several key feminist ideas. The contrast between its worldview to which we women claimed co-ownership, and the actual practice within SDS, undoubtedly stimulated consciousness and action. It is no accident that after a week of immersion in the Port Huron Statement and the relatively benign environment of the convention, I found myself excruciatingly intolerant of the blatant sexism I encountered in SDS.

From a feminist perspective it is significant that the Port Huron Statement starts with a statement of who we are, followed by a section delineating values. This beginning is one of the most eloquent and lasting parts of the Statement. Rather than lead with a classic Marxist analysis of economic factors, we chose to open with an evocative description of our own lives and the moral lessons we had derived from them. The quest for orienting human values is seen as the first task of a social movement. Working outward from concrete, immediate experience to derive general values, and using those values as criteria for comprehending structures and evaluating events, are procedures of thought common among women, that would later become hallmarks of feminist process.

The specific values enumerated in the Port Huron Statement spoke, without naming women as referents, to our thwarted aspirations, and our approach to remedying our situation. The trademark concept of the New Left and the Statement—participatory democracy—held special promise for women as we began to confront the rigidity, emptiness, and inaccessibility of institutions of decision making. Emphasis on the need to radically alter the very structures of decision processes was adopted early on by feminists as we sought to get some control over our lives. Participatory democracy provided a model for people with common concerns to come together to talk, to argue, to decide on issues of importance to them. Of course, it is now clear how vague this concept is and how difficult to implement. Yet it is equally clear that without a radical shift in the structure and process of decision making, no real democracy can emerge. While it does not provide a solution, the idea of participatory democracy at least correctly names the problem and offers a provocative model that moves in the right direction.

For women the need for participatory democracy was concrete and immediate; we had little or no control over when and whether to have babies, when and with whom to have sex, or what job options to pursue. We had little access to the seats of power, in government, in the military, in industry, or in our own political organization, SDS. As radical women, we came to understand that reformist accommodations and tokenism within existing white, male, ruling-class institutions would do little to change our situation. This understanding was to come a few years later, but our comprehension of the need for structural transformation of decision making and our experiments in practicing it within our own groups can be traced to the Port Huron Statement and the ongoing dialogue that it spawned about what participatory democracy meant and how it could be put into practice.

The high priority placed by the Port Huron Statement on relatedness and community was also congruent with female values. The assertion that people had "unrealized potential" but had been manipulated into incompetence went to the heart of women's bitterness. The depersonalization of the male-dominated public sphere, and the isolation and disengagement of feminine home life, are eloquently decried.

Other sections of the Port Huron Statement also had special application to women. When the Statement attacks in loco parentis, it is attacking a doctrine that imposed a Victorian double standard on women students. Rules, such as the then common curfews for women, ostensibly aimed at protecting helpless women from uncontrollable men, were actually used to rationalize the limitation of women's freedom and autonomy. And when the Statement points out the contradiction between educational purpose and the social purposes of university life (for women, to find a suitable husband), it is illuminating a particularly female version of the "let's pretend" irrelevance of much university experience. On the other hand, as the Statement points out, universities offered a growing number of students real opportunities for intellectual and organizational development. As graduation approached, newly confident college-educated women faced a world that expected them to settle for low-status, low-paying, unchallenging stopgap jobs. Their real social task was to "catch" that eligible, upwardly mobile man, through whom they would attain identity and security, and to whom they were to devote their lives. The Port Huron Statement spoke to women faced with this situation, validating our desire to use university-gained skills to engage in public life. The Statement held out the right promise to women at the right time: through political involvement we could create lives of meaning that would further develop our skills. SDS's inability to keep that promise catapulted many women in and around SDS into the formation of a radical, autonomous women's movement.

By painting an image of an ideal democracy in which all members participated in decisions affecting their daily lives, the Port Huron Statement intensified and clarified for women the contradiction between what could be and what was. The idea that people working collectively can change the course of history and have the right to do so (a traditional left idea given contemporary application by the Port Huron Statement) gave impetus to women in SDS as a feminist viewpoint began to emerge from our experience. The Port Huron Statement, while eradicating women from its categories of thought, gave us rudiments of an intellectual and moral groundwork with which we could begin to conceptualize our own situation.

The breadth and audacity of the Port Huron Statement and the depth of the SDS commitment to radical change offered hope for a better world for all people. That inclusiveness and basic soundness (and the urgency many felt about the Vietnam War) kept many women in SDS for several years before our anger and effectiveness forced us to separate. This was a good thing, although it cost us a great deal to stay. It allowed us, in our politically formative years, to develop a full political consciousness cognizant of issues and dilemmas faced by others, and it helped us develop the habit of seeing connections among the plethora of issues with which we were constantly flooded. At our best, women who lived that experience have been able to infuse the feminist movement with these valuable qualities of mind.

We were a generation of generalists in a world growing more and more atomized and obscure, and the Port Huron Statement reflected our conviction that atomization and obscurantism endangered the last hope for a meaningful and a humane culture. We were right. In recent decades the world has slipped further from the possibility of an empowered, participating public. Manipulation is in full sway; its technology so sophisticated and pervasive that it boggles the imagination to think of undoing its control over our minds and lives. Activism abounds, but is splintered and isolated, attempting to make change, single issue by single issue. The obstacles to creating a broad-based, nonsectarian radical movement of vision and relevance seem overwhelming. Yet there are signs that create hope: an upsurge in student activism, the perseverance and growth of women's organizations, the tenaciousness of numerous single-issue or constituency groups, many the legacy of the 1960s, and the lasting interest of young people in the music and politics of our movement.

As I have written I have had young people on my mind. If a new movement is to emerge, the lead will come from the young, who, in spite of far more constricted economic opportunities than we faced, decide to devote themselves, at least for a time, to changing history. The greatest value I can imagine for this volume's republication of the Port Huron Statement is that it will offer inspiration to young activists, not to accept our ideas, but to rethink the world for themselves, and to act reflectively, courageously, and collectively to change it, as best they can.

Chapter 10

Putting Participatory Democracy into Action

Jennifer Frost

The community organizing efforts of the Students for a Democratic Society began in 1963, the year following the Port Huron Statement. SDS aimed to build "an interracial movement of the poor" under the auspices of its Economic Research and Action Project (ERAP) to demand changes in state and society and abolish poverty in America. Over the next few years, New Left organizers established sixteen community organizing projects in low-income, racially diverse neighborhoods; the largest, most successful, and longest-lasting projects were located in Chicago, Cleveland, Newark, and Boston.[1] The ERAP projects were a central focus of SDS between 1963 and 1965, and they gave members, according to a former participant, "a sense of presence in the real world."[2] Community organizing also garnered early SDS political and media attention and contributed to its first period of sustained membership growth—before the anti–Vietnam War movement began.[3]

Although community organizing was an important part of the New Left "activist repertoire," less attention has been paid to it than to the student and antiwar movements in histories of SDS. Historian Sara Evans and sociologist Wini Breines saw the community projects as important sites for the emergence of the women's liberation movement and the welfare rights movement, and for "prefigurative politics."[4] But most scholars either briefly mention the projects or completely ignore them. In New Left scholarship, as in life, the larger student and antiwar movements with their mass demonstrations, student sit-ins, and university takeovers eclipsed quiet, less dramatic community organizing efforts.[5]

But there are good reasons to pay attention to ERAP. Community organizing in the urban North represented a direct attempt on SDS's part to respond and contribute to the civil rights movement. It is now well known that the struggle for racial equality gave the New Left its initial spark and direction, provided a training ground for SDS activists, and fostered close personal and organizational ties between SDS and other student organizations focused on civil rights and direct action, such as the Student Nonviolent Coordinating Committee (SNCC). By embodying a commitment to "putting your body on the line" for the values in which one believed, SNCC's activism created a mystique that inspired and intrigued members of SDS. As Tom Hayden asked in the spring of 1963, "Can the methods of SNCC be applied to the North?"[6] For white New Leftists, ERAP organizing also provided a new way to relate to the civil rights struggle, as the projects initially focused on poor whites. SDS activists envisioned organizing around shared economic inequality as a way to bring black and white Americans together across differences of race, providing a strategic complement to the work of civil rights activists.

Community organizing also represented SDS's attempt to formulate and implement a strategy for social change that synthesized insights and lessons from the labor movement, the Old Left, and the civil rights movement. "An Interracial Movement of the Poor?"—the position paper written for ERAP by Carl Wittman and Tom Hayden a year after the Port Huron Statement in 1963—outlined a strategy for building a social movement of poor Americans through community organizing. "We believe," Wittman and Hayden argued, "that nothing less than a wholly new organized political presence in the society is needed to break the problems of poverty and racism."[7] While this strategy provided a starting point for the community projects, once in the field organizers ended up exploring and experimenting with alternative social movement strategies and revealed the process of defining a new social movement paradigm in the 1960s.

Furthermore, ERAP challenges the view that the New Left, in seeing the state as co-optative at best, failed to define a social democratic alternative to the welfare state.[8] To be sure, New Left organizers questioned whether they should seek alliances with, or maintain a hostile distance from, the state; whether they could engage in reform activities that implicitly legitimated the system without compromising their political vision or risking co-optation. Yet, these questions did not mean they eschewed engagement with the state or refused to rethink its contours and content. For community organizers, the state is "the only game in town," and campaigns in the various ERAP projects sought an expanded and more participatory welfare state. The transformation—rather than the abandonment—of the American welfare state emerges as a goal of SDS's community organizing.

Most significantly, these experiences and the political lessons learned emerged precisely from how the ERAP projects put the Port Huron Statement's core concept—participatory democracy—into action. Participatory democracy envisioned a society in which citizens shared in the decisions shaping their lives, and participatory democracy, as an ideal and a practice, profoundly influenced organizing in the projects. I focus on three aspects: the motivations of participants, the organizing process and strategy, and the definition of goals vis-à-vis the state, or the politics of the self, of the social, and of the state.[9] While some of this may sound familiar from memoirs and histories of the New Left, what is less familiar is the crucial contribution of community residents in the various neighborhoods. A dynamic series of encounters, negotiations, and conflicts between New Left organizers and community residents shaped how participatory democracy played out in these projects.

Politics of the Self

Putting participatory democracy into action motivated the New Left activists who volunteered for ERAP's community organizing. "Politics," according to the Port Huron Statement, "has the function of bringing people out of isolation and into community, thus being a necessary, though not sufficient, means of finding meaning in personal life."[10] Wittman and Hayden restated this principle in "An Interracial Movement of the Poor": "The meaningful participation in politics, the moral reconstruction that comes from cooperation in positive work . . . [is] the main social basis for a democratic America."[11] In response to the call for volunteers for the first summer of organizing in 1964—"We are asking each person . . . to consider [whether] one should devote a summer, if not a lifetime, in a personal engagement with the problems of America's dispossessed"[12]—ERAP was "swamped" with applications. Some 120 organizers went into the field that first summer, a number equal to 20 percent of SDS's total membership (although not all volunteers belonged to SDS at the time).[13]

Dave Strauss, a University of Michigan student, was one of them. As he recalled, "The civil rights movement is exploding all over the place, and we're sitting there saying, you know, 'wait a minute, if we just stay on campus we're not gonna be there when we're needed. A lot of civil rights organizations are starting to say people need to work with whites, that's us. We're white, why don't we do that.'" Carol Glassman also remembered why she joined. She had just graduated from Smith College, where she had taken a course on problems in the American economy, written a seminar paper on poverty, read Michael Harrington's *The Other America*, and expressed solidarity with the civil rights movement, and then she had a conversation with SDS leader Lee Webb about ERAP organizing to build an interracial movement of the poor. "It really is like I was an adding machine and all the stuff had been put in and nobody had pushed the equals button, and that conversation with Lee, there it all was. That was the first time I really felt like all the things I thought and felt just came together in some way that made sense to me."[14] For Strauss, Glassman, and others, the ERAP projects offered an opportunity to engage in organizing work that felt personally meaningful and politically significant.

The community residents who participated in the projects felt the same. Just as in the civil rights movement, the local people in ERAP were often "empowered personalities" before they even met a New Left organizer, but there is no doubt ERAP activism "took their empowerment to another level."[15] The projects created a context in which they developed confidence, skills, and experience, and these attributes, in turn, provided a spur to political activism and a means for upward mobility. A significant group continued in their work after the end of SDS's community organizing and later spoke of the way their involvement transformed their lives. In 1964, Lillian Craig was a welfare mother in Cleveland when "Sharon Jeffrey knocked on my door and asked me if I was registered to vote. I asked her in, and after awhile I told her I was on welfare. That's how our friendship began." Craig related feeling ashamed and silenced about her status as a single mother on welfare. "I am nobody, and nobody cares, and there is no escape," she remembered feeling. But through her involvement in SDS's community organizing, Craig felt she had received "good basic training": "I had learned that I could do things." "You have skills that you don't know about," she later contended. "You can get involved in your immediate community, and then go from there."[16]

In Chicago, Dovie Coleman and her niece Dovie Thurman expressed similar sentiments. Thurman said she "was organized by Rennie Davis" outside a welfare office and recalled how she spoke at her very first meeting:

> I stood up and made a couple of statements. "I'm sick and tired of this welfare system. I don't know what to do about it, but I want to fight, too. It's doing the same to all of us." It was my first encounter speaking to a group of people, and I got a big hand. . . . At the next meeting I was nominated to be chairperson. Just that quick. What was most exciting was somebody wanted me. I didn't even know what a chairperson was. I had a lot inside of me that I always wanted to say, but I never knew how to get it out. I didn't use to be a person that would speak out a lot. 'Cause I was angry that night, it just came out real easy.[17]

She and her aunt became active in the JOIN Community Project, and Dovie Coleman later wrote of finding "freedom of mind" through organizing. "When I began to organize other people for the first time in my life I began to feel free. . . . I want other people to feel the way I do."[18] For these women, participation meant both personal and political transformation. Along with New Left organizers, they confirmed, and lived, participatory democracy's synthesis of moral values, personal life, and politics.

Politics of the Social

The process of organizing the community projects also reflected a commitment to participatory democracy. Echoing a long American tradition, the Port Huron Statement called for decision making to occur through a variety of "public groupings," of which community organizations could be one type.[19] Wittman and Hayden elaborated on this idea in "An Interracial Movement of the Poor," believing neighborhood-based forums and discussions could establish a basis for participatory democracy and "possibly the seed for a different society."[20] Crucially, this commitment meant that community residents should have a role in determining the shape and direction of the ERAP projects. "Let the People Decide" became the favorite ERAP slogan. To ensure grassroots participation, New Left organizers dedicated themselves to listening to and taking seriously the ideas and requests of community residents, which came to be called organizing from the bottom up.

Perhaps the best known aspect of how participatory democracy shaped the organization of the community projects was decision making by consensus. But in keeping with criticisms then and now, consensus decision making did not always meet the needs of ERAP's community constituency. To achieve consensus, meetings were initially unstructured, without rules of procedure, and open-ended until the last person had the last word. But unstructured meetings demanded much time, a commodity in short supply for community members, especially women with domestic and childcare responsibilities. New Left organizers further discovered that apparent consensus could hide disagreement and even misunderstanding among community residents, given that in situations of unequal power, the costs of, and ability to, participate were not distributed equally. Over time, a number of projects, including Chicago and Cleveland, moved to ensure clearer accountability in how meetings were run and decisions made, including adopting parliamentary procedures to ensure a more democratic outcome.[21]

Yet, the more significant outcomes of the process of community organizing in ERAP were in the area of strategy. The initial ERAP strategy for building an interracial movement of the poor focused on organizing a constituency of jobless men, reflecting the influence of the political paradigm of the Old Left and the labor movement. From the start, however, the projects attracted more women than men. The projects' preferred methods of recruitment, the door-to-door canvass or leafleting at welfare offices, contributed to this development, as women were the first and easiest to meet, as happened with Lillian Craig, Dovie Thurman, and Dovie Coleman.[22] Moreover, because initial discussions focused on community problems—problems that particularly concerned women, as the caretakers of households and families—New Left organizers found women residents more receptive. For many women residents, the lack of community resources typical of low-income neighborhoods hindered their ability to carry out domestic responsibilities. In keeping with a twentieth-century tradition, they also saw such problems as theirs to solve, viewing community improvement as a logical extension of women's domestic responsibilities.[23] And, indeed, a number of women contacted by New Left organizers were already doing so as leaders in their communities. Although not without conflict from some male SDS members, women ended up forming the largest and most active membership and providing the most consistent leadership for the projects.[24]

As part of this development, the projects began to define new issues for organizing. SDS had initially considered unemployment to be the priority issue for mobilizing community residents. Organizing around unemployment "[means] the movement is immediately political," asserted Wittman and Hayden in "An Interracial Movement of the Poor."[25] Few neighborhood residents responded to this issue, however. What SDS believed the poor needed—jobs for men—contrasted with what their actual constituency of neighborhood women, men, and children considered to be their primary concerns. Taken together, residents in Boston, Newark, Cleveland, and Chicago voiced problems with Aid to Families with Dependent Children (popularly known as "welfare"), housing, urban renewal, children's welfare, police brutality, as well as jobs. As a result, organizers began to shift their priority from the issue of unemployment to the issues raised by residents. Carol Glassman, for example, stressed "the need to listen to the community to learn what the issues should be."[26] Yet, many organizers questioned whether the issues proposed by community residents had "political" content and could contribute to social change. For Steve Max, organizing around such issues was clearly "non-political community work." Richard Rothstein wondered whether the focus on "immediate grievances" and "non-radical issues" was politically "a step or more backwards" for ERAP.[27] In the end, organizers justified the shift from unemployment to a multiplicity of organizing issues as practical, principled, and political. There were constituencies for issues such as welfare, urban renewal, and children's issues, and organizing around these issues of concern to residents was consistent with participatory democracy. Organizers also came to see these issues as connected to fundamental social, economic, and political inequalities and, thus, political.

A similar shift occurred with service provision. From the beginning of the ERAP projects, New Left organizers consistently received requests for service work from community residents. Residents asked for aid with bureaucratic procedures, such as dealing with caseworkers, tracking down late or lost checks, and filling out forms. A reduced, delayed, or missing payment could cause tremendous hardship for poor people living on a minimum budget and from check to check. Even so, organizers feared that help on such issues was not a "political" activity.[28] These fears reflected the dominant view that politics and services were, or should be, separate activities, that an opposition existed between "making change" and "helping people."[29] Despite these concerns and criticisms, they decided that engaging in service work was a concrete, practical way to meet the immediate, felt needs of low-income residents and consistent with participatory democracy. Over time, they also began to understand service provision as political. It brought community residents into the projects, built a neighborhood base and reputation for the projects, fostered trust between residents and organizers, and helped to shift the balance of power between welfare state institutions and community residents. As Elvie Jordan of the Cleveland project's Welfare Grievance Committee stated:

> Before I started working with the Welfare Grievance Committee I had the feeling that any time I would attempt to go to the Welfare Department for anything I would be embarrassed and insulted before I could get over to them why I was there or why I called. [With the Welfare Grievance Committee] you learn how to gain the respect of the Welfare Department. And as long as we have this respect we can work with the Welfare Department to make this a better welfare system.[30]

In the case of Jordan and others, participating in service activity contributed to a greater sense of personal competence, control, and political efficacy.

In a parallel development, New Left organizers initially set out to build an all-encompassing solidarity in the projects by drawing upon community members' status as poor Americans. They believed a collective identity as "the poor" would structure and give shape to political mobilization and expression in the projects. After all, as Connie Brown observed, the "central issue of the development of a radical movement" was "the forging of a new identity."[31] But constructing a collective identity out of shared poverty was primarily a goal of New Left organizers rather than neighborhood participants, who only rarely chose to represent themselves as "the poor" or even as "poor people." For example, when Chicago participant Dorothy Perez dictated an article for the JOIN newsletter, she used "we" and "us" to refer to Uptown residents; but the organizer typing her article parenthetically inserted "(the poor)" after every occurrence.[32] In keeping with participatory democracy, residents instead preferred and organizers endorsed a common citizenship, or identity as "the people" or Americans, as a basis for solidarity in the community projects, although this could be inflected with class, race, gender, and geographical meaning. "As citizens of America we should fight for decent communities. Just because we are poor," Mrs. Alcantar of the Chicago project declared, "we should not have to live in slums and be pushed around because we are Puerto Rican, Mexican, hillbillies or colored."[33]

Politics of the State

From the beginning, SDS's ultimate goal for community organizing under the auspices of ERAP was to solve the problem of poverty in the United States by transforming the welfare state along social democratic lines—a goal that was shared by many on the liberal-labor left and appeared in the Port Huron Statement. "A program against *poverty* must be just as sweeping as the nature of poverty itself. It must not be just palliative, but directed to the abolition of the structural circumstances of poverty."[34] In the Port Huron Statement and in later ERAP publications, SDS activists called for national economic planning. Direct government intervention in labor markets and manpower policy, they believed, was necessary. "It is time for a reexamination of the way in which resources are presently allocated in our society," one ERAP conference proposal stated. To this end, the United States needed to develop institutions of local, state, and national planning.[35] Beyond economic planning, the Port Huron Statement urged that "existing institutions should be expanded so the welfare state cares for *everyone's* welfare according to need."[36] ERAP writings specified the need for full and fair (nondiscriminatory) employment and a guaranteed income apart from employment for all Americans; SDS's community organizing projects incorporated these twin goals into the demand for "jobs or income now."

In keeping with participatory democracy, SDS also contended that planning and programs to end poverty must be and could be organized democratically. At this point, as Richard Flacks notes, SDS was grappling with the "macro-political meanings of participatory democracy" and attempting to envision a state and economy open and responsive to people's voices and needs.[37] The expansion of public authority to resolve the problem of

poverty thus needed to be accompanied by the extension of political participation, including to poor Americans themselves. Economic questions could
not be separated from political ones, or economic justice, from democratic
participation. As a result, once the ERAP projects were under way, organizers broadened their agenda for welfare state transformation from national
planning and "jobs or income now" to incorporate the multiplicity of
needs and concerns articulated by community residents.

In pursuing the goal of welfare state transformation, ERAP activists
gained impetus from President Lyndon Johnson's declaration of a "war on
poverty" in January 1964. Together with the successes of the civil rights
movement, this proposal for the largest expansion in welfare state programs
since the New Deal contributed to a mood of possibility and urgency
among community organizers. They would be "frontline soldiers in a *real*
war on poverty," ERAP recruitment advertisements emphasized in 1965.[38]
The community projects could be a means of shaping the War on Poverty
on the local level. Some raised fears of co-optation, arguing that involvement in the War on Poverty would preempt or sidetrack ERAP from its
larger goals, but most did not question this involvement. In fact, as SDS
president Todd Gitlin contended, they believed that "if radicals are *not*
participants" in local War on Poverty efforts, "then assuredly [such efforts]
will be co-opted."[39]

As a result, between 1964 and 1968, New Left organizers launched
numerous campaigns that incorporated both substantive and participatory
aims—that is, that sought both tangible goods and benefits from welfare
state institutions and an open, decentralized welfare state. For example, in
their campaigns around welfare, project activists demanded adequate benefits, free school lunches, higher clothing and rent allowances, and an
improved food stamp program, as well as recipients' right "to change and
run the welfare system." In Chicago, Dorothy Perez called for a voice in
administration, arguing that "recipients have a right to help make the decisions that affect their lives so radically."[40] ERAP campaigns aimed at halting
urban renewal took a similar approach. Basing their campaigns on federal
legislation mandating citizen participation, or approval, of renewal programs and the rehousing of residents displaced by renewal efforts, they
sought to realize adequate housing for all citizens and to redesign poor
neighborhoods with the participation and according to the needs and interests of local residents. In Cleveland, participants envisioned new low-and
moderate-income housing, medical clinics, schools, parks, playgrounds,

and public swimming pools. Such facilities, they maintained, would allow "people [to] have interesting, happy lives here."[41]

ERAP's War on Poverty campaigns exemplified most clearly this goal of transforming the American welfare state through expansion and participation. Activists first set out to ensure that local poverty programs adhere to the provision mandating "maximum feasible participation of the poor" and even quoted Sargent Shriver, head of the Office of Economic Opportunity (OEO), on the importance of participation. They believed that without the direction and participation of low-income residents, the poverty war would fail to target the sustaining conditions of poverty: the political powerlessness and social marginalization felt and lived by those in poverty.[42] After all, Richard Rothstein argued: "The demand for an end to poverty and the demand for participation of the poor in that fight are in reality one."[43] Demands for participation resonated within communities. Chicago resident Junior Brown wrote of the War on Poverty: "The people of Uptown should make the decisions about what they know."[44] Demands by ERAP activists in all of the cities took seriously what could have been seen as "rhetorical preambles" about citizen involvement and joined civil rights and other community activists in strengthening grassroots pressure on local and government officials to fulfill these promises of democratic participation.[45]

In addition to calling for participation in the poverty war, the community projects put forth their own programs for solving the problem of poverty in the United States. Federal policy makers' understanding of poverty as a product of blocked economic opportunities and personal handicaps, activists argued, failed to confront underlying structural inequalities.[46] "People like me and millions of others are not being reached by the War on Poverty program," protested Dovie Coleman. "I'm a Negro woman, 45, needs a job and can't get one. When are you going to start listening to me?"[47] In Cleveland, a woman welfare recipient asked of the poverty program: "What can [it] offer me? Does it raise wages to $2 an hour? Will it retrain me for a good job with decent wages?"[48] By advancing their own program proposals for the War on Poverty based on the needs and concerns of residents, the community projects revealed the limitations and inadequacies of state-initiated solutions to the problems of poverty in the United States.

Of course, SDS's community organizing under ERAP did not succeed in building an interracial movement of the poor or ending poverty in

America. The resulting recognition of the difficulties of cross-class, interracial organizing, and frustration and anger with local government officials and liberal policy makers, had real, and complicated, consequences for New Left organizers and SDS.[49] Yet, as social movement scholars Frances Fox Piven and Richard A. Cloward have noted, "What was won must be judged by what was possible," and the community organizing tradition has always been one of small victories and large defeats.[50]

However, the community projects yielded interactions and outcomes among New Left organizers and community participants that should be remembered. Their transformative vision of the welfare state, a vision that sought to redefine and expand what constituted a public responsibility and democratic participation in America, to redefine citizenship rights, is one that remains relevant to the problem of economic inequality today.[51] Their evolving organizing strategy opened up the "old" political paradigm to the multiplicity of constituencies, issues, and identities that signaled a new way of building and understanding social movements.[52] What ended during the 1960s was the notion that there was only one vehicle for achieving social change, and what began, or reopened, and is still with us, was a debate on the strategy for fundamental social transformation. Finally, personal and political change occurred for many participants, just as has happened in many social movements and organizing efforts, past and present.

An illustrative example of this process is David Strauss's recollection of a resident he and other New Left organizers encountered in Cleveland, Beulah "Boots" Neal, a welfare recipient. "What we did the first year for her was move her," Strauss recalls. "Every few weeks she was moving again, and we got to go and move her, her refrigerator and stove." When he first met her, he remembers thinking, " 'This is absurd. Why are we working with this person?' . . . And then one day it seemed like she just decided to commit to the stuff that Sharon Jeffrey kept talking to her about, and she did it with a lot of integrity."[53] Boots Neal ended up joining the Cleveland project's welfare rights group. "We are trying hard to better ourselves," she explained, "by working together as a group."[54] For Neal, the Cleveland project provided impetus, focus, and resources for her community activism. The help and time organizers gave to her resulted in an active member of the Cleveland project, but such successes felt very small. "At the time," Strauss remembers, the effort organizers put into people like Boots Neal "looked like a waste of time," for it did not produce what organizers had hoped. "I think most of us had the mass movement idea of change. The civil rights movement . . . the Russian Revolution, sitdown strikes of the '30s. That's how you change things. It's hard to measure what we were doing against those things." By January 1967, when he left the Cleveland project, he took this sense of failure with him. "I incorrectly felt that I hadn't any skills, that I hadn't learned anything. That wasn't true, but I didn't know that." Only later, reflecting back, did he realize that the "model we were using was actually a pretty good one, which is that you are probably going to change people one person at a time." "Moving Boots Neal," he now says, "was a good thing."[55]

For participants like Dave Strauss and Boots Neal, the 1960s marked a beginning, not the end, of struggles for democracy and social change. This history of SDS, ERAP, and community organizing reminds us of what, despite great historical and political obstacles, the New Left attempt to put the Port Huron Statement's participatory democracy into action made possible in the 1960s.

Chapter 11

Port Huron and the New Left Movements
in Federal Germany

Michael Vester

In this essay, I am looking backward and forward. I am looking backward to the Port Huron conference of 1962 and its relations to the early New Left movements for participatory democracy in Europe and especially in Federal Germany. In these movements, the relations between the American and the German student organizations—both were called SDS—played a special role. But this essay also looks beyond the early and mid-1960s. After describing the common and parallel roots and forms of the two movements, it proceeds to describe and explain why, on the political level, the German movements developed differently. They did not suffer the same series of severe and demoralizing political setbacks the American movements had to endure, starting with the assassinations of the Kennedys and of Martin Luther King and continuing under the Nixon, Reagan, and Bush administrations. Despite many obstacles, the German movements could flourish and expand by taking advantage of great openings for participatory politics that were connected with the rise of Willy Brandt to chancellorship in the 1960s and lasted well into the 1980s. In a way, this showed that participatory democracy is not only a great human ideal but also a strategic political alternative rooted in the contradictory dynamics of our societies.

From Frankfurt to Port Huron

In October 1961, I had come from Frankfurt to study sociology in the United States. I was twenty-one years old, having just finished my year on the national board of the German Socialist Student Federation, the Sozialistische Deutsche Studentenbund, or SDS. As its vice chairman I had been responsible for developing a new international network of socialist student and youth organizations, so I had already been in correspondence with some young leftists in the United States. In this network, we understood ourselves as parts of a new, unorthodox political current that came from England and, already in 1958, had named itself the "New Left."[1] As Edward Thompson put it later, this "British 'new left' was among the first of this international family. It began in the mid fifties as a strongly political movement, taking hostile views of both orthodox social democracy and communism, and since 1960 it [had] gone through many mutations."[2]

In 1961, the New Left current consisted of dissidents inside and outside the old socialist international organizations in the developed countries, in the newly independent nations of the third world, and in communist Eastern Europe. All these activists of a younger generation had a sense that decolonization and John F. Kennedy's election as president symbolized a new political opening. They were anxious to contest the bureaucratic stalemate and authoritarian domination they saw all about them. The new mood was manifest in the protest movements of Japanese and Turkish students, of the English and German Easter marches for nuclear disarmament, and by the civil rights movements emerging in the United States and in South Africa.

They did not expect change to come from powerful organizational structures, theoretical credos, or charismatic leaders. Instead it would arise from real social movements and mobilizations that were a product of the contemporary historic situation. But there *was* also a new appreciation of social theory, as shown in several journals. Most important became the British journal *new left review*, founded in 1960, as a fusion of two preceding New Left magazines founded in 1957, *The New Reasoner* (organized from Yorkshire by Edward Thompson together with John Saville, Doris Lessing, Raymond Williams, and other dissidents of communism), which had introduced the term "New Left," and *Universities and Left Review* (organized from Oxford by Stuart Hall and other young left-wing intellectuals). Simultaneously, in Germany and Italy many dissidents of the early twentieth-century revolutionary left were rediscovered, among them António Gramsci, Rosa Luxemburg, Wilhelm Reich, and Karl Korsch.

Arriving in New York with this background, I immediately contacted our fraternal organizations.[3] Most important to contact were Al Haber, president of Students for a Democratic Society, and, a little later Bob Ross, the vice president, and Dick Flacks, who also was very active in transforming SDS into a New Left organization and movement. Contacts also extended to socialists such as Michael Harrington and representatives of the Young People's Socialist League in New York.

In discussions with Al Haber, I immediately found that both of us, as well as many friends on both sides of the Atlantic, were electrified by *out of apathy*, a 1960 collection of New Left essays edited by Edward Thompson as the first volume of "New Left Books."[4] This book offered to the amorphous currents of the New Left a common definition of the historical situation and the role of the New Left to "find a way out of apathy."[5] It was not a declaration of principles but—as I shall develop a little further later in this essay—it was a concrete analysis of the manifold social contradictions of "'bastard' capitalism" that prevailed in society. When the book appeared in Europe, it immediately became the most important signal of a new and liberating practical *and* intellectual departure. Thus, it reached a wider international audience than even C. Wright Mills, with his famous essay "A Letter to the New Left,"[6] which appeared later in 1960 and was read mainly in Britain and the United States. After we discovered that we shared the same political enthusiasms, Al Haber and I began to cooperate and correspond closely.

Al Haber must have had the impact of *out of apathy* in mind when, in early December 1961, he told me that the Students for a Democratic Society was planning its own public statement that expressed the new ideas and applied them to the situation in America and a new generation of young activists. Tom Hayden, who was asked to formulate this statement, produced a first draft of nine pages that was circulated for discussion in March 1962.[7] From Bowdoin College, where I was in residence, I sent a comment on the draft that was also circulated.[8] I urged Tom to formulate more clearly the effort "to transform the struggle against armament into a struggle for a genuine democracy." And I indicated that Hayden's draft, following Mills, may have put too much emphasis on the role of intellectuals as agents of social change. In my view, "the intellectuals by themselves, can be a motor of social change, but *not the agency*, the moving power itself." That was still a task for the labor movement.[9] In an enormous final effort, Tom transformed his draft into a fully developed manifesto—so that we had no alternative but to understate our ambitions by simply denoting it as a "statement," taking its name from the locality where we met to discuss and formulate the penultimate draft.

The ambitious stance of the Port Huron Statement—to express the political perspectives of a whole younger generation—might well have been thought presumptuous had it not been for the authority we achieved by our participation in and identification with the new movements rising around the world. In the Statement, this is also reflected in the language we adopted to give a fresh but erudite diagnosis of the historical situation that was markedly different from the dogmatic stereotypes of the Old Left. In the atmosphere of the New Frontier rhetoric characteristic of the early Kennedy administration, we felt encouraged to proclaim a new historical departure. The Statement became a great synthesis of what was discussed since the international New Left had come into existence at the end of the 1950s. It linked an analysis of the advanced, affluent capitalist societies with that of their new social and political contradictions. It understood that these contradictions translated into a generational conflict, as well as a set of tensions that had a decided class, gender, and racial component.

But the Statement also went further. The term "participatory democracy" was offered as an integrative formula of the emerging movements. It allowed us to look back to the long history of struggles for civic, communal, trade union, and economic democracy and for personal emancipation in many countries. At the same time, the term became a common denominator for the manifold new movements renewing those traditions of genuine economic and social democracy. The slow but steady spreading of participatory grassroots activity among the younger generation gave the idea of participatory democracy the appearance of what, in 1961, Raymond Williams called a "long revolution."[10]

Indeed, after decades of neoconservative restoration, that spirit is still alive, manifested by the international chain reaction of new democratic movements that began with the Arab Spring in 2011. Take, for example, the Spanish movement M15, which began on May 15, 2011, and has been active in sixty cities. Its manifesto, *Democracia Real Ya!* (Real Democracy, Now!), demanded "the political participation of citizens through direct channels" instead of the corrupt two-party oligarchy that has long governed Spain. M15 called for an end to the current system that privileged the "accumulation of money, not regarding efficiency and the welfare of society, wasting resources, destroying the planet, creating unemployment and unhappy consumers." Of course, the return of emancipatory and participatory movements is one not just of ideas but of the underlying changes taking place in everyday cultures and social structures. These changes are represented by a new, well-educated generation whose emancipatory aspirations have been frustrated by an arrogant elite of increasingly undemocratic meme.

In 1962 and through the rest of the 1960s we found no contradiction between unionist, socialist, antiracialist, feminist, and youth-cultural movements. This coincidence was, in a way, symbolized by the fact that we adopted this manifesto in a recreation camp at Lake Huron that had been run by Michigan trade unionists, the United Automobile Workers especially, in the years after the great industrial upheavals of the Great Depression.

For me, Port Huron itself was mainly a social event, where I spent hours meeting other young people, often sitting on the grass between the primitive cabins of the camp with its unlimited view over Lake Huron. I do not remember well the discussions or the presence of Arnold Kaufman, who had written that famous essay about participatory democracy that gave our statement its historical slogan.[11] But I remember the people, more or less fifty persons around the age of twenty, mostly from liberal colleges and universities, but also people active and committed to the new peace and civil rights movements. Among them were many practical activists, like Ann Pearl Avery, a courageous young woman with whom I discussed her Student Nonviolent Coordinating Committee experience in Birmingham, Alabama, and who later was to continue the Freedom Walk of William Lewis Moore after he had been assassinated, in April 1963, on a Mississippi highway.[12] Among the Port Huron participants, I was the only representative of a foreign fraternal organization, the German SDS. But such conversations and shared commitments generated, between activists of both organizations, the beginning of a great friendship.

The German contribution in preparing the Statement is more completely described and documented in Martin Klimke's book *The Other Alliance*.[13] My responsibility was to contribute the European and international experiences. This included the German SDS perspectives and analyses on the Cold War, formulated by our group in the city of Berlin whose political division between the Eastern and Western blocs had been "cemented" by the infamous Berlin Wall since August 13, 1961.

Our analysis to end the Cold War by diplomatic recognition of East Germany and subsequent diplomatic negotiations was not very popular at that time. The main obstacle to overcoming the Cold War was formulated in the so-called Hallstein Doctrine of the conservative West German government, which insisted that a diplomatic recognition of the East German state, the Deutsche Demokratische Republik (DDR), would be a moral support to an un-democratic regime and an insurmountable obstacle to a future reunification of Germany. To study the problem of diplomatic recognition more fully, I took part in a course on international law at Bowdoin. Advised by Arthern Daggett, I developed a paper in which I could demonstrate that, by the criteria of international law as well as by selected cases, diplomatic recognition had nothing to do with moral political recognition but generally had been a way to ease tensions. When Al Haber asked me to contribute a paper on Berlin, I integrated this perspective into a ten-page political analysis that formulated its essence in its title: "Berlin: Why Not Recognize the Status Quo?" On February 6, I sent it to Al, and already on February 13, he responded that he had sent it to Bob Ross for comments and would "have it included in the TURN TOWARD PEACE packet." Turn Toward Peace was a cooperative, national effort of some sixty peace and liberal internationalist organizations, formally chaired by Norman Thomas.[14]

Much of this same analysis made its way into the Port Huron Statement in the section entitled "What Is Needed," devoted to ending the Cold War. The ideas of diplomatic recognition, military disengagement, ending nuclear tests and armament, and creating demilitarized zones between the Eastern and Western blocs were included in the subsequent discussion papers preparing the Statement and later also integrated in its text.[15] The Statement closely followed my paper and additional texts to explain for an American audience how the non-communist left in Germany saw the problem of that nation's reunification. It argued that "we should recognize that an authoritarian Germany's insistence on reunification, while knowing the impossibility of achieving it with peaceful means, could only generate increasing frustrations among the population and nationalist sentiments which frighten its Eastern neighbors." To avoid this, we were for the status quo—that is, the mutual diplomatic recognition of the two German states and the Berlin status—in order to diminish Cold War tensions. Moreover, following my suggestions, this section of the Port Huron Statement emphasized that the Cold War was not merely a problem of Soviet-American conflict: "Even if Washington and Moscow were in favor of disengagement, both Adenauer and Ulbricht would never agree to it because Cold War keeps their parties in power." Our solution included a series of "disarmament experiments," of which the most important would be the military disengagement by both world powers from Poland, Czechoslovakia, and the two Germanys. By undermining the Russian argument for tighter controls in East Europe based on the "menace of capitalist encirclement," such diplomacy, "geared to the needs of democratic elements in the satellites," would develop a real bridge between East and West, not unlike the Ost-Politik perused by Willy Brandt seven years later.

On my contribution, Tom Hayden later commented: "We saw the Cold War only inside of the United States; United States versus Soviet Union. We were not thinking of the people on the ground in-between the super-powers. So if you read the Port Huron Statement, you'll see a German SDS influence on this long section about why the Cold War had to be ended and why it had to be ended with the involvement of European social movements. . . . Michael Vester . . . I credit him with conceiving and writing the entire Cold War section of the Port Huron statement."[16]

The Statement's text made clear that politically, "as democrats," its authors were "in basic opposition to the communist system"—which, of course, was also the position of the German SDS.[17] However, this did not help us much in Germany, where we had used the phrase "Blind Anticommunism" to criticize the way in which hostility to the Soviet Union was used to shore up a conservative and constrained political culture at home. There, in an atmosphere of Cold War polarization, the Social Democratic Party (SPD) was in the process of expelling SDS members from party membership on the pretext that we were communists, which we definitely were not. Reconciliation did not take place until after 1969, when Willy Brandt became head of a new government and the Kennedy spirit of a new departure finally spread to Germany. Brandt received the Nobel Peace Prize in 1971 for his efforts to lower Cold War tensions, almost exactly the same politics of détente and mutual diplomatic recognition that we had advocated in the early 1960s and which had been part of our Port Huron analysis for reducing fears of war and expanding the realm of human freedom at the height of the Cold War.

From Port Huron to Frankfurt

As it happens in wonderful friendships, the transport of ideas also went the other direction, from West to East. Soon after Port Huron I returned to Frankfurt, where we continued building the new international network of

New Left youth and student organizations.[18] Our collective efforts were made all the more urgent by the radically unstable times: the continuing Cold War confrontations in and over Berlin, the nuclear tests conducted by both the Soviets and the United States, the conflicts in Algeria and South Africa, and the eruption of movements against dictatorial regimes around the world.

Frankfurt in the early 1960s was a city where the New Left and the international socialist movement exchanged ideas and formulated plans for action. The critical social philosophy of the Frankfurt School of Sociology was very important for us. But the student left of the Frankfurt University was also embedded in the political culture of a city that was a main center for the left within the labor union movement, within the Social Democratic Party and within the socialist youth organizations. This included also many left-wing democratic socialists of the older generation who had been perse- cuted or driven into emigration during the Nazi years. In such a milieu, ideas and ideologies of those seeking to build workers' democracy, to create institutions fostering anti-authoritarian education and undogmatic social- ism, had been handed down and restudied as an alternative to authoritarian communism and the mainstream right-wing Social Democracy of postwar Germany. In these discussions the rediscovery of the ideas and ideals of Rosa Luxemburg and Wilhelm Reich were of prime importance.

The Frankfurt Institute of Social Research was responsive to this culture in important fields of empirical research, especially those bearing on the democratic potential of the West German population and especially its working class. We were interested in this because our underlying common aim was to prevent a return of fascism in Germany. In cooperation with the labor union left, professors Ludwig von Friedeburg, Gerhard Brandt, and Manfred Teschner coordinated substantial research in industrial sociol- ogy and on workers' mentality. Jürgen Habermas, von Friedeburg, and oth- ers coordinated equally influential studies on students' attitudes toward democracy and on educational chances. Many of us studied related topics and would continue such research later, when we won teaching posts at the university level. Others carried on the Institute's work in feminist studies, initiated by Helge Pross. Especially important for us were the studies of authoritarian and democratic personality formation initiated by Theodor W. Adorno, Erich Fromm, and Wilhelm Reich. They motivated many of us to become active in education as a field of democratic, non-authoritarian pedagogics. Monika Seifert-Mitscherlich and her friends founded the first anti-authoritarian kindergarten in Frankfurt, which was soon followed by similar foundings all over the country.[19] Since the mid-1960s and, to an even larger extent, in the 1970s, many of us became teachers in schools, universities, and in the free youth movement, labor movement, and adult education, combining this with new programs and styles of democratic political education. Since the 1970s, the Frankfurt School studies of changing attitudes toward democracy and of class mentalities were also carried on, especially at the University of Hannover, where the approaches of Adorno, Fromm, and Reich were combined with the approaches of Pierre Bourdieu and the New Left cultural studies.[20] Many of the younger generation of Frankfurt sociologists became influential when scholars from the Institute moved to other universities and into politics.

Institutionalizing Workers' Participation in Postwar Germany

Among the Frankfurt socialist students as well as among the younger generation of Institute teachers, the question of enhancing democratic participation, both civic and industrial, was of keen interest. In pursuit of this aim, we relied not only on the new youth and intellectual movements of that era but also on the working-class intelligentsia, especially those who were functionaries of the big industrial unions whose leaders had played important roles in the resistance to fascism. This was also the common base of the West European socialist left in general, with whom we closely cooperated through frequent meetings, conferences, and the interchange of publications.

In Federal Germany after World War II, the industrial unions had organized big strike movements that succeeded in laying the fundaments of a strong welfare state and ensuring a voice for organized workers in the governance of the enterprise for which they worked. Astonishingly enough, this working-class progress came when conservative governments were in power. From 1949 to 1963 these were headed by the conservative Catholic Konrad Adenauer, who tried to develop a new conservatism that was responsive to working-class demands and therefore a bulwark against the appeals of communism or the return of the Nazis. He also initiated a sort of conservative international that, through common European institutions, ensured that Germany would remain a nation wedded to parliamentary institutions and formal democratic rights for its citizens. Simultaneously, he designed a conservative variant of the social democratic welfare state, pioneered by the Swedes and the British, in order to avoid severe social and political ruptures.

Some observers of West Germany in this era have forgotten that the Adenauer years did not merely bring a rise in the standard of living of the German working class. The industrial recovery of Federal Germany was also accompanied by a remarkable increase of individual and collective rights and democratic participation in capitalist enterprises. Immediately after the war, the British military government, appointed by a Labour government in London, had already supported workers' participation in its part of West Germany. After the foundation of the Federal Republic of Germany, in 1949, big organized demonstrations of the metalworkers and the miners in the Ruhr district moved the conservative parliamentary majority to concede the Mitbestimmungsgesetz ("participation act") of 1951, which gave employee representatives 50 percent of the seats on the supervisory boards of the coal and steel corporations. One year later, the same majority conceded the Betriebsverfassungsgesetz ("enterprise constitutional act"), which gave strong minority rights to elected employees' representations.

The introduction of *Mitbestimmung,* which, in full, means "democratic participation in decision making," into Federal Germany's industries served as a prime example of participatory empowerment in Arnold Kaufman's famous essay of 1960, "Human Nature and Participatory Democracy," which gave the Port Huron Statement its central slogan. Mitbestimmung was one of the rare empirical cases of participation that Kaufman could name in support of his thesis at that time.[21] In a highly ambitious assault upon the work of Walter Lippmann, Sigmund Freud, Melanie Klein, Erich Fromm, Joseph Schumpeter, Robert Michels, and others skeptical of the human capacity for democratic and rational decision making, Kaufman argues that the main justification for a "democracy of participation" is the "contribution it can make to the development of human powers of thought, feeling and action. In this respect it differs, and differs quite fundamentally, from a representative system incorporating all sorts of institutional features designed to safeguard human rights and ensure social order. *This distinction is all-important.*"[22]

However, Kaufman saw one weakness in the theories of democratic participation put forth by cooperative socialist G. D. H. Cole and pragmatist philosopher John Dewey: they never developed "an empirical defense" of the "proposition that participation contributes to personal development."[23] Consequently, Kaufman sought an empirical program to study practical examples of democratic participation defined by the criteria that it "essentially involves actual preliminary deliberation (conversations, debate, discussion) and that in the final decision each participant has a roughly equal formal say."[24]

Kaufman's intervention came in a historical situation where, since the late 1950s, the possibility of workers' participation was discussed internationally as an alternative to authoritarian structures in state-socialist as well as in capitalist enterprises. This discussion was spurred by the widely noted "experiments in Germany, Yugoslavia, Poland and elsewhere."[25] In his essay, Kaufman refers to an international symposium on "Workers' Participation in Management," held in 1956 by the International Sociological Association.[26] Controversy at the symposium centered on the syndicalist assumption that "workers could assume managerial functions with good results both for the workers themselves and for the larger society."[27] Kaufman cites German sociologist Ralf Dahrendorf as asserting that "the appointment of workers to managerial or quasi-managerial positions is bound to defeat its own ends," but also mentions a more optimistic participant who considered "the possibility of eliminating conflict through an extensive rotation of managerial jobs. All agree that the issue is fundamental for the future of workers' participation."[28]

The empirical research Kaufman had pleaded for was done by scholars of West German industrial sociology and the sociology of work who, especially in Göttingen and in Frankfurt, produced large empirical studies on how Mitbestimmung had reshaped authority structures in industry and how workers' social consciousness had been altered.[29] Their students, of which I was one, further developed this research in the 1970s, founding new research centers concerned with industrial and labor relations at a variety of other universities.

Toward a New Participatory Mobilization

Around 1960 in Germany, the participatory elements of Mitbestimmung were still embedded in a societal context with many constraints, including a paternalistic family model and the conservative consensus fostered by the Cold War. In the view of the unions as well as in our own view, these achievements were strong but not sufficient.

How could we break this oppressive sense of containment? When, also around 1960, most of the local SDS groups began to feel and think of themselves as part of a New Left, we developed a multilevel idea of how to mobilize people for participatory politics. First, many SDS members became active in workers' education and the politics of the big industrial labor unions. Second, many of us tried to build a national "left wing" or "labor wing" inside the Social Democratic Party, which soon proved successful in Frankfurt, Göttingen, Hamburg, Marburg, and Berlin. This was not easy, because at that very time the national SPD organization tried to expel its SDS members under the pretext that we were communists. And, third, we joined forces with the most critical and active parts of all progressive democratic organizations. Beyond the labor unions, SPD, and leftist socialist youth organizations (The Red Falcons and The Friends of Nature), we joined with other activists who had turned left during the Cold War conflict: student government leaders, activists from the student presses at high schools and universities, and even activists from various boy and girl scout organizations.

What I was not conscious of at that time was that this development owed much indirectly to John Dewey. After 1945, the American military government in Germany, by recommendation of Dewey-oriented advisers, had done much to reform education, including the election of student representatives as training in democratic participation. This had given many of my generation, including myself, the chance to become participatory activists in the schools, in the universities, and in the student press. Later, many of those individuals became activists within left politics and the social movements of the 1960s and 1970s in Federal Germany.

By combining these different levels of engagement, the German SDS mobilized and coordinated working-class and general youth activities, especially in the fields of labor movement education in the high schools and universities. In the early 1960s this was a rather slow process, but in the mid-1960s it gained momentum because it merged with the broad worldwide cultural youth revolts directed against authoritarianism of all kinds. This historical coincidence of socio-structural changes and active political groups finally, in 1969, led to the sweeping electoral victory of Willy Brandt, which in turn opened space for many institutional reforms demanded by the social movements of the New Left.

These beginnings were connected with a socialist-inflected, transatlantic labor internationalism. One outstanding representative of that tradition was our friend Hans Matthöfer,[30] grandson of a Polish immigrant and functionary in the Frankfurt headquarters of the Union of the Metal Industry Employees, the IG Metall. Matthöfer had spent a year working with the United Automobile Workers and was much at home in the discussions in the United States. This had been during his term as trade union attaché at the Organisation of European Economic Co-operation (OEEC) in Paris and in Washington, D.C., from 1957 to 1961. When he returned to the Frankfurt headquarters of IG Metall in October 1960, he received salaries from both occupations for a time. One of those he donated to the SDS national organization in 1960 and 1961 when it lost its financial support from the SPD and from the national youth budget because of its alleged communist sympathies.

In Frankfurt, Matthöfer directed the educational department of the IG Metall from 1960 until 1972. In that union, with its 2.2 million members, he organized the large educational program that remained an important field of participatory politics. In the 1960s, Matthöfer also made important contributions in organizing the workers of the Ford Motor Company and other firms in Germany and in the union's big campaign for participation in the workplace (*Mitbestimmung am Arbeitsplatz*). And, since the Frankfurt left-wing Social Democracy sent him to the Federal parliament in 1961, he also became important in building the left wing of the party on the national level and representing it in the governments headed by Social Democrat chancellors Willy Brandt and Helmut Schmidt from 1969 to 1982.

The strivings for workers' participation after World War II were, in a way, echoing the tradition of the democratic workers' councils formed during the German Revolution of November 1918. They had been decisive in introducing full parliamentarian democracy and the idea of industrial democracy to Germany. Many of the leftist union activists who now fought for Mitbestimmung had been influenced by this tradition and also by their experience as part of the resistance against the Hitler regime. After World War II, such participatory workers' movements were not limited to Federal Germany. They remained a strong strain within the European and Latin American labor movement, especially in Italy, France, and Britain as well as in Chile and in the Portuguese and Nicaraguan revolutions in the late 1970s.

On the theoretical and political level, Peter von Oertzen, a political scientist from Göttingen, was the most important partisan of participatory democracy. His studies of workers' councils and on workers' participation gave a fundamental orientation to much of the German SDS and proved influential in the field of union education.[31] In 1963, he moved to the University of Hanover to become head of the political science department. In 1970, after the growing young socialist movement gained a left majority in the Hannover region of the SPD, he became head of the Lower Saxony SPD and influential also on the national committee of SPD.[32] As minister of culture in Lower Saxony (1970–74) he also had many enemies, especially after he greatly expanded comprehensive high schools (which opened higher education to working-class children) and introduced democratic participation into the universities, an initiative that was, in part, rejected by the Federal Constitutional Court.

A parallel development occurred in the Federal State of Hesse that was strongly influenced by the Frankfurt left. Here, under a Social Democratic government, Frankfurt sociologist Ludwig von Friedeburg became minister of culture (1969–74) and also introduced radical educational reforms that, in the new comprehensive schools, undermined the old class privileges associated with higher education.

Learning from the New Anglo-Saxon Developments

In the early 1960s, the German SDS had started a new national magazine, *neue kritik*, which was edited in Frankfurt and reflected a general New Left internationalism and vanguardism.[33] The magazine included an increasing number of articles on new political developments and theoretical discussions in the world to which we were connected by our new international networks as well as by visitors and students who came from other countries in Europe, Africa, Asia, and Latin America. To make these impulses known was a deliberate policy of the New Left–oriented SDS national committee. After my return from the United States, as an editor of *neue kritik*, I wrote a series of comprehensive articles on the United States, with special attention offered to the peace and civil rights movements and to the changes and problems of American capitalism and politics until the Kennedy era.[34] This opened larger discussions that highly extended the "range and intensity of the American influence on the German SDS."[35] This influence reached a European level after 1963 when, with the help of the Italian, British, and

French left-wing socialists, the international network edited the *International Socialist Journal.*

Anglo-Saxon developments were especially important for the younger generation of Frankfurt sociologists even before I went to the United States. In 1961, we got Gerhard Brandt from the Frankfurt Institute to write a review of *out of apathy.*[36] As already mentioned, this was the book that convinced me that I shared much in common with Al Haber and other American radicals. In Germany it proved an exceedingly important introduction to New Left thought in Great Britain. It was the answer to new challenges that had made the old left helpless: the astonishing revival of capitalism and conservatism after 1945 and the improvements of working-class living standards, which supported the widespread assumption that capitalism now could provide endless growth and a material and mental integration of the working class into petty-bourgeois or consumerist schemes.

Against this assumption, the authors maintained that there were still contradictions in capitalism and conflicts between classes, but that these could be grasped only by developing an undogmatic understanding of Marx and an opening to what could be learned about Keynesian economics and the everyday culture of the working class. Raphael Samuel explained the contradictions of "bastard capitalism," which was still based on external repression and on an "internal colonization."[37] Stuart Hall explained the severe limits to postwar "working-class prosperity."[38] Alasdair MacIntyre criticized C. Wright Mills's image of society as "a machine in which individuals are trapped" because they allegedly are "not agents but victims."[39] Kenneth Alexander, well aware of the nature of new "managerial" capitalism, criticized the exhaustion of ideas in the old labor movement and argued for a revitalized labor movement based on "power at the base" and a renewed quest for "workers' control."[40] He called for "what the New Left has called 'reformist tactics within a revolutionary strategy.'"[41] E. P. Thompson, who would soon publish *The Making of the English Working Class,* criticized "gradual piecemeal reform" as well as the dogmatic "cataclysmic model of revolution."[42] For Thompson, it was "not the violence of a revolution which decides its extent and consequences, but the maturity and activity of the people."[43] This "demands also a break with the parliamentary fetishism which supposes that all advance must wait upon legislative change. Most popular gains have been won, in the first place, by direct action; direct action to increase wages, improve working conditions, shorten hours, build co-ops, found nursery schools. . . . What is required is a new sense of immediacy."[44]

Another important Anglo-Saxon impulse by which our discussions were influenced came from the left-wing Keynesian analysis on the changes taking place within capitalism since the Great Depression and the heyday of the New Deal. Especially important was the work of Joan Robinson in Britain and John Kenneth Galbraith in the United States. For this fresh analysis, important suggestions were given by Helge Pross in her seminars in Frankfurt and later in her book on the rise of managerial capitalism.[45] She made us familiar with the American discussion of the move toward corporate capitalism from Adolf Berle and Gardiner Means up to John Kenneth Galbraith's most advanced studies on the contradictions of American capitalism, especially the rise of private affluence amid public sector poverty. The discussion of Galbraith, which had been opened by a critical article of mine in 1961,[46] was further developed into a broader analysis of the new phase of capitalist development in 1963. My essays made extensive use of the new discussions in the English and American left.[47] They described the apparent stabilization of postwar capitalism by Keynesian state intervention (combined with rising armament and welfare expenditures) and the rise of mass consumption (connected with an "internal colonization" of everyday life by capitalism)[48] and showed that this stabilization was not definite but produced new risks, instabilities, and social conflicts. I summed up with a Millsian flourish my critique of Galbraith's *American Capitalism: The Concept of Countervailing Power*, his influential 1952 study: "The countervailing powers are like hyenas fighting for prey. The hegemony of the power elite remains untouched."[49] The discussions were continued at the Frankfurt Institute for Social Research, especially in a seminar held in 1964/65 by Jürgen Habermas, who was generally very interested in efforts to import left-wing Anglo-Saxon scholarship to Frankfurt.

C. Wright Mills was indeed a pathbreaking intellectual pioneer to many of us—and also a subject of much controversy. Tom Hayden finished his master's thesis on Mills at the University of Michigan in 1964, the same year I completed my sociological diploma thesis on Mills under the supervision of Helge Pross.[50] In the United States, Mills remained for many years something of an icon on the student left, but in Germany his ideas had become a source of debate in 1962 and 1963, the years during which *The Power Elite* and *The Sociological Imagination* were first published in German.[51]

The Sociological Imagination, which contained Norman Birnbaum's informative introduction to Mills, was not controversial. It was warmly welcomed by the younger generation of radical sociologists, who endorsed Mills's criticism of positivist empiricism personified by Paul F. Lazarsfeld, as well as of grand sociological theorizing, as developed by Talcott Parsons. We also welcomed Mills's *Power Elite*, which seemed to many a sophisticated new way of explaining how a contemporary ruling class exercises power.

But Mills's idea that intellectuals were now the prime agents of social change became part of our vivid and passionate debate on the future of the working class and of our own role as intellectuals working for social change. Manfred Liebel and I initiated the controversy in 1963 and 1964.[52] We did not question Mills's idea that a Keynesian war economy had helped generate a new ruling elite composed of an alliance of big corporations, the state apparatus, and the military, an uneasy constellation that offered the world an irresponsible risk of nuclear war. We also did not question the idea that there was widespread apathy toward politics because ordinary people mostly did not link their private grievances to public causes and because the mass media did not offer alternatives to the prevalent Cold War political culture.

But we differed with Mills because we did not see all this as a one-dimensional and irresistible tendency in either America or Europe. Like the authors of *out of apathy*, we insisted that capitalism was still contradictory and participative action on the part of the working classes was still a possibility leading us out of resignation. For us, the role of critical intellectuals in the media and in politics was not to *replace* the working classes but to help them to understand that their private grievances had political causes—a formula taken from Mills that remained important for the larger movements to come. At the SDS national conference in 1963, Liebel, who then was elected president of the organization, presented this critique in an important paper on the role of intellectuals in the Federal Republic.[53] We continued the debate on Mills,[54] and, in my diploma thesis in 1964,[55] I added a theoretical critique based on contemporary unorthodox Marxian theories as well as the early cultural studies of the English New Left. The latter were especially influenced by Raymond Williams's book *Culture and Society*, which insisted that social classes were still separated by differing "class cultures."[56] I argued that on the surface, Mills's arguments, which were based on the work of Max Weber, represented a valid description of society, but there were also latent dynamics leading to change inside modern capitalism that might alter class relations. These could be better explained by those New Left concepts that postulated that participatory movements could still transform power relations and consciousness.

In 1964 we had to defend our position another time. In the Frankfurt summer semester, Herbert Marcuse came from the United States to present his new book, *One-Dimensional Man*.[57] Our SDS group had an extra discussion with him in the crammed hall of the Walter Kolb student house. Marcuse started with a passionate attack on our position and especially a paper written by me that argued that there was still a potential for socialist change within the working classes.[58] He condemned this as surrendering to the right-wing leadership of a reformist social democracy. Instead, he defended the idea, made famous in *One-Dimensional Man*, that radical change could only come from those who were oppressed by or excluded from the benefits of the affluent society, such as racial minorities and colonial subjects who had been repressed and deprived of their humanity.

This created a difficult situation because many of us had been enthusiastic readers of Marcuse's philosophical writings on Marx. Now, we defended ourselves against our mentor but understood that Marcuse may well have been unduly influenced by the disappointing recent history of trade unionism in the United States. He was not at all familiar with the new situation in Europe, where space seemed to be opening up for social and political mobilization of the working classes. Marcuse would gain a certain influence later in the 1960s, especially among movement activists a half generation younger than us, whose hopes for a revolutionary transformation were linked to third-world insurgencies and the awakening of racial and ethnic minorities still marginalized in the nations of the first world. But a working-class-oriented New Left remained strong in Germany, the United Kingdom, and the rest of Western Europe, where those of us in the academy did many studies involving the sociology of work and the everyday culture of class. In contrast to both Marcuse and the old, social democratic left, we argued that economic immiseration was hardly the only injustice facing the working class, because the experience of social injustice in *all* its dimensions, not only the economic but also the moral and the political, was decisive in shaping consciousness. For this approach our discussions of Anglo-Saxon scholarship again became influential, especially the monumental studies of E. P. Thompson and of Barrington Moore.[59] At the same time, in Europe there was substantial research on structural change within the working class, showing that the "affluent workers" and the growing groups of technical experts and white-collar workers did not represent an end of class but a new stage of class society in which institutionalized conflicts and a more rational understanding of class interests became important, while at the same time militant conflicts might still take place.[60]

American Direct Actionism Splitting the German Left

In the 1960s, our aim—perhaps idealistic—was still to reconcile or combine the different currents in many of the new social movements. The Frankfurt group, which had trebled its membership to almost two hundred, continued its cooperation with the unions and the working-class intelligentsia but remained open to an appreciation of the importance of new social groups and forms of direct action. In *neue kritik* I published articles on the Free Speech Movement at Berkeley, the anti-Vietnam protests, and the rising tide of African American militancy. These reports helped to pave the way for others to go to the United States and participate in movement activity there. These included Günter Amendt, who also wrote about Berkeley[61] and became a most important writer on the sexual liberation movement, and Karl-Dietrich ("KD") Wolff, the last national president of our SDS in 1969. Looking back, KD Wolff remembered my activity: "without him, I might at the time not even have heard about [what was going on in the United States]. He wrote about stuff going on in the States, in the movement, the civil rights movement. He wrote in the magazine *neue kritik*. And he was the first to write articles where I read about the Free Speech Movement at Berkeley."[62]

Movement politics in the United States had an enormous impact on the young left in Germany and helped precipitate a split in our organization from top to bottom. Until 1965, the German SDS had been an explosive but unified mixture of changing and controversial orientations, many connected with the new international movements. The big groups in Frankfurt, Berlin, and Göttingen were now the leaders of a new majority that wanted to break free from the small intellectual ghettos and bureaucratic organizational forms in order to explore a new anti-authoritarian and participatory movement strategy. I was asked to formulate these basic principles for the SDS majority in an article for *neue kritik*. Titled "The Strategy of Direct

Action," it appeared in June 1965, in the midst of ardent debates that preceded the national SDS conference of that year.[63] It developed the perspective that the still prevailing apathy of the popular majority toward politics could not be overcome by propagating from above the abstract intellectual ideas or doctrines of those who were already convinced. The left could only leave its complacent ghetto when it tried to mobilize people by raising issues germane to their everyday experiences and grievances. These might well be "single-purpose movements," which some socialists in Germany still disdained, but the Americans understood that such popular mobilizations could touch the lives of far more people than a formal socialist organization. To gain moral support and to carry the cause into politics, strict nonviolence and grassroots democratic participation would be the best approach.

Two perspectives were central to this strategy. In its introduction, the article argued against the authoritarian scheme that divided society between an elite of leaders and a mass of followers, a view that was dominant not only on the political right but also in the authoritarian parts of the left. Against this view, the article summed up the most advanced findings of the American sociology of personal influence and of mass communication that I had become acquainted with in my academic year at Bowdoin. This sociology, largely developed by European émigré scholars such as Joseph T. Klapper, Paul F. Lazarsfeld, and Elihu Katz, argued that the everyday consciousness of most ordinary people was by no means the result of coercion, seduction, or manipulation from the mass media, prestigious authorities, or outright demagogues. Instead, everyday consciousness was developed relatively autonomously by the people; they did not form a uniform and dependent mass but were divided between more democratic and more authoritarian groups—differing according to their social relations and mental predispositions or, as we might say today with Bourdieu, class milieus and habitus.[64] This meant that democratic, emancipative, and reflective behavior among ordinary people still had great potential, certainly sufficient to justify our strategies designed to encourage participatory mobilization from below.

The bulk of the essay offered a narrative analysis of the demonstrations, marches, and participatory movements that had been so prominently reported in the American press until spring 1965. For Germans on the left they seemed to prove that participatory mobilization had a promising democratic and emancipative future. The American SDS movement, now growing rapidly on many campuses, seemed to offer an example for the German New Left. For me it had been a great thing since 1963 to receive on a regular basis the *SDS Bulletin,* predecessor of the *New Left Notes.* Together with newspapers like the *New York Times,* the *SDS Bulletin* offered vivid reports on the growth of student radicalism and the demonstrations and campus strikes taking place in the United States. In the civil rights movements, in the ghettos and in the universities, these protests and mobilizations were successful because they were so participatory. Of course, in Germany and Great Britain, nonviolent protests, like the Easter marches against nuclear armaments, had not been unknown. But in the United States these protests seemed fresh and new if only because they attracted a much enlarged set of participants and not only those who were already convinced.

I argued that there were at least three kinds of new, "direct" actions. First, the civil rights movement had made massive civil disobedience a powerful weapon, initially in the Montgomery bus boycott, then in the sit-ins at segregated restaurants, and finally in the effort to register black voters in the South. By taking immense personal risks while remaining entirely nonviolent, the individuals who participated in this movement made a compelling moral appeal to the general public, especially to the liberal mainstream and the newspapers and broadcast networks that shaped public consciousness. Indeed, the fact that young white men and women, like Tom Hayden and other SDS members, had joined with SNCC in the South, courting jail, beatings, and police violence, proved a compelling story to the big liberal media.

Second, the article described how issues of poverty, slum housing, poor schools, and political powerlessness in the urban North were brought to public attention when SDS began its community organizing work, sometimes involving rent boycotts, in African American ghettos in the North. These initiatives, which Tom Hayden and other SDS activists saw as pioneering an innovative approach to the distribution of power at the local community level, became increasingly attractive to those of us in Germany searching for a new way to make our politics tangible and actionable.

A third leap forward to be reported in Germany was how the new methods of the civil rights movements were brought to the universities. In February 1965 Günter Amendt had already reported in *neue kritik* how the Berkeley Free Speech Movement had brought the nonviolent methods of the SNCC civil rights activists into the university and thereby mobilized thousands of students at Berkeley and also won much support from part of the liberal public.[65] In my June 1965 article on direct action I could report to German readers a further breakthrough: the American peace movement had moved into the universities. In Ann Arbor, an SDS stronghold, students and professors had discussed America's involvement in the Vietnam War throughout a whole night at the university—and thus invented a new kind of academic phenomenon, the teach-in. With the help of student radio stations all over the United States, the Ann Arbor initiative had caused an avalanche of coordinated teach-ins on America's foreign politics at universities in thirty-five U.S. states. It was important to show German readers how these teach-ins deployed the rationality of academic discourse to discuss political alternatives to the Johnson administration's Vietnam War policy and in the process win a hearing from mainstream liberals, including the *New York Times*'s James Reston, who praised the teach-ins for offering a "serious and responsible debate" and a "model of what can be accomplished in a vast, democratic continental society, when modern instruments of communications are used to discuss fundamental questions of public policy."[66]

The teach-in method rapidly swept over to Europe with the *Guardian*, which praised a set of London events as a new form of criticism that was more adequate for our times than traditional methods of marching, shouting, demolishing embassy windows, or burning libraries.[67] Many German SDS members, especially those with experience in high school and working-class youth groups, were enthusiastic proponents of this form of direct action, but the first attempts to follow the American example were rather conventional and academic. In my article I pointed out that a Berlin teach-in on Vietnam had failed to excite the public, in part because it was organized as a routine panel discussion, without the provocative element, characteristic of the Anglo-Saxon teach-ins, whereby students and professors occupied symbolically "forbidden" space, such as public plazas and whole university buildings.

My advocacy of direct participatory action evoked enormous controversy and played a role in generating a fierce leadership contest within SDS. Normally, a mere article would not have had such a consequence, but by popularizing the American example, I deepened the already existing controversies inside the German SDS. The organization polarized into two coalitions or camps. These were the "Traditionalists," who had much support in Marburg and were led by the SDS national chairman Helmut

Schauer (who had succeeded Liebel in October 1964), and the "anti-authoritarians," whose leadership came from the Frankfurt, Berlin, and Göttingen student groups. Schauer saw himself as a traditional socialist and a Marxist who wanted SDS to form alliances with parties, unions, and other organizations in order to defeat an impending set of emergency laws that the government was about to pass. In this context he thought direct action reckless and self-defeating. At the SDS national convention in October 1965, the Frankfurt group therefore broke with the traditionalists and made a majority coalition with the Berlin group, which, by admitting Rudi Dutschke and his friends to membership, had also turned to the anti-authoritarian left. We were also allied with a Munich group of which many members were influenced by the provocative Situationist International, whose confrontations and occupations would soon become of spectacular note in Berlin. But as this coalition could not yet present a candidate for the presidency, Schauer was reelected as chairman.

We had not expected this split within the organization. Initially, the intention of the Frankfurt group, of which I was chairman for a while, had been to mediate any potential conflicts. We had attempted to win over the traditionalist members by explaining why participation and emancipation were also the essence of socialist and Marxian thinking. But Schauer rebuffed this effort and later accused those of us in the Frankfurt group of selling out socialism to anarchism. Until 1966, there followed a series of lengthy articles in *neue kritik*. Schauer defended socialist traditionalism (of course in its non-communist strain), starting from the view that capitalism was bound to collapse in a crisis and that it was an illusion to appeal to the left-liberal mainstream. Instead, SDS, as the only socialist organization in Germany, should mobilize and expand its membership by developing a program and an organizational nucleus with a clear socialist outlook.[68] This implied that in the end an economic crisis would enable a socialist party to win a parliamentary majority and thereby introduce socialist change by political measures from above.

This seemed a battle plan taken right out of the nineteenth century. It reproduced the German old left socialist tradition, which differed markedly from what we had experienced at Port Huron, where a nondogmatic combination of Marxian, Keynesian, and Dewey-oriented thinking and of participatory and humanist traditions became the basis for a set of principles to be deployed not as a dogmatic blueprint but heuristically—that is, as the tools for a fresh, experience- and data-based analysis of the situation. At the 1966 national convention, Schauer was replaced by Reimut Reiche, a young Frankfurt SDS activist who had analyzed the social structural dimensions of the Berkeley and Berlin student revolts in *neue kritik*.[69] His election as chairman signaled a fundamental change, away from programs and parties and toward movements and participation. Now, the anti-authoritarian majority transformed SDS into a real social movement with all sorts of public actions and campaigns.

In Frankfurt we developed two sorts of campaigns that soon spread all over the country. On the one hand we were highly active in support of anti-imperialist and anticolonial movements in the third world, especially in terms of our opposition to the U.S. war in Vietnam. The other dimension was the everyday experience of the younger generation to which our actions were directed. As already mentioned, we founded the first anti-authoritarian kindergartens and supported new movements of high school students and of young apprentices in their opposition against authoritarian structures and sexual morals. Amendt's and Reiche's books on sexual liberation sold many hundreds of thousands of copies.[70] We conducted sit-ins in the universities and on tramway rails, occupied empty houses as part of the squatters movement, and welcomed both the sexual revolution and the rise of late 1960s feminism, including those protests directed against male leaders of SDS. From Berlin came the more spectacular political actions. Very soon, the protests against the Shah of Iran and against America's war in Vietnam made the German student movement a mass phenomenon, one that could challenge the established social and political powers until at least the 1980s, and even then remained a force that stood in opposition to the neoliberal rollback of the decades that followed.

This enormous escalation of participatory movements of all kinds cannot be explained, in unilateral fashion, as the mere product of voluntaristic group activism. To understand this big success as well as its setbacks, we must turn to the experience of the younger generation as it was mediated through the deeper changes then taking place in the fundamental structure of society. Our experience as activists in the early and mid-1960s had taught us modesty. We came to understand that ideology and leadership in and of themselves had little power to change the world. In Germany from 1960 on, the ingredients—the ideas and potential leaders—for a radical oppositional movement were present, but they could not get a wider hearing until after 1965, when other changes also came to our country. The spectacular student rebellions of the late 1960s were therefore only the tip of a huge iceberg. The base of the iceberg that drifted to scratch the keel of the *Titanic* was much wider. The mobilization of actors with very different backgrounds in many different countries arose entirely spontaneously and in an uncoordinated manner. They can be explained not by mere intellectual insemination, but only by understanding the parallel structural changes then taking place within many of the advanced capitalist countries in the two decades after World War II. As the class structure shifted, so too would the experience of everyday life and the political culture in which radicals, in both Germany and the United States, sought a wider influence.

Opening the Field of Political Action

In Germany, these changes coincided with a remarkable political opening for the left. Here, we find a striking contrast to the experience of the United States. When reading the historic outlines on the 1960s written by Todd Gitlin, Dick Flacks, and Tom Hayden,[71] I was again shocked by that series of demoralizing political setbacks that took place during that decade. These started with the assassination of John F. Kennedy in 1963, the subsequent refusal of the Democratic Party to incorporate into its structure the political wing of the civil rights movement, and the progressive entanglement of President Lyndon B. Johnson in the Vietnam War. In 1968 hope was again destroyed when, a few months after Martin Luther King's assassination, Robert Kennedy too was assassinated. Because the Democratic Party could not mobilize its progressive potential, a Republican, Richard Nixon, became president. And this came only two years after Ronald Reagan, who was to crush the student movement at Berkeley, was elected governor in California.

Developments in Germany formed a striking contrast to this demoralizing sequence of setbacks in the United States. Until the 1970s or even the 1980s, many authoritarian initiatives could be turned into public mobilizations that significantly enlarged the ground for alternative politics. This pattern showed itself first in 1962, when the conservative government's arrest of editors at the liberal weekly *Der Spiegel*—on a charge of treason for their investigative reporting on security issues—provoked an outcry that led to an expansion of civil liberties and a shift away from Federal Germany's authoritarian political culture. Thus, in October 1963 Chancellor Konrad Adenauer was forced to resign. With him fell the architect and symbol of authoritarian conservatism. While social space would soon be closed for the American movements, it opened in Germany.

The pattern repeated itself in 1967 when, during the student protests against the visit of the Shah of Iran in Berlin, a police bullet killed a student, Benno Ohnesorg. This event was followed by an avalanche of direct student and civic protest actions in Germany and other European countries. The same dynamic reappeared in the spring of 1968 when the Berlin student leader, Rudi Dutschke, was killed. There were huge blockades against the Springer press, the stronghold of conservative attacks against the radical student movement. But, in contrast to the right-wing backlash that followed the antiwar protests at the 1968 Democratic National Convention in Chicago, comparatively few government reprisals, legal or political, were launched against the young German left. Instead, the German movements translated into new political majorities in regional elections, especially in Willy Brandt's great electoral victories in 1969 and even more sweeping in 1972, just one year after the Chancellor was awarded a Nobel Prize for peace that reduced the possibility of a Cold War confrontation in Europe.

How had this been possible? Of course, the burning memory of the incredible crimes in Germany's Nazi past, had, by mobilizing international and national public opinion, in the long run inhibited a return of outright right-wing extremist politics in Federal Germany. Moreover, the new conservatism designed by Adenauer, though gradual and incremental, had done much to replace German nationalism with a European integration project, while at the same time taming a capitalist economy through the construction of a robust, though conservative welfare state that offered the working class a set of participatory rights in industry governance.

This political context helped to open a space for New Left action in Germany after 1960. Because there was not such a sustained and successful backlash from the right or from the conservative center, the strivings of the social movements could be increasingly translated into influence in democratic institutions. Thus did movement activists become increasingly well organized in the left-wing youth section of the Social Democratic Party, the Young Socialists or so-called Jusos. They determinedly pursued anti-authoritarian, participatory politics and successfully began to conquer many sections of the party. This had already started in Frankfurt very early, in 1961, when the Jusos had helped elect Hans Matthöfer, the protagonist of participatory trade union politics, to the Bundestag. This policy accelerated from the mid-1960s on, resulting in the growth of a strong, mainly

Juso-based left wing in the SPD and in the Social Democratic factions of the Federal and State parliaments. This was combined with a successful mobilization of the liberal intelligentsia—journalists, writers, actors, film makers, and so on, as C. Wright Mills had envisaged.

This joint liberal and left mobilization was the precondition for Willy Brandt's huge progressive electoral victories in in 1969 and 1972, which, as many of us thought, paralleled the Kennedy presidential election of 1960 and the opening to the left that it symbolized. The Brandt years brought a remarkable expansion of welfare state and civil rights politics. Hans Matthöfer, that old friend of the League for Industrial Democracy, stuck to his antifascist and participatory convictions even when he became a member of the governments of Brandt and of his Social Democratic successor, Helmut Schmidt. Actively supporting the resistance against Franco's fascist regime in Spain, Matthöfer was honored with the nickname "Deputy of Barcelona." In 1973, when he was parliamentary secretary in the Ministry of Economic Co-operation, he publicly attacked the military putschists of Chile as a "gang of murderers"—and helped many people to get out of Chile with the assistance of the German embassy. In 1974, he became minister of research and technology, launching a huge research program on the "humanization of work" designed to expand employees' rights and participation; it also had lasting effects in creating influential research institutes of industrial and labor sociology.

Like the Swedish developments of the early 1970s, German changes at that same time also translated a considerable number of movement aims into legislation, ending legal discrimination of women and the criminalization of homosexuality and of abortion; enlarging the participatory rights of pupils, apprentices, and students; expanding and opening schools and universities for the popular classes; raising welfare state benefits; and increasing employee rights in the workplace. But there were also politics of containment. Under Brandt, measures were taken to keep so-called extremists out of educational institutions.

After Brandt's resignation, from 1974 to 1982, the governments of the right-wing Social Democratic Chancellor, Helmut Schmidt, systematically continued these containment politics. Students' and employees' rights to participate in the self-government of universities were cancelled. Also, the Mitbestimmungsgesetz of 1976 was a brake and containment on employees' participation in management—because managers now received seats on the employees' bench in the administrative boards. The right-wing majority of the SPD defended the construction of nuclear power plants and, in the late 1970s, cooperated with the United States to develop highly controversial plans to station medium-range nuclear missiles on German soil.

As a consequence, the left and liberal forces that had brought Brandt to power now lost influence in the political parties, but they gained much additional ground in the growing social movements, in the alternative youth cultures and in the liberal public opinion and mass media. The liberal-left current was a loose connection of individuals and groups. But its left part had an organizational nucleus, the Socialist Bureau (SB), located in Offenbach near Frankfurt. Founded in 1969, it took the role the SDS had fulfilled until its disintegration which began in 1968 and ended with its formal self-dissolution in 1971. The SB united the undogmatic left activists who had worked in the SDS, in the Easter marches, and in the labor youth organizations since the early 1960s. It coordinated people through a monthly journal, published several magazines directed to specific professional groups like the social workers and the labor union activists, and organized numerous public initiatives and direct actions through which an increasing number of writers, journalists, and other intellectuals, including Nobel laureate Heinrich Böll, were mobilized.

Although the German left was often divided in the 1970s, it was not defeated or marginalized. Because of its New Left principles, its commitment to participatory democracy and nonviolence, the Socialist Bureau found rising general support for its programs. This enabled the political tendency to join forces with the left-liberal mainstream when, after the 1973 oil crisis, rising civic mobilizations were caused by the ecological and social risks of modernization and growth, recurring unemployment, insufficient civic rights and participation, urban and infrastructural problems, and nuclear armament and energy. And of course, with its participatory principles, the SB current also constituted an attractive alternative to the Maoists and the terrorist cells that had arisen at the end of the 1960s. When, after 1977, these fundamentalist groups collapsed, the SB current gained an uncontested hegemony on the left. From 1979 to the early 1980s a huge peace, intercultural, antinuclear, and ecological movement arose, often linked to feminist and multicultural initiatives and even a "second youth revolt." It was widely supported by the growing left currents in the churches, in the labor unions, and among liberal opinion leaders.

This progress provoked an escalation of the existing conflicts between the different wings inside the established political parties. In these confrontations the movement activists began to form their own political camp, separated by deep cleavages from the old party majorities. Since 1980, they began to form a separate "Green" party that soon commanded a stable electorate of between 5 and 10 percent of the voters. Many movement sympathizers also remained inside the old parties, forming strong "green" wings, especially within the SPD. Simultaneously, civic participation was professionalized and institutionalized. Acceptance by the left part of the mainstream implied an increase of political realism, of institutionalization, and of adapting utopian idealism to practical, everyday ways of life.

This progress, however, also provoked more countermobilizations from the right, encouraged by the electoral victories of Margaret Thatcher in Britain and Reagan in the United States. The Free Democratic Party became the spearhead of neoliberalism in Germany. In 1982, it left the government of Helmut Schmidt to form a majority government with the Christian Democrats (CDU) headed by Helmut Kohl until 1998. Kohl promised "a spiritual and moral turn," but, as in the decades before, German development took a course that differed markedly from the British and U.S. developments. Welfare state securities were eroded too, but at a much slower pace, due to the counterpressure of the labor unions as well as the labor wing and voters of the CDU itself. Also, the return to authoritarian politics (in the fields of gender, immigration, civil rights, democratic participation, ecology, and foreign politics) was limited by strong counterpressures from the "Greens" and the "green" wings in all political camps.

The scales were tipped only gradually toward the neoliberal side, but they were tipped continuously, especially from the 1990s on. After 1989, the external confrontations that had given the alternative and New Left currents in Germany their attraction and their energy were replaced by another set of political constellations. The Cold War was over and so too, it now seemed, virtually any alternative to global capitalism. For a time a neoliberal current proved near hegemonic. But much remained of the democratic culture generated by the participatory New Left in the 1960s: with its large milieu basis, that current retained its role as one factor among a plurality of camps in a united twenty-first-century Germany.

PART IV

Lessons and Legacies

Chapter 12

Did We Learn How to Make Participatory Collectives Work?

Jane Mansbridge

The experience of participatory democracy after the Port Huron Statement holds several lessons for activists today. It is true that the conditions today are different, but the transcendent goals of the Statement still capture the imagination and the heart. It is also true that the practice of participatory democracy that developed after the Statement went far beyond what its framers intended. But that practice—of "horizontal," direct assembly, egalitarian, consensus democracy, inspired by the Port Huron goals has nevertheless become standard, first in participatory collectives in the United States in the 1970s and later in many emerging radical collectives around the world, in sharp contrast to traditional nineteenth- and early twentieth-century practices on the left.

The practices of direct assembly, egalitarian, consensus democracy have considerable advantages in mobilization, because they have the potential to bring into participation as equals many whose primary experience in politics has been one of marginalization. The euphoria of being "heard" for the first time and exercising "power with" on an equal basis with others energizes and transforms the participants. On the less positive side, these features also have the problems of taking much time and often failing to deliver on the promises, implied or explicit, of absolute equality and unanimity. These practices of participatory democracy thus usually require some thinking through as collectives move from mobilization to continuing work.

Stepping back reflectively from the practices that followed from the Port Huron Statement, I suggest here that its goals may be pursued most effectively by tailoring the practices of participatory equality and consensus to the context, pursuing political equality when it is most important to preserve equal respect, produce opportunities for individual development, and protect conflicting interests, and pursuing consensus when it is most important to assure commitment and unity, engage the previously marginalized, get answers right, and give assured power to permanent minorities. We still need to identify ways of pursuing the goals best while reducing the costs, and ways to transition effectively from moments of high mobilization to moments of more routinized work.

Differences and Similarities: Then and Now

When we compare the era of the Port Huron Statement with conditions now in the United States, the first big difference is that in the 1960s, the economy was booming. When I was a graduate student getting a Ph.D. in 1962, I did not worry about taking time off from my studies for activism. My fallback position if I did not finish my dissertation was to make sandals in Harvard Square. The need for a professional job was not pressing. It simply was nowhere in our minds that there might not always be readily available low-paying, relatively interesting jobs that would let you pay the rent now and perhaps lead to better paying jobs later.

Second, the adolescent bulge was beginning at the time of the Port Huron Statement. By 1975, the number of individuals aged fifteen to twenty-five was bigger in the population pyramid of the United States than it had ever been before or is likely to be again. Culturally and politically, young people had come into their own.

The sense of affluence and power that began with the Port Huron Statement's sense of being "bred in at least modest comfort"[1] and continued into the economic boom of the late 1960s could not be more different from today. In the Boston Occupy demonstration of March 15, 2012, one hand-lettered sign, carried by a college-aged young woman, read: "The light at the end of the tunnel has been turned off." The Occupy protests were sparked at least in part by this despair. Political scientists call this pattern the "J curve"—a significant downturn after a long expansion—and it is sometimes the spark for revolution.[2] If today is a time for revolution, it will be a revolution fueled by despair, not hope.

The similarities between the eras have more to do with participatory movement dynamics, particularly the internal dynamics of participatory organization. The Occupy movement and other contemporary movements use consensus and direct assembly procedures that developed first in the small participatory democracies inspired by the Port Huron Statement, then evolved further in the women's movement, in the anti-antinuclear movement, in the alter-globalization movement, and most recently in the "horizontalist" movements in Latin America, in the European and World Social Forums, and in movements such as 15M in Spain (named from its first call to action on the fifteenth of May in 2011 and also called the *Indignados,* against the new austerity policies). New participatory procedures, such as hand gestures like "twinkling" that facilitate communication and consensus in large groups, developed abroad and then played an important role in the 2011 Occupy movement in the United States.[3] Occupy added its own innovation, the "people's mic," in which everyone within hearing repeats loudly what the speaker says every few words. This technique not only lets the speaker be heard but also, incidentally, makes each speaker's contribution more concise, brings attention to each individual's speech, and provides a kind of affirmation and respect even in the midst of disagreement. Refinements such as these, developed over the years, have supplemented but not replaced the basic dynamics of direct assembly con sensus democracy developed in the participatory collectives of the late 1960s and early 1970s, which were inspired by the Port Huron Statement's "search for truly democratic alternatives to the present, and a commitment to social experimentation with them."[4]

The participatory collectives that arose in the decade after the Port Huron Statement differed from Occupy in one basic organizational respect. The Occupy encampments were not collectives aimed at accomplishing any defined piece of work. They were mobilization efforts, drawing into intense interaction anyone with the time and inclination to be drawn. Their general assemblies were open to all, and they did not expect to continue in any given form or with any given collection of people for any set period. They were open-ended in composition, in content, and in their time horizons. By contrast, almost all of the participatory collectives in the early 1970s had specific tasks they wanted to accomplish and made decisions that bound their members. Still, the Occupy decisions—made by direct assembly and consensus, like the decisions of many of today's more spontaneously formed protest movements—were intended to bind those who continued in the camp, at least until those assembled made a conflicting decision. To the degree that Occupiers saw their procedures as applicable to more permanent organizations and as prefiguring future democratic possibilities,[5] the lessons from the participatory collectives of the "long Sixties" may be helpful.

In the late 1960s and early 1970s, young people had hope and time. Real change seemed possible. Thousands of participatory collectives formed across the country. Free schools, food co-ops, bike repair collectives, legal collectives, drug counseling collectives, women's centers—all hoped to change and prefigure the future by creating the "democratic alternatives" that the Statement had called for. These collectives made their decisions by "participatory democracy," by which their members meant a combination of direct face-to-face assembly democracy and consensus decision making, with the goal of equality in the process.

Yet the collectives often ran into organizational trouble. In Boston from 1967 to 1973, I belonged to a food co-op and two feminist collectives, and had many friends in free schools, legal co-ops, and other participatory collectives. In many of these collectives I saw bitter fights over some taking informal positions of leadership and others not feeling sufficiently included. Many broke up under mutual recriminations about the "power trips" of some and the insufficient commitments of others. I saw collectives ground to a halt by individuals who stubbornly held out against consensus. But I also saw people included who would never have been so active in a traditional organization with majority votes and a president, vice president, secretary, and treasurer. I could see in others and feel in myself the engagement and excitement of making decisions so directly.

Based in those experiences, my research for *Beyond Adversary Democracy* had in its DNA a self-help manual for participatory democrats.[6] My minimal goal in that work was to reduce to some degree the mutual recriminations that so often tore apart the groups I knew by showing that all groups with these ends faced the same structural problems.[7] In the end, based on what the people I had interviewed had told me, I concluded that the problems of many participatory collectives were conceptual as well as structural. The problems stemmed not only from the practical difficulties of making decisions by consensus and with the aim of absolute equality among members, but also from a conceptual failure that derived from mapping assumptions taken from the democracy of the nation-state onto the democracy of a small group.

Research in Two Working Participatory Democracies

At the beginning of my research, having decided that a "best-case" strategy would yield the most useful results, I set out to find such best cases, and after many preliminary observations settled on a town meeting in a small Vermont town that I call "Selby" and an urban drug hotline that I call "Helpline." The town was the only one I found in which the middle class did not dominate. The workplace was the only one I found that was both highly participatory and highly functional—and it has lasted to this day, although with a new mandate to provide services for low-income people. In both places I observed meetings, collected archival data, and interviewed the members—one of every five adults in a town of about 350 adults and all but one of the forty-one members of the workplace.

I looked most closely at the patterns of inequality and the quality of deliberation. Regarding equality, I found that in the town, the patterns of attendance at its direct assembly were somewhat more equal on the dimension of class than the patterns of attendance in voting in national elections. Yet although this little town with only one paved town road was predominantly working class, the *upper* working class—of, for example, self-employed plumbers and carpenters—participated noticeably more than the *lower* working class—of, for example, people whose farms were very small or who worked for minimum wages on a non-unionized assembly line. So although this was the most egalitarian town meeting I could find, attendance at the meeting was still correlated with the assessed valuation of one's house and men spoke notably more than women at the meeting.[8]

In Helpline, the alternative workplace, the members were so committed to participatory equality that, in addition to taking equal salaries, they spent an average of seven paid hours—almost a whole day—per week in meetings. Yet even after all this effort, when at the end of the interview I asked each member of the group to distribute the names of all the members around a bulls-eye I'd drawn with a "center of power" in the middle, all of the thirty-three who participated in this exercise distributed the names unequally around the concentric circles. (One of the nonparticipants insisted that the distribution was equal.) On a questionnaire I distributed, reporting oneself as relatively low in "say" and "power" in the organization had a significant relationship with both class and gender.[9]

In short, in neither the town nor the alternative workplace was participatory democracy the cure for inequalities of class and gender. The quality of deliberation reflected these inequalities. In both the town meeting and the workplace, the less educated and the women talked less often. Qualitatively, those people also seemed to fear humiliation more and be more easily silenced. These class and gender dynamics arose even in a workplace collective composed of only forty-one people who worked together, were highly committed to equality, broke each meeting down into small groups, and implemented many exercises for creating equality, building community, and breaking down barriers.

What lessons can be learned from these two direct assembly democracies? I will address here primarily the lessons to be learned from efforts to achieve equality in power and efforts to decide by consensus. Trying to reduce inequality to the absolute minimum is expensive—in time, effort, and other costs to the system. Trying to produce absolute consensus is also expensive in time, effort, and the potential for deadlock. The most general lesson we can learn is contextual—when to expend the efforts required for greater equality or more full and genuine consensus, and when not to expend as much effort in these directions. To learn these lessons, we need to see equal power and consensus not as ends in themselves but as means to deeper ends. When the means do not conduce to those ends, those means lose much of their value.

Equal Power

Equal power, I argue, is usually implicitly valued, and should be valued, not as an end in itself but as a means to the three important ends of equal respect, personal development, and the protection of interests.[10] If this is the case, it will not usually be worth paying the costs of pushing for greater equality if a collective has already established relationships of equal respect, opportunities for personal development, and, on important issues, common interests or relatively common interests among the members.

The first, and probably most important, end is equal respect. In every culture friendship is based on equal respect, and since at least the ancient Greeks, friendship has been the informal, everyday model for good participatory democracies.[11] But unequal power can undermine equal respect. In contexts where unequal power threatens to undermine equal respect in a collective, participatory democrats have good reason to pursue greater equality in power in order to make respect more equal.

Sometimes the desires of some people to run things ("power trips" in the language of the 1960s) make others feel less than equal and weaken the solidarity of a collective based implicitly on the equal respect of friendship. Yet sometimes the sources of respect in an organization have little to do with power. In academic departments, for example, the greatest respect may derive from good scholarship, while the department chair gets relatively little respect simply from having more power. At Helpline, the greatest respect derived from doing a good job on the street with the people Helpline worked with—being a good therapist, counselor, or first responder. It did not derive from being an administrator, although the administrators in the collective in fact had more informal power. Because respect was so closely tied to accomplishing the immediate goals of the organization, the good therapists, counselors, and first responders got far more respect than the administrators. In short, if a collective already has many sources of mutual respect, it may not need to equalize power in order to equalize respect.

The second important reason for trying to equalize power in a participatory collective is so that each can develop as fully as possible within that organization. Participation in our polity and in our workplaces helps us develop what the Port Huron Statement called our "unfulfilled capacities for reason, freedom, and love" and our "unrealized potential for self-cultivation, self-direction, self-understanding, and creativity."[12] Here too, however, a collective may already provide many opportunities for developing these important potentials—through the work itself as well as through participation in decision making. When opportunities to develop lie around waiting to be picked up, the collective does not need to equalize power even more in order to provide full opportunities to develop. Some efforts to make participation more equal may even undermine other possibilities for members to realize their potential through their work. Time spent in participation may well subtract from time spent in activities that might develop one's potential more.[13]

This second goal—the developmental goal—of participation was extremely important both in the Port Huron Statement and in the work of the early theorists of participatory democracy—for example, Arnold Kaufman, the young and brilliant philosopher at the University of Michigan whose life was cut short in a plane crash and whose thinking influenced the Statement. In 1960, Kaufman first articulated the principles of participatory democracy. He coined the term "participatory democracy" (along with the term "deliberative democracy," which did not come into general use until much later). In his pathbreaking 1960 article, Kaufman wrote that the most significant justifying function of a democracy of participation "is and always has been, not the extent to which it protects or stabilizes a community, but the contribution it can make to the development of human powers of thought, feeling, and action." As he explained, "The main justifying function of participation is the development of man's essential powers—inducing human dignity and respect, and making men responsible by developing their powers of deliberate action."[14] The Port Huron Statement, and after that Carole Pateman and other theorists of participatory democracy, took up and reinforced the point that the primary aim, the main justifying function, of participatory democracy was self-development.[15]

A third reason for equalizing power is a reason—self-protection—that Arnold Kaufman and Carole Pateman explicitly distinguished from the developmental aim of participation and either implicitly or explicitly denigrated. Yet in the actual participatory collectives that emerged in the 1960s, self-protection was a major reason for members' insistence on both high degrees of equality and strict consensus. Fear of the more powerful imposing their interests on the less powerful drove in great part the continuing insistence in many collectives that the distribution of power was never equal enough. Then as now, members of participatory collectives often insist on as much equality as possible because they do not trust any representatives—formal or informal—not to betray them. That sense of distrust was palpable, for example, when I attended the General Assembly of Boston Occupy on November 17, 2011, when it was deciding whether or not to choose representatives to represent the group in the negotiations with the city over leaving the encampment.

In a group that has primarily common interests, however, this self-protective function of equal power is not so necessary. On issues of relatively common interest, the *self-protective* reasons for equal power lose their force. Indeed, an insistence on equalizing power more and more can be counterproductive by taking time and energy away from other activities that could help the members promote their individual and collective interests. Because in practice the members of many small participatory collectives do have relatively common interests on many issues that come before them for decision, it is often not useful to insist on political equality in those moments.

In sum, although participatory collectives reject the majority rule and representative government of the larger society, they often paradoxically import into their small communities of relatively common interest assumptions from national politics—of conflicting interests, and therefore the need for self-protection—that do not apply greatly in a small and relatively homogeneous collective. Recalibrating to their own contexts, participatory groups can save the stress and effort of equalizing power for the three moments when inequalities of power are most likely to (1) generate unequal respect, (2) curtail the possibilities for every member's full development, and (3) permit dominance in situations of conflicting interests. Collectives can use those criteria to judge in any given context whether or not the unequal power of some actually undermines equal respect, the capacity of others to run things if they want to, and the capacity of all to protect their interests when that protection is important.

Consensus

The use of consensus also is more or less important for democracy depending on the context. Consensus has several advantages. It increases commitment (because each individual "owns" the policy by agreeing to it personally), promotes unity (because no policy can be adopted without the active acquiescence of every member), reassures the previously marginalized by guaranteeing a form of respect for each individual (because it gives each person a veto), and encourages listening (because the threat of a veto creates incentives to hear each individual out and try to understand what each means), which in turn illuminates differences and divergent opinions, elicits new information, facilitates mutual understanding, and produces more accurate outcomes. Finally, consensus protects minority input and interests.

Consensus also has several disadvantages. It gives great weight to the status quo, which always benefits one subgroup more than another. It also

takes time, creates anxiety and anger when time is short, sometimes prevents the full recognition of dissent, and creates incentives for several
undemocratic or dysfunctional patterns: socially coercing recalcitrant
members, devising verbal formulas that obscure existing divisions, and
using the potential veto as a bargaining chip. Given these advantages and
disadvantages, consensus can be more or less useful to participatory collectives depending on the context, which may vary widely. I list some of the
most important contextual needs below.

1. Commitment
   A group often needs consensus functionally when it will ask sacrifices
   of its members.[16] Full and genuine agreement is particularly important in, for example, a nonviolent action facing arrest, where the
   defection of a few might unravel the will of those on the fence and
   the defection of the fence-sitters may then undermine the will of the
   group as a whole. As Bob Ross points out, consensus can be critically
   important "when the stakes are extremely high, and the members of
   the group risk legal or physical jeopardy."[17]

2. Unity
   A group also needs consensus functionally when its members must
   present a united front formally. An academic department might need
   unanimity in taking a case to the dean or a political party in taking
   a presidential candidate to the people. In Helpline, one of the cases
   I studied, some members had the job of caring for the young children of drug users. The children exploited divisions among the caregivers when those caregivers had not previously agreed on their
   policy through genuine consensus.

3. Past experiences with oppression
   Members with past experiences of being disempowered often find
   the individual veto that consensus provides reassuring and empowering. Such a veto is both self-protective and encouraging, giving a
   voice to those who have not in the past had such voice.[18] The original
   activists in SDS who hammered out the Port Huron Statement
   mostly had some political experience and at least in some cases were
   not intimidated by Robert's Rules of Order.[19] Less experienced members may need not only the protection of the veto and the respect
   that it symbolizes and enforces, but also the developmental benefits
   and skills that the experience of consensus can teach. Many have

found experience with consensus a "source of transformation in their lives, a place where they learned to use their 'voice' and identify and demand their personal 'needs.'"[20] A good consensus process can teach each participant to understand better what he or she really wants and needs, along with the kind of patience that develops from tolerance rather than powerlessness, the greater understanding of others' needs, wants, strengths, and foibles, and the capacity for seeing which elements of what another can give can meet one's own needs. A history of oppression may not have allowed members to develop such skills.

Far short of a history of oppression, everyday experiences with standard majority-rule democracy (despite its parliamentary procedures having often been designed to protect minorities and facilitate deliberation) may have led many participants in those processes to perceive democracy as boring, manipulable by elites, and an arena primarily for those who like that sort of thing. One woman Argentinian activist reported in 2004: "I think back to previous activist experiences I had and remember a powerful feeling of submission." By contrast, the consensus and direct democracy of the new "horizontal" organization in which she was participating gave her a feeling of freedom and the capacity "to enjoy myself."[21]

4. High costs of not listening or being wrong

   Whenever it is crucial to bring out information from all participants, the listening that consensus promotes increases in value. The same dynamic applies when the costs of being wrong are high. In a murder trial, for example, where the penalty is life imprisonment or death, the greater accuracy derived from requiring consensus is usually worth the extra time and the possibility of deadlock.

5. Permanent minorities

   Whenever a group has permanent minorities that under majority rule will lose every time, consensus gives the permanent minority a veto and encourages the majority to discover side payments sufficient to produce agreement. To take an example from the scale of the nation-state, in Belgium, French speakers, who tend also to be Catholic and more agriculturally based, would lose under majority rule in every instance involving their major cultural and economic interests to the Dutch-speaking Protestant industrial majority. They thus build forms of consensus into their democracies. Segmented societies that govern themselves through various forms of consensus usually achieve that consensus not by insisting on substantive agreement in every case but by allowing "side payments," in which a package that gives something to everyone can be agreed upon by all.[22]

6. Low contextual costs

Just as the benefits of consensus vary by context, so do its costs. The costs of consensus are lowest when the status quo is acceptable, there is sufficient time for decision making, the group is small, common interests are likely, the group is experienced in consensus or has good facilitators, the group has low turnover, and within the consensual process some institutions (such as facilitation) are designed to bring out conflict.[23]

Conclusion

After the clarion call of the Port Huron Statement for a "search for truly democratic alternatives to the present, and a commitment to social experimentation with them," participatory collectives of many kinds emerged and continue to emerge in the United States, Europe, and Latin America. These collectives have developed over the years an international set of conventions and practices for encouraging participation and facilitating democratic equality. These practices were not envisioned by the original framers of the Port Huron Statement,[24] but their tenacity, spread, and elaboration suggest that they emerged not only from the fantasies of journalists or the simple mistakes of the inexperienced, but also because they have many benefits, particularly in certain contexts. The claim that these practices of participatory democracy are the best and purest forms of democracy is simply incorrect.[25] These forms are, it is true, the original form of democracy, very probably practiced for 98 percent of human existence by the males in hunter-gatherer tribes. They are also the form that people often adopt quickly in small informal groups with common interests. They are the form that many indigenous and relatively small groups still practice today. But democracy is a practice that incorporates many values, and the various versions that have evolved to accommodate relatively egalitarian decision making in extremely large groups such as nation-states incorporate practices crafted to capture many of these values, including those of equality, freedom, and non-manipulation about which the members of participatory collectives care most deeply. These large-scale forms of democracy do not derive simply from elite manipulation over the centuries, and they are to some degree open to reform.

Each generation can invent practices that bring the human capacity to do democracy closer to our goals. I argue here that those practices usually vary, and should vary, by the function of any given collective and by the context. The Occupy movement, which stressed mobilization rather than organizational continuity, adopted not only direct assembly democracy and consensus but also the new international consensus signals, which allow large numbers of people to participate meaningfully even while only one speaks at a time. The intensely participatory procedures of the Occupy movement also generated a commitment, creativity, and excitement that brought the facts about inequality in the United States to the public with unprecedented speed. As Occupy grew and began to have difficulties making binding decisions in a large group, it began to have problems in using these procedures to meet its own goals of equality, freedom, and community. As other participatory collectives in the future begin the process of forging their own versions of democracy, it may help to learn from the experiences of the collectives of the "long Sixties," which took their inspiration from the words and some of the underlying spirit of the Port Huron Statement, if not from its drafters' intent. The lessons learned from the experience of that generation's participatory collective practices include those summarized here, suggesting when practices such as trying to achieve highly equal power and consensus bring the greatest benefits and when they have the greatest costs.

Chapter 13

Participatory Democracy and the Fate
of Occupy Wall Street

James Miller

On the afternoon of August 2, 2011, a group of self-selected activists, about sixty in all, met at Bowling Green, a park in downtown Manhattan with the famous bronze statue of a snorting bull, installed in 1989 as a tribute to the financial power of nearby Wall Street.

The people had gathered by the bull in response to a call for a general assembly, to organize an occupation of Wall Street, set to start on September 17. They came from a variety of political backgrounds. Some were students, others were union organizers. There were socialists, but a surprising number were conservatives, libertarians committed to "leaderless resistance" and also allied with Ron Paul. Still more were avowed anarchists, including David Graeber, a fifty-year-old professor of anthropology and a veteran activist.

Expecting an open assembly, Graeber and some friends from 16beaver, a downtown arts collective, discovered instead a group of conventional organizers with megaphones and placards, trying to rally participants for a conventional march that would make conventional demands. In response, Graeber and his group retreated to a corner of the park to discuss alternative steps. Sitting in a circle, they debated how they might better organize a Wall Street occupation. Graeber proposed implementing one of the most radical forms of direct democracy conceivable: a daily general assembly where virtually all decisions would be made without voting, by consensus— and formally subject to veto by a single "block," if anyone felt a proposed decision violated an ethical principle.[1]

It seemed quixotic. But Graeber's vision prevailed. Against all odds, the movement that he helped to launch—Occupy Wall Street—briefly changed the political conversation in America. It compelled the media to pay fresh attention to voices on the left. Despite a lack of explicit demands, it "reignited hope in the possibility of a free society," in part by exemplifying, in the words of one participant, a new world that is "participatory and democratic to the core."[2]

In this way, Occupy Wall Street resurrected a recurring feature of the international left since the 1960s: an overriding commitment to participatory democracy, understood as the making of decisions in a face-to-face community of friends and not through elected representatives.

The brief eruption of Occupy movements around the world offered a welcome reminder that politics is not just about elections and voting; and proof, if proof were needed, that the Port Huron Statement—the 1962 manifesto of Students for a Democratic Society (SDS), which first popularized the ideal of participatory democracy—has left a living legacy, however paradoxical.

As I wrote a quarter-century ago in my book *"Democracy Is in the Streets": From Port Huron to the Siege of Chicago,* perhaps the most important result of the most utopian 1960s experiments with participatory democracy, at least in my view, was to demonstrate "the incompatibility of rule by consensus with accountable, responsible government in a large organization—or even in a small group of people with divergent interests and a limited patience for endless meetings."[3] In fact, the young people who drafted the Port Huron Statement never meant to propose rule-by-consensus as a working definition of participatory democracy—that understanding evolved later in the decade, and was fiercely contested at the time, not least by pragmatic veterans of the Port Huron conference. Yet even this modest lesson about the limits of rule-by-consensus has proved hard to learn, perhaps because, as I also wrote, "for anyone who joined in the search for a democracy of individual participation—and certainly for anyone who remembers the happiness and holds to the hopes that the quest itself aroused—the sense of what politics can mean will never be quite the same again."[4]

The result, for many subsequent groups on the global left, has been an unstable political idealism, an amalgam of direct action and direct democracy, with many of the virtues of a utopian and romantic revolt—passion, moral conviction, a shared joy in the joining of battle—but also some of the vices: above all, an obsession with directly democratic processes and an addiction to creating ever more intense situations of felt personal liberation, regardless of the wider political ramifications.

Take, for example, the case of the Movement for a New Society—an important model for many subsequent activists committed to a radical understanding of participatory democracy. An offshoot of a Quaker direct action group, the organization, founded in the early 1970s, was inspired by the direct democratic experiments of the Student Nonviolent Coordinating Committee and Students for a Democratic Society in the 1960s, and also by Gandhi's pacifist injunction to "be the change you want to see."[5] A strict adherence to rule by consensus became perhaps the group's most distinctive feature, its preferred means of acting and also an end in itself, because organizing direct actions via consensus was *the* way (indeed, perhaps the only way) to show that direct democracy, individual freedom, and a society based on principles of solidarity are possible in practice.

The problem, as George Lakey, the tutelary spirit of Movement for a New Society, ruefully acknowledged in retrospect (the group dissolved in 1988), was that rule by consensus had some perverse consequences. "While an organization is new and vital," Lakey remarked years later, "consensus decision-making can be valuable for encouraging unity. In the longer run, however, consensus can be a conservative influence, stifling the prospects of organizational change"—not least because any one person can "block" any change that is proposed.[6] At the same time, an obsession with the purity of the process of participation slowly but surely began to erode the group's capacity to engage constructively with the larger social and economic world, in part by crippling its capacity to exploit the full range of political tactics in a democracy, from protests to the mechanics of electioneering.

Veterans of the Movement for a New Society, and activists inspired by its example, played key roles in organizing the anti–World Trade Organization demonstrations in Seattle in 1999—and they also played large roles in the Occupy Wall Street movement in 2011. Though the general assemblies that became the hallmark of the Occupy movement were not uniformly organized in every single city, most of them followed characteristic rules that were meant, in part, to solve some of the problems that had arisen in previous direct democratic experiments.[7]

Avowedly anti-authoritarian, nonhierarchical, and leaderless, the OWS assemblies generally adhered to rule-by-consensus as an end in itself and as the best way to show that direct democracy really is workable. The assemblies were avowedly free associations: they were formally open to *any*one, no matter his or her political, ethnic, or religious affiliation. In principle, anyone might join and participate, just as anyone might exit at any time. The assemblies thus enshrined, in a radical form, the autonomy of each individual in the association: "Every person is free to do as they wish."[8]

While the freedom of the individual was in principle inviolable in the assemblies, another goal was to forge, through consensus, a new form of *collective* freedom. Naturally, the assemblies could not hope to realize this goal without some help. Since leaders were not formally acknowledged, help took the form of so-called facilitators, individuals trained to foster what one guide to the process called "Collective Thinking," a form of thinking

> diametrically opposed to the kind of thinking propounded by the present system. When faced with a decision, the normal response of two people with differing opinions tends to be confrontational. They each defend their opinions with the aim of convincing their opponent, until their opinion has won or, at most, a compromise has been reached. The aim of Collective Thinking, on the other hand, is to construct. That is to say, two people with differing ideas work together to build something new. The onus is therefore not on my idea or yours; rather it is the notion that two ideas together will produce something new, something that neither of us had envisaged beforehand. This focus requires of us that we actively listen.[9]

If a single person blocks consensus, the group must listen even more carefully and seek to find common ground in a way that might win over the individual with objections; "Prejudice and ideology must be left at home." Another goal was to forge a "new subjectivity," expressed in a new form of political speech.[10]

In its first few weeks of existence, in the fall of 2011, the New York City General Assembly seemed to succeed in some of its most utopian objectives: as supporters of OWS chanted in the street, "This is what democracy looks like!"

The joy of collectively creating a new political space was palpable in the earliest firsthand accounts of those who occupied Zuccotti Park on September 17: "If you want to see what real democracy, run horizontally, with full participation, looks like, you should be here," wrote one Occupier the next day.[11] Here was a real, and striking, alternative to simply pulling levers to choose between candidates selected in advance by others, and often selected precisely in order to defend the interests of an oligarchic elite. "There is an energy and an amazing consensus process working with 50+ people in general assembly several times a day," wrote another participant a few days later, marveling at how the group was successfully "making decisions about how to run the occupation—from when to do marches, to how to communicate, to ideas about food, art, entertainment, and all kind of issues that anyone can bring up."[12]

The first surge of enthusiasm gradually waned. As time passed and the Occupiers dug in, the general assembly in New York became bogged down in logistical details. A great deal of time and energy was devoted to making sure the Occupiers had sleeping bags and food and were able to clear garbage from the site. Meetings often lasted for hours. To keep the assembly moving, the facilitators became ever more forceful in setting an agenda and limiting the scope of debate. Sometimes the group resorted to a form of "modified consensus," which instead of unanimity required a supermajority of at least two-thirds. Even then, anyone had a right to veto a proposal if a participant felt it violated some fundamental principle that might cause them to quit the group.

Effective decision making on many matters, both logistical and political, simultaneously devolved to a number of decentralized "working groups" that met separately and fell under the effective control of various individuals who assumed de facto power within the movement. (As David Graeber has explained, "Consensus only works if working groups or collectives don't feel they need to seek constant approval from the larger group, if initiative arises from below.")[13] The groups working on direct action naturally put a premium on solidarity and discretion, not an open airing of doubts and disagreements. (At a New School occupation in November 2011, for example, the direct action working group that planned the occupation worked largely in secret and effectively functioned as a cadre controlled by vanguard activists, with no formal accountability to the school's general assembly.)

In an effort to acknowledge such problems, the general assembly in Zuccotti Park voted to institute an Operational "Spokes Council," which began to meet regularly in November 2011, on nights when the general assembly was not in session. In this way, among others, the occupation in New York City by the end of 2011 had slowly turned from "experiences of visionary inspiration," in the words of David Graeber, to "a much slower, painstaking struggle of creating alternative institutions."[14]

This process in turn virtually ground to a halt in the early months of 2012, as small groups of neo-anarchists, most notably those active in Oakland, California, and those in New York City inspired by the Oakland Occupation, kept searching for confrontational experiences of visionary inspiration—at the time, it seemed as if the painstaking task of creating a sustainable movement had proved too painful, and boringly pragmatic, for many followers who had been inspired by Occupy Wall Street in its early months.[15] Even worse, the police department in cities like New York proved adept at infiltrating various groups working on direct action, and arresting activists before they could act. A planned May Day blockade of New York City's bridges and tunnels failed to materialize—and after a brief, last hurrah in September 2012, New York City's utopian experiment in rule-by-consensus was effectively finished—the latest in a long line of failures on the international left to elaborate new forms of horizontal self-governance that can transcend the consensus model and solve some of its manifold problems.

The first and perhaps most obvious problem is scale. It is one thing to create a participatory community of 500 or 1,000—or even a democracy of 40,000 direct participants, as the Athenians did in the fifth and fourth centuries B.C. It is quite another thing to imagine direct, participatory interaction in large and complex societies on the scale of the United States. Perhaps one can envision a federation of nested assemblies, but any serious effort to implement such a structure will require a delegation of authority and the selection of representatives—in short, the creation of an *indirect* democracy, much more intricate and extensive than the Spokes Council, and at some distance from most participants.[16]

Even more challenging is the fact that many of the protesters' concerns—for example, systemic debt, structural unemployment, the unfettered power of finance capital, global warming—involve dilemmas that can be addressed best by new forms of global and transnational regulation and governance, not by local assemblies.

It is also true that the self-selected participants in these general assemblies represented but a tiny fraction of the 99 percent they claimed to embody, if only symbolically. Working people and parents with small children were unlikely and often unable to commit to spending hours on weekday evenings at a general assembly. The most active participants in the movement tended to be white and well educated, which predictably produced collective hand-wringing over the lack of racial and economic diversity.

In any case, the very conditions of the general assembly's existence—it was, after all, a free association of self-selected participants—meant that these experiments in participatory democracy never had to confront seriously the toughest challenge to democratic ideals in a complex and large modern society. That challenge is one of coping with participants who hold radical, often incommensurable differences of opinion, including different views on whether or not social justice requires less income inequality, never mind the abolition of capitalism.

One glance at the world we actually live in should suffice to remind us of the many other things people do *not* share: notably moral beliefs and religious convictions, but also a passion for political participation. (As Hannah Arendt once remarked, one of "the most important negative liberties we have enjoyed since the end of the ancient world" is "freedom from politics, which was unknown to Rome or Athens and which is politically the most relevant part of our Christian heritage.")[17]

The larger a group, the more ineradicable such diversity will be, unless the group is willing to resort to coercion, in an effort to force unity and political participation (as has happened routinely in a great many avowedly democratic and socialist organizations and states over the years).

In other words, I seriously doubt that experiments in rule-by-consensus, like New York's general assembly in the fall of 2011, will *ever* generate the kinds of alternative institutions that are needed to meet the challenges of our current situation. Instead of single-mindedly pursuing a new form of "collective thinking" through endless meetings meant to forge consensus, I think we would do better to explore as well new ways to institute viable forms of modus vivendi—and this will entail fostering a tolerant ethos that accepts, and can acknowledge, that there are many incompatible forms of life, not always democratic or participatory, in which humans can flourish.[18]

Unfortunately, negotiating a modus vivendi with people whose beliefs you deplore, or devising new forms of international cooperation, may well seem boring and dull, certainly in comparison with the pleasures of direct action.

As David Graeber has observed, so-called Black Bloc tactics, including vandalism and street fighting with police, can be heady, even transporting: "It is a way to create one fleeting moment when autonomy is real and immediate, a space of liberated territory, in which the laws and arbitrary power of the state no longer apply, in which we draw the lines of force ourselves."[19] After the "whole world is watching" showdown between police and protesters in Chicago in August 1968, the most militant partisans of participatory democracy, similarly electrified by the feeling of liberation through direct action, heaped scorn on the dreary compromises involved in electoral politics.

This brings me to perhaps the most insidious paradox of participatory democracy, when a movement that pursues its aims through polarizing protests simultaneously demands consensus in its organs of self-government. The paradox unfolds as follows. The success of a polarizing movement hinges on obtaining publicity and sympathetic attention from outsiders. The surest way to obtain such publicity is through demonstrations that prompt a disproportionate and unjust response from the authorities. Meanwhile, back in the general assembly, the demand for consensus willy-nilly puts the most uncompromising militants—including many of those who in fact have spurred the growth of the movement and have become militant activists by taste as well as political conviction—in a position in which they can veto the tactics and strategy proposed by more cautious comrades. The group becomes polarized; but consensus remains the holy grail of the assembly meetings, and the moderates in the group are by definition inclined to compromise. So they silence their reservations—and in some cases simply choose to drop out of the movement. As a result, the consensus view that prevails is generally the most radical alternative on offer (an extreme illustration of what Cass Sunstein has called "the law of group polarization").[20]

Disagreements disappear, at least for public consumption. Indeed, in the New York general assemblies in the fall of 2011, "ideological" disputes were informally discouraged, since any open debate—for example, over the value of Black Bloc tactics or the meaning of the group's ostensible commitment to nonviolent civil disobedience—might undermine the group's solidarity and also, potentially, infringe on the autonomy of the most militant individuals in the association. Although insiders all knew who the most articulate leaders of the different factions were, none of these de facto leaders could be held accountable, since, according to the group's professed principles, there *were* no leaders.

And yet the dream of a more participatory democracy will doubtless survive the latest round of disappointing results, just as it did the setbacks of the 1960s in the United States, and the momentary defeats of the 1990s around the world. Veterans of Occupy Wall Street have already begun to debate the pros and cons of rule of consensus, and to explore other ways to foster a more democratic society.[21]

And who knows? If tomorrow's radical democrats can avoid fetishizing the demand for consensus, and instead elaborate a more nuanced and capacious understanding of what a more participatory democracy can actually mean in practice in a wider range of different institutional contexts, deploying rule-by-consensus only in those few situations where it may be both useful and feasible, a new generation of activists may yet prove able to forge a movement that is broader and open to a greater diversity of opinion: one that is able to build broad coalitions by welcoming advocates of moderation, pragmatism, and tolerance, and not just the voluptuaries of unrestrained direct action and "collective thinking."

In any case, a yearning for radical social change is not going to disappear anytime soon—especially since the injustices and pervasive sense of powerlessness that provoked both the New Left and the Occupy movement still remain unaddressed, more than a half-century after the Port Huron Statement made a democracy of individual participation seem a palpable possibility, if only a new generation could measure up to the task.

Chapter 14

Radical Democracy as a Real Utopia

Erik Olin Wright

Upon rereading the Port Huron Statement for the first time in decades, I was struck by how contemporary much of it sounds. Near the beginning, in the introductory section entitled "Agenda for a Generation," the following appears: "In this is perhaps the outstanding paradox: we ourselves are imbued with urgency, yet the message of our society is that there is no viable alternative to the present . . . beneath the stagnation of those who have closed their minds to the future, is the pervading feeling that there simply are no alternatives, that our times have witnessed the exhaustion not only of Utopias, but of any new departures as well."

A little later the theme continues, perhaps referencing Daniel Bell's *The End of Ideology: On the Exhaustion of Political Ideas in the Fifties*, which had been published just two years earlier: "It has been said that our liberal and socialist predecessors were plagued by vision without program, while our own generation is plagued by program without vision. . . . Theoretic chaos has replaced the idealistic thinking of old—and, unable to reconstitute theoretic order, people have condemned idealism itself. Doubt has replaced hopefulness—and people act out a defeatism that is labeled realistic. The decline of utopia and hope is in fact one of the defining features of social life today."

Today, as in 1962, social and moral progress requires utopian thought embedded in practical action. Since the early 1990s I have been directing a research initiative called the Real Utopias Project. The historical moment for its creation was framed by the demise of the state socialist regimes of Eastern Europe and the rise of neoliberalism. The central objective was to contribute to revitalizing a vision of emancipatory alternatives to dominant institutions in the context of capitalist triumphalism.

In the preface of the first book in the project I wrote the following:

> We now live in a world in which . . . radical visions are mocked rather than taken seriously. Along with the postmodern rejection of "grand narratives" there is an ideological rejection of grand designs, even by those on the left of the political spectrum. This need not mean an abandonment of deeply egalitarian emancipatory values, but it does reflect a cynicism about the human capacity to realize those values on a substantial scale. This cynicism, in turn, weakens progressive political forces in general. The Real Utopias project is an attempt at countering this cynicism by sustaining and deepening serious discussion of radical alternatives to existing institutions.[1]

The idea of "real utopias" is thus animated by the same basic impulse expressed by the crafters of the Port Huron Statement in 1962: we need a way of thinking about social transformation that simultaneously holds on to our deepest utopian aspirations for a just and humane world and embraces the practical tasks and dilemmas of real-world institution-building and thus makes possible new departures. The "real" in real utopia is meant to express two ideas. First, in thinking about institutional designs and experimentation we must be attentive to the problem of the viability of alternatives, not just their desirability, and this means worrying about unintended consequences, self-destructive dynamics, and normative trade-offs. Second, the practical work of emancipatory social transformation should be deeply informed by real-world institutional innovations and experiments that embody, if only in partial and incomplete ways, utopian aspirations.

One crucial task for social research is to study such experiments and innovations to understand the conditions for their replicability and scala-bility as well as their internal limits, dilemmas, and contradictions. What this means is that the vision of an emancipatory alternative to existing structures of domination and inequality is defined not just by idealized future possibilities, but by those relations and practices in the world as it is that prefigure those possibilities. There are many diverse examples in the world today, including:

- Worker cooperatives, in which workers own and manage, through democratic means, the firms in which they work.
- Participatory budgeting, in which the priorities and projects for portions of municipal budgets are determined through direct participation of citizens in neighborhood assemblies and budget committees.
- Wikipedia and other peer-to-peer forms of production, in which people cooperate to produce something to meet human needs through collaborative, participatory, horizontal networks.
- Open-source software, creative commons, copy-left, and other devices through which intellectual property rights are treated as a common good rather than private property.
- Community-controlled land trusts in which land is used for things like community-based forms of urban agriculture and low-cost housing.

The idea of real utopias is thus a specific way of approaching the problem of emancipatory social change and social justice. It shares with ordinary policy reform the goal of finding practical ways of changing existing institutions and creating new institutions in ways that improve the lives of people. It differs from policy reform in trying to systematically connect immediate reforms with a broader vision of systemic transformation, immediate steps with a final destination. This is very much of a piece with the proposals for a transformation of the role of the public sector in promoting public goods in the Port Huron Statement or the "nonreformist reforms" some radicals put forward in the 1970s. These were reforms that were not simply desirable in and of themselves, but which opened the space for further transformations and pointed toward a fundamentally different kind of society.[2]

We face three tasks in developing a theoretical and practical agenda for real utopias. First, as in the opening sections of the Port Huron Statement, it is crucial to elaborate the normative foundations for real utopian alternatives to existing institutions. Second, in order to understand the dilemmas and possibilities for new institutions, it is necessary to understand the core institutional designs and structural principles of such alternatives and how they work in practice. And third, in order to turn these aspirations into practical politics, we need to develop a theory of transformation.

In my work on envisioning real utopias, I argue for two foundational normative principles. The first is a strong egalitarian principle of social justice, the second an egalitarian principle of democratic empowerment. Both of these are congruent with the core moral values elaborated in the Port Huron Statement.

Social justice: In a socially just society, all people would have equal access to the social and material means necessary for living a flourishing life. Three ideas are critical in this formulation. First, the ultimate good in the principle is human flourishing. A variety of interconnected terms are invoked in discussions of egalitarianism: welfare, well-being, happiness, as well as flourishing. In practical terms it probably does not matter which is used, but human flourishing seems to me to be the most encompassing. Second, the egalitarian notion of fairness is captured by the idea of equal *access*, not equal opportunity. Equal opportunity has three problems: first, it is consistent with a lottery; second, it pays no attention to how unequal the outcomes—equal opportunity to thrive or starve is still equal opportunity; third, it is consistent with what is called "starting-gate equality," which takes a very punitive view toward people who screw up early in life. Equal access to the conditions to live a flourishing life avoids these problems. Finally, the principle of social justice refers to both material and social conditions necessary to flourish, not just material conditions. This means that issues of social recognition and social exclusion insofar as they affect human flourishing, and not just access to resources, are issues of social justice.

Democracy: In a fully democratic society, all people would have broadly equal access to the necessary means to participate meaningfully in decisions about things that affect their lives. This is very close to the definition of democracy in the Port Huron Statement: "that the individual share in those social decisions determining the quality and direction of his life."[3] This includes both the freedom of individuals to make choices that affect their own lives as separate persons, and their capacity to participate in collective decisions that affect their lives as members of a broader community. Individual liberty and collective democracy are thus rooted in the same core value: people should have as much control as possible over things that affect their lives.

Together these can be called *radical democratic egalitarianism.* They constitute the critical standards we can use to judge existing institutions and to evaluate proposals and experiments in emancipatory alternatives.

The full realization of these democratic egalitarian ideals is necessarily anticapitalist, for capitalism intrinsically obstructs both normative principles: the deep inequalities of wealth and income inherent in capitalist markets obstruct equal access of people to the social and material conditions necessary to live flourishing lives; the removal of a vast array of critical economic decisions that affect our lives from collective control by giving private wealth holders the direct power over those decisions blocks the realization of the democratic principle. So, taking democratic egalitarian principles seriously requires moving beyond capitalism.

The question, then, is how to conceive of democratic egalitarian institutional arrangements that can effectively transcend capitalism? The historical record of efforts to go beyond capitalism is not very encouraging. The failure of the grand anticapitalist revolutionary projects of the twentieth century is one of the reasons why many people in the twenty-first century believe that there is no alternative. There is not time here for me to systematically elaborate the framework I have been working on for this task, but here is the central idea. Capitalism needs to be contrasted with two other kinds of economic systems, statism and socialism. These three systems differ in many ways, but one particularly salient difference is the way power is organized over production, distribution, and investment. In capitalism, power over economic activity is anchored in private ownership of capital; in statism it is anchored in state power; and in socialism it is anchored in what I call *social power*, power rooted in the capacity of people to form voluntary associations and engage in collective action for common purposes.

No real economic system is ever characterized by a single form of power; all systems are hybrids of capitalist, statist, and socialist elements, configured in complex forms of interdependence and hierarchy. To call an economy "capitalist" is shorthand for saying it is a complex hybrid of capitalist, statist, and socialist power relations within which capitalism is dominant. In these terms the possibility of socialism revolves around the problem of enlarging and deepening the role of social power in the economic system hybrid and narrowing and weakening the capitalist component. In more familiar terms this means building economic democracy.

Using these ideas, one can construct a kind of menu of different structural configurations through which social power can be enhanced within economic systems. The most familiar, which corresponds to classic socialist ideas, can be called *statist socialism*. In statist socialism, state power directly controls economic activity—investment, production, and distribution—but is itself effectively subordinated to social power through mechanisms of effective democratic accountability. This is not a variant of the Soviet economic structure, for in the Soviet Union state power dominated social power. In these terms, the Soviet Union was an example of an authoritarian statist economy, not statist socialism.

Statist socialism remains a relevant structural configuration for transcending capitalism. It is, in fact, the institutional configuration that gets the most attention in the Port Huron Statement, where most of the explicit proposals for a change in the economy center on expanding the role of the state in directly meeting human needs and providing a wide range of public goods. The Port Huron Statement only occasionally suggests other ways of effectively subordinating the economy to democratic rule.

However, other configurations exist: "Social capitalism" is a structural configuration in which economic power continues to directly govern investment production and distribution (that is, firms remain capitalist), but economic power is itself significantly constrained by the direct exercise of social power. The system of solidarity finance in Quebec is an example: unions allocate part of their pension funds not to the stock market but to direct investment in firms in the manner of private equity investors. In exchange, unions usually get representation on the board of directors and other forms of influence over the conduct of firms. The stronger the presence of such representation of social power within a firm, the less purely capitalist the firm becomes.[4] A second configuration is the *social economy*. Here social power, often in the form of community-based associations, directly organizes economic activity to satisfy human needs. Examples would include things like urban farms anchored in community land trusts, community-based and democratically governed daycare centers, and Wikipedia. A third structural configuration is what can be termed the *cooperative market economy,* in which individual worker-owned cooperatives form networks connected to other worker-cooperatives as well as consumer cooperatives, credit unions, and specialized cooperative-facilitating institutions. A good example is the famous Mondragon cooperatives in the Basque region of Spain, where more than a hundred worker-owned firms collaborate to produce a wide range of industrial goods and services. The key to the robust success of Mondragon is not just that individual firms are owned by their workers, but that these firms form a strong network of cooperatives that support each other in all sorts of ways.[5]

The model of real utopias elaborated here is very much in the spirit of the Port Huron Statement's declaration that "The search for truly democratic alternatives to the present, and a commitment to social experimentation with them, is a worthy and fulfilling human enterprise, one which moves us and, we hope, others today."[6] The key implication of this way of thinking about alternatives to capitalism is that there are many different institutional forms through which democratic egalitarian principles can be advanced within a capitalist economic system that push the system in a more deeply democratic direction. Some of these work through the state, others do not. Some work through capitalist firms, reducing their capitalist character; others construct entirely noncapitalist forms of organization. Cumulatively they can potentially erode the capitalist character of the functioning of the system as a whole, and thus we can describe economies as more or less capitalist. A *social* socialism—a democratic economy—is one in which social power has encroached sufficiently on capitalist power relations to become the dominant form of power through which investment, production, and distribution are determined.

There are very good reasons, of course, to be skeptical that such an encroachment on capitalism is possible in the world today. Even mild reforms to impose statist constraints on capital are vigorously blocked, so the idea of a gradual erosion of capitalist power through an incremental metamorphosis of the system may seem pretty far-fetched. Yet strategies of transformation that imagine some radical, decisive break in the systemic structures of capitalism are also wildly implausible. Once again we are faced with the perennial question: *What is to be done?*

I do not have a convincing answer to that question. What I can offer is an approach to thinking about strategies for emancipatory social transformation. Anticapitalist struggles have historically involved three strategic logics, three ways of thinking about the process through which emancipatory transformations can actually be brought about. These might be labeled as the ruptural, interstitial, and symbiotic strategic logics.[7]

Ruptural strategies attempt to create a radical break in institutions, a historical discontinuity, especially around the control over state power. This logic is most associated with revolutionary socialists and communists. The vision of transformation sees the power relations within existing institutions as constituting insurmountable barriers, and thus they must be destroyed before real alternatives can be built: smash first, build second.

Interstitial strategies, in contrast, seek to build new forms of social empowerment in the niches, spaces, and margins of capitalist society, often where they do not seem to pose any immediate threat to dominant classes and elites. Contemporary examples include initiatives to expand the social economy and worker cooperatives, to create fair trade networks, and to

foster a wide range of innovative practices in the use of information technologies such as Wikipedia, Creative Commons, and open-source software.
Interstitial strategies involve ways of building institutions of social empowerment that are most deeply embedded in civil society. Instead of "smash
the state," the slogan is "ignore the state." Interstitial strategies are at the
center of some anarchist approaches to social change, and they play a big
practical role in the activities of many community activists, but socialists in
the Marxist tradition have often disparaged such efforts, seeing them as
palliative or merely symbolic, offering little prospect of serious challenge to
the status quo.

Finally, *symbiotic* strategies use existing institutions to solve problems
in ways that expand the weight for social power in the economy. Symbiotic
strategies are at the center of nonreformist reforms and are associated with
the left of the social democratic tradition. Instead of "smash" or "ignore"
the state, the slogan is "use the state." Such strategies are inherently contradictory, for they both solve problems in a pragmatic way, thus in some
ways strengthening the existing economic system and expand the space for
social power.

Any plausible scenario for transcending capitalism probably involves
aspects of all three logics, modulated by historical contexts and opportunities. In the present era in the United States, the most promising possibilities
involve mainly an articulation of symbiotic and interstitial strategies. One
example is the effort at introducing participatory budgeting mechanisms in
some American cities.[8] Participatory budgeting is a symbiotic reform, creating new mechanisms for problem solving and resource allocation in the
local state in a way that expands the possibility for grassroots associations
to be directly involved in local democracy. This in turn potentially expands
the space in which city budgets can be used to expand the space for interstitial strategies of various sorts. Another example would be the new initiatives
for community economic development in Cleveland that involve the city
government supporting the formation of worker cooperatives to provide
services for large local institutions. These efforts are meant to solve certain
practical problems in the local economy, but they also challenge the model
of capitalist investment as the only basis for job creation and economic
organization.

I do not know how effective, even in the long run, such interstitial and
symbiotic strategies can be in shifting the power configurations of capitalism; I do not think anyone really knows what the limits of possibility are

or what it really would take to break through them. But I do believe that whatever those ultimate limits might be, the prospects for eventually challenging them will be greater to the extent that within capitalism we continually try to expand the space for democratic, participatory alternatives. This was the central real utopian vision of the Port Huron Statement half a century ago. It remains as relevant today as it was then.

Chapter 15

Philosophical and Political Roots
of the American New Left

Richard Flacks

By the summer of 1960, a critical mass of young people on a number of campuses were searching for a political identity rooted in the left. They had been galvanized to thought and action by the southern civil rights movement, the fight against the remnants of McCarthyism, and the growing worldwide debate about nuclear testing and the arms race. The urgency and possibility of action was heightened by the fact that students in a number of other countries were seizing the historical initiative. And, along with such issues and models of action, was the idea that a "new left" could be created—an idea expressed in the writings of a range of dissident intellectuals.

This is the context in which Al Haber and his small group of young comrades in Ann Arbor decided to create a national New Left organization. This group soon included Tom Hayden, the exceptionally articulate, charismatic, highly ambitious editor of the *Michigan Daily* of the University of Michigan (probably the most respected student newspaper in the country). Hayden's travels, especially in the South but also across the North, persuaded him that an American student movement might be in the wind. He envisioned this movement as an autonomous self-organized force that could catalyze social change and capture the imagination of large numbers. Hayden persuaded the others in Haber's initial circle not only to create an organizational center for this emergent movement, but to produce a manifesto that would define its intellectual and moral direction. Their immediate hope was to enable students engaged in the civil rights struggle to see a common political agenda with those concerned with ending the Cold War. Inspired by the British New Left, Hayden imagined that this new organization could challenge and overcome the dead-ends of the Old Left.[1]

In early 1962, Hayden drafted a sixty-page document that combined an effort to sketch a vision of social possibility, rooted in shared values, with an effort to define a new agenda for social policy and a sketch of a strategy to promote that agenda. This draft was the basis for the intense days of discussion and debate at Port Huron, which provided Hayden with formal guidelines for revision to create the final Statement. This circulated widely during the rest of the 1960s, and the Statement is one of the key texts for understanding the American New Left.

Despite the eclectic and even diffuse character of the Port Huron Statement, it expressed a central idea embodied in the phrase "participatory democracy." Here are the relevant passages (I have retained the now archaic gendered language of the original):

As a *social system* we seek the establishment of a democracy of individual participation, governed by two central aims: that the individual share in those social decisions determining the quality of his life; that society be organized to encourage independence in men and provide the media for their common participation.

In a participatory democracy, the political life would be based in several root principles:

that decision-making of basic social consequence be carried
on by public groupings;
that politics be seen positively, as the art of collectively
creating an acceptable pattern of social relations; that
politics has the function of bringing people out of
isolation and into community:
that the political order should serve to clarify problems in a
way instrumental to their solution . . . channels should be
commonly available to relate men to knowledge and to

> power so that private problems . . . are formulated as
> general issues.

The economic sphere would have as its basis the principles:

> that the economic experience is so personally decisive that
> the individual must share in its full determination; that
> the economy itself is of such social importance that its
> major resources and means of production should be open
> to democratic participation and subject to democratic
> social regulation. . . . [All] major social
> institutions—cultural, educational, rehabilitative . . .
> should be generally organized with the well-being and
> dignity of man as the essential measure of success.[2]

Unlike European New Left formulations, the Port Huron Statement does not explicitly speak of "socialism" and its revitalization as a goal. Some have argued that the absence of the word "socialism" masks the real intent of the authors—that is, to advance a socialist agenda that would not be burdened by the deep American aversion to the word. Indeed, some participants in the gathering and in the early New Left saw the matter in those terms. But the notion that the language of the Statement is a kind of "cover" for socialism misses the fact that the stress on participatory democracy and individual self-realization was intended, by Hayden and others present, to articulate a social vision that incorporates the full range of American radical traditions, not just the socialist legacy. The vision intends to embrace anarchism, pacifism, radical democracy, libertarianism—and to deliberately efface the historical cleavages among these.

Intellectual Roots of Port Huron: C. Wright Mills

I would like to highlight several particular intellectual sources for the ideological orientation expressed at Port Huron. An immediate model and resource was the work of C. Wright Mills, widely known as a maverick sociologist, who died at age forty-two, two months before the meeting at Port Huron. In the year after Port Huron, Hayden wrote his master's thesis on Mills. The language of the Statement is quite consciously resonant with

Mills's style—a style that is both muscular and academic, with strong moral challenges couched in direct address to the reader. More important than stylistic borrowing was that the Statement as a whole tried to fulfill Mills's call for the cultivation of "sociological imagination"—an effort, as Mills defined it, to "link private troubles to public issues," to locate personal discontent in social structure and history.[3]

Accordingly, although the Statement deals at passionate length with burning issues of economic inequality and racial injustice, of war and the threat of war, it is the issue of apathy itself, of the "developed indifference to public affairs," that is its central, urgent concern. The Statement analyzes the sources of apathy as having much to do with the loss of awareness of social alternatives, with a prevailing belief that there were no means by which positive change could be realized, a belief that was coupled to a pervasive desire to protect postwar affluence that change might threaten. These beliefs are seen in the Statement as symptoms of the fact that people in general feel themselves to be at the mercy of History made at the top of institutions over which the great mass have no control. "Participatory democracy" essentially asserts a vision derived from this diagnosis. Society must be organized so that people can participate in the decisions that affect them: the people, not elites, should be positioned to make their own history; the separation between history and everyday life must be bridged. All of these themes—about the pervasiveness of popular apathy and the urgent need to challenge it, about the separation between history and daily life as the source of apathy, about the domination of history by a power elite—are at the heart of Mills's own work. In *The Sociological Imagination*, for example, he expressed this preoccupation this way: "The frequent absence of engaging legitimation and the prevalence of mass apathy are surely two of the central political facts about the Western societies today."[4]

Mills could not, however, find potential agencies of and for democratic change within the structure of contemporary politics. He emphasized the exhaustion of the left, of the labor movement, and of the Marxism that saw in a unified working class the essential agency of change in capitalist society. Near the end of his life, in essays he wrote about the New Left (referring to what was happening in Britain), he began to assert the distinctive autonomous leadership that could be played by intellectuals—particularly young ones—in both West and East, and in the third world as well. He took hope from the New Left in Britain, from dissenting voices in the communist bloc, and from the Cuban revolution—seeing all of these as expressions not of the working class, but of a rising stratum of the intelligentsia that would have both the strategic position and the mass to force a sense of responsibility and accountability on the power elites of West and East. He sought to mobilize an autonomous intellectual resistance in his pamphlet-like books, *The Causes of World War III* and *Listen Yankee!*[5]

In this way, Mills began to give theoretical legitimation to the emerging generational uprising. His work also provided a kind of theoretical recognition of the increasing importance of the intellectuals (or what Mills called the "cultural apparatus") as a social force—a perspective later elaborated by many analysts' efforts to discern a "new class" based in what came to be called the "knowledge," "information," or "postindustrial" society.[6]

The Port Huron Statement explicitly takes issue with Mills with respect to the question of agency. The manifesto strongly emphasizes the historical importance of mass movements that Mills only dimly acknowledged. In the United States, it was clear that the civil rights movement was, as the Statement says, providing a path out of apathy, not only for African Americans but for the broader left as well. In addition to the civil rights movement, the Statement explores the potential of the nascent peace movement and the rise of a new liberalism within electoral politics. Instead of emphasizing, as Mills seemed to, the critical potential of autonomous, individual intellectual rebels, the Statement stresses the university as a site of "overlooked social influence," seeing it as providing space and intellectual resources for creating theory, knowledge, and activist energy that could foster a new left. Moreover, instead of seeing intellectuals as an independent force for change, the manifesto—and the strategic outlook that SDS subsequently evolved in general—envisioned an alliance between radical intellectuals and grassroots social movements. And, contrary to Mills's tendency to criticize traditional leftist deference to the labor movement, SDS, in the early 1960s, hoped that the trade union movement might revive and help fashion a new progressive coalition. In short, if C. Wright Mills was a key intellectual inspiration for the early New Left, it is clear that its founders were able to scrutinize his intellectual legacy in sharply critical ways.

It is worth mentioning that, after Port Huron, Tom Hayden entered the graduate program in political science at the University of Michigan. His master's thesis there, entitled "Radical Nomad," was a lengthy critical examination of the work of C. Wright Mills that still can be profitably read as a guide to Mills's value and limitations as a political guide.[7]

C. Wright Mills's doctoral dissertation was entitled "A Sociological Account of Pragmatism."[8] It is striking that, although Mills was deeply grounded in the classic European works of social theory, his first philosophical love was the pragmatism of Charles Peirce, William James, G. H. Mead, and John Dewey. What we might call the "cognitive praxis" of the early New Left in the United States has strong links to that philosophical tradition, in part because of Mills's transmission of it. The phrase *cognitive praxis* was first coined by sociologists Ron Eyerman and Andrew Jamison in their 1991 book *Social Movements*.[9] They used the term to point to the ways in which movements make use of ideas to construct a collective identity, and the ways in which such identity and such ideas can help interpret both the activity of the movement and its social and cultural effects.

Indeed, the Port Huron Statement represents just such a crucial linkage between a set of ideas and the movement that would make creative use of them.

Port Huron Statement: More Dewey Than Marx

The phrase "participatory democracy" and the Port Huron Statement's treatment of that theme derives from the influence of Arnold Kaufman, a philosophy professor at the University of Michigan who had taught Hayden and other early SDS members. Kaufman used the term to signify that "democracy" as defined in conventional liberal discourse was far too limited. Kaufman was a critic of mainstream political theorizing that accepted a definition of "democracy" limited to electoral choice and sought to counter all theoretical perspectives that conceived of human nature as incompatible with democratic participation. His lectures passionately argued that that both social and personal fulfillment required a "participatory" conception of democracy—and the extension of democratic process to all arenas of human decision. It was precisely participation that would provide conditions for human beings to learn how to be socially rational and capable of self-government.[10]

Kaufman studied philosophy at Columbia and took courses with C. Wright Mills. He had considerable association with the British New Left and identified with its project.[11] Through his philosophy courses, Tom Hayden was awakened to the theme of participatory democracy and its centrality for the revitalization of the left. He and Al Haber invited Kaufman to

talk at Port Huron, and one of the evenings of that week was spent listening
to Kaufman read from a manuscript he was working on that sketched a
model of participatory citizenship. The Statement has passages that were
clearly shaped by his influence. Kaufman as well as Mills was following a
path that had been marked out by John Dewey. Both sensed that Dewey's
pragmatism contained important keys to the re-creation of the left in the
United States.

John Dewey

Dewey was of course one of the great intellectual figures in American culture. During his exceptionally long and enormously productive life (he died
at age ninety-two in 1951), Dewey was very much a mainstream public
intellectual, a highly visible and popular commentator on issues big and
small. His influence on American schooling, on religious thought, and on
American national identity was large. Yet he was also a man of the left, a
position somewhat surprising for an American public figure who so successfully navigated the mainstream. It is worth noting that one of his long-
standing organizational involvements was active membership in SDS's
parent organization, the League for Industrial Democracy (LID), which he
helped to found. Dewey served as LID president and then honorary president in the 1940s.

From his early teaching days at the University of Chicago until his
death, Dewey was involved in a variety of causes and organizations identified with the left, from defending rights of labor (helping to found the
teachers' union in the early 1930s) to opposing Stalinist dictatorship. In the
1920s and 1930s he wrote much about radicalism—with the constant
theme that America needed a left that was authentically rooted in its own
history, culture, and language. His quest for a dynamic American radicalism was carried out in action as well as writing; for example, he worked
actively during the early 1930s to create a new political party of the left.

In other words, it is clear that for much of his life Dewey was searching
for a "new left," an alternative to the ideology and practice of the established socialist organizations of his day. And what motivated that search, if
I am reading him correctly, was a deep sense that a radical political and
cultural force was needed if democracy in its fullest sense was to be made
possible. Dewey's definition of democracy was explicitly participatory and

would have an echo in the phrasing used by the drafters of the Statement: "All those who are affected by social institutions must have a share in producing and managing them." He argued that such participation is necessary both for the general welfare and for the fullest development of individuals, and that such a principle should be applied not only in the political sphere as we conventionally understand it but in the spheres of family and child raising, in the school, in business, and in the church. Such democratizing was justified by the fact that, in the long run, only people affected by decisions can judge what is best for them. But it was equally justified by the ways in which participation made possible the growth of the person. Full personhood depends on being able to gain the knowledge, form the judgments, and articulate the reasons for one's choices. Democratic participation provides the opportunity for such growth and demands as well as the acceptance of personal responsibility.[12]

One of Dewey's seminal political works, *The Public and Its Problems*, written in 1927, envisions the potentiality for a democratic public as the center of political decision making. All of the forces of modern industrial society, he argued, are arrayed against such a public. Yet he insists on the possibility that people will seek to reestablish community—including efforts to locate political initiative in face-to-face interaction. Dewey saw that the threat to democratic potential lay not only in traditional forms of despotism, and not only in social inequality deriving from capitalist political economy—but also in the growth of large-scale bureaucratic organization, mass media, and the monopolization of knowledge by experts. This work strikingly anticipates much of the current discussion about the decline of the public sphere.

In his lifetime John Dewey was often criticized from the left as a reformist who failed to recognize that capitalism itself was responsible for so many of the pathologies he denounced in American society. Such criticism was leveled against him, in part because of his resistance to Marxism, in part because of his antagonism to the Stalinist left, in part because his positions on key issues were in fact reformist. Moreover, Dewey's writing was often, perhaps deliberately, fuzzy. But his own search for an authentic and viable American left, channeled through the writings of C. Wright Mills and the teaching of Arnold Kaufman, provided the foundation for the New Left project as the Port Huron Statement defined it. For Dewey struggled to solve the very same problem that the 1960s New Left tried to address: how to create a radical political and cultural alternative that would be relevant to the American mainstream and to the realities of twentieth-century industrial society.

Dewey did not solve this problem. Indeed, his emphasis on the town meeting as a model for participatory democracy was hardly an adequate basis for creating a relevant left alternative. Neither did Mills, whose pessimism about agency and social movements made him a poor guide to understanding the potentials for social change that were brewing at the time of his death. The Port Huron Statement built on Dewey and Mills but advanced beyond their efforts, because it began to identify potential sources of agency—and thus actually served as the basis for a "cognitive praxis" for a new left—which neither Dewey nor Mills had been able to do.[13]

Looking for Political Strategy

The Port Huron Statement was much more of a manifesto than a guide to political action. But a second SDS statement, adopted a year later, called "America and the New Era" did offer a more politically strategic outlook. That document (which I helped draft) argued that the main political threat to democratic possibility in the United States was not the traditional right, but rather the consolidation of a highly flexible reformism by the dominant political, corporate, and institutional elites typified in the early 1960s by the Kennedys and figures ranging from progressive industrialists like IBM's Tom Watson to mandarin intellectuals such as Arthur Schlesinger, John Kenneth Galbraith, and Robert McNamara, first of Ford, then of the U.S. Department of Defense, and still later head of the World Bank. It was a point that Mills had already anticipated, in *The Power Elite*, where he argued that the national elites had appropriated liberal rhetoric and accommodation to a welfare state to justify their policies. His analysis was greatly extended by students at the University of Wisconsin under the tutelage of William Appleman Williams. The Madison work, much of it first published in *Studies on the Left*, which had been founded in 1959, argued that early in the twentieth century, a "corporate liberalism" constituted the ideology and praxis of key business leaders and their intellectual allies. Their purpose was to blunt grassroots protest by a combination of moderate reform, timely concession, and subtle repression, and that the same perspective had been utilized to justify and advance American global empire. Members of SDS and others in the early New Left observed that the same strategy was being applied by the Kennedys to channel and contain the southern civil rights struggle.[14]

As defined by the early New Left, "corporate liberalism" referred to the emergence of advanced, bureaucratically organized technique and expertise to anticipate discontent and engineer consent. By 1964, the New Left's identity was being shaped by struggle against such control. "Participatory democracy" provided the basis for a moral and an action critique of corporate liberalism. That critique was embodied in the manifestos of SDS and in the militant activism of the Student Nonviolent Coordinating Committee in the South, insisting upon a political voice for the poor rather than simply demanding material concessions, challenging the legitimacy of top-down styles of leadership, and making use of civil disobedience and direct action alongside efforts to use the ballot box. Beginning in September 1964, the Free Speech Movement at Berkeley challenged what it explicitly labeled corporate liberal management of the "multiversity"; indeed, University of California president Clark Kerr, the liberal, pro-labor theorist of a managerial capitalism, came to symbolize much of what the Free Speech Movement sought to challenge. In the mid-1960s, the organizing efforts of SDS in poor communities of the North aimed at creating community unions of the poor to challenge the bureaucratic welfare state and emerging corporate partnership with urban political machines.

"America and the New Era" saw what it called a "new insurgency" as the key to a strategy for change. And it drew from Appleman Williams a particular strategic hope—that domestic social movements would not only affect domestic policy, but change American global priorities as well: "A serious effort by serious men attacking our domestic problems with the pressure of a popular movement behind them would be nothing less than a reordering of priorities for our society. . . . [It] would require a vast shift of resources away from the arms race and away from efforts to implement an American grand Design on the world . . . the poor and disposed . . . could force a cessation of the arms race. The objective meaning of their demands . . . would be to make continued support for massive military programs untenable."[15] Such linking of internal renewal with an end to cold war and empire was one of Williams's central conclusions about how to read the lessons of U.S. history.

For the architects of the Port Huron Statement, the concept of "corporate liberalism" turned out to be an inadequate guide to either the ideology or the politics of the U.S. ruling class. Clark Kerr, for example, never held the confidence of California's business elite, and even as he fought student radicals at Berkeley he was the object of investigation and defamation by J. Edgar Hoover's Federal Bureau of Investigation. Meanwhile, the relative prosperity that had characterized American capitalism in the early postwar decades was replaced by a far harsher economic climate. As the 1960s turned into the 1970s, the alleged liberalism of corporate elites was being replaced by a turn away from the welfare state and corporate-labor collaboration and toward a more classic commitment to state-assisted profit maximization, what many would later call neoliberalism. By the 1980s, the once moribund far right had been restored to political viability, and many of the political activists who had grown up in the early New Left turned their energies in later years to a defense of those welfare state policies they had once thought both oppressive and inadequate. Likewise, they sought to defend or restore a social contract that, in the 1960s, they had believed to be a source of elite collaboration and managerial hegemony.

Participatory Democracy as Cognitive Praxis

If many of the democratic hopes and strategic perspectives of the 1960s were shattered by the rise of global neoliberalism during the remaining decades of the twentieth century, the central theme of the Port Huron Statement remains, I think, highly relevant.

"Participatory democracy" has, since the early 1960s, been central to the consciousness and practice of social movements in many parts of the world. As several contributions in this volume point out, the action and language of occupations, uprisings, and movements all over the world are built upon, often consciously, a number of possible implications and uses of the "participatory democratic" impulse.

John Dewey never spelled out in any systematic way how a vision of participatory democracy might be realized in actual society. And it is often claimed that the New Left conceived of participatory democracy as the mere fostering of small-group, face-to-face interaction as its political ideal—and therefore failed to figure out how to make such a new democracy a basis for practical action at the national and global levels. But such notions miss a great deal about the thinking and practices of new social movements during the past few decades, so I would like to conclude these reflections with a sketch of the varying practical uses that the vision, as Dewey, Kaufman, and Port Huron articulated it, continues to inspire:

First, participatory democracy sets a standard for evaluating every institutional arrangement, by posing such questions as: To what extent do those affected by decisions and operations have a voice in governance? To what extent are the rules by which members' activity is controlled set by them? To what extent are members free to express dissent or challenge institutional authority? Increasingly, the legitimation of institutional authority structures depends on providing some semblance of a democratic response to such questions. Established authority is particularly vulnerable to questions about voice and participation because any individual can raise them—and even small groups can take actions that make such questions potent. Mass mobilizations may follow from such actions, but the questions do not necessarily require such mobilization to generate real consequences.

Second, participatory democracy justifies protest—if all individuals have the right to a voice, then the use of direct action to achieve voice is a valid contribution to the democratic process when established arrangements block access to decision making. Such action is even more justifiable and politically effective when the institutional authority being challenged claims to be liberal. Under these conditions, the purpose of protest can be framed as an effort to pressure liberal authority to live up to its claims.

Third, participatory democracy as cognitive praxis compels efforts to fuse personalistic moral action with political strategy. The initiation of nonviolent direct action by small groups has traditionally been based on moral claims—as acts of conscience, moral witness, and truth-speaking. But the value of such action as a framework for practical strategy depends on the response of others affected by the injustices being protested. Activists may persuade through processes of "organizing"—and "organizing" was, of course, highly honored in the New Left. But they may also persuade through direct action—what anarchists used to call the "propaganda of the deed." The cognitive praxis derived from participatory democracy calls on those engaged in moral witness to evaluate the strategic, political effects of their action. Thus, for example, Rosa Parks's refusal to comply with segregation rules on the bus in Montgomery was a profound act of moral resistance—but it was also a powerful act of persuasive communication that mobilized thousands of others to gain voice.

Fourth, participatory democracy provides a logic for articulating "structural" or "nonreformist" reforms. The classic dichotomy—"reformist" versus "revolutionary"—has often been a dead-end debate on the left. Popular mobilization within industrial capitalist societies is usually based on demands for "reform"; "revolutionary" appeals rarely move masses. But the achievement of concessions is often prematurely demobilizing. Partici-patory democracy enables the evaluation of demands and concessions in terms of their potential, not only for righting a particular injustice, but for broadening opportunity for democratic participation in general. From this perspective, *the aim of collective action is democratization*—a redistribution of power so that those now voiceless will have regular voice. Participatory democracy as cognitive praxis leads activists to frame demands in terms of their democratizing potential, and to negotiate settlements that advance democratization.

Fifth, participatory democracy implies that collective grievances should not simply be advanced through established channels of representation—even if the formal mechanisms of electoral democracy are in place. It is often assumed that social movements emerge when conventional electoral channels are blocked, and that in a healthy democracy grievances are electorally expressed. Participatory democracy, however, holds out the pos-sibility that grassroots social movements can be an integral feature of demo-cratic functioning. Movements permit voice not so much in the choice of representatives but directly in decisions: social movement organizations can be ongoing players in a wide range of negotiations, planning processes, and policy arenas, and such participation can be guaranteed by law. Moreover, participatory democracy provides a strong critique of the traditional assumptions of both social-democratic and Marxist lefts about political development. The classic assumptions were that lefts mature by forming a political party that serves as the primary vehicle of popular grievance and aspiration, that the measure of left success is the growth of such a party, and that its fulfillment lies in the coming to power of such a party. Participatory democracy provides an alternative scenario in which the primary vehicles for popular expression are movements, which operate both independently and in coalition. In this scenario, left-wing "success" may be measured not by the expanding organizational power of a party, but by the reshaping of policy, both governmental and institutional, and by the fostering of new norms and rules governing social practice.

Sixth, participatory democracy defines the left's historic role not by whether its leaders are popular and installed in government but by whether the institutional structures of daily life are becoming more democratic. These include the structures of intimate, "private" life as well as those at the "macro" level. Democratizing processes are extended to both the relations between sexes and other primary relations: family life, the raising of children, schools at all levels, local community governance, the operation of workplaces and enterprises, the relations between professionals and their clients, the relations of inmates in prisons and asylums, and the relation of mass media to a variegated set of publics. Such democratizing entails structural transformations and cultural conflicts and also, at a material level, the provision by the society of opportunity and resources for all members to be able to exercise citizenship.

Seventh, participatory democracy redefines modes of thinking about political strategy. As Dewey incessantly suggested, social action must be carried on in a spirit of continuous experimentation, not by insisting on particular formulas or dogmas. All of the classic debates on the left about strategy—for example, to what extent campaigns should be waged locally or nationally, electorally or extra-parliamentarily, on the terrain of culture or within the arenas of politics as normally understood—cannot be settled a priori. Nor need the processes involved always be coordinated. Participatory democracy implies that no single leadership has the moral right or practical possibility to claim authority to direct democratization. Certainly, organizational centers are necessary for sustaining social movements, but the spirit of participatory democracy constantly challenges movement leaderships to decentralize, to be self-critical, to refuse to follow the logic of the "iron law of oligarchy." Participatory democracy provides the grounds for ongoing internal critique within movements.

Finally, participatory democracy calls on intellectuals to fundamentally question their own social roles—to break out of closed intellectual circles so that their work is widely accessible, to democratize the institutions in which they are embedded, to foster expert knowledge in the constituencies to which they are connected, and to closely monitor their own habits of elitism.

These themes constituted the defining cognitive praxis of the American New Left in its early days. Taken together, they represented, quite consciously, a "pragmatist" rather than "Marxist" perspective. It is possible to construct a "pragmatist Marxism,"[16] but such a fusion was not undertaken by new leftists. Instead, insofar as the U.S. New Left stressed the need to learn from and respond to lived experience, to be experimental and nondogmatic about issues of strategy, to be open and heterodox ideologically, to emphasize the educative character of social action, to refuse any large-scale theory of history, to question authority, to maintain organizational fluidity, to emphasize face-to-face decision making, to stress personal growth as a measure of political validity, it was John Dewey's project that was being implemented.

One of the major ironies of the 1960s New Left was that the very cognitive praxis that, at the start of the decade, enabled the radical renewal may have contributed to later decline and disorientation. The spirit of participatory democracy helped foster a climate in which efforts to establish a viable ongoing organizational structure and effective leadership for the New Left, and to sustain a critical and valid collective appraisal of social reality, could not be readily taken. The New Left's early leaders characteristically backed away from asserting ongoing control, based on a principle of leadership rotation; efforts to establish organizational coherence were usually resisted as too restrictive and inauthentic. Participatory democracy seemed to require leaderlessness, structurelessness, decision making by "consensus" rather than majority vote. Yet, by the end of the decade, the mass movement that the New Left had spawned was so diffuse, and the need for some sense of direction so acute, that many New Left activists turned away in disgust and impatience from structureless "democracy" to embrace authoritarian ideological formulations, and it tried to revive the very vanguardism of Lenin and Mao that the early SDS had staunchly opposed.

Among others, James Miller has argued that this tragic cycle was inherent in the cognitive praxis defined in the Port Huron days.[17] My own direct experience suggests instead that growing irrationalism within SDS and the late 1960s New Left was, rather, a product of our "youth" and inexperience, exacerbated by the general sense of social disintegration that pervaded the society during that tumultuous era.

The 1960s New Left did not have the time and space to work out a political practice that would validate its cognitive praxis. The latter has not disappeared, however. In the succeeding fifty years, a host of writings in many languages have elaborated and deepened the principles and themes of participatory democracy that I sketched above. In the same period, in many countries, locally based activist projects deriving from feminism, environmentalism, and a wide variety of other so-called new social movements have advanced and deepened the dynamics of grassroots participation. The relevance of participatory democracy to collective action and social organization, far from being in the past, awaits a fuller realization.

The Port Huron Statement

Introductory Note: This document represents the results of several months of writing and discussion among the membership, a draft paper, and revision by the Students for a Democratic Society national convention meeting in Port Huron, Michigan, June 11–15, 1962. It is presented as a document with which SDS officially identifies, but also as a living document open to change with our times and experiences. It is a beginning: in our own debate and education, in our dialogue with society.

INTRODUCTION: AGENDA FOR A GENERATION

We are people of this generation, bred in at least modest comfort, housed now in universities, looking uncomfortably to the world we inherit.

When we were kids the United States was the wealthiest and strongest country in the world: the only one with the atom bomb, the least scarred by modern war, an initiator of the United Nations that we thought would distribute Western influence throughout the world. Freedom and equality for each individual, government of, by, and for the people—these American values we found good, principles by which we could live as men. Many of us began maturing in complacency.

As we grew, however, our comfort was penetrated by events too troubling to dismiss. First, the permeating and victimizing fact of human degradation, symbolized by the Southern struggle against racial bigotry, compelled most of us from silence to activism. Second, the enclosing fact of the Cold War, symbolized by the presence of the Bomb, brought awareness that we ourselves, and our friends, and millions of abstract "others" we knew more directly because of our common peril, might die at any time. We might deliberately ignore, or avoid, or fail to feel all other human problems, but not these two, for these were too immediate and crushing in their impact, too challenging in the demand that we as individuals take the responsibility for encounter and resolution.

While these and other problems either directly oppressed us or rankled our consciences and became our own subjective concerns, we began to see complicated and disturbing paradoxes in our surrounding America. The declaration "all men are created equal . . ." rang hollow before the facts of Negro life in the South and the big cities of the North. The proclaimed peaceful intentions of the United States contradicted its economic and military investments in the Cold War status quo.

We witnessed, and continue to witness, other paradoxes. With nuclear energy whole cities can easily be powered, yet the dominant nation states seem more likely to unleash destruction greater than that incurred in all wars of human history. Although our own technology is destroying old and creating new forms of social organization, men still tolerate meaningless work and idleness. While two-thirds of mankind suffers undernourishment, our own upper classes revel amidst superfluous abundance. Although world population is expected to double in forty years, the nations still tolerate anarchy as a major principle of international conduct and uncontrolled exploitation governs the sapping of the earth's physical resources. Although mankind desperately needs revolutionary leadership, America rests in national stalemate, its goals ambiguous and tradition-bound instead of informed and clear, its democratic system apathetic and manipulated rather than "of, by, and for the people."

Not only did tarnish appear on our image of American virtue, not only did disillusion occur when the hypocrisy of American ideals was discovered, but we began to sense that what we had originally seen as the American Golden Age was actually the decline of an era. The worldwide outbreak of revolution against colonialism and imperialism, the entrenchment of totalitarian states, the menace of war, overpopulation, international disorder, supertechnology—these trends were testing the tenacity of our own commitment to democracy and freedom and our abilities to visualize their application to a world in upheaval.

Our work is guided by the sense that we may be the last generation in the experiment with living. But we are a minority—the vast majority of our people regard the temporary equilibriums of our society and world as eternally-functional parts. In this is perhaps the outstanding paradox: we ourselves are imbued with urgency, yet the message of our society is that there is no viable alternative to the present. Beneath the reassuring tones of the politicians, beneath the common opinion that America will "muddle through," beneath the stagnation of those who have closed their minds to the future, is the pervading feeling that there simply are no alternatives, that our times have witnessed the exhaustion not only of Utopias, but of any new departures as well. Feeling the press of complexity upon the emptiness of life, people are fearful of the thought that at any moment things might thrust out of control. They fear change itself, since change might smash whatever invisible framework seems to hold back chaos for them now. For most Americans, all crusades are suspect, threatening. The fact that each individual sees apathy in his fellows perpetuates the common reluctance to organize for change. The dominant institutions are complex enough to blunt the minds of their potential critics, and entrenched enough to swiftly dissipate or entirely repel the energies of protest and reform, thus limiting human expectancies. Then, too, we are a materially improved society, and by our own improvements we seem to have weakened the case for further change.

Some would have us believe that Americans feel contentment amidst prosperity—but might it not better be called a glaze above deeply-felt anxieties about their role in the new world? And if these anxieties produce a developed indifference to human affairs, do they not as well produce a yearning to believe there *is* an alternative to the present, that something *can* be done to change circumstances in the school, the workplaces, the bureaucracies, the government? It is to this latter yearning, at once the spark and engine of change, that we direct our present appeal. The search for truly democratic alternatives to the present, and a commitment to social experimentation with them, is a worthy and fulfilling human enterprise, one which moves us and, we hope, others today. On such a basis do we offer this document of our convictions and analysis: as an effort in understanding and changing the conditions of humanity in the late twentieth century, an effort rooted in the ancient, still unfulfilled conception of man attaining determining influence over his circumstances of life.

Values

Making values explicit—an initial task in establishing alternatives—is an activity that has been devalued and corrupted. The conventional moral terms of the age, the politician moralities—

"free world," "people's democracies"—reflect realities poorly, if at all, and seem to function more as ruling myths than as descriptive principles. But neither has our experience in the universities brought us moral enlightenment. Our professors and administrators sacrifice controversy to public relations; their curriculums change more slowly than the living events of the world; their skills and silence are purchased by investors in the arms race; passion is called unscholastic. The questions we might want raised—what is really important? can we live in a different and better way? if we wanted to change society, how would we do it?—are not thought to be questions of a "fruitful, empirical nature," and thus are brushed aside.

Unlike youth in other countries we are used to moral leadership being exercised and moral dimensions being clarified by our elders. But today, for us, not even the liberal and socialist preachments of the past seem adequate to the forms of the present. Consider the old slogans; Capitalism Cannot Reform Itself, United Front Against Fascism, General Strike, All Out on May Day. Or, more recently, No Cooperation with Commies and Fellow Travellers, Ideologies Are Exhausted, Bipartisanship, No Utopias. These are incomplete, and there are few new prophets. It has been said that our liberal and socialist predecessors were plagued by vision without program, while our own generation is plagued by program without vision. All around us there is astute grasp of method, technique—the committee, the ad hoc group, the lobbyist, that hard and soft sell, the make, the projected image—but, if pressed critically, such expertise is incompetent to explain its implicit ideals. It is highly fashionable to identify oneself by old categories, or by naming a respected political figure, or by explaining "how we would vote" on various issues.

Theoretic chaos has replaced the idealistic thinking of old—and, unable to reconstitute theoretic order, men have condemned idealism itself. Doubt has replaced hopefulness—and men act out a defeatism that is labeled realistic. The decline of utopia and hope is in fact one of the defining features of social life today. The reasons are various: the dreams of the older left were perverted by Stalinism and never recreated; the congressional stalemate makes men narrow their view of the possible; the specialization of human activity leaves little room for sweeping thought; the horrors of the twentieth century, symbolized in the gas-ovens and concentration camps and atom bombs, have blasted hopefulness. To be idealistic is to be considered apocalyptic, deluded. To have no serious aspirations, on the contrary, is to be "tough-minded."

In suggesting social goals and values, therefore, we are aware of entering a sphere of some disrepute. Perhaps matured by the past, we have no sure formulas, no closed theories—but that does not mean values are beyond discussion and tentative determination. A first task of any social movement is to convince people that the search for orienting theories and the creation of human values is complex but worthwhile. We are aware that to avoid platitudes we must analyze the concrete conditions of social order. But to direct such an analysis we must use the guideposts of basic principles. Our own social values involve conceptions of human beings, human relationships, and social systems.

We regard *men* as infinitely precious and possessed of unfulfilled capacities for reason, freedom, and love. In affirming these principles we are aware of countering perhaps the dominant conceptions of man in the twentieth century: that he is a thing to be manipulated, and that he is inherently incapable of directing his own affairs. We oppose the depersonalization that reduces human beings to the status of things—if anything, the brutalities of the twentieth century teach that means and ends are intimately related, that vague appeals to "posterity" cannot justify the mutilations of the present. We oppose, too, the doctrine of human incompetence because it rests essentially on the modern fact that men have been "competently" manipulated into incompetence—we see little reason why men cannot meet with increasing skill the complexities and responsibilities of their situation, if society is organized not for minority, but for majority, participation in decision-making.

Men have unrealized potential for self-cultivation, self-direction, self-understanding, and creativity. It is this potential that we regard as crucial and to which we appeal, not to the human potentiality for violence, unreason, and submission to authority. The goal of man and society should be human independence: a concern not with image of popularity but with finding a meaning in life that is personally authentic: a quality of mind not compulsively driven by a sense of powerlessness, nor one which unthinkingly adopts status values, nor one which represses all threats to its habits, but one which has full, spontaneous access to present and past experiences, one which easily unites the fragmented parts of personal history, one which openly faces problems which are troubling and unresolved: one with an intuitive awareness of possibilities, an active sense of curiosity, an ability and willingness to learn.

This kind of independence does not mean egotistic individualism—the object is not to have one's way so much as it is to have a way that is one's own. Nor do we deify man—we merely have faith in his potential.

Human relationships should involve fraternity and honesty. Human interdependence is contemporary fact; human brotherhood must be willed however, as a condition of future survival and as the most appropriate form of social relations. Personal links between man and man are needed, especially to go beyond the partial and fragmentary bonds of function that bind men only as worker to worker, employer to employee, teacher to student, American to Russian.

Loneliness, estrangement, isolation describe the vast distance between man and man today. These dominant tendencies cannot be overcome by better personnel management, nor by improved gadgets, but only when a love of man overcomes the idolatrous worship of things by man. As the individualism we affirm is not egoism, the selflessness we affirm is not self-elimination. On the contrary, we believe in generosity of a kind that imprints one's unique individual qualities in the relation to other men, and to all human activity. Further, to dislike isolation is not to favor the abolition of privacy; the latter differs from isolation in that it occurs or is abolished according to individual will.

We would replace power and personal uniqueness rooted in possession, privilege, or circumstance by power and uniqueness rooted in love, effectiveness, reason, and creativity. As a *social system* we seek the establishment of a democracy of individual participation, governed by two central aims: that the individual share in those social decisions determining the quality and direction of his life; that society be organized to encourage independence in men and provide the media for their common participation.

In a participatory democracy, the political life would be based in several root principles:

that decision-making of basic social consequence be carried on by public groupings;
that politics be seen positively, as the art of collectively creating an acceptable pattern of social relations;
that politics has the function of bringing people out of isolation and into community, thus being a necessary, though not sufficient, means of finding meaning in personal life;
that the political order should serve to clarify problems in a way instrumental to their solution; it should provide outlets for the expression of personal grievance and aspiration; opposing views should be organized so as to illuminate choices and

facilitate the attainment of goals; channels should be commonly available to relate men to knowledge and to power so that private problems—from bad recreation facilities to personal alienation—are formulated as general issues.

The economic sphere would have as its basis the principles:

that work should involve incentives worthier than money or survival. It should be educative, not stultifying; creative, not mechanical; self-directed, not manipulated, encouraging independence; a respect for others, a sense of dignity and a willingness to accept social responsibility, since it is this experience that has crucial influence on habits, perceptions and individual ethics;

that the economic experience is so personally decisive that the individual must share in its full determination;

that the economy itself is of such social importance that its major resources and means of production should be open to democratic participation and subject to democratic social regulation.

Like the political and economic ones, major social institutions—cultural, education, rehabilitative, and others—should be generally organized with the well-being and dignity of man as the essential measure of success.

In social change or interchange, we find violence to be abhorrent because it requires generally the transformation of the target, be it a human being or a community of people, into a depersonalized object of hate. It is imperative that the means of violence be abolished and the institutions—local, national, international—that encourage nonviolence as a condition of conflict be developed.

These are our central values, in skeletal form. It remains vital to understand their denial or attainment in the context of the modern world.

The Students

In the last few years, thousands of American students demonstrated that they at least felt the urgency of the times. They moved actively and directly against racial injustices, the threat of war, violations of individual rights of conscience and, less frequently, against economic manipulation. They succeeded in restoring a small measure of controversy to the campuses after the stillness of the McCarthy period. They succeeded, too, in gaining some concessions from the people and institutions they opposed, especially in the fight against racial bigotry.

The significance of these scattered movements lies not in their success or failure in gaining objectives—at least not yet. Nor does the significance lie in the intellectual "competence" or "maturity" of the students involved—as some pedantic elders allege. The significance is in the fact the students are breaking the crust of apathy and overcoming the inner alienation that remain the defining characteristics of American college life.

If student movements for change are rarities still on the campus scene, what is commonplace there? The real campus, the familiar campus, is a place of private people, engaged in their notorious "inner emigration." It is a place of commitment to business-as-usual, getting ahead, playing it cool. It is a place of mass affirmation of the Twist, but mass reluctance toward the controversial public stance. Rules are accepted as "inevitable," bureaucracy as "just circumstances," irrelevance as "scholarship," selflessness as "martyrdom," politics as "just another way to make people, and an unprofitable one, too."

Almost no students value activity as a citizen. Passive in public, they are hardly more idealistic in arranging their private lives: Gallup concludes they will settle for "low success, and won't risk high failure." There is not much willingness to take risks (not even in business), no setting of dangerous goals, no real conception of personal identity except one manufactured in the image of others, no real urge for personal fulfillment except to be almost as successful as the very successful people. Attention is being paid to social status (the quality of shirt collars, meeting people, getting wives or husbands, making solid contacts for later on); much too, is paid to academic status (grades, honors, the med school rat-race). But neglected generally is real intellectual status, the personal cultivation of the mind.

"Students don't even give a damn about the apathy," one has said. Apathy toward apathy begets a privately-constructed universe, a place of systematic study schedules, two nights each week for beer, a girl or two, and early marriage; a framework infused with personality, warmth, and under control, no matter how unsatisfying otherwise.

Under these conditions university life loses all relevance to some. Four hundred thousand of our classmates leave college every year.

But apathy is not simply an attitude; it is a product of social institutions, and of the structure and organization of higher education itself. The extracurricular life is ordered according to *in loco parentis* theory, which ratifies the Administration as the moral guardian of the young.

The accompanying "let's pretend" theory of student extracurricular affairs validates student government as a training center for those who want to spend their lives in political pretense, and discourages initiative from more articulate, honest, and sensitive students. The bounds and style of controversy are delimited before controversy begins. The university "prepares" the student for "citizenship" through perpetual rehearsals and, usually, through emasculation of what creative spirit there is in the individual.

The academic life contains reinforcing counterparts to the way in which extracurricular life is organized. The academic world is founded in a teacher-student relation analogous to the parent-child relation which characterizes *in loco parentis*. Further, academia includes a radical separation of student from the material of study. That which is studied, the social reality, is "objectified" to sterility, dividing the student from life—just as he is restrained in active involvement by the deans controlling student government. The specialization of function and knowledge, admittedly necessary to our complex technological and social structure, has produced and exaggerated compartmentalization of study and understanding. This has contributed to: an overly parochial view, by faculty, of the role of its research and scholarship; a discontinuous and truncated understanding, by students, of the surrounding social order; a loss of personal attachment, by nearly all, to the worth of study as a humanistic enterprise.

There is, finally, the cumbersome academic bureaucracy extending throughout the academic as well as extracurricular structures, contributing to the sense of outer complexity and inner powerlessness that transforms the honest searching of many students to a ratification of convention and, worse, to a numbness of present and future catastrophes. The size and financing systems of the university enhance the permanent trusteeship of the administrative bureaucracy, their power leading to a shift within the university toward the value standards of business and administrative mentality. Huge foundations and other private financial interests shape the underfinanced colleges and universities, not only making them more commercial, but less disposed to diagnose society critically, less open to dissent. Many social and physical scientists, neglecting the liberating heritage of higher learning, develop "human relations" or "morale-producing" techniques for the corporate economy, while others exercise their intellectual skills to accelerate the arms race.

Tragically, the university could serve as a significant source of social criticism and an initiator of new modes and molders of attitudes. But the actual intellectual effect of the college experience is hardly distinguishable from that of any other communications channel—say, a television set—passing on the stock truths of the day. Students leave college somewhat more "tolerant" than when they arrived, but basically unchallenged in their values and political orientations. With administrators ordering the institutions, and faculty the curriculum, the student learns by his isolation to accept elite rule within the university, which prepares him to accept later forms of minority control. The real function of the educational system—as opposed to its more rhetorical function of "searching for truth"—is to impart the key information and styles that will help the student get by, modestly but comfortably, in the big society beyond.

The Society Beyond

Look beyond the campus, to America itself. That student life is more intellectual, and perhaps more comfortable, does not obscure the fact that the fundamental qualities of life on the campus reflect the habits of society at large. The fraternity president is seen at the junior manager levels; the sorority queen has gone to Grosse Pointe: the serious poet burns for a place, any place, or work; the once-serious and never serious poets work at the advertising agencies. The desperation of people threatened by forces about which they know little and of which they can say less; the cheerful emptiness of people "giving up" all hope of changing things; the faceless ones polled by Gallup who listed "international affairs" fourteenth on their list of "problems" but who also expected thermonuclear war in the next few years: in these and other forms, Americans are in withdrawal from public life, from any collective effort at directing their own affairs.

Some regard this national doldrums as a sign of healthy approval of the established order— but is it approval by consent or manipulated acquiescence? Others declare that the people are withdrawn because compelling issues are fast disappearing—perhaps there are fewer breadlines in America, but is Jim Crow gone, is there enough work and work more fulfilling, is world war a diminishing threat, and what of the revolutionary new peoples? Still others think the national quietude is a necessary consequence of the need for elites to resolve complex and specialized problems of modern industrial society—but, then, why should *business* elites help decide foreign policy, and who controls the elites anyway, and are they solving mankind's problems? Others, finally, shrug knowingly and announce that full democracy never worked anywhere in the past— but why lump qualitatively different civilizations together, and how can a social order work well if its best thinkers are skeptics, and is man really doomed forever to the domination of today?

There are no convincing apologies for the contemporary malaise. While the world tumbles toward the final war, while men in other nations are trying desperately to alter events, while the very future qua future is uncertain—America is without community, impulse, without the inner momentum necessary for an age when societies cannot successfully perpetuate themselves by their military weapons, when democracy must be viable because of its quality of life, not its quantity of rockets.

The apathy here is, first *subjective*—the felt powerlessness of ordinary people, the resignation before the enormity of events. But subjective apathy is encouraged by the *objective* American situation—the actual structural separation of people from power, from relevant knowledge, from pinnacles of decision-making. Just as the university influences the student way of life, so do major social institutions create the circumstances in which the isolated citizen will try hopelessly to understand his world and himself.

The very isolation of the individual—from power and community and ability to aspire— means the rise of a democracy without publics. With the great mass of people structurally remote and psychologically hesitant with respect to democratic institutions, those institutions themselves attenuate and become, in the fashion of the vicious circle, progressively less accessible to those few who aspire to serious participation in social affairs. The vital democratic connection between community and leadership, between the mass and the several elites, has been so wrenched and perverted that disastrous policies go unchallenged time and again.

Politics without Publics

The American political system is not the democratic model of which its glorifiers speak. In actuality it frustrates democracy by confusing the individual citizen, paralyzing policy discussion, and consolidating the irresponsible power of military and business interests.

A crucial feature of the political apparatus in America is that greater differences are harbored within each major party than the differences existing between them. Instead of two parties presenting distinctive and significant differences of approach, what dominates the system is a natural interlocking of Democrats from Southern states with the more conservative elements of the Republican party. This arrangement of forces is blessed by the seniority system of Congress which guarantees congressional committee domination by conservatives—ten of 17 committees in the Senate and 13 of 21 in House of Representatives are chaired currently by Dixiecrats.

The party overlap, however, is not the only structural antagonist of democracy in politics. First, the localized nature of the party system does not encourage discussion of national and international issues: thus problems are not raised by and for people, and political representatives usually are unfettered from any responsibilities to the general public except those regarding parochial matters. Second, whole constituencies are divested of the full political power they might have: many Negroes in the South are prevented from voting, migrant workers are disenfranchised by various residence requirements, some urban and suburban dwellers are victimized by gerry-mandering, and poor people are too often without the power to obtain political representation. Third, the focus of political attention is significantly distorted by the enormous lobby force, composed predominantly of business interests, spending hundreds of millions each year in an attempt to conform facts about productivity, agriculture, defense, and social services, to the wants of private economic groupings.

What emerges from the party contradictions and insulation of privately held power is the organized political stalemate: calcification dominates flexibility as the principle of parliamentary organization, frustration is the expectancy of legislators intending liberal reform, and Congress becomes less and less central to national decision-making, especially in the area of foreign policy. In this context, confusion and blurring is built into the formulation of issues, long-range priorities are not discussed in the rational manner needed for policymaking, the politics of personality and "image" become a more important mechanism than the construction of issues in a way that affords each voter a challenging and real option. The American voter is buffeted from all directions by pseudo-problems, by the structurally-initiated sense that nothing political is subject to human mastery. Worried by his mundane problems which never get solved, but constrained by the common belief that politics is an agonizingly slow accommodation of views, he quits all pretense of bothering.

A most alarming fact is that few, if any, politicians are calling for changes in these conditions. Only a handful even are calling on the President to "live up to" platform pledges; no one is demanding structural changes, such as the shuttling of Southern Democrats out of the Democratic Party. Rather than protesting the state of politics, most politicians are reinforcing and aggravating that state. While in practice they rig public opinion to suit their own interests, in word and ritual they enshrine "the sovereign public" and call for more and more letters. Their speeches and campaign actions are banal, based on a degrading conception of what people want to hear. They respond not to dialogue, but to pressure: and knowing this, the ordinary citizen sees even greater inclination to shun the political sphere. The politician is usually a trumpeter to "citizenship" and "service to the nation," but since he is unwilling to seriously rearrange power relationships, his trumpetings only increase apathy by creating no outlets. Much of the time the call to "service" is justified not in idealistic terms, but in the crasser terms of "defending the free world from communism"—thus making future idealistic impulses harder to justify in anything but Cold War terms.

In such a setting of status quo politics, where most if not all government activity is rationalized in Cold War anti-communist terms, it is somewhat natural that discontented, super-patriotic groups would emerge through political channels and explain their ultra-conservatism as the best means of Victory over Communism. They have become a politically influential force within the Republican Party, at a national level through Senator Goldwater, and at a local level through their important social and economic roles. Their political views are defined generally as the opposite of the supposed views of communists: complete individual freedom in the economic sphere, non-participation by the government in the machinery of production. But actually "anticommunism" becomes an umbrella by which to protest liberalism, internationalism, welfarism, the active civil rights and labor movements. It is to the disgrace of the United States that such a movement should become a prominent kind of public participation in the modern world—but, ironically, it is somewhat to the interests of the United States that such a movement should be a public constituency pointed toward realignment of the political parties, demanding a conservative Republican Party in the South and an exclusion of the "leftist" elements of the national GOP.

The Economy

American capitalism today advertises itself as the Welfare State. Many of us comfortably expect pensions, medical care, unemployment compensation, and other social services in our lifetimes. Even with one-fourth of our productive capacity unused, the majority of Americans are living in relative comfort—although their nagging incentive to "keep up" makes them continually dissatisfied with their possessions. In many places, unrestrained bosses, uncontrolled machines, and sweatshop conditions have been reformed or abolished and suffering tremendously relieved. But in spite of the benign yet obscuring effects of the New Deal reforms and the reassuring phrases of government economists and politicians, the paradoxes and myths of the economy are sufficient to irritate our complacency and reveal to us some essential causes of the American malaise.

We live amidst a national celebration of economic prosperity while poverty and deprivation remain an unbreakable way of life for millions in the "affluent society," including many of our own generation. We hear glib reference to the "welfare state," "free enterprise," and "shareholder's democracy" while military defense is the main item of "public" spending and obvious oligopoly and other forms of minority rule defy real individual initiative or popular control. Work, too, is often unfulfilling and victimizing, accepted as a channel to status or plenty, if not a way to pay the bills, rarely as a means of understanding and controlling self and events. In work and leisure the individual is regulated as part of the system, a consuming unit, bombarded by hard-sell, soft-sell, lies and semi-true appeals and his basest drives. He is always told what he is supposed to enjoy while being told, too, that he is a "free" man because of "free enterprise."

The Remote Control Economy: We are subject to a remote control economy, which excludes the mass of individual "units"—the people—from basic decisions affecting the nature and organization of work, rewards, and opportunities. The modern concentration of wealth is fantastic. The wealthiest one percent of Americans own more than 80 percent of all personal shares of stock.[1] From World War II until the mid-Fifties, the 50 biggest corporations increased their manufacturing production from 17 to 23 percent of the national total, and the share of the largest 200 companies rose from 30 to 37 percent. To regard the various decisions of these elites as purely economic is short-sighted: their decisions affect in a momentous way the entire fabric of social life in America. Foreign investments influence political policies in under-developed areas—and our efforts to build a "profitable" capitalist world blind our foreign policy to mankind's needs and destiny. The drive for sales spurs phenomenal advertising efforts; the ethical drug industry, for instance, spent more than $750 million on promotions in 1960, nearly four times the amount available to all American medical schools for their educational programs. The arts, too, are organized substantially according to their commercial appeal, aesthetic values are subordinated to exchange values, and writers swiftly learn to consider the commercial market as much as the humanistic marketplace of ideas. The tendency to over-production, to gluts of surplus commodities, encourages "market research" techniques to deliberately create pseudo-needs in consumers—we learn to buy "smart" things, regardless of their utility—and introduces wasteful "planned obsolescence" as a permanent feature of business strategy. While real social needs accumulate as rapidly as profits, it becomes evident that Money, instead of dignity of character, remains a pivotal American value and Profitability, instead of social use, a pivotal standard in determining priorities of resource allocation.

Within existing arrangements, the American business community cannot be said to encourage a democratic process nationally. Economic minorities not responsible to a public in any democratic fashion make decisions of a more profound importance than even those made by Congress. Such a claim is usually dismissed by respectful and knowing citations of the ways in

---

1. Statistics on wealth reveal the "have" and "have not" gap at home. Only 5 percent of all those in the $5,000 or less bracket own any stock at all. In 1953 personally owned wealth in the U.S. stood at $1 trillion. Of this sum, $309.2 billion (30.2 percent) was owned by 1,659,000 top wealth-holders (with incomes of $60,000 or more). This elite comprised 1.04 percent of the population. Their average gross estate estimate was $182,000, as against the national average of $10,000. They held 80 percent of all corporation stock, virtually all state and local bonds, and between 10 and 33 percent of other types of property: bonds, real estate, mortgages, life insurance, unincorporated businesses, and cash. They received 40 percent of property incomes, rent, interest dividends. The size of this elite's wealth has been relatively constant: 31.6 percent (1922), 30.6 percent (1939), 29.8 percent (1949), 30.2 percent (1958).

which government asserts itself as keeper of the public interest at times of business irresponsibility. But the real, as opposed to the mythical, range of government "control" of the economy includes only:

1. some limited "regulatory" powers—which usually just ratify industry policies or serve as palliatives at the margins of significant business activity;

2. a fiscal policy built upon defense expenditures as pump-priming "public works"—without a significant emphasis on peaceful "public works" to meet social priorities and alleviate personal hardships;

3. limited fiscal and monetary weapons which are rigid and have only minor effects, and are greatly limited by corporate veto: tax cuts and reforms; interest rate control (used generally to tug on investment by hurting the little investor most); tariffs which protect non-competitive industries with political power and which keep less-favored nations out of the large trade mainstream, as the removal of barriers reciprocally with the Common Market may do disastrously to emerging countries outside of Europe; wage arbitration, the use of government coercion in the name of "public interest" to hide the tensions between workers and business production controllers; price controls, which further maintains the status quo of big ownership and flushes out little investors for the sake of "stability";

4. very limited "poverty-solving" which is designed for the organized working class but not the shut-out, poverty-stricken migrants, farm workers, the indigent unaware of medical care or the lower-middle class person riddled with medical bills, the "unhireables" of minority groups or workers over 45 years of age, etc.

5. regional development programs—such as the Area Redevelopment Act—which have been only "trickle down" welfare programs without broad authority for regional planning and development and public works spending. The federal highway program has been more significant than the "depressed areas" program in meeting the needs of people, but is generally too remote and does not reach the vicious circle of poverty itself.

In short, the theory of government's "countervailing" business neglects the extent to which government influence is marginal to the basic production decisions, the basic decision-making environment of society, the basic structure or distribution and allocation which is still determined by major corporations with power and wealth concentrated among the few. A conscious conspiracy—as in the case of price rigging in the electrical industry—is by no means generally or continuously operative but power undeniably does rest in comparative insulation from the public and its political representatives.

The Military-Industrial Complex: The most spectacular and important creation of the authoritarian and oligopolistic structure of economic decision-making in America is the institution called "the military-industrial complex" by former President Eisenhower—the powerful congruence of interest and structure among military and business elites which affects so much of our development and destiny. Not only is ours the first generation to live with the possibility of world-wide cataclysm—it is the first to experience the actual social preparation for cataclysm, the general militarization of American society. In 1948 Congress established Universal Military Training, the first peacetime conscription. The military became a permanent institution. Four years earlier, General Motors' Charles E. Wilson had heralded the creation of what he called the "permanent war economy," the continuous use of military spending as a solution to economic problems unsolved before the post-war boom, most notably the problem of the seventeen million jobless after eight years of the New Deal. This has left a "hidden crisis" in the allocation of resources by the American economy.

Since our childhood these two trends—the rise of the military and the installation of a defense-based economy—have grown fantastically. The Department of Defense, ironically the world's largest single organization, is worth $160 billion, owns 32 million acres of America and employs half the 7.5 million persons directly dependent on the military for subsistence, has an $11 billion payroll which is larger than the net annual income of all American corporations. Defense spending in the Eisenhower era totaled $350 billion and President Kennedy entered office pledged to go even beyond the present defense allocation of 60 cents from every public dollar spent. Except for a war-induced boom immediately after "our side" bombed Hiroshima, American economic prosperity has coincided with a growing dependence on military outlay—from 1941 to 1959 America's Gross National Product of $5.25 trillion included $700 billion in goods and services purchased for the defense effort, about one-seventh of the accumulated GNP. This pattern has included the steady concentration of military spending among a few corporations. In 1961, 86 percent of Defense Department contracts were awarded without competition. The ordnance industry of 100,000 people is completely engaged in military work; in the aircraft industry, 94 percent of 750,000 workers are linked to the war economy; shipbuilding, radio and communications equipment industries commit 40 percent of their work to defense; iron and steel, petroleum, metal-stamping and machine shop products, motors and generators, tools and hardware, copper, aluminum and machine tools industries all devote at least 10 percent of their work to the same cause.

The intermingling of Big Military and Big Industry is evidenced in the 1,400 former officers working for the 100 corporations who received nearly all the $21 billion spent in procurement by the Defense Department in 1961. The overlap is most poignantly clear in the case of General Dynamics, the company which received the best 1961 contracts, employed the most retired officers (187), and is directed by a former Secretary of the Army. A *Fortune* magazine profile of General Dynamics said: "The unique group of men who run Dynamics are only incidentally in rivalry with other U.S. manufacturers, with many of whom they actually act in concert. Their chief competitor is the USSR. The core of General Dynamics corporate philosophy is the conviction that national defense is a more or less permanent business." Little has changed since Wilson's proud declaration of the Permanent War Economy back in the 1944 days when the top 200 corporations possessed 80 percent of all active prime war-supply contracts.

Military-Industrial Politics: The military and its supporting business foundation have found numerous forms of political expression, and we have heard their din endlessly. There has not been a major Congressional split on the issue of continued defense spending spirals in our lifetime. The triangular relation of the business, military and political arenas cannot be better expressed than in Dixiecrat Carl Vinson's remarks as his House Armed Services Committee reported out a military construction bill of $808 million throughout the 50 states, for 1960–61: "There is something in this bill for everyone," he announced. President Kennedy had earlier acknowledged the valuable anti-recession features of the bill.

Imagine, on the other hand, $808 million suggested as an anti-recession measure, but being poured into programs of social welfare: the impossibility of receiving support for such a measure identifies a crucial feature of defense spending: it is beneficial to private enterprise, while welfare spending is not. Defense spending does not "compete" with the private sector; it contains a natural obsolescence; its "confidential" nature permits easier boondoggling; the tax burdens to which it leads can be shunted from corporation to consumer as a "cost of production." Welfare spending, however, involves the government in competition with private corporations and contractors; it conflicts with immediate interests of private pressure groups; it leads to taxes on business. Think of the opposition of private power companies to current proposals for river and valley development, or the hostility of the real estate lobby to urban renewal; or the attitude of the American Medical Association to a paltry medical care bill; or of all business lobbyists to foreign aid; these are the pressures leading to the schizophrenic public-military, private-civilian economy of our epoch. The politicians, of course, take the line of least resistance and thickest support: warfare, instead of welfare, is easiest to stand up for: after all, the Free World is at stake (and our constituency's investments, too).

Automation, Abundance, and Challenge: But while the economy remains relatively static in its setting of priorities and allocation of resources, new conditions are emerging with enormous implications: the revolution of automation, and the replacement of scarcity by the potential of material abundance.

Automation, the process of machines replacing men in performing sensory, motoric and complex logical tasks, is transforming society in ways that are scarcely comprehensible. By 1959, industrial production regained its 1957 "pre-recession" level—but with 750,000 fewer workers required. In the Fifties as a whole, national production enlarged by 43 percent but the number of factory employees remained stationary, seven tenths of one percent higher than in 1947.[2] Automation is destroying whole categories of work—impersonal thinkers have efficiently labeled this "structural unemployment"—in blue-collar, service, and even middle management occupations. In addition it is eliminating employment opportunities for a youth force that numbers one million more than it did in 1950, and rendering work far more difficult both to find and do for people in the forties and up. The consequences of this economic drama, strengthened by the force of post-war recessions, are momentous: five million becomes an acceptable unemployment tabulation, and misery, uprootedness and anxiety become the lot of increasing numbers of Americans.

But while automation is creating social dislocation of a stunning kind, it paradoxically is imparting the opportunity for men the world around to rise in dignity from their knees. The dominant optimistic economic fact of this epoch is that fewer hands are needed now in actual production, although more goods and services are a real potentiality. The world could be fed, poverty abolished, the great public needs could be met, the brutish world of Darwinian scarcity could be brushed away, all men could have more time to pursue their leisure, drudgery in work could be cut to a minimum, education could become more of a continuing process for all people, both public and personal needs could be met rationally. But only in a system with selfish

---

2. The electronics industry lost 200,000 of 900,000 workers in the years 1953–57. In the steel industry, productive capacity has increased 20 percent since 1955, while the number of workers has fallen 17,000. Employment in the auto industry decreased in the same period from 746,000 to 614,000. The chemical industry has enlarged its productive powers 27 percent although its work force has dropped by 3 percent. A farmer in 1962 can grow enough to feed 24 people, where one generation ago only 12 could be nourished. The United States Bureau of the Census used 50 statisticians in 1960 to perform the service that required 4,100 in 1950.

production motives and elitist control, a system which is less welfare than war-based, undemocratic rather than "stockholder participative" as "sold to us," does the potentiality for abundance become a curse and a cruel irony:

1. Automation brings unemployment instead of mere leisure for all and greater achievement of needs for all people in the world—a crisis instead of economic utopia. Instead of being introduced into a social system in a planned and equitable way, automation is initiated according to its profitability. American Telephone and Telegraph holds back modern telephone equipment, invented with public research funds, until present equipment is *financially* unprofitable. Colleges develop teaching machines, mass-class techniques, and TV education to replace teachers: not to proliferate knowledge or to assist the qualified professors now, but to "*cut costs in education* and make the academic community more *efficient* and less *wasteful*." Technology, which could be a blessing to society, becomes more and more a sinister threat to humanistic and rational enterprise.

2. Hard-core poverty exists just beyond the neon lights of affluence, and the "have-nots" may be driven still further from opportunity as the high-technology society demands better education to get into the production mainstream and more capital investment to get into "business." Poverty is shameful in that it herds people by race, region, and previous condition of infortune into "uneconomic classes" in the so-called free society— the marginal worker is made more insecure by automation and high education requirements, heavier competition for jobs, maintaining low wages or a high level of unemployment. People in the rut of poverty are strikingly unable to overcome the collection of forces working against them: poor health, bad neighborhoods, miserable schools, inadequate "welfare" services, unemployment and underemployment, weak political and union organization.

3. Surplus and potential plenty are wasted domestically and producers suffer impoverishment because the real needs of the world and of our society are not reflected in the market. Our huge bins of decomposing grain are classic American examples, as is the steel industry which, in the summer of 1962, is producing at 53 percent of capacity.

The Stance of Labor: Amidst all this, what of organized labor, the historic institutional representative of the exploited, the presumed "countervailing power" against the excesses of Big Business? The contemporary social assault on the labor movement is of crisis proportions. To the average American, "big labor" is a growing cancer equal in impact to Big Business—nothing could be more distorted, even granting a sizable union bureaucracy. But in addition to public exaggerations, the labor crisis can be measured in several ways. First, the high expectations of the newborn AFL-CIO of 30 million members by 1965 are suffering a reverse unimaginable five years ago. The demise of the dream of "organizing the unorganized" is dramatically reflected in the AFL-CIO decision, just two years after its creation, to slash its organizing staff in half. From 15 million members when the AFL and the CIO merged, the total has slipped to 13.5 million. During the post-war generation, union membership nationally has increased by four million—but the total number of workers has jumped by 13 million. Today only 40 percent of all non-agricultural workers are protected by any form or organization. Second, organizing conditions are going to worsen. Where labor now is strongest—in industries—automation is leading to an attrition of available work. As the number of jobs dwindles, so does labor's power of bargaining, since management can handle a strike in an automated plant more easily than the older mass-operated ones.

More important perhaps, the American economy has changed radically in the last decade, as suddenly the number of workers producing goods became fewer than the number in "nonproductive" areas—government, trade, finance, services, utilities, transportation. Since World War II "white collar" and "service" jobs have grown twice as fast as have "blue collar" production jobs. Labor has almost no organization in the expanding occupational areas of the new economy, but almost all of its entrenched strength in contracting areas. As big government hires more, as business seeks more office workers and skilled technicians, and as growing commercial America demands new hotels, service stations and the like, the conditions will become graver still. Further, there is continuing hostility to labor by the Southern states and their industrial interests—meaning "runaway" plants, cheap labor threatening the organized trade union movement, and opposition from Dixiecrats to favorable labor legislation in Congress. Finally, there is indication that Big Business, for the sake of public relations if nothing more, has acknowledged labor's "right" to exist, but has deliberately tried to contain labor at its present strength, preventing strong unions from helping weaker ones or from spreading or unorganized sectors of the economy. Business is aided in its efforts by proliferation of "right-to-work" laws at state levels (especially in areas where labor is without organizing strength to begin with), and anti-labor legislation in Congress.

In the midst of these besetting crises, labor itself faces its own problems of vision and program. Historically, there can be no doubt as to its worth in American politics—what progress there has been in meeting human needs in this century rests greatly with the labor movement. And to a considerable extent the social democracy for which labor has fought externally is reflected in its own essentially democratic character: representing millions of people, not millions of dollars; demanding their welfare, not eternal profit.

Today labor remains the most liberal "mainstream" institution—but often its liberalism represents vestigial commitments, self-interestedness, unradicalism. In some measure labor has succumbed to institutionalization, its social idealism waning under the tendencies of bureaucracy, materialism, business ethics. The successes of the last generation perhaps have braked, rather than accelerated labor's zeal for change. Even the House of Labor has bay windows: not only is this true of the labor elites, but as well of some of the rank-and-file. Many of the latter are indifferent unionists, uninterested in meetings, alienated from the complexities of the labor-management negotiating apparatus, lulled to comfort by the accessibility of luxury and the opportunity of long-term contracts. "Union democracy" is not simply inhibited by labor leader elitism, but by the unrelated problem of rank-and-file apathy to the tradition of unionism. The crisis of labor is reflected in the co-existence within the unions of militant Negro discontents and discriminatory locals, sweeping critics of the obscuring "public interest" marginal tinkering of government and willing handmaidens of conservative political leadership, austere sacrificers and business-like operators, visionaries and anachronisms—tensions between extremes that keep alive the possibilities for a more militant unionism. Too, there are seeds of rebirth in the "organizational crisis" itself: the technologically unemployed, the unorganized white collar men and women, the migrants and farm workers, the unprotected Negroes, the poor, all of whom are isolated now from the power structure of the economy, but who are the potential base for a broader and more forceful unionism.

Horizon. In summary: a more reformed, more human capitalism, functioning at three-fourths capacity while one-third of America and two-thirds of the world goes needy, domination of politics and the economy by fantastically rich elites, accommodation and limited effectiveness by the labor movement, hard-core poverty and unemployment, automation confirming the dark ascension of machine over man instead of shared abundance, technological change being intro-duced into the economy by the criteria of profitability—this has been our inheritance. However inadequate, it has instilled quiescence in liberal hearts—partly reflecting the extent to which misery has been over-come but also the eclipse of social ideals. Though many of us are "affluent," poverty, waste, elitism, manipulation are too manifest to go unnoticed, too clearly unnecessary to go accepted. To change the Cold War status quo and other social evils, concern with the challenges to the American economic machine must expand. Now, as a truly better social state becomes visible, a new poverty impends: a poverty of vision, and a poverty of political action to make that vision reality. Without new vision, the failure to achieve our potentialities will spell the inability of our society to endure in a world of obvious, crying needs and rapid change.

THE INDIVIDUAL IN THE WARFARE STATE

Business and politics, when significantly militarized, affect the whole living condition of each American citizen. Worker and family depend on the Cold War for life. Half of all research and development is concentrated on military ends. The press mimics conventional cold war opinion in its editorials. In less than a full generation, most Americans accept the military-industrial structure as "the way things are." War is still pictured as one more kind of diplomacy, perhaps a gloriously satisfying kind. Our saturation and atomic bombings of Germany and Japan are little more than memories of past "policy necessities" that preceded the wonderful economic boom of 1946. The facts that our once-revolutionary 20,000 ton Hiroshima Bomb is now paled by 50 megaton weapons, that our lifetime has included the creation of intercontinental ballistic mis-siles, that "greater" weapons are to follow, that weapons refinement is more rapid than the development of weapons of defense, that soon a dozen or more nations will have the Bomb, that one simple miscalculation could incinerate mankind: these orienting facts are but remotely felt. A shell of moral callous separates the citizen from sensitivity of the common peril: this is the result of a lifetime saturation with horror. After all, some ask, where could we begin, even if we wanted to? After all, others declare, we can only assume things are in the best of hands. A coed at the University of Kentucky says, "we regard peace and war as fairy tales." And a child has asked in helplessness, perhaps for us all, "Daddy, why is there a cold war?"

Past senselessness permits present brutality; present brutality is prelude to future deeds of still greater inhumanity; that is the moral history of the twentieth century, from the First World War to the present. A half-century of accelerating destruction has flattened out the individual's ability to make moral distinction, it has made people understandably give up; it has forced private worry and public silence.

To a decisive extent, the means of defense, the military technology itself, determines the political and social character of the state being defended—that is, defense mechanism themselves in the nuclear age alter the character of the system that creates them for protection. So it has been with America, as her democratic institutions and habits have shriveled in almost direct proportion to the growth of her armaments. Decisions about military strategy, including the monstrous decision to go to war, are more and more the property of the military and the indus-trial arms race machine, with the politicians assuming a ratifying role instead of a determining one. This is increasingly a fact not just because of the installation of the permanent military, but because of constant revolutions in military technology. The new technologies allegedly require military expertise, scientific comprehension, and the mantle of secrecy. As Congress relies more and more on the Joint Chiefs of Staff, the existing chasm between people and decision-makers becomes irreconcilably wide, and more alienating in its effects.

A necessary part of the military effort is propaganda: to "sell" the need for congressional appropriations, to conceal various business scandals, and to convince the American people that the arms race is important enough to sacrifice civil liberties and social welfare. So confusion prevails about the national needs, while the three major services and the industrial allies jockey for power—the Air Force tending to support bombers and missilery, the Navy, Polaris and carriers, the Army, conventional ground forces and invulnerable nuclear arsenals, and all three feigning unity and support of the policy of weapons and agglomeration called the "mix." Strategies are advocated on the basis of power and profit, usually more so than on the basis of national military needs. In the meantime, Congressional investigating committees—most notably the House Un-American Activities Committee and the Senate Judiciary Committee—attempt to curb the little dissent that finds its way into off-beat magazines. A huge militant anticommunist brigade throws in its support, patriotically willing to do anything to achieve "total victory" in the Cold War; the government advocates peaceful confrontation with international Communism, then utterly pillories and outlaws the tiny American Communist Party. University professors withdraw prudently from public issues; the very style of social science writing becomes more qualified. Needs in housing, education, minority rights, health care, land redevelopment, hourly wages, all are subordinated—though a political tear is shed gratuitously—to the primary objective of the "military and economic strength of the Free World."

What are the governing policies which supposedly justify all this human sacrifice and waste? With few exceptions they have reflected the quandaries and confusion, stagnation and anxiety, of a stalemated nation in a turbulent world. They have shown a slowness, sometimes a sheer inability to react to a sequence of new problems.

Of these problems, two of the newest are foremost: the existence of poised nuclear weapons and the revolutions against the former colonial powers. In the both areas, the Soviet Union and the various national communist movements have aggravated international relations in inhuman and undesirable ways, but hardly so much as to blame only communism for the present menacing situation.

Deterrence Policy

The accumulation of nuclear arsenals, the threat of accidental war, the possibility of limited war becoming illimitable holocaust, the impossibility of achieving final arms superiority or invulnerability, the approaching nativity of a cluster of infant atomic powers; all of these events are tending to undermine traditional concepts of power relations among nations. War can no longer be considered as an effective instrument of foreign policy, a means of strengthening alliances, adjusting the balance of power, maintaining national sovereignty, or preserving human values. War is no longer simply a forceful extension of foreign policy; it can obtain no constructive ends in the modern world. Soviet or American "megatonnage" is sufficient to destroy all existing social structures as well as value systems. Missiles have (figuratively) thumbed their nosecones at national boundaries. But America, like other countries, still operates by means of national defense and deterrence systems. These are seen to be useful so long as they are never fully used: unless we as a national entity can convince Russia that we are willing to commit the most heinous action in human history, we will be forced to commit it.

Deterrence advocates, all of them prepared at least to threaten mass extermination, advance arguments of several kinds. At one pole are the minority of open partisans of preventive war—who falsely assume the inevitability of violent conflict and assert the lunatic efficacy of striking the first blow, assuming that it will be easier to "recover" after thermonuclear war than to recover now from the grip of the Cold War. Somewhat more reluctant to advocate initiating a war, but perhaps more disturbing for their numbers within the Kennedy Administration, are the many advocates of the "counterforce" theory of aiming strategic nuclear weapons at military installations—though this might "save" more lives than a preventive war, it would require drastic, provocative and perhaps impossible social change to separate many cities from weapons sites, it would be impossible to ensure the immunity of cities after one or two counterforce nuclear "exchanges," it would generate a perpetual arms race for less vulnerability and greater weapons power and mobility, it would make outer space a region subject to militarization, and accelerate the suspicions and arms build-ups which are incentives to precipitate nuclear action.

Others would support fighting "limited wars" which use conventional (all but atomic) weapons, backed by deterrents so mighty that both sides would fear to use them—although underestimating the implications of numerous new atomic powers on the world stage, the extreme difficulty of anchoring international order with weapons of only transient invulnerability, the potential tendency for a "losing side" to push limited protracted fighting on the soil of underdeveloped countries. Still other deterrence artists propose limited, clearly defensive and retaliatory, nuclear capacity, always potent enough to deter an opponent's aggressive designs—the best of deterrence stratagems, but inadequate when it rests on the equation of an arms "stalemate" with international stability.

All the deterrence theories suffer in several common ways. They allow insufficient attention to preserving, extending, and enriching democratic values, such matters being subordinate rather than governing in the process of conducting foreign policy. Second, they inadequately realize the inherent instabilities of the continuing arms race and balance of fear. Third, they operationally tend to eclipse interest and action towards disarmament by solidifying economic, political and even moral investments in continuation of tensions. Fourth, they offer a disinterested and even patriotic rationale for the boondoggling, belligerence, and privilege of military and economic elites. Finally, deterrence stratagems invariably understate or dismiss the relatedness of various dangers; they inevitably lend tolerability to the idea of war by neglecting the dynamic interaction of problems—such as the menace of accidental war, the probable future tensions surrounding the emergence of ex-colonial nations, the imminence of several new nations joining the "Nuclear Club," the destabilizing potential of technological breakthrough by either arms race contestant, the threat of Chinese atomic might, the fact that "recovery" after World War III would involve not only human survivors but, as well, a huge and fragile social structure and culture which would be decimated perhaps irreparably by total war.

Such a harsh critique of what we are doing as a nation by no means implies that sole blame for the Cold War rests on the United States. Both sides have behaved irresponsibly—the Russians by an exaggerated lack of trust, and by much dependence on aggressive military strategists rather than on proponents of nonviolent conflict and coexistence. But we do contend, as Americans concerned with the conduct of our representative institutions, that our government has blamed the Cold War stalemate on nearly everything but its own hesitations, its own anachronistic dependence on weapons. To be sure, there is more to disarmament than wishing for it. There are inadequacies in international rule-making institutions—which could be corrected. There are faulty inspection mechanisms—which could be perfected by disinterested scientists. There is Russian intransigency and evasiveness—which do not erase the fact that the Soviet Union, because of a strained economy, an expectant population, fears of Chinese potential, and interest in the colonial revolution, is increasingly disposed to real disarmament with real controls. But there is, too, our own reluctance to face the uncertain world beyond the Cold War, our own shocking assumption that the risks of the present are fewer than the risks of a policy re-orientation to disarmament, our own unwillingness to face the implementation of our rhetorical commitments to peace and freedom.

Today the world alternatively drifts and plunges towards a terrible war—when vision and change are required, our government pursues a policy of macabre dead-end dimensions—conditioned, but not justified, by actions of the Soviet bloc. Ironically, the war which seems so close will not be fought between the United States and Russia, not externally between two national entities, but as an international civil war throughout the unrespected and unprotected *civitas* which spans the world.

The Colonial Revolution

While weapons have accelerated man's opportunity for self-destruction, the counter-impulse to life and creation are superbly manifest in the revolutionary feelings of many Asian, African and Latin American peoples. Against the individual initiative and aspiration, and social sense of organicism characteristic of these upsurges, the American apathy and stalemate stand in embar-rassing contrast.

It is difficult today to give human meaning to the welter of facts that surrounds us. That is why it is especially hard to understand the facts of "underdevelopment": in India, man and beast together produced 65 percent of the nation's economic energy in a recent year, and of the remaining 35 percent of inanimately produced power almost three-fourths was obtained by burning dung. But in the United States, human and animal power together account for only one percent of the national economic energy—that is what stands humanly behind the vague term "industrialization." Even to maintain the misery of Asia today at a constant level will require a rate of growth tripling the national income and the aggregate production in Asian countries by the end of the century. For Asians to have the (unacceptable) 1950 standard of Europeans, less than $2,000 per year for a family, national production must increase 21-fold by the end the century, and that monstrous feat only to reach a level that Europeans find intolerable.

What has America done? During the years 1955–57 our total expenditures in economic aid were equal to one-tenth of one percent of our total Gross National Product. Prior to that time it was less; since then it has been a fraction higher. Immediate social and economic development is needed—we have helped little, seeming to prefer to create a growing gap between "have" and "have not" rather than to usher in social revolutions which would threaten our investors and out military alliances. The new nations want to avoid power entanglements that will open their countries to foreign domination—and we have often demanded loyalty oaths. They do not see the relevance of uncontrolled free enterprise in societies without accumulated capital and a sig-nificant middle class—and we have looked calumniously on those who would not try "our way." They seek empathy—and we have sided with the old colonialists, who now are trying to take credit for "giving" all the freedom that has been wrested from them, or we "empathize" when pressure absolutely demands it.

With rare variation, American foreign policy in the Fifties was guided by a concern for foreign investment and a negative anti-communist political stance linked to a series of military alliances, both undergirded by military threat. We participated unilaterally—usually through the Central Intelligence Agency—in revolutions against governments in Laos, Guatemala, Cuba, Egypt, Iran. We permitted economic investment to decisively affect our foreign policy: fruit in Cuba, oil in the Middle East, diamonds and gold in South Africa (with whom we trade more than with any African nation). More exactly: America's "foreign market" in the late Fifties, including exports of goods and services plus overseas sales by American firms, averaged about $60 billion annually. This represented twice the investment of 1950, and it is predicted that the same rates of increase will continue. The reason is obvious: *Fortune* said in 1958, "foreign earnings will be more than double in four years, more than twice the probable gain in domestic profits." These investments are concentrated primarily in the Middle East and Latin America, neither region being an impressive candidate for the long-run stability, political caution, and lower-class tolerance that American investors typically demand.

Our pugnacious anti-communism and protection of interests has led us to an alliance inappropriately called the "Free World." It included four major parliamentary democracies: ourselves, Canada, Great Britain, and India. It also has included through the years Batista, Franco, Verwoerd, Salazar, De Gaulle, Boun Oum, Ngo Diem, Chiang Kai Shek, Trujillo, the Somozas, Saud, Ydigoras—all of these non-democrats separating us deeply from the colonial revolutions.

Since the Kennedy administration began, the American government seems to have initiated policy changes in the colonial and underdeveloped areas. It accepted "neutralism" as a tolerable principle; it sided more than once with the Angolans in the United Nations; it invited Souvanna Phouma to return to Laos after having overthrown his neutralist government there; it implemented the Alliance for Progress that President Eisenhower proposed when Latin America appeared on the verge of socialist revolutions; it made derogatory statements about the Trujillos; it cautiously suggested that a democratic socialist government in British Guiana might be necessary to support; in inaugural oratory, it suggested that a moral imperative was involved in sharing the world's resources with those who have been previously dominated. These were hardly sufficient to heal the scars of past activity and present associations, but nevertheless they were motions away from the Fifties. But quite unexpectedly, the President ordered the Cuban invasion, and while the American press railed about how we had been "shamed" and defied by that "monster Castro," the colonial peoples of the world wondered whether our foreign policy had really changed from its old imperialist ways (we had never supported Castro, even on the eve of his taking power, and had announced early that "the conduct of the Castro government toward foreign private enterprise in Cuba" would be a main State Department concern). Any heralded changes in our foreign policy are now further suspect in the wake of the Punta Del Este foreign minister's conference where the five countries representing most of Latin America refused to cooperate in our plans to further "isolate" the Castro government.

Ever since the colonial revolution began, American policy makers have reacted to new problems with old "gunboat" remedies, often thinly disguised. The feeble but desirable efforts of the Kennedy administration to be more flexible are coming perhaps too late, and are of too little significance to really change the historical thrust of our policies. The hunger problem is increasing rapidly mostly as a result of the worldwide population explosion that cancels out the meager triumphs gained so far over starvation. The threat of population to economic growth is simply documented: in 1960–70 population in Africa south of the Sahara will increase 14 percent; in South Asia and the Far East by 22 percent; in North Africa 26 percent; in the Middle East by 27 percent; in Latin America 29 percent. Population explosion, no matter how devastating, is neutral. But how long will it take to create a relation of thrust between America and the newly-developing societies? How long to change our policies? And what length of time do we have?

The world is in transformation. But America is not. It can race to industrialize the world, tolerating occasional authoritarianisms, socialisms, neutralisms along the way—or it can slow the pace of the inevitable and default to the eager and self-interested Soviets and, much more importantly, to mankind itself. Only mystics would guess we have opted thoroughly for the first. Consider what our people think of this, the most urgent issue on the human agenda. Fed by a bellicose press, manipulated by economic and political opponents of change, drifting in their own history, they grumble about "the foreign aid waste," or about "that beatnik down in Cuba," or how "things will get us by" . . . thinking confidently, albeit in the usual bewilderment, that Americans can go right on like always, five percent of mankind producing forty percent of its goods.

Anti-Communism

An unreasoning anti-communism has become a major social problem for those who want to construct a more democratic America. McCarthyism and other forms of exaggerated and conservative anti-communism seriously weaken democratic institutions and spawn movements contrary to the interests of basic freedoms and peace. In such an atmosphere even the most intelligent of Americans fear to join political organizations, sign petitions, speak out on serious issues. Militaristic policies are easily "sold" to a public fearful of a democratic enemy. Political debate is restricted, thought is standardized, action is inhibited by the demands of "unity" and "oneness" in the face of the declared danger. Even many liberals and socialists share static and repetitious participation in the anti-communist crusade and often discourage tentative, inquiring discussion about "the Russian question" within their ranks—often by employing "stalinist," "stalinoid," trotskyite" and other epithets in an oversimplifying way to discredit opposition.

Thus much of the American anti-communism takes on the characteristics of paranoia. Not only does it lead to the perversion of democracy and to the political stagnation of a warfare society, but it also has the unintended consequence of preventing an honest and effective approach to the issues. Such an approach would require public analysis and debate of world politics. But almost nowhere in politics is such a rational analysis possible to make.

It would seem reasonable to expect that in America the basic issues of the Cold War should be rationally and fully debated, between persons of every opinion—on television, on platforms and through other media. It would seem, too, that there should be a way for the person or an organization to oppose communism *without* contributing to the common fear of associations and public actions. But these things do not happen; instead, there is finger-pointing and comical debate about the most serious of issues. This trend of events on the domestic scene, towards greater irrationality on major questions, moves us to greater concern than does the "internal threat" of domestic communism. Democracy, we are convinced, requires every effort to set in peaceful opposition the basic viewpoints of the day; only by conscious, determined, though difficult, efforts in this direction will the issue of communism be met appropriately.

Communism and Foreign Policy

As democrats we are in basic opposition to the communist system. The Soviet Union, as a system, rests on the total suppression of organized opposition, as well as on a vision of the future in the name of which much human life has been sacrificed, and numerous small and large denials of human dignity rationalized. The Communist Party has equated falsely the "triumph of true socialism" with centralized bureaucracy. The Soviet state lacks independent labor organizations and other liberties we consider basic. And despite certain reforms, the system remains almost totally divorced from the image officially promulgated by the Party. Communist parties through-out the rest of the world are generally undemocratic in internal structure and mode of action. Moreover, in most cases they subordinate radical programs to requirements of Soviet foreign policy. The communist movement has failed, in every sense, to achieve its stated intentions of leading a worldwide movement for human emancipation.

But present trends in American anti-communism are not sufficient for the creation of appropriate policies with which to relate to and counter communist movements in the world. In no instance is this better illustrated than in our basic national policy-making assumption that the Soviet Union is inherently expansionist and aggressive, prepared to dominate the rest of the world by military means. On this assumption rests the monstrous American structure of military "preparedness"; because of it we sacrifice values and social programs to the alleged needs of military power.

But the assumption itself is certainly open to question and debate. To be sure, the Soviet state has used force and the threat of force to promote or defend its perceived national interests. But the typical American response has been to equate the use of force—which in many cases might be dispassionately interpreted as a conservative, albeit brutal, action—with the initiation of a worldwide military onslaught. In addition, the Russian-Chinese conflicts and the emergence of rifts throughout the communist movement call for a re-evaluation of any monolithic interpre-tations. And the apparent Soviet disinterest in building a first-strike arsenal of weapons challenges the weight given to protection against surprise attack in formulations of American policy toward the Soviets.

Almost without regard to one's conception of the dynamics of Soviet society and foreign policy, it is evident that the American military response has been more effective in deterring the growth of democracy than communism. Moreover, our prevailing policies make difficult the encouragement of skepticism, anti-war or pro-democratic attitudes in the communist systems. America has done a great deal to foment the easier, opposite tendency in Russia: suspicion, suppression, and stiff military resistance. We have established a system of military alliances which are even of dubious deterrence value. It is reasonable to suggest that "Berlin" and "Laos" have been earth-shaking situations partly because rival systems of deterrence make impossible the withdrawal of threats. The "status quo" is not cemented by mutual threat but by mutual fear of receding from pugnacity—since the latter course would undermine the "credibility" of our deter-ring system. Simultaneously, while billions in military aid were propping up right-wing Laotian, Formosan, Iranian and other regimes, American leadership never developed a purely political policy for offering concrete alternatives to either communism or the status quo for colonial revolutions. The results have been: fulfillment of the communist belief that capitalism is stagnant, its only defense being dangerous military adventurism; destabilizing incidents in numerous developing countries; an image of America allied with corrupt oligarchies counterposed to the Russian-Chinese image of rapid, though brutal, economic development. Again and again, America mistakes the static area of defense, rather than the dynamic area of development, as the master need of two-thirds of mankind.

Our paranoia about the Soviet Union has made us incapable of achieving agreements abso-lutely necessary for disarmament and the preservation of peace. We are hardly able to see the possibility that the Soviet Union, though not "peace loving," may be seriously interested in disarmament.

Infinite possibilities for both tragedy and progress lie before us. On the one hand, we can continue to be afraid, and out of fear commit suicide. On the other hand, we can develop a fresh and creative approach to world problems which will help to create democracy at home and establish conditions for its growth elsewhere in the world.

Discrimination

Our America is still white.

Consider the plight, statistically, of its greatest nonconformists, the "nonwhites" (a Census Bureau designation).

Literacy: One of every four "nonwhites" is functionally illiterate; half do not complete elementary school; one in five finishes high school or better. But one in twenty whites is functionally illiterate; four of five finish elementary school; half go through high school or better.

Salary: In 1959 a "nonwhite" worker could expect to average $2,844 annually; a "nonwhite" family, including a college-educated father, could expect to make $5,654 collectively. But a white worker could expect to make $4,487 if he worked alone; with a college degree and a family of helpers he could expect $7,373. The approximate Negro-white wage ratio has remained nearly level for generations, with the exception of the World War II employment "boom" which opened many better jobs to exploited groups.

Work: More than half of all "nonwhites" work at laboring or service jobs, including one-fourth of those with college degrees; one in 20 works in a professional or managerial capacity. Fewer than one in five of all whites are laboring or service workers, including one in every 100 of the college-educated; one in four is in professional or managerial work.

Unemployment: Within the 1960 labor force of approximately 72 million, one of every 10 "nonwhites" was unemployed. Only one of every 20 whites suffered that condition.

Housing: The census classifies 57 percent of all "nonwhite" houses substandard, but only 27 percent of white-owned units so exist.

Education: More than fifty percent of America's "nonwhite" high school students never graduate. The vocational and professional spread of curriculum categories offered "nonwhites" is 16 as opposed to the 41 occupations offered to the white student. Furthermore, in spite of the 1954 Supreme Court decision, of all "nonwhites" educated, 80 percent are educated actually, or virtually, under segregated conditions. And only one of 20 "nonwhite" students goes to college as opposed to the 1:10 ratio for white students.

Voting: While the white community is registered above two-thirds of its potential, the "nonwhite" population is registered below one-third of its capacity (with even greater distortion in areas of the Deep South).

Even against this background, some will say progress is being made. The facts bely it, however, unless it is assumed that America has another century to deal with its racial inequalities.

Others, more pompous, will blame the situation on "those people's inability to pick themselves up," not understanding the automatic way in which such a system can frustrate reform efforts and diminish the aspirations of the oppressed. The one-party system in the South, attached to the Dixiecrat-Republican complex nationally, cuts off the Negro's independent powers as a citizen. Discrimination in employment, along with labor's accommodation to the "lily-white" hiring practices, guarantees the lowest slot in the economic order to the "nonwhite." North or South, these oppressed are conditioned by their inheritance and their surroundings to expect more of the same: in housing, schools, recreation, travel, all their potential is circumscribed, thwarted and often extinguished. Automation grinds up job opportunities, and ineffective or non-existent retraining programs make the already-handicapped "nonwhite" even less equipped to participate in "technological progress."

Horatio Alger Americans typically believe that the "nonwhites" are being "accepted" and "rising" gradually. They see more Negroes on television and so assume that Negroes are "better off." They hear the President talking about Negroes and so assume they are politically repre-sented. They are aware of black peoples in the United Nations and so assume that the world is generally moving toward integration. They don't drive through the South, or through the slum areas of the big cities, so they assume that squalor and naked exploitation are disappearing. They express generalities about "time and gradualism" to hide the fact that they don't know what is happening.

The advancement of the Negro and other "nonwhites" in America has not been altogether by means of the crusades of liberalism, but rather through unavoidable changes in social struc-ture. The economic pressures of World War II opened new jobs, new mobility, new insights to Southern Negroes, who then began great migrations from the South to the bigger urban areas of the North where their absolute wage was greater, though unchanged in relation to the white man of the same stratum. More important than the World War II openings was the colonial revolu-tion. The world-wide upsurge of dark peoples against white colonial domination stirred the aspiration and created an urgency among American Negroes, while simultaneously it threatened the power structure of the United States enough to produce concessions to the Negro. Produced by outer pressure from the newly-moving peoples rather than by the internal conscience of the Federal government, the gains were keyed to improving the American "image" more than to reconstructing the society that prospered on top of its minorities. Thus the historic Supreme Court decision of 1954, theoretically desegregating Southern schools, was more a proclamation than a harbinger of social change—and is reflected as such in the fraction of Southern school districts which have desegregated, with Federal officials doing little to spur the process.

It has been said that the Kennedy administration did more in two years than the Eisenhower administration did in eight. Of this there can be no doubt. But it is analogous to comparing whispers to silence when positively stentorian tones are demanded. President Kennedy leapt ahead of the Eisenhower record when he made his second reference to the racial problem; Eisen-hower did not utter a meaningful public statement until his last month in office when he men-tioned the "blemish" of bigotry.

To avoid conflict with the Dixiecrat-Republican alliance, President Kennedy has developed a civil rights philosophy of "enforcement, not enactment," implying that existing statutory tools are sufficient to change the lot of the Negro. So far he has employed executive power usefully to appoint Negroes to various offices, and seems interested in seeing the Southern Negro registered to vote. On the other hand, he has appointed at least four segregationist judges in areas where voter registration is a desperate need. Only two civil rights bills, one to abolish the poll tax in five states and another to prevent unfair use of literacy tests in registration, have been proposed—the President giving active support to neither. But even this legislation, lethargically supported, then defeated, was intended to extend only to Federal elections. More important, the Kennedy interest in voter registration has not been supplemented with interest in giving the Southern Negro the economic protection that only trade unions can provide.

It seems evident that the President is attempting to win the Negro permanently to the Democratic Party without basically disturbing the reactionary one-party oligarchy in the South. Moreover, the administration is decidedly "cool" (a phrase of Robert Kennedy) toward mass nonviolent movements in the South, though by the support of racist Dixiecrats the Administration makes impossible gradual action through conventional channels. The Federal Bureau of Investigation in the South is composed of Southerners and their intervention in situations of racial tension is always after the incident, not before. Kennedy has refused to "enforce" the legal prerogative to keep Federal marshals active in Southern areas before, during and after any "situations" (this would invite Negroes to exercise their rights and it would infuriate the Southerners in Congress because of its "insulting" features).

While corrupt politicians, together with business interests happy with the absence of organized labor in Southern states and with the $50 billion in profits that results from paying the Negro half a "white wage," stymie and slow fundamental progress, it remains to be appreciated that the ultimate wages of discrimination are paid by individuals and not by the state. Indeed the other sides of the economic, political and sociological coins of racism represent their more profound implications in the private lives, liberties and pursuits of happiness of the citizen. While hungry nonwhites the world around assume rightful dominance, the majority of Americans fight to keep integrated housing out of the suburbs. While a fully interracial world becomes a biological probability, most Americans persist in opposing marriage between the races.

While cultures generally interpenetrate, white America is ignorant still of nonwhite America—and perhaps glad of it. The white lives almost completely within his immediate, close-up world where things are tolerable, there are no Negroes except on the bus corner going to and from work, and where it is important that daughter marry right. White, like might, makes right in America today. Not knowing the "nonwhite," however, the white knows something less than himself. Not comfortable around "different people," he reclines in whiteness instead of preparing for diversity. Refusing to yield objective social freedoms to the "nonwhite," the white loses his personal subjective freedom by turning away "from all these damn causes."

White American ethnocentrism at home and abroad reflect most sharply the self-deprivation suffered by the majority of our country which effectively makes it an isolated minority in the world community of culture and fellowship. The awe inspired by the pervasiveness of racism in American life is only matched by the marvel of its historical span in American traditions. The national heritage of racial discrimination via slavery has been a part of America since Christopher Columbus' advent on the new continent. As such, racism not only antedates the Republic and the thirteen Colonies, but even the use of the English language in this hemisphere. And it is well that we keep this as a background when trying to understand why racism stands as such a steadfast pillar in the culture and custom of the country. Racial-xenophobia is reflected in the admission of various racial stocks to the country. From the nineteenth century Oriental Exclusion

Acts to the most recent up-dating of the Walter-McCarren Immigration Acts, the nation has shown a continuous contemptuous regard for "nonwhites." More recently, the tragedies of Hiroshima and Korematsu, and our cooperation with Western Europe in the United Nations, add treatment to the thoroughness of racist overtones in national life.

But the right to refuse service to anyone is no longer reserved to the Americans. The minority groups, internationally, are changing places.

WHAT IS NEEDED?

How to end the Cold War? How to increase democracy in America? These are the decisive issues confronting liberal and socialist forces today. To us, the issues are intimately related, the struggle for one invariably being a struggle for the other. What policy and structural alternatives are needed to obtain these ends?

1. *Universal controlled disarmament must replace deterrence and arms control as the national defense goal.*

The strategy of mutual threat can only temporarily prevent thermonuclear war, and it cannot but erode democratic institutions here while consolidating oppressive institutions in the Soviet Union. Yet American leadership, while giving rhetorical due to the ideal of disarmament, persists in accepting mixed deterrence as its policy formula: under Kennedy we have seen first-strike and second-strike weapons, counter-military and counter-population inventions, tactical atomic weapons and guerilla warriors, etc. The convenient rationalization that our weapons *potpourri* will confuse the enemy into fear of misbehaving is absurd and threatening. Our own intentions, once clearly retaliatory, are now ambiguous since the President has indicated we might in certain circumstances be the first to use nuclear weapons. We can expect that Russia will become more anxious herself, and perhaps even prepare to "preempt" us, and we (expecting the worst from the Russians) will nervously consider "preemption" ourselves. The symmetry of threat and counter-threat lead not to stability but to the edge of hell.

It is necessary that America make disarmament, not nuclear deterrence, "credible" to the Soviets and to the world. That is, disarmament should be continually avowed as a national goal; concrete plans should be presented at conference tables; real machinery for a disarming and disarmed world—national and international—should be created while the disarming process itself goes on. The long-standing idea of unilateral initiative should be implemented as a basic feature of American disarmament strategy: initiatives that are graduated in their risk potential, accompanied by invitations to reciprocate when done regardless of reciprocation, openly planned for a significant period of future time. Their function should not be to strip America of weapons, but to induce a climate in which disarmament can be discussed with less mutual hostility and threat. They might include: a unilateral nuclear test moratorium, withdrawal of several bases near the Soviet Union, proposals to experiment in disarmament by stabilization of zone of controversy; cessation of all apparent first-strike preparations, such as the development of 41 Polaris submarines by 1963 while naval theorists state that about 45 constitute a provocative force; inviting a special United Nations agency to observe and inspect the launchings of all American flights into outer space; and numerous others.

There is no simple formula for the content of an actual disarmament treaty. It should be phased: perhaps on a region-by-region basis, the conventional weapons first. It should be conclusive, not open-ended, in its projection. It should be controlled: national inspection systems are adequate at first, but should be soon replaced by international devices and teams. It should be more than denuding: world or at least regional enforcement agencies, an international civil ser-vice and inspection service, and other supranational groups must come into reality under the United Nations.

2. *Disarmament should be seen as a political issue, not a technical problem.*

Should this year's Geneva negotiations have resulted (by magic) in a disarmament agree-ment, the United States Senate would have refused to ratify it, a domestic depression would have begun instantly, and every fiber of American life would be wrenched drastically: these are indica-tions not only of our unpreparedness for disarmament, but also that disarmament is not "just another policy shift." Disarmament means a deliberate shift in most of our domestic and foreign policy.

A. It will involve major changes in economic direction. Government intervention in new areas, government regulation of certain industrial price and investment practices to pre-vent inflation, full use of national productive capacities, and employment for every per-son in a dramatically expanding economy all are to be expected as the "price" of peace.

B. It will involve the simultaneous creation of international rulemaking and enforce-ment machinery beginning under the United Nations, and the gradual transfer of sovereignties—such as national armies and national determination of "international" law—to such machinery.

C. It will involve the initiation of an explicitly political—as opposed to military—foreign policy on the part of the two major superstates. Neither has formulated the political terms in which they would conduct their behavior in a disarming or disarmed world. Neither dares to disarm until such an understanding is reached.

3. *A crucial feature of this political understanding must be the acceptance of status quo possessions.*

According to the universality principle all present national entities—including the Vietnams, the Koreans, the Chinas, and the Germanys—should be members of the United Nations as sovereign, no matter how desirable, states.

Russia cannot be expected to negotiate disarmament treaties for the Chinese. We should not feed Chinese fanaticism with our encirclement but Chinese stomachs with the aim of making war contrary to Chinese policy interests. Every day that we support anti-communist tyrants but refuse to even allow the Chinese Communists representation in the United Nations marks a greater separation of our ideals and our actions, and it makes more likely bitter future relations with the Chinese.

Second, we should recognize that an authoritarian Germany's insistence on reunification, while knowing the impossibility of achieving it with peaceful means, could only generate increas-ing frustrations among the population and nationalist sentiments which frighten its Eastern neighbors who have historical reasons to suspect Germanic intentions. President Kennedy him-self told the editor of *Izvestia* that he fears an independent Germany with nuclear arms, but American policies have not demonstrated cognizance of the fact that Chancellor Adenauer too is interested in continued East-West tensions over the Germany and Berlin problems and nuclear arms precisely because this is the rationale for extending his domestic power and his influence upon the NATO-Common Market alliance.

A world war over Berlin would be absurd. Anyone concurring with such a proposition should demand that the West cease its contradictory advocacy of "reunification of Germany through free elections" and "a rearmed Germany in NATO." It is a dangerous illusion to assume that Russia will hand over East Germany to a rearmed re-united Germany which will enter the Western camp, although this Germany might have a Social Democratic majority which could prevent a reassertion of German nationalism. We have to recognize that the cold war and the incorporation of Germany into the two power blocs was a decision of both Moscow and Washington, of both Adenauer and Ulbricht. The immediate responsibility for the Berlin wall is Ulbricht's. But it had to be expected that a regime which was bad enough to make people flee is also bad enough to prevent them from fleeing. The inhumanity of the Berlin wall is an ironic symbol of the irrationality of the cold war, which keeps Adenauer and Ulbricht in power. A reduction of the tension over Berlin, if by internationalization or by recognition of the status quo and reducing provocations, is a necessary but equally temporary measure which could not ultimately reduce the basic cold war tension to which Berlin owes its precarious situation. The Berlin problem cannot be solved without reducing tensions in Europe, possibly by a bilateral military disengagement and creating a neutralized buffer zone. Even if Washington and Moscow were in favor of disengagement, both Adenauer and Ulbricht would never agree to it because cold war keeps their parties in power.

Until their regimes' departure from the scene of history, the Berlin status quo will have to be maintained while minimizing the tensions necessarily arising from it. Russia cannot expect the United States to tolerate its capture by the Ulbricht regime, but neither can America expect to be in a position to indefinitely use Berlin as a fortress within the communist world. As a fair and bilateral disengagement in Central Europe seems to be impossible for the time being, a mutual recognition of the Berlin status quo, that is, of West Berlin's and East Germany's security, is needed. And it seems to be possible, although the totalitarian regime of East Germany and the authoritarian leadership of West Germany until now succeeded in frustrating all attempts to minimize the dangerous tensions of cold war.

The strategy of securing the status quo of the two power blocs until it is possible to depolarize the world by creating neutralist regions in all trouble zones seems to be the only way to guarantee peace at this time.

4. *Experiments in disengagement and demilitarization must be conducted as part of the total disarming process.*

These "disarmament experiments" can be of several kinds, so long as they are consistent with the principles of containing the arms race and isolating specific sectors of the world from the Cold War power-play. First, it is imperative that no more nations be supplied with, or locally produce, nuclear weapons. A 1959 report of the National Academy of Arts and Sciences predicted that 19 nations would be so armed in the near future. Should this prediction be fulfilled, the prospects of war would be unimaginably expanded. For this reason the United States, Great Britain and the Soviet Union should band against France (which wants its own independent deterrent) and seek, through United Nations or other machinery, the effective prevention of the spread of atomic weapons. This would involve not only declarations of "denuclearization" in whole areas of Latin America, Africa, Asia and Europe, but would attempt to create inspection machinery to guarantee the peaceful use of atomic energy.

Second, the United States should reconsider its increasingly outmoded European defense framework, the North Atlantic Treaty Organization. Since its creation in 1949, NATO has assumed increased strength in overall determination of Western military policy, but has become less and less relevant to its original purpose, which was the defense of Central Europe. To be sure, after the Czech coup of 1948, it might have appeared that the Soviet Union was on the verge of a full-scale assault on Europe. But that onslaught has not materialized, not so much because of NATO's existence but because of the general unimportance of much of Central Europe to the Soviets. Today, when even American-based ICBMs could smash Russia minutes after an invasion of Europe, when the Soviets have no reason to embark on such an invasion, and when "thaw sectors" are desperately needed to brake the arms race, one of the least threatening but most promising courses for America would be toward the gradual diminishment of the NATO forces, coupled with the negotiated "disengagement" of parts of Central Europe.

It is especially crucial that this be done while America is entering into favorable trade relations with the European Economic Community: such a gesture, combining economic ambition with less dependence on the military, would demonstrate the kind of competitive "co-existence" America intends to conduct with the communist-bloc nations. If the disengaged states were the two Germanies, Poland and Czechoslovakia, several other benefits would accrue. First, the United States would be breaking with the lip-service commitment to "liberation" of Eastern Europe which has contributed so much to Russian fears and intransigence, while doing too little about actual liberation. But the end of "liberation" as a proposed policy would not signal the end of American concern for the oppressed in East Europe. On the contrary, disengagement would be a real, rather than a rhetorical, effort to ease military tensions, thus undermining the Russian argument for tighter controls in East Europe based on the "menace of capitalist encirclement." This policy, geared to the needs of democratic elements in the satellites, would develop a real bridge between East and West across the two most pro-Western Russian satellites. The Russians in the past have indicated some interest in such a plan, including the demilitarization of the Warsaw pact countries. Their interest should be publicly tested. If disengagement could be achieved, a major zone could be removed from the Cold War, the German problem would be materially diminished, and the need for NATO would diminish, and attitudes favorable to disarming would be generated.

Needless to say, these proposals are much different than what is currently being practiced and praised. American military strategists are slowly acceding to the NATO demand for an independent deterrent, based on the fear that America might not defend Europe from military attack. These tendencies strike just the opposite chords in Russia than those which would be struck by disengagement themes: the chords of military alertness, based on the fact that NATO (bulwarked by the German Wehrmacht) is preparing to attack Eastern Europe or the Soviet Union. Thus the alarm which underlies the NATO proposal for an independent deterrent is likely itself to bring into existence the very Russian posture that was the original cause of fear. Armaments spiral and belligerence will carry the day, not disengagement and negotiation.

The Industrialization of the World

Many Americans are prone to think of the industrialization of the newly developed countries as a modern form of American *noblesse*, undertaken sacrificially for the benefit of others. On the contrary, the task of world industrialization, of eliminating the disparity between have and have-not nations, is as important as any issue facing America. The colonial revolution signals the end of an era for the old Western powers and a time of new beginnings for most of the people of the earth. In the course of these upheavals, many problems will emerge: American policies must be revised or accelerated in several ways.

1. *The United States' principal goal should be creating a world where hunger, poverty, disease, ignorance, violence, and exploitation are replaced as central features by abundance, reason, love, and international cooperation.*

To many this will seem the product of juvenile hallucination: but we insist it is a more realistic goal than is a world of nuclear stalemate. Some will say this is a hope beyond all bounds: but it is far better to us to have positive vision than a "hard headed" resignation. Some will sympathize, but claim it is impossible: if so, then, we, not Fate, are the responsible ones, for we have the means at our disposal. *We should not give up the attempt for fear of failure.*

2. *We should undertake here and now a fifty-year effort to prepare for all nations the conditions of industrialization.*

Even with far more capital and skill than we now import to emerging areas, serious prophets expect that two generations will pass before accelerating industrialism is a worldwide act. The needs are numerous: every nation must build an adequate infrastructure (transportation, communication, land resources, waterways) for future industrial growth; there must be industries suited to the rapid development of differing raw materials and other resources; education must begin on a continuing basis for everyone in the society, especially including engineering and technical training; technical assistance from outside sources must be adequate to meet present and long-term needs; atomic power plants must spring up to make electrical energy available. With America's idle productive capacity, it is possible to begin this process immediately without changing our military allocations. This might catalyze a "peace race" since it would demand a response of such magnitude from the Soviet Union that arms spending and "coexistence" spending would become strenuous, perhaps impossible, for the Soviets to carry on simultaneously.

3. *We should not depend significantly on private enterprise to do the job.*

Many important projects will not be profitable enough to entice the investment of private capital. The total amount required is far beyond the resources of corporate and philanthropic concerns. The new nations are suspicious, legitimately, of foreign enterprises dominating their national life. World industrialization is too huge an undertaking to be formulated or carried out by private interests. Foreign economic assistance is a national problem, requiring long range planning, integration with other domestic and foreign policies, and considerable public debate and analysis. Therefore the Federal government should have primary responsibility in this area.

4. *We should not lock the development process into the Cold War: we should view it as a way of ending that conflict.*

When President Kennedy declared that we must aid those who need aid because it is right, he was unimpeachably correct—now principle must become practice. We should reverse the trend of aiding corrupt anti-communist regimes. To support dictators like Diem while trying to destroy ones like Castro will only enforce international cynicism about American "principle," and is bound to lead to even more authoritarian revolutions, especially in Latin America where we did not even consider foreign aid until Castro had challenged the status quo. We should end the distinction between communist hunger and anti-communist hunger. To feed only anticommunists is to directly fatten men like Boun Oum, to incur the wrath of real democrats, and to distort our own sense of human values. We must cease seeing development in terms of communism and capitalism. To fight communism by capitalism in the newly-developing areas is to fundamentally misunderstand the international hatred of imperialism and colonialism and to confuse the needs of 19th century industrial America with those of contemporary nations.

Quite fortunately, we are edging away from the Dullesian "either-or" foreign policy ultimatum towards an uneasy acceptance of neutralism and nonalignment. If we really desire the end of the Cold War, we should now welcome nonalignment—that is, the creation of whole blocs of nations concerned with growth and with independently trying to break out of the Cold War apparatus.

Finally, while seeking disarmament as the genuine deterrent, we should shift from financial support of military regimes to support of national development. Real security cannot be gained by propping up military defenses, but only through the hastening of political stability, economic growth, greater social welfare, improved education. Military aid is temporary in nature, a "shoring up" measure that only postpones crisis. In addition, it tends to divert the allocations of the nation being defended to supplementary military spending (Pakistan's budget is 70% oriented to defense measures). Sometimes it actually creates crisis situations, as in Latin America where we have contributed to the growth of national armies which are opposed generally to sweeping democratization. Finally, if we are really generous, it is harder for corrupt governments to exploit unfairly economic aid—especially if it is so plentiful that rulers cannot blame the absence of real reforms on anything but their own power lusts.

5. *America should show its commitment to democratic institutions not by withdrawing support from undemocratic regimes, but by making domestic democracy exemplary.*

Worldwide amusement, cynicism and hatred toward the United States as a democracy is not simply a communist propaganda trick, but an objectively justifiable phenomenon. If respect for democracy is to be international, then the significance of democracy must emanate from America shores, not from the "soft sell" of the United States Information Agency.

6. *America should agree that public utilities, railroads, mines, and plantations, and other basic economic institutions should be in the control of national, not foreign, agencies.*

The destiny of any country should be determined by its nationals, not by outsiders with economic interests within. We should encourage our investors to turn over their foreign holdings (or at least 50 percent of the stock) to the national governments of the countries involved.

7. *Foreign aid should be given through international agencies, primarily the United Nations.*

The need is to eliminate political overtones, to the extent possible, from economic development. The use of international agencies, with interests transcending those of American or Russian self-interest, is the feasible means of working on sound development. Second, internationalization will allow more long-range planning, integrate development plans adjacent countries and regions may have, and eliminate the duplication built into national systems of foreign aid. Third, it would justify more strictness of supervision than is now the case with American foreign aid efforts, but with far less chance of suspicion on the part of the developing countries. Fourth, the humiliating "hand-out" effect would be replaced by the joint participation of all nations in the general development of the earth's resources and industrial capacities. Fifth, it would eliminate national tensions, e.g. between Japan and some Southeast Asian areas, which now impair aid programs by "disguising" nationalities in the common pooling of funds. Sixth, it would make easier the task of stabilizing the world market prices of basic commodities, alleviating the enormous threat that decline in prices of commodity exports might cancel out the gains from foreign aid in the new nations. Seventh, it would improve the possibilities of non-exploitative development, especially in creating "soft-credit" rotating-fund agencies which would not require immediate progress or financial return. Finally, it would enhance the importance of the United Nations itself, as the disarming process would enhance the UN as a rule-enforcement agency.

8. *Democratic theory must confront the problems inherent in social revolutions.*

For Americans concerned with the development of democratic societies, the anti-colonial movements and revolutions in the emerging nations pose serious problems. We need to face these problems with humility: after 180 years of constitutional government we are still striving for democracy in our own society. We must acknowledge that democracy and freedom do not magically occur, but have roots in historical experience; they cannot always be demanded for any society at any time, but must be nurtured and facilitated. We must avoid the arbitrary projection of Anglo-Saxon democratic forms onto different cultures. Instead of democratic capitalism we should anticipate more or less authoritarian variants of socialism and collectivism in many emergent societies.

But we do not abandon our critical faculties. Insofar as these regimes represent a genuine realization of national independence, and are engaged in constructing social systems which allow for personal meaning and purpose where exploitation once was, economic systems which work for the people where once they oppressed them, and political systems which allow for the organization and expression of minority opinion and dissent, we recognize their revolutionary and positive character. Americans can contribute to the growth of democracy in such societies not by moralizing, nor by indiscriminate prejudgment, but by retaining a critical identification with these nations, and by helping them to avoid external threats to their independence. Together with students and radicals in these nations we need to develop a reasonable theory of democracy which is concretely applicable to the cultures and conditions of hungry people.

TOWARDS AMERICAN DEMOCRACY

Every effort to end the Cold War and expand the process of world industrialization is an effort hostile to people and institutions whose interests lie in perpetuation of the East-West military threat and the postponement of change in the "have not" nations of the world. Every such effort, too, is bound to establish greater democracy in America. The major goals of a domestic effort would be:

1. *America must abolish its political party stalemate.*

Two genuine parties, centered around issues and essential values, demanding allegiance to party principles shall supplant the current system of organized stalemate which is seriously inadequate to a world in flux. It has long been argued that the very overlapping of American parties guarantees that issues will be considered responsibly, that progress will be gradual instead of intemperate, and that therefore America will remain stable instead of torn by class strife. On the contrary: the enormous party overlap itself confuses issues and makes responsible presentation of choice to the electorate impossible, that guarantees Congressional listlessness and the drift of power to military and economic bureaucracies, that directs attention away from the more fundamental causes of social stability, such as a huge middle class, Keynesian economic techniques and Madison Avenue advertising. The ideals of political democracy, then, the imperative need for flexible decision-making apparatus makes a real two-party system an immediate social necessity. What is desirable is sufficient party disagreement to dramatize major issues, yet sufficient party overlap to guarantee stable transitions from administration to administration.

Every time the President criticizes a recalcitrant Congress, we must ask that he no longer tolerate the Southern conservatives in the Democratic Party. Every time a liberal representative complains that "we can't expect everything at once" we must ask if we received much of anything from Congress in the last generation. Every time he refers to "circumstances beyond control" we must ask why he fraternizes with racist scoundrels. Every time he speaks of the "unpleasantness of personal and party fighting" we should insist that pleasantry with Dixiecrats is inexcusable when the dark peoples of the world call for American support.

2. *Mechanisms of voluntary association must be created through which political information can be imparted and political participation encouraged.*

Political parties, even if realigned, would not provide adequate outlets for popular involvement. Institutions should be created that engage people with issues and express political preference, not as now with huge business lobbies which exercise undemocratic *power*, but which carry political *influence* (appropriate to private, rather than public, groupings) in national decision-making enterprise. Private in nature, these should be organized around single issues (medical care, transportation systems reform, etc.), concrete interest (labor and minority group organizations), multiple issues or general issues. These do not exist in America in quantity today. If they did exist, they would be a significant politicizing and educative force bringing people into touch with public life and affording them means of expression and action. Today, giant lobby representatives of business interests are dominant, but not educative. The Federal government itself should counter the latter forces whose intent is often public deceit for private gain, by subsidizing the preparation and decentralized distribution of objective materials on all public issues facing government.

3. *Institutions and practices which stifle dissent should be abolished, and the promotion of peaceful dissent should be actively promoted.*

The first Amendment freedoms of speech, assembly, thought, religion and press should be seen as guarantees, not threats, to national security. While society has the right to prevent active subversion of its laws and institutions, it has the duty as well to promote open discussion of all issues—otherwise it will be in fact promoting real subversion as the only means to implementing ideas. To eliminate the fears and apathy from national life it is necessary that the institutions bred by fear and apathy be rooted out: the House Un-American Activities Committee, the Senate Internal Security Committee, the loyalty oaths on Federal loans, the Attorney General's list of subversive organizations, the Smith and McCarren Acts. The process of eliminating these blighting institutions is the process of restoring democratic participation. Their existence is a sign of the decomposition and atrophy of participation.

4. *Corporations must be made publicly responsible.*

It is not possible to believe that true democracy can exist where a minority utterly controls enormous wealth and power. The influence of corporate elites on foreign policy is neither reliable nor democratic; a way must be found to subordinate private American foreign investment to a democratically-constructed foreign policy. The influence of the same giants on domestic life is intolerable as well; a way must be found to direct our economic resources to genuine human needs, not the private needs of corporations nor the rigged needs of maneuvered citizenry.

We can no longer rely on competition of the many to ensure that business enterprise is responsive to social needs. The many have become the few. Nor can we trust the corporate bureaucracy to be socially responsible or to develop a "corporate conscience" that is democratic. The community of interest of corporations, the anarchic actions of industrial leaders, should become structurally responsible to the people—and truly to the people rather than to an ill-defined and questionable "national interest." Labor and government as presently constituted are not sufficient to "regulate" corporations. A new re-ordering, a new calling of responsibility is necessary: more than changing "work rules" we must consider changes in the rules of society by challenging the unchallenged politics of American corporations. Before the government can really begin to control business in a "public interest," the public must gain more substantial control of government: this demands a movement for political as well as economic realignments. We are aware that simple government "regulation," if achieved, would be inadequate without increased worker participation in management decision-making, strengthened and independent regulatory power, balances of partial and/or complete public ownership, various means of humanizing the conditions and types of work itself, sweeping welfare programs and regional *public* government authorities. These are examples of measures to re-balance the economy toward public—and individual—control.

5. *The allocation of resources must be based on social needs. A truly "public sector" must be established, and its nature debated and planned.*

At present the majority of America's "public sector," the largest part of our public spending, is for the military. When great social needs are so pressing, our concept of "government spending" is wrapped up in the "permanent war economy."

In fact, if war is to be avoided, the "permanent war economy" must be seen as an "*interim* war economy." At some point, America must return to other mechanisms of economic growth besides public military spending. We must plan economically in peace. The most likely, and least desirable, return would be in the form of private enterprise. The undesirability lies in the fact of inherent capitalist instability, noticeable even with bolstering effects of government intervention. In the most recent post-war recessions, for example, private expenditures for plant and equipment dropped from $16 billion to $11.5 billion, while unemployment surged to nearly six million. By good fortune, investments in construction industries remained level, else an economic depression would have occurred. This will recur, and our growth in national per capita living standards will remain unsensational while the economy stagnates.

The main *private* forces of economic expansion cannot guarantee a steady rate of growth, nor acceptable recovery from recession—especially in a demilitarizing world. Government participation in the economy is essential. Such participation will inevitably expand enormously, because the stable growth of the economy demands increasing "public" investments yearly. Our present outpour of more than $500 billion might double in a generation, irreversibly involving government solutions. And in future recessions, the compensatory fiscal action by the government will be the only means of avoiding the twin disasters of greater unemployment and a slackening rate of growth. Furthermore, a close relationship with the European Common Market will involve competition with numerous planned economies and may aggravate American unemployment unless the economy here is expanding swiftly enough to create new jobs.

All these tendencies suggest that not only solutions to our present social needs but our future expansion rests upon our willingness to enlarge the "public sector" greatly. Unless we choose war as an economic solvent, future public spending will be of a non-military nature—a major intervention into civilian production by the government. The issues posed by this development are enormous:

A. How should public vs. private domain be determined? We suggest these criteria: 1) when a resource has been discovered or developed with public tax revenues, such as a space communications system, it should remain a public source, not be given away to private enterprise; 2) when monopolization seems inevitable, the public should maintain control of an industry; 3) when national objectives contradict seriously with business objectives as to the use of the resource, the public need should prevail.

B. How should technological advances be introduced into a society? By a public process, based on publicly-determined needs. Technological innovations should not be postponed from social use by private corporations in order to protect investment in older equipment.

C. How shall the "public sector" be made public, and not the arena of a ruling bureaucracy of "public servants"? By steadfast opposition to bureaucratic coagulation, and to definitions of human needs according to problems easiest for computers to solve. Second, the bureaucratic pileups must be at least minimized by local, regional, and national economic *planning*—responding to the interconnection of public problems by comprehensive programs of solution. Third, and most important, by experiments in *decentralization,* based on the vision of man as master of his machines and his society. The personal capacity to cope with life has been reduced everywhere by the introduction of technology that only minorities of men (barely) understand. How the process can be reversed—and we believe it can be—is one of the greatest sociological and economic tasks before human people today. Polytechnical schooling, with the individual adjusting to several work and life experiences, is one method. The transfer of certain mechanized tasks back into manual forms, allowing men to make whole, not partial, products, is not unimaginable. Our monster cities, based historically on the need for mass labor, might now be humanized, broken into smaller communities, powered by nuclear energy, arranged according to community decision. These are but a fraction of the opportunities of the new era: serious study and deliberate experimentation, rooted in a desire for human fraternity, may now result in blueprints of civic paradise.

6. *America should concentrate on its genuine social priorities: abolish squalor, terminate neglect, and establish an environment for people to live in with dignity and creativeness.*

A. A program against poverty must be just as sweeping as the nature of poverty itself. It must not be just palliative, but directed to the abolition of the structural circumstances of poverty. At a bare minimum it should include a *housing* act far larger than the one supported by the Kennedy Administration, but one that is geared more to low- and middle-income needs than to the windfall aspirations of small and large private entrepreneurs, one that is more sympathetic to the quality of communal life than to the efficiency of city-split highways. Second, *medical care* must become recognized as a lifetime human right just as vital as food, shelter and clothing—the Federal government should guarantee health insurance as a basic social service turning medical treatment into a social habit, not just an occasion of crisis, fighting sickness among the aged, not just by making medical care financially feasible but by reducing sickness among children and younger people. Third, existing institutions should be expanded so the welfare state cares for *everyone's* welfare according to need *Social Security* payments should be extended to everyone and should be proportionately greater for the poorest. A *minimum wage* of at least $1.50 should be extended to all workers (including the 16 million currently not covered at all). Programs for equal *educational opportunity* are as important a part of the battle against poverty.

B. A full-scale public initiative for civil rights should be undertaken despite the clamor among conservatives (and liberals) about gradualism, property rights, and law and order. The executive and legislative branches of the Federal government should work by enforcement *and* enactment against any form of exploitation of minority groups. No Federal cooperation with racism is tolerable—from financing of schools, to the development of Federally-supported industry, to the social gatherings of the President. Laws hastening school desegregation, voting rights, and economic protection for Negroes are needed right now. The moral force of the Executive Office should be exerted against the Dixiecrats specifically, and the national complacency about the race question generally. Especially in the North, where one-half of the country's Negro people now live, civil rights is not a problem to be solved in isolation from other problems. The fight against poverty, against slums, against the stalemated Congress, against McCarthyism, are all fights against the discrimination that is nearly endemic to all areas of American life.

C. The promise and problems of long-range *Federal economic development* should be studied more constructively. It is an embarrassing paradox that the Tennessee Valley Authority is a wonder to foreign visitors but a "radical" and barely influential project to most Americans. The Kennedy decision to permit private facilities to transmit power from the $1 billion Colorado River Storage Project is a disastrous one, interposing privately-owned transmitters between public-owned power generators and their publicly (and cooperatively) owned distributors. The contrary trend, to public ownership of power, should be generated in an experimental way.

The Area Redevelopment Act of 1961 is a first step in recognizing the underdeveloped areas of the United States. It is only a drop in the bucket financially and is not keyed to public planning and public works on a broad scale. It consists only of a few loan programs to lure industries and some grants to improve public facilities to lure these industries. The current public works bill in Congress is needed—and a more sweeping, higher-priced program of regional development with a proliferation of

"TVAs" in such areas as the Appalachian region are needed desperately. However, it has been rejected already by Mississippi because of the improvement it bodes for the unskilled Negro worker. This program should be enlarged, given teeth, and pursued rigorously by Federal authorities.

D. We must meet the growing complex of "city" problems; over 90 percent of Americans will live in urban areas in the next two decades. Juvenile delinquency, untended mental illness, crime increase, slums, urban tenantry and non-rent controlled housing, the isolation of the individual in the city—all are problems of the city and are major symptoms of the present system of economic priorities and lack of public planning. Private property control (the real estate lobby and a few selfish landowners and businesses) is as devastating in the cities as corporations are on the national level. But there is no comprehensive way to deal with these problems now midst competing units of government, dwindling tax resources, suburban escapism (saprophitic to the sick central cities), high infrastructure costs and no one to pay them.

The only solutions are national and regional. "Federalism" has thus far failed here because states are rural-dominated; the Federal government has had to operate by bootlegging and trickle-down measures dominated by private interests, and the cities themselves have not been able to catch up with their appendages through annexation or federation. A new external challenge is needed, not just a Department of Urban Affairs but a thorough national *program* to help the cities. The *model* city must be projected—more community decision-making and participation, true integration of classes, races, vocations—provision for beauty, access to nature and the benefits of the central city as well, privacy without privatism, decentralized "units" spread horizontally with central, regional, democratic control—provision for the basic facility-needs, for everyone, with units of planned *regions* and thus public, democratic control over the growth of the civic community and the allocation of resources.

E. *Mental health* institutions are in dire need; there were fewer mental hospital beds in relation to the numbers of mentally-ill in 1959 than there were in 1948. Public hospitals, too, are seriously wanting; existing structures alone need an estimated $1 billion for rehabilitation. Tremendous staff and faculty needs exist as well, and there are not enough medical students enrolled today to meet the anticipated needs of the future.

F. Our *prisons* are too often the enforcers of misery. They must be either re-oriented to rehabilitative work through public supervision or be abolished for their dehumanizing social effects. Funds are needed, too, to make possible a decent prison environment.

G. *Education* is too vital a public problem to be completely entrusted to the province of the various states and local units. In fact, there is no good reason why America should not progress now toward internationalizing rather than localizing, its educational system—children and young adults studying everywhere in the world, through a United Nations program, would go far to create mutual understanding. In the meantime, the need for teachers and classrooms in America is fantastic. This is an area where "minimal" requirements hardly should be considered as a goal—there always are improvements to be made in the educational system, e.g., smaller classes and many more teachers for them, programs to subsidize the education of the poor but bright, etc.

H. America should eliminate *agricultural policies* based on scarcity and pent-up surplus. In America and foreign countries there exist tremendous needs for more food and balanced diets. The Federal government should finance small farmers' cooperatives, strengthen programs of rural electrification, and expand policies for the distribution of agricultural surpluses throughout the world (by Food-for-Peace and related UN programming). Marginal farmers must be helped to either become productive enough to survive "industrialized agriculture" or given help in making the transition out of agriculture—the current Rural Area Development program must be better coordinated with a massive national "area redevelopment" program.

I. Science should be employed to constructively transform the conditions of life throughout the United States and the world. Yet at the present time the Department of Health, Education, and Welfare and the National Science Foundation together spend only $300 million annually for scientific purposes in contrast to the $6 billion spent by the Defense Department and the Atomic Energy Commission. One-half of all research and development in America is directly devoted to military purposes. Two imbalances must be corrected—that of military over non-military investigation, and that of biological-natural-physical science over the sciences of human behavior. Our political system must then include planning for the human use of science: by anticipating the political consequences of scientific innovation, by directing the discovery and exploration of space, by adapting science to improved production of food, to international communications systems, to technical problems of disarmament, and so on. For the newly-developing nations, American science should focus on the study of cheap sources of power, housing and building materials, mass educational techniques, etc. Further, science and scholarship should be seen less as an apparatus of conflicting power blocs, but as a bridge toward supranational community: the International Geophysical Year is a model for continuous further cooperation between the science communities of all nations.

Alternatives to Helplessness

The goals we have set are not realizable next month, or even next election—but that fact justifies neither giving up altogether nor a determination to work only on immediate, direct, tangible problems. Both responses are a sign of helplessness, fearfulness of visions, refusal to hope, and tend to bring on the very conditions to be avoided. Fearing vision, we justify rhetoric or myopia. Fearing hope, we reinforce despair.

The first effort, then, should be to state a vision: what is the perimeter of human possibility in this epoch? This we have tried to do. The second effort, if we are to be politically responsible, is to evaluate the prospects for obtaining at least a substantial part of that vision in our epoch: what are the social forces that exist, or that must exist, if we are to be at all successful? And what role have we ourselves to play as a social force?

1. In exploring the existing social forces, note must be taken of the Southern civil rights movement as the most heartening because of the justice it insists upon, exemplary because it indicates that there can be a passage out of apathy.

This movement, pushed into a brilliant new phase by the Montgomery bus boycott and the subsequent nonviolent action of the sit-ins and Freedom Rides, has had three major results: first, a sense of self-determination has been instilled in millions of oppressed Negroes; second, the movement has challenged a few thousand liberals to new social idealism; third, a series of important concessions have been obtained, such as token school desegregation, increased Administration help, new laws, desegregation of some public facilities.

But fundamental social change—that would break the props from under Jim Crow—has not come. Negro employment opportunity, wage levels, housing conditions, educational privileges—these remain deplorable and relatively constant, each deprivation reinforcing the impact of the others. The Southern states, in the meantime, are strengthening the fortresses of the status quo, and are beginning to camouflage the fortresses by guile where open bigotry announced its defiance before. The white-controlled one-party system remains intact; and even where the Republicans are beginning under the pressures of industrialization in the towns and suburbs, to show initiative in fostering a two-party system, all Southern state Republican Committees (save Georgia) have adopted militant segregationist platforms to attract Dixiecrats.

Rural dominance remains a fact in nearly all the Southern states, although the reapportionment decision of the Supreme Court portends future power shifts to the cities. Southern politicians maintain a continuing aversion to the welfare legislation that would aid their people. The reins of the Southern economy are held by conservative businessmen who view human rights as secondary to property rights. A violent anti-communism is rooting itself in the South, and threatening even moderate voices. Add the militaristic tradition of the South, and its irrational regional mystique and one must conclude that authoritarian and reactionary tendencies are a rising obstacle to the small, voiceless, poor, and isolated democratic movements.

The civil rights struggle thus has come to an impasse. To this impasse, the movement responded this year by entering the sphere of politics, insisting on citizenship rights, specifically the right to vote. The new voter registration stage of protest represents perhaps the first major attempt to exercise the conventional instruments of political democracy in the struggle for racial justice. The vote, if used strategically by the great mass of now-unregistered Negroes theoretically eligible to vote, will be a decisive factor in changing the quality of Southern leadership from low demagoguery to decent statesmanship.

More important, the new emphasis on the vote heralds the use of *political* means to solve the problems of equality in America, and it signals the decline of the shortsighted view that "discrimination" can be isolated from related social problems. Since the moral clarity of the civil rights movement has not always been accompanied by precise political vision, and sometimes not even by a real political consciousness, the new phase is revolutionary in its implications. The intermediate goal of the program is to secure and insure a healthy respect and realization of Constitutional liberties. This is important not only to terminate the civil and private abuses which currently characterize the region, but also to prevent the pendulum of oppression from simply swinging to an alternate extreme with a new unsophisticated electorate, after the unhappy example of the last Reconstruction. It is the *ultimate* objectives of the strategy which promise profound change in the politics of the nation. An increased Negro voting rate in and of itself is not going to dislodge racist controls of the Southern power structure; but an accelerating movement through the courts, the ballot boxes, and especially the jails is the most likely means of shattering the crust of political intransigency and creating a semblance of democratic order, on local and state levels.

Linked with pressure from Northern liberals to expunge the Dixiecrats from the ranks of the Democratic Party, massive Negro voting in the South could destroy the vice-like grip reactionary Southerners have on the Congressional legislative process.

2. The broadest movement for *peace* in several years emerged in 1961–62. In its political orientation and goals it is much less identifiable than the movement for civil rights: it includes socialists,
pacifists, liberals, scholars, militant activists, middle-class women, some professionals, many students, a few unionists. Some have been emotionally single-issue: Ban the Bomb. Some have been
academically obscurantist. Some have rejected the System (sometimes both systems). Some have
attempted, too, to "work within" the system. Amidst these conflicting streams of emphasis,
however, certain basic qualities appear. The most important is that the "peace movement" has
operated almost exclusively through peripheral institutions—almost never through mainstream
institutions. Similarly, individuals interested in peace have nonpolitical social roles that cannot
be turned to the support of peace activity. Concretely, liberal religious societies, anti-war groups,
voluntary associations, ad hoc committees have been the political unit of the peace movement;
and its human movers have been students, teachers, housewives, secretaries, lawyers, doctors,
clergy. The units have not been located in spots of major social influence; the people have not
been able to turn their resources fully to the issues that concern them. The results are political
ineffectiveness and personal alienation.

The organizing ability of the peace movement thus is limited to the ability to state and
polarize issues. It does not have an institution or the forum in which the conflicting interests can
be debated. The debate goes on in corners; it has little connection with the continuing process of
determining allocations of resources. This process is not necessarily centralized, however much
the peace movement is estranged from it. National policy, though dominated to a large degree
by the "power elites" of the corporations and military, is still partially founded in consensus. It
can be altered when there actually begins a shift in the allocation of resources and the listing of
priorities by the people in the institutions which have social influence, e.g., the labor unions and
the schools. As long as the debates of the peace movement form only a protest, rather than an
opposition viewpoint within the centers of serious decision-making, then it is neither a movement of democratic relevance, nor is it likely to have any effectiveness except in educating more
outsiders to the issue. It is vital, to be sure, that this educating go on (a heartening sign is the
recent proliferation of books and journals dealing with peace and war from newly-developing
countries); the possibilities for making politicians responsible to "peace constituencies" becomes
greater.

But in the long interim before the national political climate is more open to deliberate, goal-
directed debate about peace issues, the dedicated peace "movement" might well prepare a *local
base*, especially by establishing civic committees on the techniques of converting from military to
peacetime production. To make war and peace *relevant* to the problems of everyday life, by
relating it to the backyard (shelters), the baby (fall-out), the job (military contracts)—and making a turn toward peace seem desirable on these same terms—is a task the peace movement is
just beginning, and can profitably continue.

3. Central to any analysis of the potential for change must be an appraisal of *organized labor*. It
would be ahistorical to disregard the immense influence of labor in making modern America a
decent place in which to live. It would be confused to fail to note labor's presence today as the
most liberal of mainstream institutions. But it would be irresponsible not to criticize labor for
losing much of the idealism that once made it a driving movement. Those who expected a labor
upsurge after the 1955 AFL-CIO merger can only be dismayed that one year later, in the
Stevenson-Eisenhower campaign, the AFL-CIO Committee on Political Education was able to

obtain solicited $1.00 contributions from only one of every 24 unionists, and prompt only 40% of the rank-and-file to vote.

As a political force, labor generally has been unsuccessful in the postwar period of prosperity. It has seen the passage of the Taft-Hartley and Landrum-Griffin laws, and while beginning to receiving slightly favorable National Labor Relations Board rulings, it has made little progress against right-to-work laws. Furthermore, it has seen less than adequate action on domestic problems, especially unemployment.

This labor "recession" has been only partly due to anti-labor politicians and corporations. Blame should be laid, too, to labor itself for not mounting an adequate movement. Labor has too often seen itself as elitist, rather than mass-oriented, and as a pressure group rather than as an 18-million member body making political demands for all America. In the first instance, the labor bureaucracy tends to be cynical toward, or afraid of, rank-and-file involvement in the work of the union. Resolutions passed at conventions are implemented only by high-level machinations, not by mass mobilization of the unionists. Without a significant base, labor's pressure function is materially reduced since it becomes difficult to hold political figures accountable to a movement that cannot muster a vote from a majority of its members.

There are some indications, however, that labor might regain its missing idealism. First, there are signs within the movement: of worker discontent with the economic progress, of collective bargaining, of occasional splits among union leaders on questions such as nuclear testing or other Cold War issues. Second, and more important, are the social forces which prompt these feelings of unrest. Foremost is the permanence of unemployment, and the threat of automation. But important, too, is the growth of unorganized ranks in white-collar fields.. Third, there is the tremendous challenge of the Negro movement for support from organized labor: the alienation from and disgust with labor hypocrisy among Negroes ranging from the NAACP to the Black Muslims (crystallized in the formation of the Negro American Labor Council) indicates that labor must move more seriously in its attempts to organize on an interracial basis in the South and in large urban centers. When this task was broached several years ago, "jurisdictional" disputes prevented action. Today, many of these disputes have been settled—and the question of a massive organizing campaign is on the labor agenda again.

These threats and opportunities point to a profound crisis: either labor will continue to decline as a social force, or it must constitute itself as a mass political force demanding not only that society recognize its rights to organize but also a program going beyond desired labor legislation and welfare improvements. Necessarily this latter role will require rank-and-file involvement. It might include greater autonomy and power for political coalitions of the various trade unions in local areas; rather than the more stultifying dominance of the international unions now. It might include reductions in leaders' salaries, or rotation from executive office to shop obligations, as a means of breaking down the hierarchical tendencies which have detached elite from base and made the highest echelons of labor more like businessmen than workers. It would certainly mean an announced independence of the center and Dixiecrat wings of the Democratic Party, and a massive organizing drive, especially in the South to complement the growing Negro political drive there.

A new politics must include a revitalized labor movement; a movement which sees itself, and is regarded by others, as a major leader of the breakthrough to a politics of hope and vision. Labor's role is no less unique or important in the needs of the future than it was in the past, its numbers and potential political strength, its natural interest in the abolition of exploitation, its reach to the grass roots of American society, combine to make it the best candidate for the synthesis of the civil rights, peace, and economic reform movements.

The creation of bridges is made more difficult by the problems left over from the generation of "silence." Middle class students, still the main actors in the embryonic upsurge, have yet to overcome their ignorance, and even vague hostility, for what they see as "middle class labor" bureaucrats. Students must open the campus to labor through publications, action programs, curricula, while labor opens its house to students through internships, requests for aid (on the picket-line, with handbills, in the public dialogue), and politics. And the organization of the campus can be a beginning—teachers' unions can be advocated as both socially progressive, and educationally beneficial; university employees can be organized—and thereby an important element in the education of the student radical.

But the new politics is still contained; it struggles below the surface of apathy, awaiting liberation. Few anticipate the breakthrough and fewer still exhort labor to begin. Labor continues to be the most liberal—and most frustrated—institution in mainstream America.

4. Since the Democratic Party sweep in 1958, there have been exaggerated but real efforts to establish a liberal force in Congress, not to balance but to at least voice criticism of the conservative mood. The most notable of these efforts was the Liberal Project begun early in 1959 by Representative Kastenmeier of Wisconsin. The Project was neither disciplined nor very influential but it was concerned at least with confronting basic domestic and foreign problems, in concert with sever liberal intellectuals.

In 1960 five members of the Project were defeated at the polls (for reasons other than their membership in the Project). Then followed a "post mortem" publication of the *Liberal Papers*, materials discussed by the Project when it was in existence. Republican leaders called the book "further out than Communism." The New Frontier Administration repudiated any connection with the statements. Some former members of the Project even disclaimed their past roles.

A hopeful beginning came to a shameful end. But during the demise of the Project, a new spirit of Democratic Party reform was occurring: in New York City, Ithaca, Massachusetts, Connecticut, Texas, California, and even in Mississippi and Alabama where Negro candidates for Congress challenged racist political power. Some were for peace, some for the liberal side of the New Frontier, some for realignment of the parties—and in most cases they were supported by students.

Here and there were stirrings of organized discontent with the political stalemate. Americans for Democratic Action and the *New Republic*, pillars of the liberal community, took stands against the President on nuclear testing. A split, extremely slight thus far, developed in organized labor on the same issue. The Rev. Martin Luther King, Jr., preached against the Dixiecrat-Republican coalition across the nation.

5. From 1960 to 1962, the campuses experienced a revival of idealism among an active few. Triggered by the impact of the sit-ins, students began to struggle for integration, civil liberties, student rights, peace, and against the fast-rising right wing "revolt" as well. The liberal students, too, have felt their urgency thwarted by conventional channels: from student governments to Congressional committees. Out of this alienation from existing channels has come the creation of new ones; the most characteristic forms of liberal-radical student organizations are the dozens of campus political parties, political journals, and peace marches and demonstrations. In only a

few cases have students built bridges to power: an occasional election campaign, the sit-ins, Freedom Rides, and voter registration activities; in some relatively large Northern demonstrations for peace and civil rights, and infrequently, through the United States National Student Association whose notable work has not been focused on political change.

These contemporary social movements—for peace, civil rights, civil liberties, labor—have in common certain values and goals. The fight for peace is one for a stable and racially integrated world; for an end to the inherently volatile exploitation of most of mankind by irresponsible elites; and for freedom of economic, political and cultural organization. The fight for civil rights is also one for social welfare for all Americans; for free speech and the right to protest; for the shield of economic independence and bargaining power; for a reduction of the arms race which takes national attention and resources away from the problems of domestic injustice. Labor's fight for jobs and wages is also one against exploitation of the Negro as a source of cheap labor; for the right to petition and strike; for world industrialization; for the stability of a peacetime economy instead of the insecurity of the war economy; for expansion of the welfare state. The fight for a liberal Congress is a fight for a platform from which these concerns can issue. And the fight for students, for internal democracy in the university, is a fight to gain a forum for the issues.

But these scattered movements have more in common: a need for their concerns to be expressed by a political party responsible to their interests. That they have no political expression, no political channels, can be traced in large measure to the existence of a Democratic Party which tolerates the perverse unity of liberalism and racism, prevents the social change wanted by Negroes, peace protesters, labor unions, students, reform Democrats, and other liberals. Worse, the party stalemate prevents even the raising of controversy—a full Congressional assault on racial discrimination, disengagement in Central Europe, sweeping urban reform, disarmament and inspection, public regulation of major industries; these and other issues are never heard in the body that is supposed to represent the best thoughts and interests of all Americans.

An imperative task for these publicly disinherited groups, then, is to demand a Democratic Party responsible to their interests. They must support Southern voter registration and Negro political candidates and demand that Democratic Party liberals do the same (in the last Congress, Dixiecrats split with Northern Democrats on 119 of 300 roll-calls, mostly on civil rights, area redevelopment and foreign aid bills; the breach was much larger than in the previous several sessions). Labor should begin a major drive in the South. In the North, reform clubs (either independent or Democratic) should be formed to run against big city regimes on such issues as peace, civil rights, and urban needs. Demonstrations should be held at every Congressional or convention seating of Dixiecrats. A massive research and publicity campaign should be initiated, showing to every housewife, doctor, professor, and worker the damage done to their interests every day a racist occupies a place in the Democratic Party. Where possible, the peace movement should challenge the "peace credentials" of the otherwise-liberals by threatening or actually running candidates against them.

The University and Social Change

There is perhaps little reason to be optimistic about the above analysis. True, the Dixiecrat-GOP coalition is the weakest point in the dominating complex of corporate, military and political power. But the civil rights, peace and student movements are too poor and socially slighted, and the labor movement too quiescent, to be counted with enthusiasm. From where else can power and vision be summoned? We believe that the universities are an overlooked seat of influence.

First, the university is located in a permanent position of social influence. Its educational function makes it indispensable and automatically makes it a crucial institution in the formation of social attitudes. Second, in an unbelievably complicated world, it is the central institution for organizing, evaluating, and transmitting knowledge. Third, the extent to which academic resources presently are used to buttress immoral social practice is revealed first, by the extent to which defense contracts make the universities engineers of the arms race. Too, the use of modern social science as a manipulative tool reveals itself in the "human relations" consultants to the modern corporation, who introduce trivial sops to give laborers feelings of "participation" or "belonging," while actually deluding them in order to further exploit their labor. And, of course, the use of motivational research is already infamous as a manipulative aspect of American politics. But these social uses of the universities' resources also demonstrate the unchangeable reliance by men of power on the men and storehouses of knowledge: this makes the university functionally tied to society in new ways, revealing new potentialities, new levers for change. Fourth, the university is the only mainstream institution that is open to participation by individuals of nearly any viewpoint.

These, at least, are facts, no matter how dull the teaching, how paternalistic the rules, how irrelevant the research that goes on. Social relevance, the accessibility to knowledge, and internal openness—these together make the university a potential base and agency in a movement of social change.

1. Any new left in America must be, in large measure, a left with real intellectual skills, committed to deliberativeness, honesty, reflection as working tools. The university permits the political life to be an adjunct to the academic one, and action to be informed by reason.

2. A new left must be distributed in significant social roles throughout the country. The universities are distributed in such a manner.

3. A new left must consist of younger people who matured in the postwar world, and partially be directed to the recruitment of younger people. The university is an obvious beginning point.

4. A new left must include liberals and socialists, the former for their relevance, the latter for their sense of thoroughgoing reforms in the system. The university is a more sensible place than a political party for these two traditions to begin to discuss their differences and look for political synthesis.

5. A new left must start controversy across the land, if national policies and national apathy are to be reversed. The ideal university is a community of controversy, within itself and in its effects on communities beyond.

6. A new left must transform modern complexity into issues that can be understood and felt close-up by every human being. It must give form to the feelings of helplessness and indifference, so that people may see the political, social and economic sources of their private troubles and organize to change society. In a time of supposed prosperity, moral complacency and political manipulation, a new left cannot rely on only aching stomachs to be the engine force of social reform. The case for change, for alternatives that will involve uncomfortable personal efforts, must be argued as never before. The university is a relevant place for all of these activities.

But we need not indulge in illusions: the university system cannot complete a movement of ordinary people making demands for a better life. From its schools and colleges across the nation, a militant left might awaken its allies, and by beginning the process towards peace, civil rights, and labor struggles, reinsert theory and idealism where too often reign confusion and political barter. The power of students and faculty united is not only potential; it has shown its actuality in the South, and in the reform movements of the North.

The bridge to political power, though, will be built through genuine cooperation, locally, nationally, and internationally, between a new left of young people, and an awakening community of allies. In each community we must look within the university and act with confidence that we can be powerful, but we must look outwards to the less exotic but more lasting struggles for justice.

To turn these possibilities into realities will involve national efforts at university reform by an alliance of students and faculty. They must wrest control of the educational process from the administrative bureaucracy. They must make fraternal and functional contact with allies in labor, civil rights, and other liberal forces outside the campus. They must import major public issues into the curriculum—research and teaching on problems of war and peace is an outstanding example. They must make debate and controversy, not dull pedantic cant, the common style for educational life. They must consciously build a base for their assault upon the loci of power.

As students for a democratic society, we are committed to stimulating this kind of social movement, this kind of vision and program in campus and community across the country. If we appear to seek the unattainable, it has been said, then let it be known that we do so to avoid the unimaginable.

Notes

Introduction

1. Several books discuss this controversy and Harrington's part therein. See Michael Harrington, *Fragments of a Century* (New York: Simon and Schuster, 1973), 70–71; Maurice Isserman, *The Other American: The Life of Michael Harrington* (New York: Public Affairs, 2000), 221–44; Todd Gitlin, *The Sixties: Years of Hope, Days of Rage* (New York: Bantam Books, 1987), 109–26; James Miller, *"Democracy Is in the Streets": From Port Huron to the Siege of Chicago* (New York: Simon and Schuster, 1987), 126–40.

2. The Port Huron Statement, page 242 in this volume. Hereafter, all quotations and citations to his document are to the 1964 version, the first that SDS printed rather than mimeographed. We have reprinted it, with new pagination, as an appendix. The 1964 edition corrects spelling and typographical errors found in the 1962 version of the Statement and changes a very few phrases and words, none consequential. It is by far the most widely read and quoted version. We have retained the 1962 "Introductory Note," however, because of its directness and immediacy.

3. As quoted in Milton Viorst, *Fire in the Streets: America in the 1960s* (New York: Simon and Schuster, 1979), 176.

4. Charles Payne, *I've Got the Light of Freedom: The Organizing Tradition and the Mississippi Freedom Struggle* (Berkeley: University of California Press, 1995), 101.

5. Tom Hayden, *Writings for a Democratic Society: The Tom Hayden Reader* (San Francisco: City Lights Books, 2008), 34.

6. Gitlin, *The Sixties*, 129.

7. As quoted in Miller, *"Democracy Is in the Streets,"* 144.

8. Robert Cohen, *Freedom's Orator: Mario Savio and the Radical Legacy of the 1960s* (New York: Oxford University Press, 2009), 327.

Chapter 1. Crafting the Port Huron Statement

1. Kirpatrick Sale, *SDS* (New York: Random House, 1973), 50–51.

2. Michael Kazin, "The Port Huron Statement at Fifty," *Dissent* (Spring 2012), 83.

3. Tom Hayden, *The Port Huron Statement: The Visionary Call of the 1960s Revolution* (New York: Thunder's Mouth Press, 2005).

4. As quoted in Vivian Gornick, *Emma Goldman: Revolution as a Way of Life* (New Haven: Yale University Press, 2011), 28.

5. Twenty-first-century historians have offered a somewhat more nuanced view. See Matthew Garcia, *From the Jaws of Victory: The Triumph and Tragedy of Cesar Chavez and the Farm*

Worker Movement (Berkeley: University of California Press, 2012); and Frank Bardacke, *Trampling Out the Vintage: Cesar Chavez and the Two Souls of the United Farm Workers* (New York: Verso, 2012).

6. Many younger historians now support this perspective. See, for example, Fred Logevall's authoritative *Choosing War: The Lost Chance for Peace and the Escalation of War in Vietnam* (Berkeley: University of California Press, 2001).

7. Such revelations and more are found in Seth Rosenfeld's *Subversives: The FBI's War on Student Radicals, and Reagan's Rise to Power* (New York: Picador, 2013).

8. For more, see Kevin Boyle, *The UAW and the Heyday of American Liberalism, 1945–1968* (Ithaca, NY: Cornell University Press, 1998); and Nelson Lichtenstein, *Walter Reuther: The Most Dangerous Man in Detroit* (Urbana: University of Illinois Press, 1997).

9. Howard Zinn, *A People's History of the United States* (New York: HarperCollins, 2005), 341.

10. Noam Chomsky, *Chomsky on Anarchism* (Oakland, CA: AK Press, 2005), 410–11.

11. Micah White, *Adbusters* 98 (February 4, 2012).

Chapter 2. Two Cheers for Utopia

1. Port Huron Statement in Appendix, 275.

2. "A Letter to the New (Young) Left," *Writings for a Democratic Society: The Tom Hayden Reader* (San Francisco: City Lights Books, 2008), 21.

3. Weld in 1885, quoted in Merton L. Dillon, "The Abolitionists as a Dissenting Minority," in *Dissent: Explorations in the History of American Radicalism,* ed. Alfred F. Young (DeKalb: Northern Illinois University Press, 1968), 25.

4. Eldridge Cleaver, *Soul on Ice* (New York: McGraw-Hill, 1967), 15; Marshall Berman, *The Politics of Authenticity* (New York: Atheneum, 1970), xii.

5. http://circuitous.org/scraps/combahee.html.

6. Port Huron Statement in Appendix, 279–80.

7. Nelson Lichtenstein, *The Most Dangerous Man in Detroit: Walter Reuther and the Fate of American Labor* (New York: Basic Books, 1995), 391.

8. Tom Hayden, *Reunion* (New York: Random House, 1988), 102.

9. Carl Oglesby, "The Idea of the New Left," introduction to *The New Left Reader*, ed. Oglesby (New York: Grove Press, 1969), 3. He added that Marxism "had lost, at both the theoretical and practical levels, the power to criticize itself" (11).

10. Jim Miller, *"Democracy Is in the Streets": From Port Huron to the Siege of Chicago* (New York: Simon and Schuster, 1987), 152.

11. Port Huron Statement in Appendix, 242.

12. Wieseltier, "Beyond Tahrir," *The New Republic,* December 15, 2011, 40.

13. Port Huron Statement in Appendix, 282.

14. Oglesby, speech at antiwar march in Washington, D.C., quoted in Kirkpatrick Sale, *SDS* (New York: Random House, 1973), 243–24.

15. Port Huron Statement in Appendix, 245.

16. http://www.bartleby.com/73/1828.html. Jerry Rubin later turned the jibe into a warning.

17. By 1980, more than 12 percent of the population was in college, compared with only 2.5 percent in 1950. Doug Rossinow, *The Politics of Authenticity: Liberalism, Christianity, and the New Left in America* (New York: Columbia University Press, 1998), 255.

18. Todd Gitlin, *The Sixties* (New York: Bantam Books, 1986), 103. The rest of Savio's speech was more temperate but, inevitably, it is his brief fulmination that survives in historical memory.

19. Port Huron Statement in Appendix, 242.

20. Miller, *"Democracy Is in the Streets,"* 328.

21. Port Huron Statement in Appendix, 283.

Chapter 3. Port Huron and the Origins of the International New Left

1. Eric Hobsbawm, *Age of Extremes: A History of the World, 1914–1991* (New York: Vintage, 1994), lays out well these important motor forces.

2. Kristin Ross, *May '68 and Its Afterlives* (Chicago: University of Chicago Press, 2002). See also Jacques Baynac, *Mai Retrouvé: Contribution à l'histoire du mouvement revolutionnaire du 3 mai au 16 juin 1968* (Paris: Robert Laffont, 1978); Antoine Artous, *Retours sur Mai* (Montreuil, France: Brèche-PEWC, 1988); Michel Seidman, *The Imaginary Revolution: Parisian Students and Workers in 1968* (New York: Berghahn, 2004); and Daniel Singer, *Prelude to Revolution: France in May 1968* (Cambridge, MA: South End, 2002).

3. Eric Zolov, *Refried Elvis: The Rise of the Mexican Counterculture* (Berkeley: University of California Press, 1999); César Gilabert, *El habito de la utopia: Análisis del imaginiario sociopolítico en el movimiento estudiantíl de México, 1968* (Mexico City: Instituto Mora/Miguel Angel Porrua, 1993); Gilberto Guevara Niebla, *La Democracia en la calle: Crónica del movimiento estudiantil mexicano* (Mexico City: Siglo XXI, 1988); Evelyn P. Stevens, *Protest and Response in Mexico* (Cambridge, MA: MIT Press, 1974); Elena Poniatowska, *Massacre in Mexico* (New York: Viking, 1975).

4. Bruno Trentin, *Autunno Caldo: Il Secondo Biennio Rosso, 1968–1969* (Rome: Riuniti, 1999); Robert Lumley, *States of Emergency: Cultures of Revolt from 1968 to 1978* (London: Verso, 1990); Joanne Barkan, *Visions of Emancipation: The Italian Workers' Movement Since 1945* (New York: Praeger, 1984).

5. H. Gordon Skilling, *Czechoslovakia's Interrupted Revolution* (Princeton, NJ: Princeton University Press, 1976); Kieran Williams, *The Prague Spring and Its Aftermath: Czechoslovak Politics, 1968–1970* (New York: Cambridge University Press, 1997); Günter Bischof, Stefan Karner, and Peter Ruggenthaler, eds., *The Prague Spring and the Warsaw Pact Invasion of Czechoslovakia in 1968* (Lanham, MD: Lexington Books, 2010).

6. Tim Brown, "1968 East and West: Divided Germany as a Case Study in Transnational History," *American Historical Review* 114 (February 2009): 69–96.

7. See also J. Victor Koschmann, *Revolution and Subjectivity in Postwar Japan* (Chicago: University of Chicago Press, 1996); Eiji Oguma, *1968, Wakamono Tachi No Hanran To Sono Haikei*, vol. 1: *1968, Youth Revolt and Its Background* (Tokyo: Shinyo-sha, 2009) and Eiji Oguma, *1968, Hanran No Shuen To Sono Isan*, vol. 2: *1968, The End of the Youth Revolt and Its Legacy* (Tokyo: Shinyo-sha, 2009). Japanese titles translated by Ryoko Kosugi. See also Kazuko Tsurumi, "Some Comments on the Japanese Student Movements in the Sixties," *Journal of Contemporary History* 5 (1970): 104–12, and William Marotti, "Japan 1968: The Performance of Violence and the Theater of Protest," *American Historical Review* (February 2009): 97–135.

8. Omar Gueye, *Mai 68 au Sénégal: Senghor face au monde du travail* (unpublished dissertation, Amsterdam Institute for Social Science Research, 2014).

9. See Martin Klimke, *The Other Alliance: Student Protest in West Germany and the United States in the Global 1960s* (Princeton, NJ: Princeton University Press, 2010); Gerd-Rainer Horn,

The Spirit of '68: Rebellion in Western Europe and North America, 1956–1976 (New York: Oxford University Press, 2007); Ingrid Gilcher-Holtey, *Die 68er Bewegung: Deutschland, Westeuropa, USA* (Munich: Beck, 2001). Some books that do attempt a global reach have done so by homing in on 1968 itself; see Jens Kastner and David Mayer, eds., *Weltwende 1968? Ein Jahr aus Globalgeschichtlicher Perspektive* (Vienna: Mandelbaum, 2008); Norbert Frei, *1968: Jugendrevolte und globaler Protest* (Munich: Deutscher Taschenbuch Verlag, 2008). Jeremi Suri's *Power and Protest* examines this international moment of rebellion to make an innovative argument about state leaders' responses to student protest and their embrace of détente. See Suri, *Power and Protest: Global Revolution and the Rise of Détente* (Cambridge, MA: Harvard University Press, 2003). Also worthy of mention is Ivan Jobs's effort to trace the cultural origins of a broad European identity to the 1960s youth movements; see Richard Ivan Jobs, "Youth Movements: Travel, Protest and Europe in 1968," *American Historical Review* 114 (April 2009): 376–404.

10. Karen Dubinsky et al., eds., *New World Coming: The Sixties and the Shaping of Global Consciousness* (Toronto: Between the Lines, 2009). See also "International 68" articles in the *American Historical Review* (2009).

11. Those books that examine transnational linkages have predominantly focused on Western Europe (Germany in particular) and the United States. See Ingrid Gilcher-Holtey, *Die 68er Bewegung: Deutschland, Westeuropa, USA* (Munich: Beck, 2001); Arthur Marwick's excellent *The Sixties: Cultural Transformation in Britain, France, Italy and the United States, c. 1958–c. 1974* (Oxford: Oxford University Press, 1998); and Horn, *Spirit of '68*.

12. See, for example, James Miller, *"Democracy Is in the Streets": From Port Huron to the Siege of Chicago* (New York: Simon and Schuster, 1987); Doug Rossinow, *The Politics of Authenticity: Liberalism, Christianity and the New Left in America* (New York: Columbia University Press, 1998); Todd Gitlin, *The Sixties: Years of Hope, Days of Rage* (New York: Bantam Books, 1987). Many memoirs and autobiographies of the student New Left similarly focus on experiences with SDS; see, for example, Robert Pardun, *Prairie Radical: A Journey Through the 1960s* (Los Gatos, CA: Shire Press, 2001); and Carl Oglesby, *Ravens in the Storm: A Personal History of the 1960s Anti-War Movement* (New York: Scribner, 2008).

13. See Dan Geary, "'Becoming International Again': C. Wright Mills and a Global New Left, 1956–1962," *Journal of American History* 95 (December 2008): 710–36; and Marwick, *The Sixties*.

14. Tsurumi, "Some Comments on the Japanese Student Movement in the Sixties,"105.

15. Patricia Steinhof, "Student Conflict," in *Conflict in Japan*, ed. Ellis S. Krauss, Thomas P. Rohlen, and Patricia G. Steinhoff (Honolulu: University of Hawaii Press, 1984), 174–213; see also Ryoko Kosugi, "The Japanese Student Movement," unpublished paper in author's possession; William Marotti, "Japan 1968: The Performance of Violence and the Theater of Protest," *American Historical Review* 114 (February 2009): 97–135.

16. Horn, *Spirit of '68*, 144–45; and Geary, "Becoming International Again."

17. Klimke, *The Other Alliance*, 14.

18. Ibid., 14.

19. Skilling, *Czechoslovakia's Interrupted Revolution*, 111–19.

20. See Maurice Isserman, *If I Had a Hammer: The Death of the Old Left and the Birth of the New Left* (Urbana: University of Illinois Press, 1993).

21. Geary, "Becoming International Again," 710–19.

22. Geary, "Becoming International Again," 710–19. See also Michael Newman, *Ralph Miliband and the Politics of the New Left* (London: Merlin Press, 2002), 66–67; Horn, *Spirit of '68*, 1.

23. Vijay Prashad, *The Darker Nations: A People's History of the Third World* (New York: New Press, 2007), 45–47. See also Christopher Lee, *Making a World After Empire: The Bandung Moment and Its Political Afterlives* (Athens: Ohio University Press, 2010).

24. Odd Arne Westad, *The Global Cold War* (New York: Oxford University Press, 2006), 102–8.

25. Port Huron Statement in Appendix, 257.

26. Quinn Slobodian, *Foreign Front: Third World Politics in Sixties West Germany* (Durham, NC: Duke University Press, 2012); Van Gosse, *Where the Boys Are: Cuba, the Cold War and the Making of a New Left* (New York: Verso, 1993); Sean Mills, *The Empire Within: Postcolonial Thought and Political Activism in Sixties Montreal* (Montreal: McGill–Queens University Press, 2010).

27. Klimke, *The Other Alliance*, 66.

28. Brenda Gayle Plummer, *In Search of Power: African-Americans in the Era of Decolonization, 1956–1974* (New York: Cambridge University Press, 2013).

29. Geary, "Becoming International Again," 722. See also Lawrence Witner, *Resisting the Bomb: A History of the World Nuclear Disarmament Movement, 1954–1970* (Stanford, CA: Stanford University Press, 1997). One example of a prominent New Left activist who got his start in the peace movement was Todd Gitlin; see Gitlin, *Years of Hope, Days of Rage.*

30. Port Huron Statement in Appendix, 239.

31. Hobsbawm, *Age of Extremes.*

32. Report, "Student Explosion," Lyndon B. Johnson Library, Austin Texas, as in Klimke, *The Other Alliance,* 210.

33. Horn, *Spirit of '68,* 77–79.

34. Hideo Otake, *Shin Sayoku No Isan: Nyu Refuto Kara Postutomodann E* (*The Legacy of the New Left: From New Left to Postmodern*) (Tokyo: University of Tokyo Press, 2007), 31–32 (translated by Ryoko Kosugi). See also Kosugi, "The Japanese Student Movement"; and Tsurumi, "Some Comments on the Japanese Student Movement in the Sixties."

35. Alla Baranovsky, "The Prague Spring: A Look at Events from Above and Below" (2011), unpublished paper in author's possession. See also Günter Bischof, Stefan Karner, and Peter Ruggenthaler, eds., *The Prague Spring and the Warsaw Pact Invasion of Czechoslovakia in 1968* (Lanham, MD: Lexington Books, 2010); Kieran Williams, *The Prague Spring and Its Aftermath: Czechoslovak Politics, 1968–1970* (Cambridge: Cambridge University Press, 1997).

36. Klimke, *The Other Alliance,* 18–28.

37. Horn, *Spirit of '68.*

38. Martin Klimke details the findings of the report by CIA director Richard Helms entitled "Restless Youth" in Klimke, *The Other Alliance,* 202.

39. Hideo Otake, *Shin Sayoku No Isan: Nyu Refuto Kara Postutomodann E* (*The Legacy of the New Left: From New Left to Postmodern* (Tokyo: University of Tokyo Press, 2007), 31–32 (translated by Ryoko Kosugi); see also Kosugi, "Japanese Student Movements."

40. Horn, *Spirit of '68.*

41. Uta Poiger, *Jazz, Rock, and Rebels: Cold War Politics and American Culture in a Divided Germany* (Berkeley: University of California Press, 2000); Eric Zolov, *Refried Elvis: The Rise of the Mexican Counterculture* (Berkeley: University of California Press, 1999).

42. Zolov, *Refried Elvis,* 15.

43. Ibid., 17–60.

44. Port Huron Statement in Appendix, 241.

45. Ibid., 240.

46. Horn, *Spirit of '68*.

47. See Andreas Hess, *Die Politische Soziologie C. Wright Mills: Eine Beitrag zur politischen Ideengeschicte* (Opladen, Germany: Liske & Budrich, 1995). See also Geary, "Becoming International Again"; and Horn, *Spirit of '68*, 146–53.

48. The influence of Marcuse is evident in Guy Debord, *La Société du Spectacle* (Paris: G. Lebovici, 1967).

49. Zafer Senocak, "Turkey: The Lost Generation," reprinted in *Global 68*, Goethe-Institut, http://www.geosthe.de/ges/pok/prj/akt/wit/oeu/tur/en3045180.htm.

50. Horn, *Spirit of '68*, 77, 103.

51. Port Huron Statement in Appendix, 242.

52. See Tsurumi, "Some Comments on the Japanese Student Movement": she writes, for example, that the students who support the Zenkyoto are oriented predominantly toward existential rather than direct political goals. In other words, their emphasis is on "change within rather than change without" (111). See also Victor Koschmann, who similarly identifies the importance of "subjectivity" and the search for new selfhood within the movement; J. Victor Koschmann, *Revolution and Subjectivity in Postwar Japan* (Chicago: University of Chicago Press, 1996), and Koschmann, "Intellectuals and Politics," in *Postwar Japan as History*, ed. Andrew Gordon (Berkeley: University of California Press, 1993), 395–423. The most recent scholarship on the movement in Japan, Eiji Oguma's two-volume set, has come to similar conclusions about the movement's existentialist orientation: Oguma, *1968, Wakamono Tachi No Hanran To Sono Haikei*, vol. 1: *1968, Youth Revolt and Its Background*, and vol. 2: *1968, The End of the Youth Revolt and Its Legacy*.

53. Marotti, "Japan: 1968."

54. Brown, "1968 East and West."

55. Santiago Roncagliolo, *La Cuarta Espada: La Historia de Abimael Guzman y Sendero Luminoso* (Barcelona: Debate Publishers, 2007).

56. Koschmann, *Revolution and Subjectivity in Postwar Japan*; Oguma, *1968, Hanran No Shuen To Sono Isan*, vol. 2; and Kosugi, "The Japanese Student Movement."

57. Jeremy Varon, *Bringing the War Home: The Weather Underground, the Red Army Faction and Revolutionary Violence in the Sixties and Seventies* (Berkeley: University of California Press, 2004).

58. See Evans, "Sons, Daughters, and Patriarchy," 332.

59. Ibid., 333.

Chapter 4. The Romance of Rebellion

1. James Forman, *The Making of Black Revolutionaries* (1972; Seattle: University of Washington Press, 1997); Sara Evans, *Personal Politics: The Roots of Women's Liberation in the Civil Rights Movement and the New Left* (New York: Vintage, 1980); Clayborne Carson, *In Struggle: SNCC and the Black Awakening of the 1960s* (Cambridge, MA: Harvard University Press, 1981); Todd Gitlin, *The Sixties: Days of Hope, Days of Rage* (New York: Bantam, 1987); and Doug Rossinow, *The Politics of Authenticity: Liberalism, Christianity, and the New Left in America* (New York: Columbia University Press, 1998).

2. Miles Orvell, *The Real Thing: Imitation and Authenticity in American Culture, 1880–1940* (Chapel Hill: University of North Carolina Press, 1990); and Grace Elizabeth Hale, *A Nation of*

Outsiders: How the White Middle Class Fell in Love with Rebellion in Postwar America (New York: Oxford University Press, 2011), especially chapter 3.

3. Nat Hentoff, "Folk Finds a Voice," *Reporter* (January 4, 1962), 40; John McPhee, "Folk Singing: Sibyl with Guitar," *Time* (November 23, 1962), 56; and Hale, *Nation of Outsiders*, 88–107.

4. Brian Massumi, *Parables for the Virtual: Movement, Affect, Sensation* (Durham, NC: Duke University Press, 2002); and Sara Ahmed, *The Cultural Politics of Emotion* (New York: Routledge, 2004).

5. Walter Benjamin, *Illuminations* (New York: Schocken, 1978); and Walter Benjamin, *Walter Benjamin and Art* (New York: Continuum, 2005).

6. Hale, *Nation of Outsiders*, 49–131; Leerom Medovoi, *Rebels: Youth and the Cold War Origins of Identity* (Durham, NC: Duke University Press, 2005); Steven Watson, *The Birth of the Beat Generation: Visionaries, Rebels, and Hipsters, 1944–1960* (New York: Pantheon, 1995); George Lipsitz, "Against the Wind: Dialogic Aspects of Rock and Roll," in *Time Passages: Collective Memory and American Popular Culture* (Minneapolis: University of Minnesota, 1990), 99–132; and George Gillett, *The Sound of the City: The Rise of Rock and Roll* (New York: Da Capo, 1995).

7. Hale, *Nation of Outsiders*, 84–131; Hale, "'My Political Beliefs Are Songs': Pete Seeger in Cold War America," in Kathleen Donohue, ed., *Liberty and Justice for All? Rethinking Politics in Cold War America* (Amherst: University of Massachusetts Press, 2012); the excellent Robert Cantwell, *When We Were Good: The Folk Revival* (Cambridge, MA: Harvard University Press, 1996); and John Cohen, "A Rare Interview with Harry Smith," *Sing Out!* 19, no. 1 (April/May 1969), quote on 3.

8. Tom Hayden, *Reunion: A Memoir* (New York: Random House, 1988), 39–41; Virginia Durr, *Freedom Writer: Virginia Foster Durr, Letters from the Civil Rights Years*, ed. Patricia Sullivan (New York: Routledge, 2003), 175; James Miller, *"Democracy Is in the Streets": From Port Huron to the Siege of Chicago* (Cambridge, MA: Harvard University Press, 1994), 33–34, 185–87; Bob Zellner with Constance Curry, *The Wrong Side of Murder Creek: A White Southerner in the Freedom Movement* (Montgomery, AL: New South Books, 2008), 61; Miller, *"Democracy Is in the Streets"*; Gitlin, *The Sixties*; Wini Breines, *Community and Organization in the New Left, 1962–1968: The Great Refusal* (New York: Praeger, 1982); Maurice Isserman, *The Death of the Old Left and the Birth of the New Left* (New York: Basic Books, 1987); Sohnya Sayres, Anders Stephanson, Stanley Aronowitz, and Fredric Jameson, *The 60s Without Apology* (Minneapolis: University of Minnesota Press, 1984); Arthur Marwick, *The Sixties: Cultural Revolution in Britain, France, Italy, and the United States* (New York: Oxford University Press, 1998); and Van Gosse, *Rethinking the New Left: An Interpretative History* (New York: Palgrave, 2005).

9. Only a few students at the time knew that the National Student Association was funded and controlled by the CIA. Hayden, like other radicals, was unaware of the connection and saw NSA as a convenient forum for airing ideas and winning converts. Haber was there in 1960 too, looking for student leaders to recruit into SDS. The NSA-CIA connection was exposed in 1967. See Sol Stern, "A Short Account of International Student Politics and the Cold War with Particular Reference to the NSA, CIA, Etc.," *Ramparts*, March 1967, 29–39.

10. Hayden, *Reunion*, quote, 18; Tim Findley, "Tom Hayden: *Rolling Stone* Interview, Parts I and II," *Rolling Stone*, October 26, 1972, 36–50, quote on 38; and November 9, 1972, 28–36. See also Steven V. Roberts, "Will Tom Hayden Overcome?" *Esquire*, December 1968, 176–79, 207–9.

11. Hayden, *Reunion*, 33–52, quotes, including Cason's, 33, 39–41.

12. Hayden, *Reunion,* 33–52.

13. Haber, SDS, New York City, September 27, 1960, to Tim Jenkins, Philadelphia, all in SDS File, Folder 18, Box 9, SNCC, King Center, Atlanta.

14. Hayden, "Who Are the Student Boat-Rockers?" Mademoiselle, *August 1961*, distributed as an SDS pamphlet; SDS Microfilm, Series 1, No. 11. 38; "Southern Report #2," October 7, 1961, SDS File, Folder 18, Box 9, SNCC. See all the SDS Southern Reports, Series 1, Reel 1, Folders 11, 13, SDS microfilm.

15. Tom Hayden, *Revolution in Mississippi,* SDS Publication, 1962, Series 4B, Reel 37, Folder 159, SDS microfilm, quotes, 5, 22. See also A. L. Hopkins, "Investigation of Negro Student Demonstrators, and Adult Negro Agitators, McComb, Mississippi, October 20, 1961"; September 6, 1962, letter to Mississippi State Sovereignty Commission members; and memo on *Revolution in Mississippi*, n.d.; all in Mississippi State Sovereignty Commission Papers, http://www.mdah.state.ms.us. The memo states: "This booklet (not meant for the eyes of white people) fell into the hands of white officials." In fact, Hayden's intended audience was white students.

16. Tom Hayden, "Student Social Action: From Liberation to Community," in Mitchell Cohen and Dennis Hale, *The New Student Left: An Anthology* (Boston: Beacon Press, 1966), 270–88.

17. Sale, *SDS*, 42–70.

18. Port Huron Statement in Appendix, 239.

19. Ibid., 282.

20. I am indebted to conversations with political theorist Lawrie Balfour, Professor of Politics at the University of Virginia, for this point. See her *Democracy's Reconstruction: Thinking Politically with W. E. B. DuBois* (New York: Oxford University Press, 2011).

21. Julius Lester, "The Angry Children of Malcolm X," *Sing Out!* (October–November 1966), 21–25.

Chapter 5. The New Left and Liberalism Reconsidered

1. For details of this story, see James Miller, *"Democracy Is in the Streets": From Port Huron to the Siege of Chicago* (New York: Simon and Schuster, 1987), 111–17, 126–40; Maurice Isserman, *The Other American: The Life of Michael Harrington* (New York: Public Affairs, 2000), 234–43. As Isserman makes clear, even after the tensions at Port Huron, Harrington and SDS had friendly relations throughout the early 1960s. Later, Harrington expressed regret about his actions at Port Huron.

2. Nelson Lichenstein, "A Moment of Convergence," this volume, 95–106.

3. Port Huron Statement in Appendix, 264. The peace movement's influence on the New Left is discussed in Maurice Isserman, *If I Had a Hammer: The Death of the Old Left and the Birth of the New Left* (New York: Basic Books, 1987), 127–69. On the peace movement revival, see also Lawrence S. Wittner, *The Struggle Against the Bomb,* vol. 2: *Resisting the Bomb: A History of the World Nuclear Disarmament Movement, 1954–1970* (Stanford, CA: Stanford University Press, 1997).

4. *Speak Truth to Power: A Quaker Search for an Alternative to Violence* (Friends Service Committee, 1955). The Committee of Correspondence's organizational history is recounted in David Riesman to Rabinowitz Foundation, April 22, 1962, Box 12, HUGFP 99.16, David Riesman Papers, Harvard University Archives (henceforth referred to as "Riesman Papers"). The Bear Mountain statement is quoted in this document.

5. Riesman to Lawrence Percy, April 2, 1963, Box 12, HUGFP 99.16, Riesman Papers.

6. David Riesman with Reuel Denney and Nathan Glazer, *The Lonely Crowd: A Study of the Changing American Character* (New Haven: Yale University Press, 1950).

7. Riesman to Erich Fromm, March 14, 1962, Box 10, HUGFP 99.12, Riesman Papers.

8. TOCSIN *Prospectus* [1960], Box 67, HUGFP 99.16, Riesman Papers.

9. Seymour Martin Lipset and David Riesman, *Education and Politics at Harvard* (New York: McGraw-Hill, 1975), 207. For information on the Harvard peace movement of the early 1960s, see also Todd Gitlin, *The Sixties: Years of Hope, Days of Rage* (New York: Bantam Books, 1987), 87–104.

10. Riesman to Rabinowitz Foundation, April 22, 1962, Riesman Papers.

11. The publication's name was changed in 1963. In 1962, the Committee of Correspondence changed its name to the Council for Correspondence. To avoid confusion in the text, I have used "*Correspondent*" and "Committee of Correspondence" throughout.

12. Inside back cover, *The Correspondent,* Autumn 1964.

13. "Birthday," *Newsletter of the Council for Correspondence,* September 1961, ii.

14. Riesman to Rabinowitz Foundation, April 22, 1962, Riesman Papers.

15. Riesman to Lenore Marshall, June 3, 1962, Box 12, HUGFP 99.16, Riesman Papers.

16. "The Unhelpful Fringes" (n.d., probably late 1960), cutting from *Life,* Box 12, HUGFP 99.16, Riesman Papers.

17. *National Review,* April 10, 1962, cutting, Box 12, HUGFP 99.16, Riesman Papers.

18. Roger Hagan, email to author, October 21, 2012.

19. "Minutes of coordinating committee meeting, March, 24, 1962, New York City," Box 12, HUGFP 99.16, Riesman Papers.

20. David Riesman, "Comment on Robert Colborn's Letter," *Newsletter of the Committee of Correspondence* 6a (May 3, 1960): 7. Note that issue numbering for the publication was erratic in its early years.

21. Roger Hagan and David Riesman, "Cuba," *Newsletter of the Committee of Correspondence* 5 (May 12, 1961).

22. Roger Hagan, "Reciprocal Hardening," *Newsletter of the Council of Correspondence* 26 (May 1963): 7.

23. David Riesman, "The National Purpose," *Newsletter of the Council of Correspondence* 27 (June 1963): 11.

24. Port Huron Statement in Appendix, 273.

25. Ibid., 241–42.

26. "Dear Friends," n.d. [1960], Box, 6, HUGFP 99.16, Riesman Papers. I quote here from a draft letter announcing the Committee's formation.

27. David Riesman and Michael Maccoby, "The American Crisis," in Riesman, *Abundance for What?* (Garden City, NY: Doubleday, 1964), 47, 42.

28. Port Huron Statement in Appendix, 280. The secretary of the Liberal Project was Marcus Raskin, who counted Riesman among his mentors and participated in the Bear Mountain conference.

29. David Riesman and Michael Maccoby, "The American Crisis," *New Left Review* 1 (September–October 1960): 24–35.

30. Port Huron Statement in Appendix, 245.

31. "Report to Our Readers," *The Correspondent,* no. 28 (July–August 1963): 38.

32. *Newsletter of the Committee for Correspondence,* no. 10 (September 10, 1960): 4.

33. Port Huron Statement in Appendix, 282.

34. David Riesman, "Postscript to the Postscript," no. 9 (September 15, 1961): 31.

35. Roger Hagan to Erich Fromm, March 6, 1962, Box 10, HUGFP 99.12, Riesman Papers.

36. David Riesman, "A Problem of Reaction," *The Correspondent* 29 (November–December 1963): 54.

37. Tom Hayden, "Liberal Analysis and Federal Power," *The Correspondent* 30 (January–February 1964): 83.

38. David Riesman, "Morals and Politics," *The Correspondent* 35 (August 1965): 7.

39. Michael Maccoby, remarks at panel, "Committee of Correspondence," Conference on Public Intellectuals, Cambridge, MA, April 13, 2012.

40. Riesman to Hagan, May 11, 1970, Box 17, HUGFP 99.12, Riesman Papers. For more on Riesman's changing views on the New Left, see Daniel Geary, "Children of *The Lonely Crowd*: David Riesman, the Young Radicals, and the Splitting of Liberalism in the 1960s," *Modern Intellectual History* 10 (November 2013): 603–33.

41. As quoted in Miller, *"Democracy Is in the Streets,"* 176.

42. Carl Oglesby, "Trapped in a System," in Massimo Teodori, ed., *The New Left: A Documentary History* (London: Jonathan Cape, 1969), 182–88. See also Doug Rossinow, *Visions of Progress: The Left-Liberal Tradition in America* (Philadelphia: University of Pennsylvania Press, 2008), 240–53.

43. Robert Jay Lifton, *Witness to an Extreme Century: A Memoir* (New York: Free Press, 2011), 197–204.

44. Kenneth Keniston, *Young Radicals: Notes on Committed Youth* (New York: Harcourt & Brace, 1968).

Chapter 6. A Moment of Convergence

1. Daniel Bell, *Marxian Socialism in the United States* (1952; Ithaca, NY: Cornell University Press, 1996), 5. This edition contains a fine introduction by Michael Kazin.

2. Nelson Lichtenstein, *Walter Reuther: The Most Dangerous Man in Detroit* (Urbana: University of Illinois Press, 1997), 302–4; Kevin Boyle: *The UAW and American Liberalism* (Ithaca, NY: Cornell University Press, 1995), 40–43.

3. James Miller, *"Democracy Is in the Streets": From Port Huron to the Siege of Chicago* (New York: Simon and Schuster, 1987), 104–5; Reuther quoted in UAW-International Executive Board Minutes, June 15, 1967, in UAW-IEB Collection, 63, Walter P. Reuther Library, Wayne State University, Detroit, MI.

4. As quoted in Ben Hall, "Reutherism Marks Time on the Main Issues at UAW Convention," *Labor Action*, April 6, 1953.

5. *Proceedings of the 19th Constitutional Convention of the International Union, United Automobile, Aerospace and Agricultural Implement Workers of America*, Atlantic City, NJ, March 20–27, 1964, 48.

6. Kermit Eby, CIO educational director, quoted in B. J. Widick, *Labor Today: The Triumphs and Failures of Unionism in the United States* (New York: Houghton Mifflin, 1964), 111.

7. Frank Marquart, *An Auto Worker's Journal: The UAW from Crusade to One-Party Union* (University Park: Pennsylvania State University Press, 1975), 123.

8. Peter Levy, *The New Left and Labor in the 1960s*, (Urbana: University of Illinois Press, 1994), 11.

9. UAW-IEB Minutes, December 5, 1962, UAW-IEB Collection, Archives of Labor and Urban Affairs, Wayne State University, Detroit, MI, 113.

10. A. H. Raskin, "Walter Reuther's Great Big Union," *Atlantic Monthly,* October 1963, 85–86.

11. Lichtenstein, *Walter Reuther*, 391.

12. *Proceedings of the 18th Constitutional Convention of the International Union, United Automobile, Aerospace and Agricultural Implement Workers of America* (hereafter *UAW Convention Proceedings*), Atlantic City, NJ, May 4–10, 1962, 309.

13. *UAW Convention Proceedings,* 1962, 267–83. This was the convention at which, after much protest and insurgency among African Americans, a black was finally elected to the union's executive board.

14. Port Huron Statement in Appendix, 274.

15. *UAW Convention Proceedings*, 1962, 199.

16. Port Huron Statement in Appendix, 253.

17. Arnold Kaufman, "Human Nature and Participatory Democracy," in Carl J. Friedrich, ed., *Responsibility: NOMOS III* (New York: Liberal Arts Press, 1960), 266–89, reprinted in William E. Connolly, ed., *The Bias of Pluralism* (New York: Atherton Press, 1969).

18. Daniel Bell, "The Subversion of Collective Bargaining," *Commentary,* March 1960, 697, 711. In the late 1960s, the New England Free Press, which grew out of SDS, republished the Bell essay in pamphlet form.

19. Port Huron Statement in Appendix, 279.

20. Ibid, 279–80.

21. *UAW Convention Proceedings*, 1962, 57.

22. Port Huron Statement in Appendix, 279; Lichtenstein, *Walter Reuther*, 312.

23. Christopher Phelps, "Port Huron at Fifty: The New Left and Labor: An Interview with Kim Moody," *LABOR: Studies in Working-Class History of the Americas* 9 (Summer 2012): 25–46.

24. Port Huron Statement in Appendix, 277.

25. Ibid., 271.

26. Ibid., 270–71. It is not unlikely that Arnold Kaufman, the University of Michigan political philosopher, had introduced Hayden to the ideas found in an influential political science report of 1950 advocating more ideologically and politically coherent parties. See Committee on Political Parties, American Political Science Association, *Toward a More Responsible Two-Party System* (New York: Rinehart, 1950); and in an e-mail to the author, James Miller notes that when he was writing *"Democracy Is in the Streets,"* "I was shocked to discover how much Hayden had borrowed from his mentor Arnold Kaufman" (James Miller to Nelson Lichtenstein, personal correspondence, January 25, 2012).

27. Nicol C. Rae, "Be Careful What You Wish For: The Rise of Responsible Parties in American National Politics," *Annual Review of Political Science* 10 (2007): 169–91.

28. Lichtenstein, *Walter Reuther*, 392–93.

29. Harvey Swados, "The UAW: Over the Top or Over the Hill," in Swados, *A Radical at Large: American Essays* (London: Rupert Hart-Davis, 1968), 88–89.

30. Tom Hayden, "The Port Huron Statement, Participatory Democracy, and the History and Vision of the 1960's Student Movements," January 17, 2012, available at http://tomhayden .com.

31. Todd Gitlin, *The Sixties: Years of Hope, Days of Rage* (New York: Bantam Books, 1987), 161–62.

Chapter 7. The New Left's Love-Hate Relationship with the University

1. Port Huron Statement in Appendix, emphasis added. 239.

2. Ibid., 241.

3. Ibid., 243–45.

4. Tom Hayden, *Rebel: A Personal History of the 1960s* (Los Angeles: Red Hen Press, 2003), 74; Tom Hayden, *Student Social Action* (1966), 1–19.

5. Port Huron Statement in Appendix, 244–45.

6. Ibid., 244.

7. Ibid., 245.

8. Ibid., 282.

9. Ibid., 241.

10. Ibid., 282.

11. Ibid., 241, 244.

12. Ibid., 241, 245.

13. Ibid., 245.

14. Ibid., 282.

15. Ibid., 282.

16. Ibid., 245.

17. Hayden, *Rebel*, 72–74; Hayden, *The Port Huron Statement: The Visionary Call of the 1960s Revolution* (New York: Thunder Mountain Press, 2005), 4–5; James Miller, *"Democracy Is in the Streets": From Port Huron to the Siege of Chicago* (New York: Simon and Schuster, 1987), 111.

18. Harold Taylor, *On Education and Freedom* (Carbondale: Southern Illinois University Press, 1954), 69–70.

19. Tom Hayden, e-mails to the author, June 12 and 13, 2012, copies in author's possession.

20. Richard Flacks telephone interview with Stacie Brensilver Berman, April 2, 2012, transcript in author's possession.

21. The Port Huron Statement in Appendix, 282.

22. C. Wright Mills, "Letter to the New Left," *New Left Review,* September–October 1960, available at www.marxists.org/subects/humanism/mills-c-wright/letter.

23. The Port Huron Statement in Appendix, 282.

24. Ibid., 244.

25. Hayden, *Rebel,* 71.

26. The Port Huron Statement in Appendix, 243.

27. Ibid. (emphasis added), 243.

28. Ibid., 243.

29. Ibid., 283.

30. Ibid., 283.

31. Ibid., 280.

32. Ibid., 280.

33. Hayden, *The Port Huron Statement,* 31–32.

34. Ibid., 32.

35. Port Huron Statement in Appendix, 240, 282; Julie A. Rueben, "Reforming the University: Student Protest and the Demand for a 'Relevant' Curriculum," in Gerard J. DeGroot, ed., *Student Protest: The Sixties and After* (London: Longman, 1998), 153–68; Martha Biondi, *The Black Revolution on Campus* (Berkeley: University of California Press, 2012).

36. Port Huron Statement in Appendix, 261.

37. Ibid., 283. Robert Cohen, *Freedom's Orator: Mario Savio and the Radical Legacy of the 1960s* (New York: Oxford University Press, 2009), 327.

38. Kirkpatrick Sale, *SDS* (New York: Random House, 1973), 302–650.

39. Port Huron Statement in Appendix, 282, Derek Bok, *Universities in the Marketplace: The Commercialization of Higher Education* (Princeton, NJ: Princeton University Press, 2003); Sheila Slaughter and Gary Rhodes, *Academic Capitalism and the New Economy* (Baltimore: Johns Hopkins University Press, 2004); David L. Kirp, *Shakespeare, Einstein, and the Bottom Line: The Marketing of Higher Education* (Cambridge, MA: Harvard University Press, 2003).

40. Sale, *SDS*, 639.

41. Allan Bloom, *The Closing of the American Mind* (New York: Simon and Schuster, 1987), 336–82.

42. Clark Kerr interview with Robert Cohen and Reginald E. Zelnik, Berkeley, California, July 12, 1999, audiotape in author's possession.

43. Clark Kerr, *The Gold and the Blue: A Personal Memoir of the University of California, 1949–1967*, vol. 2: *Political Turmoil* (Berkeley: University of California Press, 2003), 212; Cohen, *Freedom's Orator*, 188–90.

44. Cohen, *Freedom's Orator*, 203–7, 274–320.

45. Kerr, *The Gold and the Blue*, vol. 2, 212, 385, n. 19.

46. Kerr, *The Gold and the Blue*, vol. 2, 161–330; Clark Kerr, "Fall of 1964 at Berkeley: Confrontation Yields to Reconciliation," in Robert Cohen and Reginald E. Zelnik, eds., *The Free Speech Movement: Reflections on Berkeley in the 1960s* (Berkeley: University of California Press, 2002), 390–95.

47. Cohen, *Freedom's Orator*, 206–7; Hayden, *The Port Huron Statement*, 165–69.

48. Cohen, *Freedom's Orator*, 199–207, 326–32, 350–57; Hayden, *The Port Huron Statement*, 49, 57–61, 165–69. On the impact that the New Left had on university reform and democratization in the South both on campus and off, see Robert Cohen and David S. Snyder, eds., *Rebellion in Black and White: Southern Student Activism in the 1960s* (Baltimore: Johns Hopkins University Press, 2013).

49. Kerr interview with Cohen and Zelnik.

50. For an example of Kerr's use of these revised terms, see his "Fall of 1964 at Berkeley" in Cohen and Zelnik, *The Free Speech Movement*, 395.

51. For examples of this New Left–bashing narrative tradition, see John Searle, "A Foolproof Scenario for Student Revolts," *New York Times Magazine*, December 29, 1968; Theodore White, *The Making of the President 1968* (New York: Harper, 1968), 248–58; Allen Matusow, *The Unraveling of America: A History of Liberalism in the 1960s* (Athens: University of Georgia Press, 2009), 308–44; Kenneth J. Heinemann, *Put Your Bodies on the Wheels: Student Revolt in the 1960s* (Chicago: Ivan Dees, 2001), 106–80.

52. Mark Rudd, *Underground: My Life with SDS and the Weather Underground* (New York: Morrow, 2009), 82, 92–93, 105.

53. Rusti Eisenberg, "The Strike: A Critical Appraisal," *Ripsaw, A Journal of the Graduate Student Union, Columbia University,* December 1968, reprinted in Immanuel Wallerstein and Paul Starr, eds., *The University Crisis Reader,* vol. 2: *Confrontation and Counterattack* (New York: Vintage, 1971).

54. Richard Flacks, telephone interview with the author, June 22, 2012, audiotape in author's possession.

55. For voluminous evidence of New Left interest in university reform, see the many documents students published demanding such reform reprinted in Wallerstein and Starr, eds., *The University Crisis Reader,* vol. 2, as well as the first volume, *The Liberal University Under Attack* (New York: Random House, 1971).

56. Note that although I am terming this the "left academic tradition" and the "academic left" because it denotes radicals based in the academy, this term is not meant to suggest that those faculty and student radicals were or wanted to be academic in the sense of Ivy Tower pedants. Their ideal was of the politically engaged radical intellectual. As Richard Flacks explains, C. Wright Mills "was in the university (in fact at Columbia—the leading sociology department), but he was not of it, being bitingly critical of the academic mainstream and strikingly different in pose and practice from your typical professor. So his persona itself was very appealing to student intellectuals of the time, who ourselves hoped to be in the university while rebelling against the merely academic." Richard Flacks, "C. Wright Mills, Tom Hayden, and the New Left," in Tom Hayden, *Radical Nomad: C. Wright Mills and His Times* (Boulder, CO: Paradigm, 2006), 4. *Radical Nomad* is the published version of Hayden's thesis, which included contemporary reflections by Flacks, Stanley Aronowitz, and Charles Lemert. On Mills's political and personal meaning to Hayden, see Tom Hayden, "Missing Mills," in *Radical Nomad,* 55–62. Richard and Mickey Flacks named their son after Mills. See Kathryn Mills and Pamela Mills, eds., *C. Wright Mills: Letters and Autobiographical Writings* (Berkeley: University of California Press, 2000), 3.

57. Hayden, *Rebel,* 71–74.

58. Port Huron Statement in Appendix, 240.

59. Hayden's *Student Social Action* is available at http://www.sds-1960s.org/documents.htm. The Potter pamphlets and the Haber and Flacks pamphlet are available in the SDS collection of pamphlets and publications, box 3, Tamiment Library, Robert F. Wagner Labor Archives, Bobst Library, New York University.

60. *Freedom's Orator,* 203–8; see FSM pamphlets in the appendix of Hal Draper, *Berkeley: The New Student Revolt* (Alameda, CA: Center for Socialist History, 2009), 217–62.

61. The Booth pamphlet is available in the SDS collection of pamphlets and publications, box 3, Tamiment Library; Wallerstein and Starr, *The University Crisis Reader,* vols. 1 and 2.

62. On the curricular innovations the student movement of the 1960s brought to the university, see Rueben, "Reforming the University."

63. Todd Gitlin, "New Chances: The Reality and Dynamic of the New Left," 14, SDS collection of pamphlets and publications, box 3, Tamiment Library.

64. Jennifer Frost, *"An Interracial Movement of the Poor": Community Organizing and the New Left in the 1960s* (New York: NYU Press, 2001).

65. Sale, *SDS,* 635–43.

66. For example, Slaughter and Rhodes, *Academic Capitalism and the New Economy;* Kirp, *Shakespeare, Einstein, and the Bottom Line;* Benjamin Ginsberg, *The Fall of the Faculty: The Rise of the All-Administrative University and Why It Matters* (New York: Oxford University Press, 2011); Ellen Schrecker, *The Lost Soul of Higher Education: Corporatization, The Assault on Academic Freedom, and the End of the American University* (New York: New Press, 2010); Elizabeth Popp Berman, *Creating the Market University: How Academic Science Became an Economic Engine* (Princeton, NJ: Princeton University Press, 2012).

67. There has recently been disagreement over the extent to which Mills was an academic dissenter. Daniel Geary argues that Mills was much more identified—and in conversation—with

mainstream sociology than those who see him as an academic outlaw have allowed. While Geary's *Radical Ambition: C. Wright Mills, the Left, and American Social Thought* (Berkeley: University of California Press, 2009) is an important book that sheds much new light on Mills's early years, his attempt to debunk the image of Mills as an academic outsider is not persuasive, and it is contradicted even by Mills's private correspondence, in which the dissident sociologist refers to himself as "intellectually, politically, morally alone. . . . I have never known what others call 'fraternity' with any group . . . neither academic nor political" (Mills and Mills, eds., *C. Wright Mills: Letters and Autobiographical Writings*, 250). Also see, John Summers, "Permanent Stranger," *Reviews in American History* 38 (2010): 348–54.

68. David Horowitz, *The Professors: The 101 Most Dangerous Academics in America* (Washington, DC: Regnery, 2006). The most penetrating critique of the slew of such right-wing jeremiads against the campus left remains Lawrence W. Levine, *The Opening of the American Mind: Canons, Culture, and History* (Boston: Beacon Press, 1996), especially 1–34.

Chapter 8. The Democratic Process at Port Huron and After

1. SLID was the distant offspring of a 1905 organization—the Intercollegiate Socialist Society—originally started by prominent intellectuals, including novelists Upton Sinclair and Jack London and the great lawyer Clarence Darrow.

2. The sit-ins that began in North Carolina on February 1, 1960, attempting to integrate lunch counters at the then-dominant discount chains, Woolworth and Kresge. Sympathy boycotts and picketing of these chains were organized at their northern (unsegregated) outlets. Ann Arbor was among the places with a vigorous movement.

3. McEldowney studied economics and became a leading consumer advocate and executive director of Consumer Action, a San Francisco–based national consumer advocacy and education membership organization. Hawley earned a Ph.D. in English and was later on the faculty at the Massachusetts Institute of Technology and a local activist in the Boston area.

4. Our tutor was Mark Chesler, then a social psychology graduate student and subsequently a lifelong member of the Sociology Department at the University of Michigan. Because of the expertise I gained, the SDS chapter at the University of Chicago later asked me to chair a very large meeting that it had called to ratify its decision to hold a sit-in over the firing of a leftist professor. I agreed (though I was personally not in favor of the tactic) and was subsequently suspended from graduate school.

5. This suggests one of those paradoxes that may appear in social movements: the ethos of participants and the contrasting behavior of leaders and organizations. My experience, including, for example, one of the summer camps heavily influenced by Communist Party culture (but not the famous Kinderland), was that teaching and practice of everyday social life was democratic and nonhierarchical. The Communist Party USA (CPUSA) was a Leninist organization, and the "leading organs" of the party were often impervious to the sentiments of the members. My parents and the people who they knew when I was a child were rank-and-filers, more or less estranged from both the Communist Party leaders and the more social democratic union leaders who dominated their workplaces. Pioneer Youth Camp, which I attended, is discussed along with Kinderland in Paul Mishler's *Raising Reds: The Young Pioneers, Radical Summer Camps, and Communist Political Culture in the United States* (New York: Columbia University Press, 1999).

6. In the spirit of setting the record straight, I should note that few among us were charmed by the Kennedy mystique. Between the Bay of Pigs invasion in April 1961, and Robert Kennedy's

request in May 1961 that the Freedom Riders "cool off," early SDS members were not knights in Camelot. See C. T. Vivian's comments in the video "C. T. Vivian on Robert Kennedy's Request for a Cooling Off Period," available at http://www.pbs.org/wgbh/americanexperience/freedom riders/people/robert-f-kennedy, and Neil R. McMillen, "Black Enfranchisement in Mississippi: Federal Enforcement and Black Protest in the 1960s," *Journal of Southern History* 43, no. 3 (1977): 359. Tom Hayden's extreme focus on the importance of the Kennedys'—John's and Robert's—and movement's fate determined by their assassinations is not widely shared by his comrades.

7. A. Javier Trevino, "Influence of C. Wright Mills on Students for a Democratic Society: An Interview with Bob Ross," *Humanity & Society* 22, no. 3 (1998): 260–77; Robert J.S. Ross, "At the Center and Edge: Notes on a Life In and Out of Sociology and the New Left," *Critical Sociology* 15, no. 2 (1988): 79–93.

8. Port Huron Statement in Appendix, 240–43.

9. See Richard Rothstein, "'Representative Democracy and SDS," *Liberation*, February 1972, 10–18. Reprinted in R. David Myers, ed., *Toward a History of the New Left: Essays from Within the Movement* (New York: Carlson, 1989), 49–62.

10. Interestingly, the person who made this comment, Dick Roman, later was a stalwart anti–Vietnam War, pro–labor rights activist who is well loved by many of those with whom he was in earlier conflict.

11. These phrases occur in a section on the economy with the subhead "Horizon." Port Huron Statement in Appendix, 254.

12. Ibid,. 252, 253.

13. See Immanuel Ness and Dario Azzellini, eds., *Ours to Master and to Own: Workers' Control from the Commune to the Present* (Chicago: Haymarket, 2011).

14. Students for a Democratic Society, *America and the New Era*, 1963. The text is available in original photo-image at http://archive.lib.msu.edu/DMC/AmRad/americanewera.pdf.

15. Dick Flacks was ANE's lead drafter with, according to Kirkpatrick Sale, "considerable help from the theoretical apparatchik: Booth, Haber, Hayden, Ross." My own memory is not so detailed. See Kirkpatrick Sale, *SDS*, 48, available at http://www.antiauthoritarian.net/sds_wuo.

16. For one good look at this history, see Jennifer Frost, *An Interracial Movement of the Poor: Community Organizing and the New Left* (New York: NYU Press, 2001). An excellent contemporary account by a leading organizer in Chicago that takes on issues of democracy and representation is Richard Rothstein, "A Short History of ERAP," available at http://content.cdlib .org/view?docId = kt4k4003k7;NAAN = 13030&doc.view = frames&chunk.id = d0e35&toc.depth = 1&toc.id = d0e35&brand = calisphere.

17. For another version, see Jim Zarichny, "History of SDS," January 1, 2005, available at http://greenhouse.economics.utah.edu/pipermail/marxism/2005-January/025769.html.

18. See Robert Ross, "Primary Groups in Social Movements: A Memoir and Interpretation," *Journal of Voluntary Action Research* 6, no. 3–4 (1977): 139–52. Reprinted as "Generational Change and Primary Groups in a Social Movement," in Jo Freeman, ed., *Social Movements of the Sixties and Seventies* New York: Longman, 1983), 177–187. Also reprinted in R. David Myers, ed., *Toward a History of the New Left*.

19. The slogan has one anchor in the Seattle/Everett confrontation of 1916. See Margaret Riddle, "Everett Massacre (1916)," 2011, available at http://www.historylink.org/_content/ printer_friendly/pf_output.cfm?file_id = 9981. Interestingly, *every* source that discusses the history of the IWW discusses its "leaders."

20. The episode can be viewed at http://www.youtube.com/watch?v = 3QZlp3eGMNI.

21. There are scholars working on this frontier, but their link to parties and movements is weak. See John Parkinson and Jane Mansbridge, eds., *Deliberative Systems: Deliberative Democracy at the Large Scale* (New York: Cambridge University Press, 2012).

Chapter 9. A Manifesto of Hope

1. Originally published in *Socialist Review* 93 (1987), 158–66. Revised in 2013.

Chapter 10. Putting Participatory Democracy into Action

1. The Chicago project began in the fall of 1963, while the other projects began during the summer of 1964; ending dates vary and are difficult to define given the continued activism of some organizers and residents, but by 1967 and 1968 all of these projects had disbanded. The national ERAP disbanded in 1965. See Jennifer Frost, *"An Interracial Movement of the Poor": Community Organizing and the New Left in the 1960s* (New York: New York University Press, 2001).

2. Carl Oglesby, quoted in Ronald Fraser, ed., *1968: A Student Generation in Revolt* (New York: Pantheon Books, 1988), 65; Gregory Nevala Calvert, *Democracy from the Heart: Spiritual Values, Decentralization, and Democratic Idealism in the Movement of the 1960s* (Eugene, OR: Communitas Press, 1991), 118.

3. James Putnam O'Brien, "The Development of a New Left in the United States, 1960–1965," Ph.D. dissertation, University of Wisconsin at Madison, 1971, 294. As Richard Flacks noted during the spring of 1964, the commitment to community organizing already had extended "the base of the organization." Richard Flacks, quoted in "National Council Minutes," April 1964, Students for a Democratic Society Records, 1958–1970, series 2A (hereafter SDS-2A), box 13, folder 10, State Historical Society of Wisconsin (SHSW).

4. Sara Evans, *Personal Politics: The Roots of Women's Liberation in the Civil Rights Movement and the New Left* (New York: Vintage Books, 1980); Wini Breines, *Community and Organization in the New Left, 1962–1968: The Great Refusal*, rev. ed. (New Brunswick, NJ: Rutgers University Press, 1989).

5. Charles M. Payne found the same for community organizing in the civil rights movement. Payne, *I've Got the Light of Freedom: The Organizing Tradition and the Mississippi Freedom Struggle* (Berkeley: University of California Press, 1995).

6. Tom Hayden, editor's note, *SDS Bulletin* [1], March–April 1963.

7. Carl Wittman and Tom Hayden, "An Interracial Movement of the Poor?" SDS pamphlet, n.d., 24, Lee D. Webb Papers, 1955–1968, box 1, folder 22, SHSW (hereafter Webb Papers).

8. David Burner, *Making Peace with the 60s* (Princeton, NJ: Princeton University Press, 1996), 11, 186–87.

9. I borrow and adapt these terms from Marianne DeKoven, *Utopia Limited: The Sixties and the Emergence of the Postmodern* (Durham, NC: Duke University Press, 2004), chapter 6.

10. Port Huron Statement in Appendix, 242.

11. Wittman and Hayden, "An Interracial Movement of the Poor?" 26.

12. ERAP brochure (Summer 1964), Students for a Democratic Society Records, 1958–1970, series 2B (hereafter SDS-2B), box 15, folder 5, SHSW.

13. Richard Rothstein, "A Short History of ERAP," *SDS Bulletin* 4 [November 1965].

14. David Strauss, interview with author, November 29, 1999; Carol Glassman, interview #1 with author, August 7, 1993.

15. Payne, *I've Got the Light of Freedom*, 331.

16. Lillian Craig, with Marge Grevatt, *Just a Woman: Memoirs of Lillian Craig* (Cleveland: Orange Blossom Press, 1981), 12, 16–17, 27, 33, 53.

17. Dovie Thurman, quoted in Studs Terkel, *Race: How Blacks and Whites Think and Feel About the American Obsession* (New York: New Press, 1992), 57–58.

18. Dovie Coleman, "SELF-EXPLANATION ON AN OVER-ALL THING**THAT'S PRESSURE," George Wiley Papers, 1949–1975, box 25, folder 1, SHSW.

19. Port Huron Statement in Appendix, 242.

20. Wittman and Hayden, "An Interracial Movement of the Poor?" 15.

21. Richard Rothstein, "Evolution of the ERAP Organizers," in Priscilla Long, ed., *The New Left: A Collection of Essays* (Boston: Porter Sargent, 1969), 272–88.

22. Cathy Wilkerson, "Rats, Washtubs, and Block Organizations," SDS pamphlet [1964], 4, Webb Papers, box 1, folder 6a.

23. Temma Kaplan, "Female Consciousness and Collective Action: The Case of Barcelona, 1910–1918," *Signs* 7 (Spring 1982): 545–66; Kathleen McCourt, *Working Class Women and Grass Roots Politics* (Bloomington: Indiana University Press, 1977); Nancy Naples, *Grassroots Warriors: Activist Mothering, Community Work, and the War on Poverty* (New York: Routledge, 1998), 181.

24. Kim Moody, "ERAP, Ideology, and Social Change," [1964–65], 2, SDS-2B, box 22, folder 13; Evans, *Personal Politics*, 141–45.

25. Wittman and Hayden, "An Interracial Movement of the Poor?" 17.

26. Carol Glassman, ERAP application, SDS-2B, box 26, folder 4.

27. Steve Max, "Words Butter No Parsnips: Remarks on the Nature of Community Political Organization," *SDS Bulletin* 2, no. 8 (May 1964); Richard Rothstein, paraphrased in "Ann Arbor Report," *ERAP Newsletter,* November 16–23, 1964.

28. "Training Institute of the Economic Research and Action Project," June 6–11, 1964, SDS-2B, box 15, folder 5.

29. Ann Withorn, *Serving the People: Social Services and Social Change* (New York: Columbia University Press, 1984), 3–5, 21–22; John H. Ehrenreich, *The Altruistic Imagination: A History of Social Work and Social Policy in the United States* (Ithaca, NY: Cornell University Press, 1985), 160.

30. Elvie Jordan, "The Welfare Grievance Committee," typescript of speech, Carol McEldowney Papers, 1964–1968, SHSW.

31. Connie Brown, "Cleveland: Conference of the Poor," *Studies on the Left* 5 (Spring 1965): 72.

32. Dorothy Perez, "The Need for JOIN," SDS-2B, box 20, folder 2. On the Chicago project's use of dictation for producing newsletters, see "JOIN Community Union: Program for 1966," p. 29, SDS-2B, box 21, folder 9.

33. Mrs. Alcantar, "What Is Our Democracy??" *JOIN Newsletter,* September 23–October 7, 1966, SDS-2B, box 20, folder 3.

34. Port Huron Statement in Appendix, 274.

35. Conference on Community Organizing for Economic Issues, "Agenda," Ann Arbor, Michigan, April 1964, SDS-2B, box 15, folder 5.

36. Port Huron Statement in Appendix, 274.

37. This project was soon "overshadowed by efforts to apply the vision to SDS's internal functioning." Richard Flacks, "What Happened to the New Left?" *Socialist Review* 19 (January–March 1989): 104; James Miller, *"Democracy Is in the Streets": From Port Huron to the Siege of Chicago* (New York: Simon and Schuster, 1987), 143. See also Robert J. Ross, "Primary Groups in Social Movements: A Memoir and Interpretation," in R. David Myers, ed., *Toward a History of the New Left: Essays from Within the Movement* (Brooklyn, NY: Carlson, 1989), 162.

38. ERAP advertisement, *SDS Bulletin* 3, no. 6 (March 1965).

39. Todd Gitlin, "President's Report," *SDS Bulletin* 2, no. 7 (April 1964).

40. "Welfare Bill of Rights," *CUFAW Newsletter,* December 1965, McEldowney Papers; JOIN, "Welfare Bill of Rights," SDS-2B, box 20, folder 1; Dorothy Perez, "Statement Before the Advisory Council on Public Welfare," March 1965, SDS-2B, box 19, folder 14.

41. "If You Live in this Area, You're in Trouble!" pamphlet, SDS-2B, box 23, folder 11; "What Do We, the People of the Near West Side, Know About Urban Renewal?" leaflet, [1966]; and "Urban Renewal Action Committee," leaflet, [1966], McEldowney Papers.

42. Sargent Shriver, quoted in *ERAP Newsletter,* December 11, 1964; "Training Program for Community Organizers, [Spring 1965], SDS-2B, box 17, folder 2.

43. Richard Rothstein, "Yale Political Notes," SDS-2B, box 21, folder 8.

44. Junior Brown, "Who Should Decide?" *ERAP Newsletter,* May 17, 1965.

45. Calvert, *Democracy from the Heart,* 117.

46. Al Haber, "War on Poverty Attacked," *SDS Bulletin* 3, no. 5 (February 1965); Wilson conference brochure, "Poverty U.S.A.," March 1964, SDS-2B, box 18, folder 1. See also Ken McEldowney, "Critique of Cleveland Poverty Proposal," *Cleveland Community Project* 1, no. 2 (November 1964), SDS-2B, box 24, folder 12.

47. Dovie Coleman, quoted in "JOIN Press Release," December 6, 1965, SDS-2B, box 21, folder 4.

48. Mother on ADC, "Statement Issued to Congressional Sub-Committee Investigating War on Poverty Program in Cleveland," *Community Union News,* [January 15, 1966], McEldowney Papers.

49. For a discussion of these issues, see Frost, *"An Interracial Movement of the Poor,"* chapter 7.

50. Frances Fox Piven and Richard A. Cloward, *Poor People's Movements: Why They Succeed, How They Fail* (New York: Vintage Books, 1979), xiii; Neil Betten and Michael J. Austin, "The Cincinnati Unit Experiment, 1917–1920," in Betten and Austin, eds., *The Roots of Community Organizing, 1917–1939* (Philadelphia: Temple University Press, 1990), 35.

51. Michael B. Katz, *The Undeserving Poor: America's Enduring Confrontation with Poverty,* 2nd ed. (New York: Oxford University Press, 2013).

52. Barbara Epstein, *Political Protest and Cultural Revolution: Nonviolent Direct Action in the 1970s and 1980s* (Berkeley: University of California Press, 1991).

53. Strauss interview.

54. "This Week's Activities of Grievance Committee Members," *Welfare Grievance Committee Newsletter,* June 28, 1966, McEldowney Papers.

55. Strauss interview.

Chapter 11. Port Huron and the New Left Movements in Federal Germany

1. The term "New Left" was especially introduced by *The New Reasoner: A Quarterly Journal of Socialist Humanism,* a journal edited by E. P. Thompson and John Saville. In the autumn 1958 edition, its "Letter to Our Readers" began: "Very slowly, and sometimes with more sound than substance, it does seem that a 'new left' is coming into being in this country." The text describes how this "new left" is made up "of the most diverse elements. . . . It's a mood still and we like it that way" (*New Reasoner,* no. 6 [Autumn 1958]: 137).

2. Edward Palmer Thompson, "Country and City" (first published in 1970), in *Persons and Polemics: Historical Essays* (London: Merlin Press, 1994), 244.

3. We had come to know each other through the social-democratic youth international, the International Union of Socialist Youth (IUSY) of which the German SDS was a member and the American SDS was an associate organization. In summer of 1959 IUSY held its international congress in Vienna visited by many representatives from Europe and the third world. As a delegate of the German SDS, I was part of its minority wing of delegates from socialist student and youth organizations that were attracted by New Left views. We used the IUSY congress as a chance to begin building a New Left network of mutual contacts. The IUSY address list gave us the chance to contact the American SDS, which had not taken part in Vienna.

4. Edward Palmer Thompson, ed., *out of apathy* (London: New Left Books, 1960). As the title of the new journal, *new left review*, also the book's title, *out of apathy*, was deliberately written in small letters on the cover and the inner title, symbolizing a political vanguardism which was closely linked to the cultural vanguardism of that time which was also represented by the authors and topics of every edition of *The New Reasoner*. This linkage was a trademark of the New Left in many countries, including Germany (see note 33).

5. Thompson, ed., *out of apathy*, 9.

6. C. Wright Mills, "Letter to the New Left," *new left review*, no. 5 (1960): 18–23.

7. Students for a Democratic Society, Convention Document #1—Manifesto Notes: A Beginning Draft (Hayden) and Convention Document #2—Manifesto Notes: Problems of Democracy (Hayden), both mimeographed and dated March 19, 1962. Documents in author's possession. Other early SDS documents can be found in the SDS collection at Wisconsin Historical Society.

8. Michael Vester, "A Note to Tom Hayden (Manifesto)," SDS mimeo, n.d. Documents in author's possession.

9. Vester, "A Note to Tom Hayden," 2, 3. The comment is discussed more fully in Martin Klimke, *The Other Alliance: Student Protest in West Germany and the United States in the Global Sixties* (Princeton, NJ: Princeton University Press 2010), 22–23.

10. Raymond Williams, *The Long Revolution* (1961; Harmondsworth: Penguin, 1965).

11. Arnold Kaufman, "Human Nature and Participatory Democracy," in Carl J. Friedrich, ed., *Responsibility: NOMOS III* (New York: Liberal Arts Press, 1960), 266–89, reprinted in William E. Connolly, ed., *The Bias of Pluralism* (New York: Atherton Press, 1969).

12. This is described in Faith S. Holsaert, Martha Prescod Norman Noonan, Judy Richardson, Betty Garman Robinson, Jean Smith Young, Dorothy M. Zellner, eds., *Hands on the Freedom Plow: Personal Accounts by Women in SNCC* (Urbane: University of Illinois Press, 2010), 449–50, 455–56.

13. Klimke, *The Other Alliance*, 10–39.

14. Al Haber told me later that my Berlin paper was also officially distributed by the National Student Association of the United States.

15. In the Port Huron Statement's section "What Is Needed?" the problem is discussed in the subsection titled "A crucial feature of this political understanding must be the acceptance of status quo possessions," and in parts of the subsection "Experiments in disengagement and demilitarization must be conducted as part of the total disarming process." Port Huron Statement in Appendix, 265.

16. Belinda Davis, Wilfried Mausbach, Martin Klimke, and Carla MacDougall, eds., *Changing the World, Changing Oneself: Political Protest and Collective Identities in West Germany and the U.S. in the 1960s and 1970s* (New York: Berghahn Books, 2010), 278, 281.

17. This first sentence in the Statement's section "Communism and Foreign Policy" is continued by further elaboration, beginning with the words: "The Soviet Union, as a system, rests on the total suppression of organized opposition, as well as on a vision of the future in the name of which much human life hast been sacrificed, and numerous small and large denials of human dignity rationalized."

18. The activities of the German SDS to develop this network are more fully described in Klimke, *The Other Alliance*, 28–39.

19. Wilma Aden-Grossmann and Monika Seifert, *Pädagogin der antiautoritären Erziehung: Eine Biographie* (Frankfurt a.m.: Brandes & Apsel, 2014).

20. Summed up in Michael Vester, Peter von Oertzen, Heiko Geiling, Thomas Hermann, and Dagmar Müller, eds., *Soziale Milieus im gesellschaftlichen Strukturwandel* (Frankfurt a.M.: Suhrkamp, 2001). A short English outline is given in Michael Vester, "Class and Culture in Germany," in Fiona Devine, Mike Savage, John Scott, and Rosemary Crompton, eds., *Rethinking Class: Cultures, Identities and Life-Styles* (Basingstoke: Palgrave Macmillan, 2005), 69–94.

21. Kaufman, *Human Nature and Participatory Democracy*, 280–82.

22. Ibid., 272.

23. Ibid., 280f. This assertion is only partly true as G. D. H. Cole, the great historian of the labor movement and of cooperative socialism, and Dewey, as a social and educational reformer, in their works presented an abundance of practical experiences and empirical examples.

24. Kaufman, *Human Nature*, 281.

25. Ibid., 282.

26. Reprinted in the *International Archives of the Sociology of Cooperation* 2 (1957): 106–82.

27. Kaufman, *Human Nature*, 282.

28. Ibid., 282.

29. Heinrich Popitz, Hans-Paul Bahrdt, Ernst August Jüres, and Hanno Kesting, *Das Gesellschaftsbild des Arbeiters* (Tübingen: Mohr, 1957); Ludwig von Friedeburg, *Soziologie des Betriebsklimas* (Frankfurt a.M.: Europäische Verlagsanstalt, 1963).

30. See Werner Abelshauser, *Nach dem Wirtschaftswunder: Der Gewerkschafter, Politiker und Unternehmer Hans Matthöfer* (Bonn: Dietz, 2009). This book is also a comprehensive history of the participatory labor union left in West Germany.

31. Peter von Oertzen, *Betriebsräte in der Novemberrevolution* (Düsseldorf: Droste 1963); Peter von Oertzen, *Analyse der Mitbestimmung—ein Diskussionsbeitrag* (Hanover: Arbeit und Leben Niedersachsen, 1965).

32. See Peter von Oertzen, *Demokratie und Sozialismus zwischen Politik und Wissenschaft* (Hanover: Offizin, 2004).

33. This was also expressed in its design. The aesthetic vanguard of design of that time was still strongly influenced by the progressive Bauhaus tradition. For *neue kritik*, Maria Fraxedas, an Argentinian graduate of the famous Hochschule für Gestaltung (Academy of Design) in Ulm, designed a cover that, by its quadratic format and the small letters of its title, signalized nonconformity with the dominant styles and politics of that time (see note 4).

34. See especially Michael Vester, "Schöne neue Welt?" *neue kritik, zeitschrift sozialistischer studenten,* no. 15 (March 1963): 3–8; Michael Vester, "Die Linke in den USA," *neue kritik, zeitschrift sozialistischer studenten,* no. 17 (July 1963): 6–14; Michael Vester, "Falsche Alternativen," *neue kritik, zeitschrift sozialistischer studenten,* no. 18 (November 1963): 5–11.

35. Klimke, *The Other Alliance*, 35.

36. Gerhard Brandt, "Die Neue Linke in England," *neue kritik—informationen*, no. 6 (June 1961): 22–30.

37. Thompson, *out of apathy*, 25.

38. Ibid., 79.

39. Ibid., 224f.

40. Ibid., 267.

41. Ibid., 275.

42. Ibid., 298f.

43. Ibid., 302.

44. Ibid., 306.

45. Helge Pross, *Manager und Aktionäre in Deutschland. Untersuchungen zum Verhältnis von Eigentum und Verfügungsmacht* (Frankfurt a.M.: Europäische Verlagsanstalt, 1965).

46. Michael Vester, "John Kenneth Galbraith und der 'Amerikanische Kapitalismus,'" *neue kritik—informationen*, no. 7 (July 1961): 18–29.

47. Vester, *Schöne neue Welt?*; Vester, *Falsche Alternativen*.

48. This concept, which I had taken from Raphael Samuel (see Klimke, *The Other Alliance*, 35), was further developed into a critique of the colonization of everyday life by Habermas (who regularly observed our discussions in Frankfurt) after 1970.

49. Vester, *Schöne neue Welt?* 8.

50. Thomas Hayden, *Radical Nomad: Essays on C. Wright Mills and His Times*, Preprint, Center for the Research on Conflict Resolution, University of Michigan (July 1964); Michael Vester, *Die politische Soziologie von C. Wright Mills*, sociological diploma thesis, University of Frankfurt am Main, December 1964.

51. C. Wright Mills, *Die amerikanische Elite* (Hamburg: Holsten, 1962) (German edition of *The Power Elite* [New York: Oxford University Press, 1956]); C. Wright Mills, *Kritik der soziologischen Denkweise* (Neuwied/Berlin: Luchterhand, 1963) (German edition of *The Sociological Imagination* [New York: Oxford University Press, 1959]).

52. See especially Manfred Liebel, "Die Rolle der Intellektuellen in der Bundesrepublik," *neue kritik, zeitschrift sozialistischer studenten*, no. 8 (November 1963): 5–8; Vester, "Schöne neue"; and Vester, "Die Linke."

53. Liebel, "Die Rolle der Intellektuellen."

54. Michael Vester, "Das Dilemma von C. Wright Mills," *neue kritik, zeitschrift sozialistischer studenten*, no. 27 (December 1964): 20–23.

55. Vester, *Schöne neue Welt?*; Vester, *Falsche Alternativen*.

56. Raymond Williams, *Culture and Society, 1780–1950* (1958; Harmondsworth: Penguin 1963).

57. Herbert Marcuse, *One-Dimensional Man: Study in the Ideology of Advanced Industrial Society* (London: Routledge & Kegan Paul, 1964) (German edition: *Der eindimensionale Mensch. Studien zur Ideologie der fortgeschrittenen Industriegesellschaft*, Darmstadt: Luchterhand, 1967).

58. In this, we followed the New Left perspective of "reformist tactics within a revolutionary strategy," as designed in *out of apathy* (see Kaufman, *Human Nature*, 282). The arguments of my chapter are developed more fully and published in an essay titled "On the Dialectics of Reform and Revolution: The Working Classes in Socialist Strategy": Michael Vester, "Zur Dialektik von Reform und Revolution: Die Arbeitnehmer in der sozialistischen Strategie," *neue kritik. zeitschrift sozialistischer studenten*, no. 34 (February 1966: 15–28.

59. Edward Palmer Thompson, *The Making of the English Working Class* (1963; Harmondsworth: Penguin, 1968); Barrington Moore, *Social Origins of Dictatorship and Democracy: Lord and Peasant in the Making of the Modern World* (Boston: Beacon Press, 1966). The German edition of Moore's book appeared in 1969. Thompson's book appeared in German translation rather late (in 1987), but was much discussed in West Germany and even in East Germany since 1970 when I published a comprehensive historical study synthesizing Thompson's research especially with the research of G. D. H. Cole and with the history of the industrial revolution and of socialist ideas before Marx. Michael Vester, *Die Entstehung des Proletariats als Lernprozess: Die Entstehung antikapitalistischer Theorie und Praxis in England, 1792–1848* (Frankfurt a.M.: Europäische Verlagsanstalt, 1970).

60. Of special importance were: Serge Mallet, *Die neue Arbeiterklasse* (1963; Neuwied: Luchterhand, 1972); John H. Goldthorpe, David Lockwood, Frank Bechhofer, and Jennifer Platt, *The Affluent Worker in the Class Structure* (Cambridge: Cambridge University Press, 1968) [German edition: *Der "wohlhabende" Arbeiter in England*, 3 vols., Munich: Goldmann, 1970/71]; Horst Kern and Michael Schumann, *Industriearbeit und Arbeiterbewusstsein* (Frankfurt a.M.: Europäische Verlagsanstalt, 1970); Siegfried Braun and Jochen Fuhrmann, *Angestelltenmentalität* (Neuwied: Luchterhand, 1970); Frank Deppe, Hellmuth Lange, and Lothar Peter, eds., *Die neue Arbeiterklasse:. Technische Intelligenz und Gewerkschaften im organisierten Kapitalismus* (Frankfurt a.M.: Europäische Verlagsanstalt, 1970); Michael Vester, "Solidarisierung als historischer Lernprozess," in Diethart Kerbs, ed., *Die hedonistische Linke: Beiträge zur Subkultur-Debatte* (Neuwied: Luchterhand, 1971).

61. Günter Amendt, "Die Studentenrevolte in Berkeley," *neue kritik. zeitschrift sozialistischer studenten,* no. 28 (February 1965): 5–7.

62. Davis et al., *Changing the World,* 299ff.

63. Michael Vester, "Die Strategie der direkten Aktion," *neue kritik. zeitschrift sozialistischer studenten,* no. 30 (June 1965): 12–20.

64. Pierre Bourdieu, *Distinction: A Social Critique of the Judgement of Taste* (1979; London: Routledge, 1984); see also Vester, *Class and Culture in Germany,* and Vester et al., *Soziale Milieus im gesellschaftlichen Strukturwandel.*

65. Amendt, "Berkeley."

66. James Reston, "Washington: An Enterprising Debate," *New York Times,* May 16, 1965, E12.

67. *Guardian,* June 12, 1965. In my article on direct action in 1965, I quoted the *Guardian* in the form of a citation (!) in my German translation of the original text of the *Guardian*'s specimen in our institute; this paraphrase is a retranslation into English.

68. Helmut Schauer, "Zur Politik des SDS," *neue kritik. zeitschrift sozialistischer studenten,* no. 30 (October 1965): 3–9; Helmut Schauer, "Einige Kernpunkte der aktuellen Diskussion im SDS," *neue kritik. zeitschrift sozialistischer studenten,* no. 33 (December 1965): 4–12.

69. Reimut Reiche, "Studentenrevolten in Berkeley und Berlin," *neue kritik. zeitschrift sozialistischer studenten,* no. 38/39 (October–December 1966): 21–27.

70. Günter Amendt, *Kinderkreuzzug oder Beginnt die Revolution in den Schulen?* (Reinbek: Rowohlt, 1968); Günter Amendt, *Sexfront* (Reinbek: Rowohlt, 1970); Reimut Reiche, *Sexualität und Klassenkampf: Zur Abwehr repressiver Entsublimierung* (Frankfurt a.M.: Verlag neue kritik, 1968).

71. Todd Gitlin, *The Sixties: Years of Hope, Days of Rage* (1987; New York: Bantam, 1993); Richard Flacks, *Making History: The American Left and the American Mind* (New York: Columbia

University Press, 1988); Thomas Hayden, *The Long Sixties: From 1960 to Barack Obama* (Boulder, CO: Paradigm, 2009).

Chapter 12. Did We Learn How to Make Participatory Collectives Work?

1. Port Huron Statement in the Appendix, 239.

2. James C. Davies, "Toward a Theory of Revolution," *American Sociological Review* 27, no. 1 (1962): 5–19.

3. For twinkling and the other hand signals, see Direct Action Conference Organizers (Amsterdam), "Shared Path, Shared Goal: A Handbook on Direct Democracy and the Consensus Decision Process" (1995), distributed by the Zhaba Facilitators' Collective in Hungary, available at http://www.zhaba.cz/uploads/media/Shared_Path.pdf. See also "Occupy Movement Hand Signals," available at http://en.wikipedia.org/wiki/Occupy_movement_hand_signals. For other innovations and refinements that have developed to make the consensus process easier, see "Consensus Decision-Making," available at http://en.wikipedia.org/wiki/Consensus_decision-making, and sources therein. Ruth Milkman, Stephanie Luce, and Penny Lewis, *Changing the Subject: A Bottom-Up Account of the Occupy Wall Street Movement in New York City* (New York: Murphy Institute, 2013), report that "Many OWS activists also drew inspiration from recent Latin American social movements, from the Zapatistas to the factory occupations in Argentina and Venezuela" (referencing Marina Sitrin, *Everyday Revolutions: Horizontalism and Autonomy in Argentina* [London: Zed Books, 2012]).

4. Port Huron Statement in the Appendix, 240.

5. "OWS was committed to non-hierarchal 'horizontalism.' This organizational form, as well as the structure of the occupation itself, were self-consciously politically prefigurative" (Milkman et al., "Changing the Subject," 4). For the concept of "prefiguring" in the 1960s, see Wini Breines, *Community and Organization in the New Left, 1962–1968: The Great Refusal* (New York: Praeger, 1962).

6. Jane Mansbridge, *Beyond Adversary Democracy* (New York: Basic Books, 1980). For earlier analyses from this research, see "Time, Emotion, and Inequality: Three Problems of Participatory Groups," *Journal of Applied Behavioral Science*, 9 (1973): 351–68, and "The Limits of Friendship," in Roland Pennock and John Chapman, eds., *Participation in Politics: NOMOS XVI* (New York: Lieber-Atherton, 1976), arguing that the participatory democratic model is based on the characteristics of friendship and hard to extend to a larger scale.

7. In *The Child from Five to Ten* (New York: Harper and Bros., 1946), Arnold Gesell and Frances Ilg concluded from close observation of children at different ages that each age had its stages and that tantrums, for example, were typical of five- and six-year-olds, not the fault of the parents or the child. Inspired by this book in my parents' library, I hoped that my description of the typical problems of participatory collectives, taken from "best case" examples, would allow members of other collectives to see that some of their problems were not necessarily the faults of their own specific members but instead common structural problems.

8. Attendance at the meeting correlated .25 with the assessed valuation of one's house (Mansbridge, *Beyond Adversary Democracy*, Table 2, p. 99). For the low percentages of women speaking at town meetings throughout Vermont, see Frank Bryan, *Real Democracy: The New England Town Meeting and How it Works* (Chicago: University of Chicago Press, 2004) and for gender and speaking in public more generally, see Christopher Karpowitz and Tali Mendelberg, *The Silent Sex: Gender, Deliberation, and Institutions* (Princeton: Princeton University Press, 2014).

9. Of the forty-one members of Helpline, I was unable to interview one; seven declined to do the exercise. On the questionnaire, reporting low "say" and "power" in the organization correlated .36 with one's perception of one's parents as "working class" and .21 with being female (Mansbridge, *Beyond Adversary Democracy*, Table 5, p. 185).

10. I define power in general as "the actual or potential causal relation between the preferences or interests of an actor or set of actors and the outcome itself" (Jane Mansbridge, with James Bohman, Simone Chambers, David Estlund, Andreas Follesdal, Archon Fung, Cristina Lafont, Bernard Manin, and José Luis Martí, "The Place of Self-Interest and the Role of Power in Deliberative Democracy," *Journal of Political Philosophy* 18, no. 1 [2010]: 64–100). This formulation encompasses the benign kind of power that Mary Parker Follett ("Power" [1925], in *Dynamic Administration: The Collected Papers of Mary Parker Follett*, ed. Henry C. Metcalf [New York: Harper, 1942]), followed by many other theorists and social movement activists, called "power-with," as well as the kind of power that John Holloway (*Change the World Without Taking Power* [London: Pluto Press, 2002]) and many others call "power-to." It also encompasses the kind of power that participatory democrats try to eliminate or equalize, and that I call "coercive power," that is, "A's preferences or interests causing B to do (or changing the probability that B will do) what B would not otherwise have done through the threat of sanction or the use of force" (Mansbridge et al., "The Place of Self-Interest"). "Equal power" here means equal coercive power. For more on kinds of power, see Jane Mansbridge, "Using Power/Fighting Power: The Polity," in Seyla Benhabib, ed., *Democracy and Difference* (Princeton: Princeton University Press, 1996). A longer treatment would advance other criteria for reasonably accepting certain inequalities of power: the continuing opportunity for the less powerful to exercise power when contexts change and the ease of communication between the less and more powerful in the organization.

11. Mansbridge, "Limits of Friendship," 246–75; see also Francesca Polletta, *Freedom Is an Endless Meeting: Democracy in American Social Movements* (Chicago: University of Chicago Press, 2002).

12. Port Huron Statement in Appendix, 241–42.

13. Carmen Sirianni has pointed out in regard to participatory democracy that although appropriate conditions might someday eliminate scarcity in material things as Marx perhaps hoped, time will always be limited ("Economies of Time in Social Theory: Three Approaches Compared," *Current Perspectives in Sociological Theory*, vol. 8, ed. John Wilson [Greenwich, CT: JAI Press, 1987], 161–95).

14. Arnold Kaufman, "Human Nature and Participatory Democracy," in Carl J. Friedrich, ed., *Responsibility: NOMOS III* (New York: Liberal Arts Press, 1960), 272, 289.

15. See Carole Pateman, *Participation and Democratic Theory* (Cambridge: Cambridge University Press, 1970).

16. For example, the Peace Brigades International, discussed in Patrick G. Coy, "Negotiating Identity and Danger Under the Gun: Consensus Decision Making on Peace Brigades International Teams," in Coy, ed., Consensus Decision-Making, Northern Ireland, and Indigenous Movements (Oxford, UK: Elsevier, 2003), 85–122.

17. See Robert J. S. Ross's chapter in this volume, "The Democratic Process at Port Huron and After."

18. See the discussions of consensus in the groups Basic Kneads, Earth First, and Peace Brigades International in Coy, ed., *Consensus Decision-Making*. See also Milkman et al., "Changing the Subject," 30, reporting the feeling of some participants in Occupy Wall Street that "my voice has never been heard before."

19. See Ross, "Democratic Process."

20. Lynne M. Woehrle, describing the experiences of the women members of a collective whole grains bakery ("Claimsmaking and Consensus in Collective Group Processes," in Coy, ed., Consensus Decision-Making, 22–23).

21. Marina Sitrin, ed., *Horizontalism: Voices of Popular Power in Argentina* (Oakland, CA: AK Press, 2006), 58.

22. See Arendt Lijphart, *Democracies: Patterns of Majoritarian and Consensus Government* (New Haven: Yale University Press, 1984), on "consociationalism" as a democratic solution to segmented societies, and James M. Buchanan and Gordon Tullock, *Calculus of Consent* (Ann Arbor: University of Michigan Press, 1971), on side payments.

23. For more on these issues, including a discussion of the problem of structurelessness (Jo Freeman, "The Tyranny of Structurelessness," *Berkeley Journal of Sociology* 17 (1972–73): 151–64; see also Jane Mansbridge, "Consensus in Context: A Guide for Social Movements," in Coy, ed., *Consensus Decision Making*, 229–53, as well as Mansbridge, *Beyond Adversary Democracy.*

24. See Ross, "Democratic Process," and James Miller, "Participatory Democracy and the Fate of Occupy Wall Street." in this volume.

25. See also the points made in Ross, "Democratic Process," and Miller, "Participatory Democracy," in this volume.

Chapter 13. Participatory Democracy and the Fate of Occupy Wall Street

1. For the instituting of participatory democracy within OWS, see David Graeber, "Enacting the Impossible: On Consensus Decision Making," *Occupied Wall Street Journal*, October 22, 2011; Drake Bennett, "David Graeber, the Anti-Leader of Occupy Wall Street," *Bloomberg Businessweek*, October 26, 2011; and Jeff Sharlet, "Inside Occupy Wall Street," *Rolling Stone*, November 10, 2011. For an invaluable survey of some of the movement's participants (based, unfortunately, on a survey conducted on May 1, 2012, months after the movement's glory days in the fall of 2011), see Ruth Milkman, Stephanie Luce, and Penny Lewis, *Changing the Subject: A Bottom-Up Account of Occupy Wall Street in New York City* (New York: Murphy Institute, CUNY, 2013).

2. Yotam Marom, "Occupy Wall Street Is Winning, So What's Next," *Metro Focus*, October 6, 2011, available at http://www.thirteen.org/metrofocus/news/2011/10/were-winning-%E2%80%93-so-what-do-we-want.

3. James Miller, *"Democracy Is in the Streets": From Port Huron to the Siege of Chicago* (New York: Simon & Schuster, 1987), 326; reiterating an argument made by others, notably Jane J. Mansbridge in *Beyond Adversary Democracy* (New York: Basic Books, 1980).

4. Miller, *"Democracy Is in the Streets,"* 328.

5. Andrew Cornell, "Anarchism and the Movement for a Free Society: Direct Action and Prefigurative Community in the 1970s and 80s," *Perspectives*, 2009, available at the Anarchist Studies website, http://anarchiststudies.org/node/292.

6. George Lakey, from an interview in 2008, quoted in Cornell, "Anarchism and the Movement for a Free Society."

7. See David Graeber, *Direct Action*, 234.

8. "Quick Guide on Group Dynamics in People's Assemblies," recommended on the New York City General Assembly website, www.nycga.net/about; document available at http://takethesquare.net/wp-content/uploads/2011/07/Quickguidetodynamicsofpeoplesassemblies_13_6_2011.pdf.

9. "Quick Guide on Group Dynamics in People's Assemblies."

10. "Quick Guide on Group Dynamics in People's Assemblies." For the goal of a "new subjectivity," see Marina Sitrin, "Horizontalism," available at http://marinasitrin.com/?page_id = 108.

11. GE, "News from the Front," available at the 16beaver website, http://www.16beaver group.org/journalisms09.23.11.htm.

12. DG, "Some Impressions from Saturday and Monday," posted at the 16beaver website.

13. David Graeber, "Some Remarks on Consensus," February 26, 2013, available at http://occupywallst.org and http://occupywallstreet.net/story/some-remarks-consensus.

14. David Graeber, "Revolution in Reverse," in *Revolutions in Reverse: Essays in Politics, Violence, Art, and Imagination* (London: Minor Compositions, 2011), 64.

15. The infatuation with Oakland's Black Bloc anarchists and their tactics provoked a heated debate; see Chris Hedges, "The Cancer in Occupy," February 6, 2012, available at http://www.truthdig.com/report/item/the_cancer_of_occupy_20120206. David Graeber—the most prominent of those infatuated—responded to Hedges with an "open letter," "Concerning the Violent Peace Police," February 9, 2012, available at http://nplusonemag.com/concerning-the-violent-peace-police.

16. Perhaps the most interesting effort to imagine such a national form of participatory democracy remains that of G. D. H. Cole, whose vision of Guild Socialism was informed by the experience of anarchosyndicalism as well as the theories of Rousseau.

17. Hannah Arendt, *On Revolution* (New York: Viking, 1963), 284.

18. Cf. John Gray, *The Two Faces of Liberalism* (New York: New Press, 2000), who has come to a similar conclusion. Similar arguments appear in the work of William Galston, Bernard Williams, and Judith Shklar. My own views have been even more deeply shaped by the example of Montaigne, which I briefly describe in *Examined Lives* (New York: Farrar, Straus and Giroux, 2011).

19. Graeber, *Direct Action,* 407.

20. Cass R. Sunstein, "The Law of Group Polarization," John M. Olin Law and Economics Working Paper No. 91, available at www.law.uchicago.edu/Publications/Working/index.html.

21. For example, see Justine Tunney, "Occupiers! Stop Using Consensus!" February 13, 2013, available at http://occupywallst.org, and the response by David Graeber, "Some Remarks on Consensus."

Chapter 14. Radical Democracy as a Real Utopia

1. Joshua Cohen and Joel Rogers, *Associations and Democracy,* ed. Erik Olin Wright (New York: Verso, 1995), xi–xii.

2. The expression "non-reformist reforms" comes from Andre Gorz, *Strategy for Labor: A Radical Proposal* (Boston: Beacon Press, 1967).

3. Port Huron Statement in Appendix, 242.

4. See Erik Olin Wright, *Envisioning Real Utopias* (New York: Verso, 2010), 225–30.

5. Three other configurations—social democratic statist regulation, associational democracy, and participatory socialism—are discussed in Wright, *Envisioning Real Utopias,* 134–43.

6. Port Huron Statement in Appendix, 240.

7. For an extended discussion of these strategic logics, see Wright, *Envisioning Real Utopias,* 303–65.

8. "Participatory budgeting" refers to a range of institutional devices through which citizens become directly involved in deciding priorities for the use of city budgets. In early 2014, participatory budgeting was being tried in Chicago, New York, and Vallejo, California. In Chicago and New York, city council members are allocated a certain amount of discretionary money to be used for capital improvements (e.g., potholes and parks) in their districts. In a number of districts in each city, council members are experimenting with having these funds allocated through a participatory process involving direct democracy. In Vallejo, a citywide participatory budget has been instituted for a portion of the city budget.

Chapter 15. Philosophical and Political Roots of the American New Left

1. Hayden's account of these activities, written twenty-five years later, appears in his memoir, *Reunion* (New York: Random House, 1988). Other studies include James Miller, *"Democracy Is in the Streets": From Port Huron to the Siege of Chicago* (New York: Simon and Schuster, 1987), 92–125; Todd Gitlin, *The Sixties: Years of Hope, Days of Rage* (New York: Bantam Books, 1987), 104–26.

2. Port Huron Statement in Appendix, 242–43.

3. See C. Wright Mills, *The Sociological Imagination,* 40th Anniversary Edition (New York: Oxford University Press, 2000).

4. Mills, *The Sociological Imagination,* 41.

5. C. Wright Mills, *The Causes of World War Three* (New York: Simon and Schuster, 1958); C. Wright Mills, *Listen Yankee!* (New York: McGraw-Hill, 1962). The writing of Mills that most directly influenced the Port Huron Statement was "Letter to the New Left," in C. Wright Mills, *Power, Politics, and People: The Collected Essays of C. Wright Mills,* ed. Irving Louis Horowitz (New York: Ballantine Books, 1963), 256ff. Cf. Tom Hayden's effort to emulate Mills explicitly: Tom Hayden, "Letter to the New (Young) Left," in M. Cohen and D. Hale, eds., *The New Student Left* (Boston: Beacon Press, 1967), 3 ff. And see Daniel Geary, " 'Becoming International Again': C. Wright Mills and the Emergence of a Global New Left, 1958–1962," *Journal of American History* 95 (2008): 710–36.

6. Cf. Daniel Bell, *The Coming of Post-Industrial Society* (New York: Basic Books, 1973); Alvin Ward Gouldner, *The Future of Intellectuals and the Rise of the New Class* (New York: Seabury Press, 1979).

7. This has been published as Tom Hayden, *Radical Nomad: C. Wright Mills and His Times* (Boulder, CO: Paradigm, 2006). The book includes a lengthy memoir in which Hayden recounts how his ideas evolved during the drafting of the Port Huron Statement and reflects on the impact of Mills's work on his own political development.

8. The dissertation, completed at the University of Wisconsin in 1940, was published in 1964: C. Wright Mills, *Sociology and Pragmatism: The Higher Learning in America* (New York: Paine-Whitman, 1964). See also Daniel Geary, *Radical Ambition: C. Wright Mills, the Left, and American Social Thought* (Berkeley: University of California Press, 2009).

9. Ron Eyerman and Andrew Jamison, *Social Movements: A Cognitive Approach* (University Park: Pennsylvania State University Press, 1991).

10. Kaufman's arguments for a politics based on participatory democracy were laid out in a number of articles in the early 1960s. Most are difficult to retrieve, but see Kaufman, "Human Nature and Participatory Democracy," in A. Friedrich, ed., *Responsibility* (New York: Liberal Arts Press, 1960), 296 ff.

11. Arnold Kaufman's life and work is depicted in Kevin Mattson, *Intellectuals in Action: The Origins of the New Left and Radical Liberalism, 1945–1970* (University Park: Pennsylvania State University Press, 2002); see especially 187 ff. Mattson provides an overview of the articles Kaufman wrote in small left-wing journals on participatory democracy and the left. I wrote an early version of this paper before Mattson's book appeared, and I was pleased to see that his far more extensive study validates my own hunches—and provides an exceedingly rich and complex analysis of the intellectual foundations of the New Left.

12. For a detailed review of Dewey's conceptualization of participatory democracy, see Robert B. Westerbook, *John Dewey and American Democracy* (Ithaca, NY: Cornell University Press, 1991. The quotation in this paragraph is from p. 433.

13. Eyerman and Jamison, *Social Movements*.

14. The key works in the development of the "corporate liberalism" analysis include: William A. Williams, *The Contours of American History* (Cleveland: World Publishing Co., [1961]); Martin Sklar, *The Corporate Reconstruction of American Capitalism, 1890–1916* (New York: Cambridge University Press, 1988); Gabriel Kolko, *The Triumph of Conservatism: A Re-interpretation of American History, 1900–1916* (New York: Free Press of Glencoe, 1963). For a detailed sense of the New Left in Madison, see Paul Buhle, ed., *History and the New Left: Madison, Wisconsin, 1950–1970* (Philadelphia: Temple University Press, 1990). Mattson's *Intellectuals in Action: The Origins of the New Left and Radical Liberalism, 1945–1970* provides a detailed account of Williams's relation to the New Left.

15. *America and the New Era* is long out of print. A pdf file containing a facsimile of the mimeograph document is available at http://archive.lib.msu.edu/DMC/AmRad/americanewera .pdf.

16. As did Dewey's well-known Marxist follower Sidney Hook. See Sidney Hook, *Toward the Understanding of Karl Marx* (Amherst, N.Y.: Prometheus Books, 2002), originally published in 1933; Christopher Phelps, *Young Sidney Hook: Marxist and Pragmatist* (Ithaca: Cornell University Press, 1997).

17. See James Miller's essay in this volume, which extends this argument to the recent Occupy movement.

Contributors

Robert Cohen is Professor of Social Studies and History at New York University. His books include *The Free Speech Movement: Reflections on Berkeley in the 1960s* (with Reginald Zelnik, 2002), *Freedom's Orator: Mario Savio and the Radical Legacy of the 1960s* (2009); *Rebellion in Black and White: Southern Student Activism in the 1960s* (with David Snyder, 2013), and *The Essential Mario Savio: Speeches and Writings that Changed America* (2014).

Richard Flacks is Research Professor of Sociology at the University of California, Santa Barbara. His books include *Playing for Change: Music and Musicians in the Service of Social Movements* (with Rob Rosenthal, 2012); *Making History: The American Left and the American Mind* (1989); and *Beyond the Barricades: The Liberated Generation Grows Up* (with Jack Whalen, 1988). He was a participant at the 1962 Port Huron conference.

Jennifer Frost is Associate Professor of History at the University of Auckland, New Zealand. She is the author of *"An Interracial Movement of the Poor": Community Organizing and the New Left in the 1960s* (2001).

Daniel Geary is the Mark Pigott Assistant Professor of U.S. History at Trinity College Dublin. He is the author of *The Moynihan Report Controversy: Race, Liberalism, and America Since the 1960s* (2015), and *Radical Ambition: C. Wright Mills, the Left, and American Social Thought* (2009).

Barbara Haber has practiced psychotherapy for thirty years. She has remained active, on and off, in progressive political projects, now especially climate change, and has returned to her first vocation, painting and drawing. She lives in the Bay Area.

Grace Elizabeth Hale is Commonwealth Professor of American Studies at the University of Virginia. She is the author of *Making Whiteness: The Culture of Segregation in the South, 1890–1940* (1999), *A Nation of Outsiders: How the White Middle Class Fell in Love with Rebellion in Postwar America* (2011), and *Cool Town: Athens, Georgia, and the Promise of Alternative Culture in Reagan's America* (2015).

Tom Hayden is a retired California state senator, author, *Nation* editor, and constant promoter of participatory democracy, living in Los Angeles. His writings are at tomhayden.com. He was the principal author of the Port Huron Statement.

Michael Kazin is Professor of History at Georgetown University as well as editor of *Dissent* and a contributing editor of the *New Republic*. His books include *American Dreamers: How the Left Changed a Nation* (2012), *A Godly Hero: The Life of William Jennings Bryan* (2007), *The Populist Persuasion: An American History* (1998), *Barons of Labor: The San Francisco Building Trades and Union Power in the Progressive Era* (1987), and *America Divided: The Civil War of the 1960s* (with Maurice Isserman, 2010).

Nelson Lichtenstein is MacArthur Foundation Chair in History and Director of the Center for the Study of Work, Labor, and Democracy at the University of California, Santa Barbara. His most recent books are *The Retail Revolution: How Wal-Mart Created a Brave New World of Business* (2010), *The Right and Labor in America: Politics, Ideology, and Imagination* (co-edited with Elizabeth Tandy Shermer, 2012), and *A Contest of Ideas: Capital, Politics, and Labor* (2013).

Jane Mansbridge is the Charles F. Adams Professor of Political Leadership and Democratic Values at the Harvard Kennedy School. She was President of the American Political Science Association in 2013–14 and winner of the American Political Science Association's James Madison Prize in 2010. She is the author of *Beyond Adversary Democracy* (1980), *Why We Lost the ERA* (1986), editor of *Beyond Self-Interest* (1990), editor of *Feminism* (with Susan Moller Okin, 1994), and editor of *Oppositional Consciousness: The Subjective Roots of Social Consciousness* (with Aldon Morris, 2001).

Lisa McGirr is Professor of History at Harvard University. Her research focuses on politics and social movements in the twentieth century. The author of the award-winning *Suburban Warriors: The Origins of the New American Right* (2001) and coeditor of *American History Now* (with Eric Foner, 2011), she is currently finishing a book on Prohibition during the 1920s.

James Miller is Professor of Politics at the New School for Social Research and the author of *"Democracy Is in the Streets": From Port Huron to the Siege of Chicago* (1988), *The Passion of Michel Foucault* (1993), and *Examined Lives: From Socrates to Nietzsche* (2011), among other books.

Robert J. S. Ross is Research Professor of Sociology at Clark University and the Mosakowski Institute for Public Enterprise. Author of *Global Capitalism: The New Leviathan* (with Kent Trachte, 1990) and *Slaves to Fashion: Poverty and Abuse in the New Sweatshops* (2004), he lectures widely on labor rights issues. He was a participant at the 1962 Port Huron Conference.

Michael Vester is Professor Emeritus of Political Science at the University of Hanover in Germany. His books include *Die neuen Arbeitnehmer* (with Christel Teiwes-Kügler et al., 2007), *Soziale Milieus im gesellschaftlichen Strukturwandel* (with Peter von Oertzen et al., 2001), *Unterentwicklung und Selbsthilfe in europäischen Regionen* (1993), *Die Frühsozialisten, 1789–1848,* vols. I/II (1970/1971), *Die Entstehung des Proletariats als Lernprozess* (1970 ff.). He was a participant at the 1962 Port Huron Conference.

Erik Olin Wright is past president of the American Sociological Association and Vilas Distinguished Professor of Sociology at the University of Wisconsin. His publications include *Classes* (1985), *Class Counts: Comparative Studies in Class Analysis* (1997), *Deepening Democracy: Institutional Innovations in Empowered Participatory Governance* (with Archon Fung, 2003), *Envisioning Real Utopias* (2010), and *American Society: How It Really Works* (with Joel Rogers, 2011).

Index

Acknowledgments

This book had its origins at a University of California, Santa Barbara, conference, "The Port Huron Statement at 50," held in February 2012. Bringing together historians, social theorists, contemporary student activists, and Port Huron veterans, attendees offered papers and comments discussing the origins, historical impact, and contemporary relevance of the New Left's founding manifesto. It was sponsored, at UCSB, by the Dick Flacks Democracy Fund, the Associated Students, the Interdisciplinary Humanities Center, and the Center for the Study of Work, Labor, and Democracy. *The Nation* and *Dissent* also endorsed the conference.

Among the participants were Miguel Albarran, Sophia Armen, Eileen Boris, Mickey Flacks, Richard Flacks, Joshua Freeman, Daniel Geary, Yoel Haile, Grace Hale, Tom Hayden, Michael Kazin, Nelson Lichtenstein, Jane Mansbridge, Ben Manski, Steve Max, Lisa McGirr, Charles McDew, James Miller, Alice O'Connor, Charles Payne, Robert Ross. Vivian Rothstein, Michael Vester, Harrison Weber, Howard Winant, Erik Olin Wright, and a spirited group of campus activists who brought the conference to a close with their reflections on past, present, and future.

In addition, we want to thank Robert Cohen, Jennifer Frost, and Barbara Haber who contributed important essays to the volume, and Christopher Phelps, whose comments on the nearly completed manuscript were highly useful. Robert Lockhart of the University of Pennsylvania Press played a key role in orchestrating the entire project from concept to print, while copyeditor Joyce Ippolito and project editor Noreen O'Connor-Abel did exemplary work helping to get the manuscript into final form. We thank James O'Brien for composing a most accurate index.